THE RIGHT TO PROTECTION FROM INCITEMENT TO HATRED

Against the backdrop of the new globalized hate speech dynamics, the nature and scope of States' obligations pursuant to international human rights law on prohibiting incitement to hatred have taken on increased importance and have become a controversial issue within multilateral human rights diplomacy. Key questions being posed in the ongoing debates over how best to respond to the new wave of hatred include whether the international legal norm against incitement to hatred, as it currently stands, is suitable to address the contemporary challenges of this phenomenon. Alternatively, does it need to be developed further? This book traces the journey of this norm in three analytical domains; its emergence, relevant supranational jurisprudence; and the recent standard-setting attempts within the UN. The book argues that five internal features of the norm had a strong influence on its difficult path within international human rights law.

Dr Mona Elbahtimy holds a PhD from the University of Cambridge, and has practical experience in multilateral human rights diplomacy.

The Right to Protection from Incitement to Hatred

AN UNSETTLED RIGHT

MONA ELBAHTIMY

CAMBRIDGE
UNIVERSITY PRESS

University Printing House, Cambridge CB2 8BS, United Kingdom

One Liberty Plaza, 20th Floor, New York, NY 10006, USA

477 Williamstown Road, Port Melbourne, VIC 3207, Australia

314–321, 3rd Floor, Plot 3, Splendor Forum, Jasola District Centre, New Delhi – 110025, India

103 Penang Road, #05–06/07, Visioncrest Commercial, Singapore 238467

Cambridge University Press is part of the University of Cambridge.

It furthers the University's mission by disseminating knowledge in the pursuit of education, learning, and research at the highest international levels of excellence.

www.cambridge.org
Information on this title: www.cambridge.org/9781108837569
DOI: 10.1017/9781108946490

First published 2021

A catalogue record for this publication is available from the British Library.

ISBN 978-1-108-83756-9 Hardback

For Selim and Nour

Contents

Acknowledgements

This monograph is the revised and updated version of my doctoral thesis submitted to the University of Cambridge. While preparing my thesis for publication, I have benefited from the great support of my family. I would like to first thank my beloved husband Mohamed for his invaluable, long-lasting, and ongoing support and patience. I am really grateful to my children, Selim and Nour, for their understanding, despite their young age, that I needed to dedicate considerable time to work on my book during the remarkably difficult year of 2020 (against the backdrop of the COVID-19 pandemic). I am deeply indebted to my brother Dr Hassan Elbahtimy; he has been an excellent and inspirational mentor, who offered important insights during the long discussions we had about the topic of this book. Words cannot express the depth of my gratitude to my dear parents, Ahmed and Amany, for their limitless love and encouragement throughout the years of my life.

Further back chronologically, it has been a pleasure to write my doctoral thesis under the supervision of Dr Barbra Metzger. She has provided valuable academic guidance and important feedback on my work throughout the three years of conducting my research. The Citadel Capital Scholarship Foundation contributed the funding that allowed me to undertake my doctoral studies at the University of Cambridge, which I immensely appreciate. Also, I would like to extend my gratitude to Ambassadors Dr Ibrahim Salama, Wael Aboulmagd, and Dr Ahmed Ihab Gamal Eldin for the valuable support they have provided me. I also appreciate the assistance of the staff of UN library in Geneva and the University of Cambridge Library. Special thanks go to the lovely couple Dr Tristram and Louisa Riley-Smith – I was lucky to write considerable parts of my doctoral thesis in their beautiful house in Fen Ditton-Cambridge.

It has been a pleasure working with Cambridge University Press, where Tom Randall has been a very supportive editor, both during the proposal stage and since then. I am also indebted to the anonymous reviewers for their constructive and helpful comments and suggestions on the proposal for this book. Special thanks go to Alan O'Dowd, who provided very expeditious and to-the-point copy-editing.

International Law

1981 African Charter on Human and Peoples' Rights, 27 June 1981, 1520 UNTS 245

1969 American Convention on Human Rights, 22 November 1969, 1144 UNTS 144

1972 Charter of the Organization of the Islamic Conference, 4 March 1972, 914 UNTS 103

2008 Charter of the Organization of the Islamic Conference, 14 March 2008, OIC Doc. OIC-CHARTER-FINAL-miscdoc-ah-08

1950 European Convention for the Protection of Human Rights and Fundamental Freedoms, 4 November 1950, CETS 5

1966 International Covenant on Civil and Political Rights, 16 December 1966, 999 UNTS 172

1965 International Convention on the Elimination of All Forms of Racial Discrimination, 21 December 1965, 660 UNTS 212

International Cases

International Materials

UN DOCUMENTS ON TRAVAUX PRÉPARATOIRES OF ARTICLE 20(2) OF THE ICCPR

A/C.3/SR.289 – General Assembly, Fifth Session (19 October 1950)

A/C.3/SR.291 – General Assembly, Fifth Session (20 October 1950)

A/C.3/SR.568 – General Assembly, Ninth Session (1 November 1954)

A/C.3/SR.570 – General Assembly, Ninth Session (2 November 1954)

A/C.3/SR.571 – General Assembly, Ninth Session (2 November 1954)

A/C.3/SR.575 – General Assembly, Ninth Session (5 November 1954)

A/C.3/SR.580 – General Assembly, Ninth Session (10 November 1954)

A/5000 – General Assembly, Sixteenth Session (5 December 1961)

A/C.3/SR.1079 – General Assembly, Sixteenth Session (20 October 1961)

A/C.3/SR.1080 – General Assembly, Sixteenth Session (23 October 1961)

A/C.3/L.932 – General Assembly, Sixteenth Session (20 October 1961)

A/C.3/SR.1071 – General Assembly, Sixteenth Session (12 October 1961)

A/C.3/SR.1072 – General Assembly, Sixteenth Session (12 October 1961)

A/C.3/SR.1073 – General Assembly, Sixteenth Session (13 October 1961)

A/C.3/SR.1078 – General Assembly, Sixteenth Session (19 October 1961)

A/C.3/SR.1081 – General Assembly, Sixteenth Session (23 October 1961)

A/C.3/SR.1082 – General Assembly, Sixteenth Session (25 October 1961)

A/C.3/SR.1083 – General Assembly, Sixteenth Session (25 October 1961)

A/C.3/SR.1084 – General Assembly, Sixteenth Session (26 October 1961)

E/CN.4/NGO/39 – Commission on Human Rights, Eighth Session (20 November 1952)

E/CN.4/223 – Commission on Human Rights, Fifth Session (23 May 1949)

E/CN.4/SR.123 – Commission on Human Rights, Fifth Session (14 June 1949)

E/CN.4/SR.379 – Commission on Human Rights, Ninth Session (19 October 1953)

E/CN.4/L.269 – Commission on Human Rights, Ninth Session (7 May 1953)

E/CN.4/SR.377 – Commission on Human Rights, Ninth Session (19 October 1953)

E/CN.4/SR.378 – Commission on Human Rights, Ninth Session (19 October 1953)

E/CN.4/41 – Commission on Human Rights, Second Session (1 December 1947)

E/CN.4/52 – Commission on Human Rights, Second Session (6 December 1947)
E/CN.4/SR.174 – Commission on Human Rights, Sixth Session (8 May 1950)
E/CN.4/Sub.2/21 – Commission on Human Rights (26 November 1947)
E/CN.4/365 – Commission on Human Rights (1950)
E/CN.4/SR.320 – Commission on Human Rights (18 June 1952)
E/CN.4/82 – Drafting Committee, Second Session (16 April 1948)
E/CN.4/82/Add.12 – Drafting Committee, Second Session (3 June 1948)
E/CN.4/AC.1/SR.28 – Drafting Committee, Second Session (18 May 1948)
E/SR.438 – Economic and Social Council, Twelfth Session (21 February 1951)

UN RESOLUTIONS

A/Res/1780 (XVII) – GA Res. 1780 (XVII), Preparation of a Draft Declaration and a Draft Convention on the Elimination of All Forms of Racial Discrimination, GA, 17th sess., 1187th mtg (7 December 1962)

A/HRC/Dec/3/103 – HRC Dec. 3/103, Global Efforts for the Total Elimination of Racism, Racial Discrimination, Xenophobia and Related Intolerance and the Comprehensive Follow-up to the World Conference against Racism, Racial Discrimination, Xenophobia and Related Intolerance and the Effective Implementation of the Durban Declaration and Programme of Action, UN Human Rights Council, 3rd sess., 14th mtg (8 December 2006)

A/HRC/Res/10/22 – HRC Res. 10/22, Defamation of Religions, Human Rights Council, 10th sess., 43rd mtg (26 March 2009)

A/HRC/Res/12/16 – HRC Res. 12/16, Freedom of Opinion and Expression, UN Human Rights Council, 12th sess., 31st mtg (2 October 2009)

A/HRC/Res/16/18 – HRC Res. 16/18, Combating Intolerance, Negative Stereotyping and Stigmatization of, and Discrimination, Incitement to Violence, and Violence against Persons Based on Religion or Belief, Human Rights Council, 16th sess., 46th mtg (24 March 2011)

A/HRC/Res/4/9 – HRC Res. 4/9, Combating Defamation of Religions, UN Human Rights Council, 4th sess., 31st mtg (30 March 2007)

A/HRC/Res/6/21 – HRC Res. 6/21, Elaboration of International Complementary Standards to the International Convention on the Elimination of All Forms of Racial Discrimination, UN Human Rights Council, 6th sess., 22nd mtg (28 September 2007)

A/HRC/Res/7/19 – HRC Res. 7/19, Defamation of Religions, UN Human Rights Council, 7th sess., 40th mtg (27 March 2008)

E/CN.4/Res/1999/82 – CHR Res. 1999/82, Defamation of Religions, UN Commission on Human Rights, 55th sess., 62nd mtg (30 April 1999)

E/CN.4/Res/2000/84 – CHR Res. 2000/84, Defamation of Religions, UN Commission on Human Rights, 56th sess., 67th mtg (26 April 2000)

E/CN.4/Res/2001/4 – CHR Res. 2001/4, Combating Defamation of Religions as a Means to Promote Human Rights, Social Harmony and Religious and Cultural Diversity, UN Commission on Human Rights, 57th sess., 61st mtg (18 April 2001)

E/CN.4/Res/2002/9 – CHR Res. 2002/9, Combating Defamation of Religions, UN Commission on Human Rights, 58th sess., 39th mtg (15 April 2002)

E/CN.4/Res/2003/4 – CHR Res. 2003/4, Combating Defamation of Religions, UN Commission on Human Rights, 59th sess., 47th mtg (14 April 2003)

E/CN.4/Res/2004/6 – CHR Res. 2004/6, Combating Defamation of Religions, UN Commission on Human Rights, 60th sess., 45th mtg (13 April 2004)

E/CN.4/Res/2005/3 – CHR Res. 2005/3, Combating Defamation of Religions, UN Commission on Human Rights, 61st sess., 44th mtg (12 April 2005)

A/Res/60/150 – GA Res. 60/150, Combating Defamation of Religions, GA, 60th sess., 64th plen. mtg (16 December 2005)

A/Res/60/164 – GA Res. 60/164, Respect for the Principles of National Sovereignty and Diversity of Democratic Systems in Electoral Processes as an Important Element for the Promotion and Protection of Human Rights, GA, 60th sess., 64th plen. mtg (16 December 2005)

A/Res/62/154 – GA Res. 62/154, Combating Defamation of Religions, GA, 62nd sess., 76th plen. mtg (18 December 2007)

A/Res/63/171 – GA Res. 63/171, Combating Defamation of Religions, GA, 63rd sess., 70th plen. mtg (18 December 2008)

A/Res/64/156 – GA Res. 64/156, Combating Defamation of Religions, GA, 65th plen. mtg (18 December 2009)

A/Res/65/224 – GA Res. 65/224, Combating Defamation of Religions, GA, 65th sess., 71st plen. mtg (21 December 2010)

UN REPORTS

A/48/18 – CERD, General Recommendation no. 15: Organized violence based on ethnic origin (Art. 4) (23 March 1993)

A/32/18 – Concluding Observations of the Committee on Elimination of Racial Discrimination: Germany, Committee on Elimination of Racial Discrimination (April 1977)

A/61/335 – Doudou Diène, Report by the Special Rapporteur on Contemporary Forms of Racism, Racial Discrimination, Xenophobia, and Related Intolerance, UN Human Rights Council (17 September 2006)

A/32/18 – Report of the Committee on Elimination of Racial Discrimination: Official Records: Thirty-Second Session (April 1977)

A/33/18 – Report of the Committee on Elimination of Racial Discrimination: Official Records: Eighteenth Session (1978)

A/62/280 – Asma Jahangir, Interim Report by the Special Rapporteur on Freedom of Religion or Belief, UN Human Rights Council (20 August 2007)

A/67/537 – Frank La Rue, Report by the Special Rapporteur on the Promotion and Protection of the Right to Freedom of Opinion and Expression, UN Human Rights Council (7 September 2012)

A/CONF.119/10 – Study on Positive Measures Designed to Eradicate All Incitement to, or Acts of, Racial Discrimination: Implementation of the International Convention on the Elimination of All Forms of Racial Discrimination, Committee on Elimination of Racial Discrimination (May 1986)

A/CONF.189/PC.1/7 – Abdelfattah Amor, Study of Special Rapporteur on Religious Intolerance (13 April 2000)

A/CONF.211/PC.4/5 – Report on Implementation of the Durban Declaration and Programme of Action and Proposal for its Enhancement, Report of the UNHCHR (24 February 2009)

A/CONF.211/PC.3/4 – Report of the Regional Preparatory Meeting for Africa for the Durban Review Conference (3 September 2008)

A/HRC/2/3 – Asma Jahangir and Doudou Die'ne, Report Further to Human Rights Council Decision 1/107 on Incitement to Racial and Religious Hatred and the Promotion of Tolerance, Report by the Special Rapporteur on Freedom of Religion or Belief and the Special Rapporteur on Contemporary Forms of Racism, Racial Discrimination, Xenophobia and Related Intolerance, UN Human Rights Council (20 September 2006)

A/HRC/2/6 – Incitement to Racial and Religious Hatred and the Promotion of Tolerance, Report of the UNHCHR, UN Human Rights Council (20 September 2006)

A/HRC/4/19 – Doudou Diène, Report by the Special Rapporteur on Contemporary Forms of Racism, Racial Discrimination, Xenophobia and Related Intolerance (12 January 2007)

A/HRC/4/WG.3/6 – Report on the Study by the Five Experts on the Content and Scope of Substantive Gaps in the Existing International Instruments to Combat Racism, Racial Discrimination, Xenophobia and Related Intolerance (27 August 2007)

A/HRC/5/10 – Doudou Diène, Report by the Special Rapporteur on Contemporary Forms of Racism, Racial Discrimination, Xenophobia and Related Intolerance on Political Platforms Which Promote or Incite Racial Discrimination, UN Human Rights Council (25 May 2007)

A/HRC/6/6 – Doudou Diène, Manifestations of Defamation of Religions and in Particular on the Serious Implications of Islamophobia on the Enjoyment of all Rights, Report of the Special Rapporteur on Contemporary Forms of Racism, Racial Discrimination, Xenophobia and Related Intolerance, UN Human Rights Council (21 August 2007)

Abbreviations

ACHPR	African Charter on Human and Peoples' Rights
ACHR	American Convention on Human Rights
ACommHPR	African Commission on Human and Peoples' Rights
Ad Hoc Committee	UN Ad Hoc Committee on the Elaboration of Complementary Standards
CERD	UN Committee on Elimination of Racial Discrimination
ECHR	European Convention on Human Rights
ECtHR	European Court of Human Rights
GA	General Assembly
HRC	Human Rights Council
HRCttee	Human Rights Committee
ICCPR	International Covenant on Civil and Political Rights
ICERD	International Convention on the Elimination of All Forms of Racial Discrimination
ICL	International Criminal Law
IHRL	International Human Rights Law
OHCHR	The Office of the High Commissioner for Human Rights
OIC	Organization of Islamic Cooperation
UDHR	Universal Declaration of Human Rights

1

Introduction

1.1 INCITEMENT TO HATRED IN A GLOBALIZED WORLD

Globalization has had clear and direct effects on the proliferation of incitement to hatred. One of the most important features of the globalized context of incitement is mass global migration. The unprecedented rise in immigration flows during the last four decades has made most modern societies – especially in the West – more racially, religiously, and culturally diverse and, consequently, has created the global challenge of managing diversity. In the period from 1980 to 2019, the total number of international migrants increased by 172 per cent worldwide.[1] The number of international migrants worldwide rose by 18 million in the period between 1970 and 1980, 27 million in 1980–1990, 54 million in 1990–2000, 64 million in 2000–2010, and 58 million in 2010–2019.[2] The migration flows have been mostly Westwards. For example, on 1 January 2018, the number of people residing in EU Member States with citizenship of a non-member country was 22.3 million.[3] In 2016, 26.3 per cent of the Australian population had been born overseas.[4] In 2018, the number of people residing in the United States who were not US citizens at birth was 44.7 million.[5]

The increasingly multicultural fabric of modern societies has provided fertile ground for social anxieties and the escalation of prejudices predicated on ethnic, national, or religious divides, thus exacerbating the potential harms of hate speech.[6]

---

[1] International Organization for Migration, Report on World Migration: Costs and Benefits 2005, p. 380; International Organization for Migration, World Migration Report 2020, p. 10.

[2] Report of the International Organization for Migration 2005, p. 380; Report of the International Organization for Migration 2020, p. 10.

[3] Eurostat website available at www.ec.europa.eu/eurostat/statisticsexplained/index.php/Migration_and_migrant_population_statistics.

[4] Available at the website of the Parliament of Australia www.aph.gov.au/About_Parliament/Parliamentary_Departments/Parliamentary_Library/pubs/rp/rp1819/Quick_Guides/PopulationStatistics.

[5] Migration Policy Institute, available at www.migrationpolicy.org/programs/data-hub/charts/immigrant-population-over-time.

[6] Michel Rosenfeld, 'Hate speech in constitutional jurisprudence: A comparative analysis', in Michael E Herz and Péter Molnár (eds.), *The Content and Context of Hate Speech: Rethinking Regulation and Responses* (Cambridge University Press, 2012), p. 283.

Intolerance of diversity – or resistance to multiculturalism – under the guise of defending national identity or combating illegal immigration has frequently taken the form of negative stereotyping, profiling, stigmatizing, and demonization of minority and migrant groups.[7] This intolerance has created an environment conducive to hate speech involving incitement to discrimination, violence, and prejudicial attitudes towards groups different from the identities constructed as *us* or *someone like us*.[8] There has also been a resurgence of political parties with racist and xenophobic agendas and rhetoric that promotes or incites hatred, discrimination, and intolerance towards ethnic and religious minorities.[9] Such political parties have exploited identity politics to exacerbate sectarian and religious tensions by criticizing the impact of mass immigration on national cultures and economic conditions; this was particularly evident following the financial crisis of 2008 and the subsequent adoption of policies of fiscal austerity by governments across the world.

The need to respect cultural diversity has started to feature in arguments about free speech and its limits, especially with regard to speech that spreads, incites, promotes, or justifies hatred based on intolerance. Setting clear boundaries between highly charged public debates on national identity and immigration, on the one hand, and hate speech, on the other, has become increasingly important in maintaining a peaceful coexistence within multicultural societies.[10] However, setting these boundaries is a difficult and controversial exercise. It calls for rethinking, and perhaps reconfiguring, long-standing assumptions about liberal democracies. More specifically, it calls into question the capacity of liberal democracies to meet the challenge of diversity by functioning as multicultural or pluralist democracies, in normative rather than merely descriptive terms.[11]

These disconcerting developments have taken place in tandem with the global war on terrorism, following the events of 11 September 2001. Counter-terrorism measures have become associated with a growing tendency to stigmatize and negatively stereotype specific minorities and immigrants, who have also been subjected to racial and religious profiling.[12] A number of recent studies have shown

---

[7] A/HRC/9/12, p. 6; A/HRC/7/19, p. 17; A/HRC/15/53, p. 5; A/67/537, para. 24.

[8] See, for example, country monitoring reports of the European Commission against Racism and Intolerance, available at www.coe.int/t/dghl/monitoring/ecri/default_en.asp.

[9] A/HRC/7/19, para. 47–50; A/HRC/7/19, p. 6; Jennifer Schweppe and Mark Austin Walters, 'Introduction: The globalization of hate', in Jennifer Schweppe and Mark Austin Walters (eds.), *The Globalization of Hate: Internationalizing Hate Crime?* (Oxford University Press, 2016), p. 3.

[10] Michael Herz and Peter Molnar, 'Introduction', in Michael Herz and Peter Molnar (eds.), *The Content and Context of Hate Speech: Rethinking Regulation and Responses* (Cambridge University Press, 2012), p. 3.

[11] Geoffrey Brahm Levey and Tariq Modood, 'The Muhammad Cartoons and Multicultural Democracies' (2009) 9(3) *Ethnicities*, 427–428.

[12] A/HRC/7/19, p. 4; Report of the Special Rapporteur on Contemporary Forms of Racism, Racial Discrimination, Xenophobia and Related Intolerance, Doudou Diène, on Political Platforms Which Promote or Incite Racial Discrimination (UN Doc. A/HRC/5/10, 25 May 2007), p. 7; European Monitoring Centre on Racism and Xenophobia, *Report of European Monitoring Centre on Racism*

a temporal relationship between widely publicized terrorist events and more localized incidents of hate.[13] These terrorist events have, in a number of cases, triggered prejudice or even physical attacks by the members of the 'victimized' group against members of the group who are perceived to share an identity with the alleged perpetrator(s).[14]

Another significant feature of the contemporary context for hate speech is the proliferation of global information and communication technologies (ICT), which have provided easily accessible and far-reaching platforms for the dissemination of identity-based prejudices and hostilities. As a result, the proliferation of hate speech in recent years has increasingly acquired a transnational nature; the sheer number of incidents and their negative repercussions have been compounded by the speed and convenience with which information can be spread and accessed, and its wide geographic reach, unfettered by national borders.[15]

Extremist individuals and organizations have successfully exploited the internet to foment hatred within a worldwide audience in ways that were not previously possible; it has become a powerful platform for extremists, creating a 'rising tide of electronic hate'.[16] Cyber (or online) hate, as a global phenomenon, refers to the use of electronic communications to express hateful comments, insults, or discriminatory remarks about a person or group of persons based on their identity.[17] The number of websites promoting hate speech on the internet has grown exponentially in the last few years. Furthermore, hateful rhetoric continues to spread via social media and online forums. With the advent of social networking sites such as Facebook and Twitter, used by hundreds of millions of people around the world, and the recent explosion in mobile computing, new and influential avenues and hubs for the diffusion of identity-based prejudices and hostilities have developed.[18] Thus, hate has flourished within the online space on a global scale.[19]

---

and *Xenophobia on Muslims in the European Union: Discrimination and Islamophobia* (2006), available at fra.europa.eu/sites/default/files/fra_uploads/156-Manifestations_EN.pdf

[13] Kathryn Benier, 'Global terrorism events and ensuing hate incidents', in Jennifer Schweppe and Mark Austin Walters (eds.), *The Globalization of Hate: Internationalizing Hate Crime?* (Oxford University Press, 2016), pp. 79–80.

[14] Benier, 'Global terrorism events', pp. 79–80.

[15] A/67/537, para. 33.

[16] Abraham H. Foxman and Christopher Wolf, *Viral Hate: Containing Its Spread on the Internet* (Palgrave Macmillan, 2013), p. ix.

[17] Chara Bakalis, 'Regulating hate crime in the digital age', in Jennifer Schweppe and Mark Austin Walters (eds.), *The Globalization of Hate: Internationalizing Hate Crime?* (Oxford University Press, 2016), p. 274.

[18] Foxman and Wolf, *Viral Hate*, p. 1.

[19] Teo Keipi, Matti Näsi, Atte Oksanen, and Pekka Räsänen, *Online Hate and Harmful Content: Cross-national Perspectives* (Routledge, 2017), p. 1.

Cyber hate has created more nuanced and complex forms of harm which go beyond traditional conceptions of 'offline' harm.[20] The prevalence of online hatred may even affect the ability of targeted individuals or groups to fully access the internet and its benefits.[21] The scope and nature of harms caused by the proliferation of cyber hate has initiated debates on the need to establish new ways of regulating online activity.

Furthermore, globalization, both in its physical dimension (as manifested in international migration) and its virtual dimension (as manifested in digital technology) has provided a new international structure that can transform local hate speech incidents into global crises with geopolitical implications.[22] National governments' responses towards specific hate speech incidents now have an international impact. This new dynamic is perhaps best exemplified by the Danish cartoon controversy; in 2005, caricatures of Prophet Muhammad were published in a relatively obscure publication in Denmark, setting off a major international crisis with wide-ranging and serious repercussions, including loss of lives in several different countries. 'The Innocence of Muslims', an amateurish and low-budget short film uploaded on YouTube in 2012 which denigrated and insulted Prophet Muhammad, triggered a similar crisis, with violent protests erupting on a global scale. In 2015, twelve people were murdered at the offices of the French satirical newspaper *Charlie Hebdo*, following publication of controversial depictions of Prophet Muhammad which echoed the earlier Danish cartoons. These crises can no longer be regarded as isolated incidents; they have triggered extreme incidents of hate-motivated violence affecting entire religious or national groups and have incited retaliatory violence between communities. Thus, hate speech now has the potential to fuel political tensions between states in addition to seriously endangering the social cohesion of many societies. Although cases of religious offence have existed historically, they were predominantly local or national affairs, whereas such cases now have the potential to escalate into global crises.

Against the background of these troubling developments, hardly a day passes without heated debate somewhere in the world regarding hate speech regulation. The question of how to determine where freedom of expression ends and incitement to hatred begins has taken on great significance and become the subject of considerable confusion. The subject of regulating incitement to hatred has resurfaced with renewed urgency, not just within political and scholarly circles, but also in wider public discourse. The globalized context of hate speech has brought into question

---

[20] Jon Garland and Corinne Funnell, 'Defining hate crime internationally: Issues and conundrums', in Jennifer Schweppe and Mark Austin Walters (eds.), *The Globalization of Hate: Internationalizing Hate Crime?* (Oxford University Press, 2016), p. 16.

[21] Bakalis, 'Regulating hate crime in the digital age', p. 274.

[22] Miklos Haraszti, 'Forward: Hate speech and the coming death of the international standard before it was born (complaints of a watchdog)', in Michael Herz and Peter Molnar (eds.), *The Content and Context of Hate Speech: Rethinking Regulation and Responses* (Cambridge University Press, 2012), p. xiii.

not just how hate is being globalized but, more specifically, how international human rights law (IHRL) should respond to this phenomenon. Most pertinently, it has called into question whether the scope of legitimate restrictions on freedom of speech within IHRL ought to be reconsidered or further developed to address hate speech.

The international norm prohibiting incitement to discrimination, hostility, or violence, which was incorporated into the International Covenant on Civil and Political Rights (ICCPR) in 1966, triggered little debate or interest until the twenty-first century. Only recently, with the additional challenges posed by globalization, has this norm attracted significant attention within the international community and assumed a prominent position within the multilateral human rights agenda. In particular, the norm has become the focus of much polarization and confrontation between Western and Islamic UN member states, regarding its exact interpretation. A major issue in these debates is whether recent changes in the scale and nature of hate speech challenges require a new balance to be struck between states' international obligations to prohibit incitement to hatred, on the one hand, and freedom of expression, on the other.

1.2 THE RIGHT TO PROTECTION FROM INCITEMENT TO DISCRIMINATION, HOSTILITY OR VIOLENCE

There are provisions relevant to incitement in three different instruments of IHRL: the Universal Declaration of Human Rights (UDHR), the International Convention on the Elimination of All Forms of Racial Discrimination (ICERD), and ICCPR. This section is concerned mainly with the ICCPR, in particular Article 20(2) as it embodies the most comprehensive concept of the international norm prohibiting incitement within IHRL, but first it is necessary to say a little about the relevant provisions of the two other instruments.

Article 7 of the UDHR obliges states to provide protection against incitement to discrimination. Such prohibition is thus integral to the definition of the right to equality and the right to non-discrimination. The Article provides protection only against one category of harms resulting from incitement which is discrimination. It does not address the other harms of incitement that Article 20(2) proscribes; which are hostility and violence.

Article 4 of ICERD obliges state parties to declare the following offences punishable by law: the dissemination and promotion of ideas based on racial superiority or hatred, incitement to racial discrimination, and incitement to and acts of racially motivated violence. Furthermore, the Article obliges states to legally prohibit the provision of assistance to racist activities and the establishment of organizations that promote and incite racial discrimination. The Article is restricted only to the racial ground of incitement and does not address the other two grounds of incitement that Article 20(2) addresses which are the religious and national grounds. The ICERD imposes wider restrictions on racist speech than the ICCPR as it does not only oblige states to prohibit incitement to racial discrimination and violence; it also prohibits the mere dissemination and promotion of ideas based on racial superiority or hatred.

Turning now to Article 20(2) of the ICCPR,[23] it states that '[a]ny advocacy of national, racial or religious hatred that constitutes incitement to discrimination, hostility or violence shall be prohibited by law'. The scope of the norm against incitement in this Article is broader than that of Article 7 of the UDHR and Article 4 of the ICERD. It proscribes incitement to three different categories of harms: (1) discrimination, (2) hostility, and (3) violence, and covers three grounds of incitement: (1) race, (2) nationality, and (3) religion.

Article 20(2) is a unique provision within the edifice of the ICCPR, standing out from the Covenant's other Articles codifying human rights. The other Articles use terms such as 'all persons' and 'everyone' and oblige states to refrain from interfering with the exercise of specific rights. The Articles codifying human rights are subject to a general provision stipulating that states adopt laws only 'as may be necessary' to give effect to these rights. Limitations on the exercise of freedoms within the Covenant are of a permissive rather than prescriptive nature, authorizing states to impose such limitations (which must be enacted in law) at their discretion. However, Article 20(2) explicitly incorporates a *positive* obligation on states to enact laws prohibiting specific expressions, rather than merely authorizing them to enact such laws. Article 20(2) is the only Article in the ICCPR whose wording incorporates the phrase 'shall be prohibited by law'.

Given the distinctive formulation of Article 20(2), a number of scholars and human rights experts have described it as an 'unusual',[24] 'cryptic',[25] 'anomalous',[26] or even an 'alien'[27] Article within the context of the ICCPR. They contend that the Article, unlike other substantive Articles of the Covenant, does not set forth or codify any specific human right but is only relevant insofar as it establishes an additional limitation on freedom of expression.[28] Partsch, for instance, considers Article 20(2) to be 'practically a fourth paragraph to Article 19', which codifies the right to freedom of

---

[23] International Covenant on Civil and Political Rights, adopted by the General Assembly Resolution 2200A (XXI) of 16 December 1966, entry into force on 23 March 1976.

[24] A/HRC/2/3, 67; Rhona K. M. Smith, *Textbook on International Human Rights* (Oxford University Press, 2009), p. 296.

[25] Jeroen Temperman, *Religious Hatred and International Law: The Prohibition of Incitement to Violence or Discrimination* (Cambridge University Press, 2015), p. 4.

[26] Nazila Ghanea, 'Nature and Means of Effective Remedies' presented to the OHCHR Expert Seminar on the Prohibition of Incitement to National, Racial or Religious Hatred in accordance with International Human Rights Law (2011), available at www.ohchr.org/Documents/Issues/Expression/ICCPR/Vienna/CRP5Ghanea.pdf.

[27] Manfred Nowak, *U.N. Covenant on Civil and Political Rights: CCPR Commentary*, 2nd ed. (N. P. Engel, 2005), p. 468.

[28] Nowak, *U.N. Covenant on Civil and Political Rights*, pp. 468, 477; Stephanie Farrior, 'Molding the Matrix: The Historical and Theoretical Foundations of International Law Concerning Hate Speech' (1996) 14 *Berkeley Journal of International Law*, 8; A/HRC/2/3, para. 67; Nazila Ghanea, 'Expression and Hate Speech in the ICCPR: Compatible or Clashing?' (2010) 5 (2–3) *Religion and Human Rights*,

expression.[29] Similarly, Nowak argues that Article 20(2) 'may easily be included' under Article 19(3) on the basis that the prohibition of advocacy of hatred is necessary for the respect of others' rights and for the protection of public order.[30] So, according to this argument, Article 20(2) of the Covenant is just *lex specialis* of Article 19(3).[31] Article 19(3) of the ICCPR expressly states that the exercise of freedom of expression carries with it special duties and responsibilities. Pursuant to the Article, two limitative areas of restrictions on this freedom are permissible, which may relate either to respect of the rights or reputations of others or to the protection of national security or of public order or of public health or morals. Article 19(3) includes a clear three-part test by which the legitimacy of restrictions imposed on the exercise of freedom of expression may be assessed. Any restrictions imposed (1) must be provided by law, (2) must pursue a legitimate aim, and (3) are necessary to the legitimate aim and proportionate.

The reluctance to conceive of Article 20(2) as setting forth a human right – or even outright rejection of this proposition – might be explained not only by its distinctive drafting, but also by its grounding in the libertarian–individualist approach to human rights. As Chapter 2 will explain in detail, the recognition of the claim to be free from the harm of hate speech as a legal human right challenges the strictly libertarian–individualist approach to rights. Article 20(2) takes effect through limiting the legitimate range of expressions available to speakers who advocate hatred and recognizes group-based harms. The norm prohibiting incitement to discrimination, hostility, or violence differs from classical liberties as it reflects an understanding of rights that is not solely based on states' obligations to refrain from certain actions infringing upon the liberties of individuals. Instead, the norm focuses on states' duties to undertake positive measures to protect the liberty and equality of group members. The libertarian–individualist approach to rights expresses unease about recognizing an obligation on states to prohibit certain expressions as a human right norm.

Notably, as Chapter 3 will demonstrate, a number of Western states that voted in the UN against the incorporation of Article 20(2) into the ICCPR also viewed the

---

177; Smith, *Textbook on International Human Rights*, p. 296; Marloes van Noorloos. *Hate Speech Revisited: A Comparative and Historical Perspective on Hate Speech Law in the Netherlands and England & Wales* (Intersentia, 2011), p. 151; I. Boerefijn, and J. Oyediran, 'Article 20 of the International Covenant on Civil and Political Rights', in Sandra Coliver (ed.), *Striking a Balance: Hate Speech, Freedom of Expression, and Non-discrimination* (Article 19, International Centre against Censorship, Human Rights Centre, University of Essex, 1992), p. 30.

[29] Karl Josef Partsch, 'Freedom of conscience and expression, and political freedoms', in Louis Henkin (ed.), *The International Bill of Rights: The Covenant on Civil and Political Rights* (Columbia University Press, 1981), p. 277.

[30] Nowak, *U.N. Covenant on Civil and Political Rights*, p. 477.

[31] Partsch, 'Freedom of conscience and expression', pp. 227, 230; Boerefijn and Oyediran, 'Article 20', p. 30; David Feldman, 'Freedom of expression', in D. J. Harris and Sarah Joseph (eds.), *The International Covenant on Civil and Political Rights and United Kingdom Law* (Oxford University Press, 1995), p. 431; Farrior, 'Molding the Matrix', 97.

Article as not being cast in terms of a justiciable right, reflecting similar biases towards the strictly libertarian–individualist approach to rights.[32] In a recent complaint before the HRCttee (*Mohamed Rabbae, A.B.S and N.A. v. Netherlands*[33]), the Netherlands argued that the Article 'is cast not in the form of a human right, but as an obligation on States to put in place legislation prohibiting the conduct described. Other articles use terms such as "all persons" and "everyone".[34] The Netherlands further argued that if Article 20(2) is conceived as establishing a human right, this would necessarily mean acknowledging a human right to specific legislation, which is not acceptable.[35]

By these interpretations, Article 20(2) of the ICCPR serves a restrictive purpose and simply represents an additional limitation on freedom of expression, rather than establishing or codifying a specific human right or empowering individuals. Such assumptions largely explain the fact that the volume of literature on the norm prohibiting incitement to hatred within the context of IHRL remains particularly thin.[36] The treatment of this norm in the existing literature has mostly been rather incidental, lacking the depth of reflective study accorded to most rights and freedoms codified in IHRL.

Conversely, this book contends that Article 20(2) codifies a separate and autonomous human right among the other rights codified in the Covenant. Despite the Article's direct relevance to other rights, in particular freedom of expression, it sets forth an independent right which is *right to protection from advocacy of national, racial, or religious hatred that constitutes incitement to discrimination, hostility, or violence.* The Article not only imposes an obligation on states to legislate against incitement to hatred but also codifies the right to protection from it.

---

[32] Farrior, 'Molding the Matrix', 40–41.

[33] *Mohamed Rabbae, A.B.S and N.A. v. Netherlands*, Communication no. 2124/2011, CCPR (14 July 2016).

[34] *Mohamed Rabbae, A.B.S and N.A. v. Netherlands*, para. 4.3.

[35] *Mohamed Rabbae, A.B.S and N.A. v. Netherlands*, para. 4.3.

[36] See, for example, Temperman, *Religious Hatred*; Lorenz Langer, *Religious Offence and Human Rights: The Implications of Defamation of Religions* (Cambridge University Press, 2014); Gregory S. Gordon, *Atrocity Speech Law: Foundation, Fragmentation, Fruition* (Oxford University Press, 2017); Wibke K. Timmermann, *Incitement in International Law* (Routledge, 2015); Erica Howard, *Freedom of Expression and Religious Hate Speech in Europe* (Routledge, 2018); Partsch, 'Freedom of conscience and expression'; Ghanea, 'Expression and Hate Speech'; Farrior, 'Molding the Matrix'; Toby Mendel, 'Does international law provide for consistent rules on hate speech?', in Michael E. Herz and Péter Molnár (eds.), *The Content and Context of Hate Speech: Rethinking Regulation and Responses* (Cambridge University Press, 2012); Noorloos, *Hate Speech Revisited*; Tarlach McGonagle, *Minority Rights, Freedom of Expression and of the Media: Dynamics and Dilemmas* (Intersentia, 2011); Nowak, *U.N. Covenant on Civil and Political Rights*; Boerefijn and Oyediran, 'Article 20'; Elizabeth F. Defeis, 'Freedom of Speech and International Norms: A Response to Hate Speech' (1992) 29 *Stanford Journal of International Law*; Eric Heinze, 'Viewpoint Absolutism and Hate Speech' (2006) 69(4) *The Modern Law Review*; Dominic McGoldrick and Thérèse O'Donnell, 'Hate-Speech Laws: Consistency with National and International Human Rights Law' (1998) 18(4) *Legal Studies*.

The distinct formulation of Article 20(2), as well as the fact that it shrinks the available zone for legitimate exercise of freedom of expression by speakers who advocate hatred, should not lead to the presumption that it does not set forth a right recognizable on its own terms. On the contrary, the protection of an independent right is what distinguishes the Article from the other provisions within the ICCPR that allow states to impose interest-based limitations on freedoms (such as paragraph 3 of Article 19). Under these other limitation provisions, states are granted discretionary power to apply limitations to the exercise of freedoms only as an option (i.e. these limitations are permissible, rather than mandatory, in nature). Conversely, the mandatory nature of states' obligations under Article 20(2) is consistent with the declaration of an independent right. The interest in being against the harm of hate speech carves out an independent right.

Moreover, the Article was inserted in the section of the Covenant dealing with substantive rights. The norm prohibiting incitement to discrimination, hostility, or violence was not subsumed under the abuse of rights doctrine (Article 5) or merged with the limitations clause of Article 19.[37] The autonomous presence of Article 20(2) in the Covenant's text corresponds with its right-declaratory nature. This contrasts with the Covenant's limitations provisions, which exist as sub-clauses within relevant Articles. Similar to other right-declaratory Articles of the Covenant, Article 20(2) also entails a negative claim vis-à-vis the state. Though it might appear prima facie as incorporating only a positive claim vis-à-vis the state to enact laws that prohibit the expressive acts described therein, Article 20(2) also obliges the state to refrain from engaging in advocacy of hatred constituting incitement to discrimination, hostility, or violence. Indeed, laws enacted pursuant to Article 20(2) should apply equally to private persons and state organs.[38]

The absolute prohibition of torture and slavery under Articles 7 and 8 of the ICCPR, respectively, have been widely acknowledged in the IHRL lexicon as duties upon states giving rise to rights to be free from torture and slavery, respectively. As with Article 20(2), neither of these Articles include the words 'right' or 'freedom'.[39] Correspondingly, the prohibition of advocacy of hatred that constitutes incitement to discrimination, hostility, or violence is the duty that gives rise to the right to protection from incitement to such harms. Such prohibition represents the right's counterpart obligation or the corollary to a right to protection free from incitement to discrimination, hostility, or violence. It should also be noted that the protection against incitement pursuant to Article 7 of the UDHR is explicitly formulated as a right: 'All are *entitled* . . . and against any incitement to such discrimination [my

---

[37]   Temperman, *Religious Hatred*, p. 81.
[38]   CCPR, General Comment no. 11 (Art. 20) (29 July 1983), para. 2; Nowak, *U.N. Covenant on Civil and Political Rights*, p. 475.
[39]   Nowak, *U.N. Covenant on Civil and Political Rights*, pp. 157, 194; Temperman, *Religious Hatred*, p. 81.

emphasis],' thus establishing the right to protection free from incitement to discrimination.[40]

The right to protection from incitement to discrimination, hostility, or violence as codified by Article 20(2) of the ICCPR comes into direct contact with a wide range of freedoms and rights: life, equality, expression, religion, association, assembly, mental and physical integrity, and group rights. It facilitates and enhances the enjoyment of these rights and freedoms. Thus, the right to protection from incitement falls squarely under the ambit of rights that maximize the *utility* of freedoms, rather than those that maximize the *range* of freedoms.[41]

Multiple dualities are features of the right to protection from incitement; it guarantees *freedom* from being subjected to incitement in order to enhance *equality* through imposing *restriction* on the exercise of freedom of expression as a fundamental *liberty*. It pushes the boundaries between the *individual*, on the one hand, and the *state*, *society*, and *groups*, on the other. The right protects the *personal* aspects of an *individual's* life, both the physical and psychological, and also embraces a highly *public* dimension in which the interests and identities of *groups* and *society* as a whole are involved. The principle affirmed in Article 5 of the ICCPR that 'no one may engage in an activity aimed at destroying the rights of others' provides the rationale for the right to protection from incitement, given that it prohibits the abuse of freedom of expression with the aim of enhancing the rights of others.[42]

The issue of determining valid justifications for recognizing specific claims as human rights has, however, been subject to extensive philosophical, legal, and political debates and remains widely contested. Traditionally, appeals have been made to natural law and the inherent dignity of human beings.[43] Currently, an increasing number of theorists focus on grounding human rights in human interests.[44] These theorists have suggested a wide range of interests, corresponding to different views of human life. However, there is limited agreement among them on the valid criteria for determining when an interest deserves recognition as – or is sufficiently important to necessitate the formulation of – a human right.[45] Such debates need not be repeated here, as this book does not investigate, at the abstract

---

[40] Temperman, *Religious Hatred*, p. 18.

[41] Feldman uses these two categories to distinguish between negative rights and positive rights. David Feldman, *Civil Liberties and Human Rights in England and Wales*, 2nd ed. (Oxford University Press, 2002), p. 13.

[42] Ghanea, 'Expression and Hate Speech', 177–178; Farrior, 'Molding the Matrix', 4–5.

[43] Richard Tuck, *Natural Rights Theories: Their Origin and Development* (Cambridge University Press, 1979).

[44] John Tobin, *The Right to Health in International Law* (Oxford University Press, 2012), p. 52.

[45] Alon Harel, 'What Demands Are Rights? An Investigation into the Relation between Rights and Reasons' (1997) 17(1) *Oxford Journal of Legal Studies*; 101–114; Tobin, *The Right to Health*, pp. 51–53; James Griffin, *On Human Rights* (Oxford University Press, 2008), pp. 179–187; Amartya Sen, 'Elements of a Theory of Human Rights' (2004) 32(4) *Philosophy & Public Affairs*, 320–325; Allen Buchanan, 'The Egalitarianism of Human Rights' (2010) 120(4) *Ethics*, 120.

level, whether the claim to be free from the harm of incitement to hatred should be elevated to the status of a human right in a moral or philosophical sense. Rather, the book uses the term 'human rights' in a positivist sense: as a legal term of art, referring to those rights codified in international human rights instruments.[46] These instruments validate and legitimize claims to protect specific interests and prevent certain harms and elevate such claims to the status of international human rights.[47] Clapham notes that 'the content of human rights is usually understood by reference to the legal catalogue of human rights we find developed through international texts'.[48] Besson also draws an important distinction: 'there are universal moral rights that exist independently from their political recognition, but human rights are those universal moral rights that are also recognized as constraints on national sovereignty by international institutions.'[49] Any critical assessment of international instruments' recognition of certain claims as human rights should therefore be distinguished from the denial of the existence of those rights as such.[50] In other words, there should be a clear distinction between the positive set of international human rights as they *are* and as they *ought to be*. While one might contest the theoretical or philosophical bases of international human rights instruments, such instruments nevertheless provide the legal grounding for human rights protection.

The ICCPR stands at the apex of IHRL[51] as 'the most authoritative expression of the contemporary and universally accepted minimum standard of human rights'.[52] The Covenant's provisions proclaim and protect legal human rights as such, rather than important interests, concerns, or aspirations.[53] State parties to the ICCPR are subject to legal obligations to respect, protect, and promote rights codified therein with regard to people within their jurisdictions. This book, by analysing rights through a positivist lens, recognizes the incorporation of Article 20(2) within the ICCPR as elevating freedom from incitement to discrimination, hostility, or violence resulting from advocacy of hatred, to the status of an international legal human right. The Article imposes rights-based, not merely interest-based, limitations on the exercise of freedoms; the protection from incitement to hatred not only represents a societal or public interest which enhances the values of tolerance, mutual respect, and dignity, but may also be properly characterized as a human right.

Recognition of Article 20(2) as codifying a human right entails the characterization of incitement laws as protecting the rights of others, rather than simply

---

[46] Feldman, *Civil Liberties and Human Rights*, p. 5.

[47] Samantha Besson, 'Human rights: Ethical, political or legal? First steps in a legal theory of human rights', in Donald Earl Childress (ed.), *The Role of Ethics in International Law* (Cambridge University Press, 2012), p. 237; Tobin, *The Right to Health*, pp. 46, 54, 58, 73, 74.

[48] Andrew Clapham, *Human Rights: A Very Short Introduction* (Oxford University Press, 2007), p. 23.

[49] Besson, 'Human rights', pp. 223–224.

[50] Besson, 'Human rights', p. 680.

[51] Rosalyn Higgins, 'The United Nations: Still a Force for Peace' (1989) 52(1) *The Modern Law Review*, 52, 1.

[52] Nowak, *U.N. Covenant on Civil and Political Rights*, p. xi.

[53] Harel, 'What Demands Are Rights?', 113.

enforcing morality. While it could be contested that the latter rationale is an appropriate objective for the law, especially under liberal theory, the former rationale cannot.[54] At the adjudication level, the violation of a right provides uncontested grounds for restricting the exercise of liberties. However, the protection of public or societal interests does not necessarily enjoy the same status; precedence is granted to the right unless there is a sufficiently severe danger, or other compelling reason, which justifies a right being trumped by such an interest.[55] Courts must apply 'an elaborate, sophisticated and rather strict test of justification' when a fundamental right is at stake in a specific case, while they tend to adopt 'a highly relaxed and deferential approach' when a mere interest is at stake.[56] Thus, interests that have not been elevated to the status of human rights 'will be less carefully scrutinized' than interests which have acquired such status.[57]

At adjudication level, treating the norm prohibiting incitement to hatred as merely an additional limitation to the exercise of freedom of expression would require ascertainment of the acceptable limits that may be imposed on that freedom when protecting the *interest* to be free from the harm caused by such incitement. In contrast, the recognition of such an interest or claim as a *right* would require adjudicatory bodies, when considering hate speech cases, to uphold the right to protection free from hateful incitement. Even when called upon to determine the legitimate limitations upon freedom of expression, they would have to consider the element of necessity pertaining to the respect of others' rights (including the right to protection from hateful incitement), rather than just the protection of public order or morals. Furthermore, the position of hate speech victims is stronger if the right to protection from hateful incitement is recognized as such; these victims, as unambiguous human rights beneficiaries, would have the legal standing to complain about rights violations.[58] Accordingly, the right to bring complaints to adjudicatory bodies would be extended not only to those convicted of hate speech offences, but also to alleged victims of hate speech. Such victims would be empowered to raise claims about human rights violations caused by lack of state protection against hate speech, either through prevention (enactment of appropriate laws), investigation, or punishment.

1.3 A NOTE ON TERMINOLOGY

The *right to protection from advocacy of national, racial, or religious hatred that constitutes incitement to discrimination, hostility, or violence* is the precise and

---

[54] Joel Feinberg, *Harmless Wrongdoing* (Oxford University Press, 1988), p. 154.

[55] Eva Brems, 'Introduction', in Eva Brems (ed.), *Conflict between Fundamental Rights* (Intersentia, 2008), p. 2; Janneke H. Gerards, 'Fundamental rights and other interests: Should it really make a difference?' in Eva Brems (ed.), *Conflict between Fundamental Rights* (Intersentia, 2008), p. 688.

[56] Gerards, 'Fundamental rights', p. 680.

[57] Gerards, 'Fundamental rights', p. 688.

[58] Temperman, *Religious Hatred*, pp. 80–81.

comprehensive description of the norm codified in Article 20(2) of the ICCPR. However, this book uses the *right to protection from incitement to discrimination, hostility, or violence* and the *right to protection from incitement to hatred* interchangeably as convenient abbreviations. The book also uses the term 'hate speech' when addressing the issue of incitement to discrimination, hostility, or violence. The term 'hate speech' enjoys a widespread currency and is frequently used in public discourse by academics, human rights practitioners, and international and regional human rights–monitoring and adjudicative bodies to refer to the issue of incitement to hatred. Nevertheless, the term is not incorporated into IHRL instruments as such, lacks an authoritative definition within the jurisprudence of supranational human rights–monitoring bodies, and has no widely endorsed definition in academic literature.[59] Hate speech is a broad or 'catch-all' term that lacks legal precision.[60] It can cover a wide and varied range of expressions targeting a group or individual on the basis of their identity, with a range of actual or potential harms. Article 20(2) does not prohibit the mere hateful content of certain expressions, nor does it ensure protection against their harms in an open-ended manner; rather, it prohibits advocacy of hatred on the basis of three potential or actual harms (incitement to discrimination, incitement to hostility, and incitement to violence). States are not required under international law to prohibit expressions that do not reach the threshold of such incitement.

Despite the fact that the term 'hate speech' is not explicitly used in IHRL instruments, academic literature has often described Article 20(2) as the main and most comprehensive provision on hate speech prohibition within IHRL.[61] Moreover, the UN Human Rights Committee (HRCttee), the body mandated by the ICCPR with monitoring states' implementation of their obligations under the Covenant, has categorized the laws that should be adopted pursuant to Article 20(2) as 'hate speech laws'. Also, the UN Committee on the Elimination of All Forms of Racial Discrimination (CERD) has been using the term 'racist hate speech' in its jurisprudence in relation to Article 4 of ICERD. The terminology of Article 20(2) has also been used in a number of attempts to define 'hate speech'.[62]

---

[59] McGonagle, *Minority Rights*, p. 317; Peter Molnar, 'Towards improved law and policy on hate speech: The clear and present danger test in Hungary', in Ivan Hare and James Weinstein (eds.), *Extreme Speech and Democracy* (Oxford University Press, 2009), p. 237; Scott J. Catlin, 'Proposal for Regulating Hate Speech in the United States: Balancing Rights under the International Covenant on Civil and Political Rights' (1994) 69 *Notre Dame Law Review*, 772.

[60] McGonagle, *Minority Rights*, p. 317.

[61] Catlin, 'Proposal for Regulating Hate Speech', 772; Farrior, 'Molding the Matrix', 3; Noorloos, *Hate Speech Revisited*, p. 141; Defeis, 'Freedom of Speech and International Norms', 57; Rosenfeld, 'Hate speech in constitutional jurisprudence', p. 273; Jeremy Waldron, *The Harm in Hate Speech* (Harvard University Press, 2012), p. 13; Mendel, 'Consistent rules on hate speech', p. 418; Heinze, 'Viewpoint Absolutism', 544.

[62] See, for example, definition of hate speech used by Noorloos in Noorloos, *Hate Speech Revisited*, p. 4; the definition of hate speech within the Committee of Ministers of the Council of Europe

1.4 MAIN ARGUMENT

Hate speech has, historically, had serious and wide-ranging ramifications on the enjoyment of human rights. There is compelling empirical evidence connecting speech inciting hostility, discrimination, and violence against particular groups with human rights violations and even genocide. Both before and during the Second World War, Nazi and fascist hate propaganda played a significant role in causing atrocities – in particular, the murder of millions of people on the basis of their race, religion, or nationality. In the post–cold war era, hate speech acted as a catalyst for a number of mass atrocities; hate speech was directly linked to genocide in both Rwanda and the former Yugoslavia. More recently, instances of hate speech have been connected – to varying degrees – with large-scale human rights violations in Kenya, Cote d'Ivoire, and Myanmar.[63] As the processes of globalization deepen, the nature and scale of the challenges resulting from hate speech have become ever more complex and wide-ranging. They are also, increasingly, acquiring a transnational character. The new wave of hate speech has transformed concerns about this phenomenon from separate national anxieties into a pressing global issue, raising the question of how an increasingly globalized world should respond. More specifically, it has raised the question of whether expanded international regulation of the norm prohibiting incitement to hatred is necessary or, indeed, feasible. This has brought renewed attention upon how IHRL has addressed hate speech. Over the last few years, states' obligations under IHRL regarding the regulation of hate speech have occupied a prominent position on the multilateral human rights agenda. In particular, recent (mostly polarized) debates within the UN have focused on the meaning and scope of the international norm prohibiting incitement to discrimination, hostility, or violence.

Despite the clear historical record of hate speech, and its contemporary transnational challenges, efforts geared towards the development of international legal standards prohibiting incitement to hatred have faced considerable difficulties. The inclusion of Article 20(2) within the ICCPR was based on fragile international agreement; furthermore, supranational hate speech jurisprudence is characterized by weaknesses and interpretational gaps, and recent standard-setting efforts at the UN reached an impasse. The precise nature and implications of the international norm prohibiting incitement to hatred continue to be contested. Moreover, the relationship of the norm to other human rights continues to cause controversy. This book analyses the difficulties confronting the international legal regulation of this norm. It provides an explanatory framework for the piecemeal development of

---

Recommendation No. (97) 20 on 'hate speech'; and the definition of hate speech used by Sumner in L. W. Sumner, 'Incitement and the regulation of hate speech in Canada: A philosophical analysis', in Ivan Hare and James Weinstein (eds.), *Extreme Speech and Democracy* (Oxford University Press, 2009), p. 208.

[63] See Gordon, *Atrocity Speech Law*, he provides a detailed historical sketch of instances of mass atrocities that were accompanied by hate speech.

international law in the area of hate speech. The problem statement of the book is therefore: why has the international regulatory framework prohibiting incitement to hatred been particularly problematic and controversial? Or, to pose the question in another way: why does the right to protection from incitement to hatred remain an unsettled right within IHRL?

This book argues that five internal features of the norm prohibiting incitement to discrimination, hostility, or violence have had a strong, direct, influence on its difficult and controversial path within IHRL. These five constitutive features are: firstly, the *'emotive'* component, which manifests itself in the forms of expression that states are entitled to prohibit pursuant to the norm (advocacy of hatred), as well as one particular category of harms justifying such prohibition (incitement to hostility); secondly, the *'incitement'* component, in which the norm's enforcement depends on proving that advocacy of hatred has an inciting effect; thirdly, the tensions between equality and liberty rights of speakers and members of targeted groups; fourthly, the *'group identity'* component, in which the norm provides protection against incitement that targets specific group identities and creates tensions between individual and group rights; and, fifthly, the *'religion'* component, in which the norm prohibits religion-based incitement, and thus embodies inherent tensions between the expressive and collective identity aspects of freedom of religion.

This book aims to expand the debate on the norm prohibiting incitement to hatred by unpacking its intrinsic qualities, which the existing literature has often overlooked by subsuming these qualities into a wider discussion of tensions between the norm and freedom of expression. The thin body of literature on this norm in the context of IHRL shies away from explaining, in a comprehensive manner, the challenges facing the development of international standards within IHRL, prohibiting incitement to hatred. This book attempts to fill the gap through the development of explanatory tools with which to enhance understanding of these challenges. It subjects the norm to detailed conceptual, legal, historical, and political scrutiny. It also contributes to a more concrete debate on this complicated human right norm by presenting a taxonomy of its multifaceted interpretation and implementation challenges.

The book argues that the aforementioned five constitutive features make it difficult for the right to protection from incitement to hatred to acquire a universal, definite, and consensual meaning. Past and contemporary international negotiations over the norm (both during the drafting of ICCPR and during more recent attempts to expand the prohibition of hate speech) indicate that the meaning and implications of the norm are deeply contested among states. The major areas of international contention are grounded mainly in different approaches to addressing the definitional uncertainties and tensions underlying these five intrinsic qualities. Moreover, these uncertainties and tensions represent the most significant obstacles to consolidation of supranational jurisprudence on incitement to hatred.

While this book does not seek to resolve the norm's definitional problems and the inherent tensions which these illuminate, it brings them together as an analytical lens through which to examine and explain the difficulties and controversies confronting the international legal regulation of the norm. The book also contends that any efforts to further develop such an international legal framework or to reach a uniform international legal response to the phenomenon of hate speech will be precluded by the problematic nature of the normative and conceptual presuppositions underlying the five constitutive features. However, there are prospects for developing technical or procedural guidance to states regarding the implementation of their national frameworks, as opposed to normative prescription or guidance on how hate speech should be addressed in their national legislation. The latter would require broad agreement on the norm-rationale of the right to protection from incitement to hatred, which is hampered by the conundrums underlying its five internal features.

1.5 METHODOLOGY AND SOURCES

This book focuses on the issue of incitement to hatred in the context of international legal regulation. It traces and analyses the challenges surrounding the emergence, interpretation, and further development of the norm prohibiting incitement to discrimination, hostility, or violence in IHRL. The book traces the norm's difficult journey through three levels of analysis: firstly, the drafting history of Article 20(2) of the ICCPR (which codifies the norm); secondly, the body of hate speech jurisprudence produced by supranational human rights–monitoring and adjudicatory bodies; thirdly, recent attempts within the UN to develop new international standards on hate speech. Focusing on these three aspects of the norm's journey to date within IHRL facilitates a rounded and comprehensive treatment, linking narratives of the norm's emergence and interpretation with a narrative of the UN's thwarted attempt at its expansion, to form a single cohesive study. The book provides a longitudinal analysis spanning multiple decades, from the late 1940s (when the norm's origins were formed during the drafting of the ICCPR) to the most recent UN negotiations aimed at creating complementary standards.

While the book uses these three analytical domains to trace the challenges that have confronted international legal regulation of the norm providing protection from incitement, it also uses an analytical lens comprised of the five intrinsic qualities of the norm to explain those challenges. In developing its analytical framework, the book focuses on the norm's internal constitution but also recognizes that these are by no means the only influences impacting its difficult path within IHRL. In fact, the content of the 'universal' in relation to norms within IHRL depends on the outcome of international political power struggles.[64] Exogenous

---

[64] Heini í Skorini, 'The OIC and freedom of expression: Justifying religious censorship norms with human rights language', in Marie Juul Petersen and Turan Kayaoglu (eds.), *The Organization of Islamic Cooperation and Human Rights* (University of Pennsylvania Press, 2019), p. 124.

factors, associated with international politics, have played an important role in contextualizing and accounting for some aspects of the norm's problematic journey within IHRL. The book takes into account international normative politics both during the international negotiations on drafting Article 20(2) of the ICCPR and during recent attempts within the UN to expand the prohibition of hate speech. The book takes full account of interactions between the norm's internal features and political dynamics, which act as important determinants shaping its evolution. In addition to academic and secondary sources, the book's analysis draws extensively on a wide variety of primary sources, including documentary and archival evidence, as well as a number of interviews.

In order to provide an account of the emergence of the norm prohibiting incitement to discrimination, hostility, or violence in IHRL, the book relies on the records of UN meetings documenting the ICCPR's travaux préparatoires. The Covenant was the subject of intensive international negotiations between 1947 and 1954 at the former UN Commission on Human Rights in Geneva. Negotiations then continued in the Third Committee of the General Assembly (GA) in New York until 1966, when the Covenant was finally adopted. The UN library at UN European headquarters in Geneva houses a comprehensive collection of all official UN meetings on human rights, including comprehensive records of ICCPR negotiations. These records provide a wealth of information regarding states' positions in a formative period of IHRL and are indispensible for any thorough historical or analytical account of how the norm emerged internationally.

This book also relies upon an analysis of the body of supranational hate speech jurisprudence which has been developed by a number of international human rights–monitoring and adjudicatory bodies.

Moreover, the book draws upon its author's participation in UN Human Rights Council (HRC) meetings in Geneva from August 2009 to October 2010. Participation in the Council's formal meetings and informal consultations, as well as the closed meetings of political and regional groups, significantly enriched the author's engagement with, and understanding of, the relevant issues and provided her with valuable practical exposure to them.

The author's direct experience of the dynamics within the HRC occurred at an important juncture of the journey of the norm prohibiting incitement to hatred, when various attempts to further develop the norm at the international level stalled. The unique opportunity to witness this important process at first hand has given the author an appreciation of the context and procedure of diplomatic negotiations at the multilateral level. In particular, she gained an insight into the tensions among the supporters and opponents of standard-setting attempts related to hate speech, beyond the perspective which could be gained by relying solely on documentary records. This direct exposure also allowed privileged access to a great deal of documentation, some of which is restricted.

The excellent recording services of the UN provided another important source of information, particularly for the study of more recent UN meetings. In addition to the author's observations, and documentary and audiovisual sources, the author also draws on a number of personal interviews with diplomats, negotiators, and senior UN staff. These interviews provided invaluable personal perspectives from actual participants, providing a nuanced account of the negotiations, as well as background on different states' positions. The interviews also allowed the author to probe behind the neutral and diplomatic language sometimes employed in official statements and written records. Interviewees expressed a preference for anonymity, which the author has fully respected.

1.6 OUTLINE

This book is divided into six chapters. This introductory chapter outlines the book's parameters. Chapter 2 then analyses the five main internal features characterizing the norm prohibiting incitement to hatred (as outlined in Section 1.4) and illustrates how these five constitutive features present major challenges to the norm's definition, effective implementation and interpretation, and related international standard-setting exercises. Chapter 2 also examines how the libertarian and egalitarian notions of freedom of expression, and the individualist and communitarian approaches to rights, address – in their different ways – the definitional uncertainties and tensions underlying the norm's five internal features, leading to different delineations of the norm's meaning and scope.

The subsequent three chapters examine, in turn, the impact of the tensions underlying these five features upon three different aspects of the troubled journey of the right to protection from incitement to hatred in IHRL. The analysis set out therein suggests that the right's five internal features provide an explanatory tool for understanding its difficult evolution within IHRL.

Chapter 3 traces the genesis of the norm prohibiting incitement to discrimination, hostility or violence in IHRL through an analysis of the drafting history of Article 20(2) of the ICCPR; it illustrates the divisions that arose and caused profound controversies among states during the drafting process. The chapter examines the historical and political setting in which the Article's negotiations took place. It identifies the states that supported the Article's inclusion in the Covenant, those which opposed this, and provides an analysis of the contentious issues that arose between them during negotiations. Notably, these issues related to the scope of permissible limitations on freedom of expression and how to reconcile freedom of expression, on the one hand, with the fight against hate speech (and the abuse of hate speech prohibitions), on the other. The following issues are also examined: the appropriateness of adding an emotional component to the right's normative content; the scope of harms caused by advocacy of hatred that justify the incorporation of restrictions in IHRL; and the appropriateness (or otherwise) of obliging states to impose legal measures to address those harms.

Chapter 4 examines the body of hate speech jurisprudence which has emerged from supranational monitoring and adjudicatory bodies, and its development. It provides an account of how the HRCttee has developed its jurisprudence on Article 20(2); more specifically, it analyses the committee's decisions on hate speech under the individual communications procedure, its General Comments, and its concluding observations and recommendations on state parties' implementation of Article 20(2). The chapter also analyses the hate speech jurisprudence of other supranational human rights–monitoring and adjudicatory bodies, namely the CERD and the ECtHR. The chapter illustrates how the five internal features of the norm prohibiting incitement to hatred have largely informed the weaknesses and interpretational gaps in the body of supranational hate speech jurisprudence to date.

Chapter 5 examines recent efforts to further develop international standards on hate speech, particularly of a religious nature, within the UN. The chapter analyses how and why these standard-setting efforts ultimately failed. It outlines the content of the proposed standards, identifies the characteristics of both the supporters and the opponents of standard-setting efforts, and analyses the main areas of contention between them, which largely related to states' polarized positions on the meaning of the norm prohibiting incitement to hatred and the need for complementary standards to Article 20(2) of the ICCPR. The suggested standards' intervention with the scope of freedom of religion and racism within IHRL proved particularly contentious. Chapter 5 illustrates how the polarized positions on standard-setting efforts were rooted in different perceptions of how to address the definitional uncertainties and tensions underlying the five internal features of the norm prohibiting incitement.

The concluding Chapter 6 summarizes the various chapters' findings in order to construct a full picture of the difficult journey of the norm prohibiting incitement to discrimination, hostility, or violence within IHRL. The chapter also provides an assessment of the norm's potential within IHRL.

2

The Right to Protection from Incitement to Hatred

An Analysis of Five Internal Features

2.1 INTRODUCTION

This chapter examines, in detail, five internal features that characterize the norm providing protection from incitement to discrimination, hostility, or violence, as codified in Article 20(2) of the International Covenant on Civil and Political Rights (ICCPR). The chapter elaborates on the dilemmas of interpretation and implementation generated by these internal features. The following sections illustrate how the minimalist and maximalist approaches to the legal regulation of hate speech perceive these five features differently. Furthermore, they clarify how the libertarian and egalitarian approaches to freedom of expression, as well as the individualist and communitarian approaches to rights, address differently the conundrums created by the five features. This ultimately generates different delineations of the meaning and scope of the norm and different views on whether or not legalistic constraints on hate speech (or, rather, quasi-legalistic restrictions) are warranted, as well as on the scope and nature of such restrictions.

2.2 THE 'EMOTIVE' COMPONENT

The international norm prohibiting incitement to hatred obliges states to legally prohibit a particular extreme emotion (*hatred*) if its expression leads, or could lead to, certain harms. Among these harms is *hostility*, another extreme emotion. Thus, the terminology referring to intense emotions describes both the content of prohibited expressions, defined in terms of advocacy of *hatred*, and the nature of one category of their harms, defined in terms of *hostility*. This book uses the term 'emotive' to describe the use of the two words *hatred* and *hostility* in constructing the content of the norm. Although the use of this term might raise terminological difficulties within an international legal framework,[1] it best captures the invisible

---

[1] The term 'emotional harm' is used in a number of academic works; see for example Harvey Teff, *Causing Psychiatric and Emotional Harm: Reshaping the Boundaries of Legal Liability* (Hart Publishing, 2009); Amnon Reichman, 'Criminalizing religiously offensive satire: Free speech, human dignity, and comparative law', in Ivan Hare and James Weinsteinn (eds.), *Extreme Speech and Democracy* (Oxford University Press, 2009), pp. 331–356.

occurrences that belong to the realms of states of mind, negative attitudes, psycho-logical states and sentiments towards abhorrence, detestation, and enmity. Article 20 (2) has brought these emotive realms under the regulation of IHRL. The *emotive* feature of the norm prohibiting incitement to hatred provokes an enduring contro-versy with regard to the interpretation and implementation of the norm, as this section will illustrate.

The right to protection from incitement to discrimination, hostility, or violence encompasses a mixture of content-based and harm-based restrictions on freedom of expression. Expressions prohibited in order to effectuate the norm are not content-neutral, but rather *emotively* charged. Indeed, proving that a particular expression amounts to advocacy of hatred is the first threshold that needs to be met in order to invoke the right to protection from incitement. In order to identify whether the expressions in question can be classified as 'hateful', one must first undertake a content analysis of these expressions, assessing the emotions or subjective attitudes underlying them. The right to protection from incitement to discrimination, hostil-ity, or violence acknowledges that hatred, as an intense emotion, can cause unwar-ranted harms if advocated. However, the mere advocacy of hatred is not prohibited unless it constitutes incitement to discrimination, hostility, or violence. The exist-ence or potential occurrence of such particular harms is the second threshold that must be met in order to invoke the right.

The *Oxford English Dictionary* defines 'hate' as 'an emotion of extreme dislike or aversion; detestation, abhorrence, hatred'.[2] Defining hate has been described as 'notoriously difficult',[3] and like entering a 'conceptual swamp'.[4] Hatred represents a distinct problem for law.[5] Attempts to define hatred, in the context of imposing legal liability on persons who express or advocate this emotion, fall short of providing clear standards on identifying 'hate'. Such attempts have also encountered the profound conceptual difficulty of distinguishing hatred from other, less intense, emotions.[6] For example, the Camden Principles on Freedom of Expression and Equality define hatred as 'intense and irrational emotions of opprobrium, enmity and detestation towards the target group'.[7] Boyle and Baldaccini describe hatred as 'a feeling, a state of mind, and not a clearly established legal interest, as is the case of

---

[2]   Oxford English Dictionary, Entry for 'Hate', available at www.oed.com/view/Entry/84550? rskey=OIQKO5&result=1#eid.

[3]   Nathan Hall, *Hate Crime* (Routledge, 2013), p. 1.

[4]   Richard A. Berk, Elizabeth A. Boyd, and Karl M. Hamner, 'Thinking more clearly about hate-motivated crimes', in Barbara Perry (ed.), *Hate and Bias Crime: A Reader* (Routledge, 2003), p. 51.

[5]   Eric Heinze, 'Toward a legal concept of hatred: Democracy, ontology, and the limits of deconstruc-tion', in Thomas Brudholm and Birgitte Schepelern Johansen (eds.), *Hate, Politics, Law: Critical Perspectives on Combatting Hate* (Oxford University Press, 2018), p. 94.

[6]   Robert Post, 'Hate speech', in Ivan Hare and James Weinstein (eds.), *Extreme Speech and Democracy* (Oxford University Press, 2009), p. 125.

[7]   ARTICLE 19: Global Campaign for Free Expression, *The Camden Principles on Freedom of Expression and Equality*, available at www.article19.org/data/files/pdfs/standards/the-camden-prin ciples-on-freedom-of-expression-and-equality.pdf, Principle 12.1.

discrimination'.[8] Parekh understands hatred as referring to 'hostility, ill will, severe contempt, rejection, a wish to harm or destroy the target group, a silent or vocal and a passive or active declaration of war against it'.[9] For Post, the qualification 'extreme' is a definitional prerequisite for hatred, since legal order is not concerned with, and cannot address, ordinary or less intense human emotions.[10] Partsch defines it as 'an active dislike, a feeling of antipathy or enmity connected with a disposition to injure'.[11]

The term 'hostility' presents another challenge to defining and interpreting the right to be protected from incitement to discrimination, hostility, or violence. In addition to the harms of discrimination and violence, hostility is one of the categories of harm that the right aims to prevent and prohibit. Given its nature as an emotion, subjective attitude, or a psychological outcome unrelated to concrete practice, hostility (as with hatred) defies objective legal definition and, as such, easily risks subjective interpretation.[12] A number of UN Special Rapporteurs claim that 'the alleged perpetrator of hate speech, the alleged victim, the average man on the street or a judge may come up with completely different definitions of what constitutes – or not – incitement to hostility'.[13]

Hostility, as a recognized non-physical harm for the purposes of legal redress, does not possess the clear illegality of violence and discrimination within national legal systems.[14] In contrast to hostility, discrimination and violence are illegal acts, definable or clearly defined in national jurisdictions and prohibited under various provisions of

---

[8]   Kevin Boyle and Anneliese Baldaccini, 'A critical evaluation of international human rights approaches to racism', in Sandra Fredman (ed.), *Discrimination and Human Rights: The Case of Racism* (Oxford University Press, 2004), p. 160.

[9]   Bhikhu Parekh, 'Is there a case for banning hate speech?', in Michael E. Herz and Péter Molnár (eds.), *The Content and Context of Hate Speech: Rethinking Regulation and Responses* (Cambridge University Press, 2012), p. 40.

[10] Post, 'Hate speech', p. 123.

[11] K. J. Partsch, 'Racial speech and human rights: Article 4 of the Convention on the Elimination of All Forms of Racial Discrimination', in Sandra Coliver (ed.), *Striking a Balance: Hate Speech, Freedom of Expression, and Non-Discrimination* (Article 19, International Centre against Censorship, Human Rights Centre, University of Essex, 1992), p. 26.

[12] Heiner Bielefeldt et al., Joint Submission to OHCHR Expert Workshop on Africa on the prohibition of incitement to national, racial or religious hatred (6–7 April 2011, Nairobi), available at www.ohchr .org/Documents/Issues/Expression/ICCPR/Nairobi/JointSRSubmissionNairobiWorkshop.pdf; Toby Mendel, *Study on International Standards Relating to Incitement to Genocide or Racial Hatred* (2006), available at www.concernedhistorians.org/content_files/file/TO/239.pdf, pp. 15, 28; Natan Lerner, *Freedom of Expression and Incitement to Group Hatred*, paper presented to OHCHR Expert workshop on the prohibition of incitement to national, racial or religious hatred (2011), available at www.ohchr.org/Documents/Issues/Expression/ICCPR/Bangkok/NatanLerner.pdf, p. 6; Paula Martins, *Freedom of Expression and Equality: The Prohibition of Incitement to Hatred in Latin America*, paper presented to OHCHR Expert workshop on the prohibition of incitement to national, racial or religious hatred (2011), available at www.ohchr.org/Documents/Issues/Expression/ICCPR/Santiago/ PaulaMartins.pdf, p. 23.

[13] Bielefeldt et al., Joint Submission to OHCHR Expert Workshop on Africa.

[14] Mendel, 'Study on international standards,' p. 39.

IHRL.[15] The prohibition of advocacy of hatred constituting incitement to discrimination or violence is 'a species of a more general rule prohibiting incitement to crime'.[16] Incitement to violence is clearly narrower and more specific than incitement to discrimination. Its prohibition thus enjoys a wider and deeper consensus than the prohibition of incitement to discrimination or hostility.[17] Physical harms, rather than emotional or intangible ones, have traditionally taken greater priority within the law.[18] Tangible, visible, and immediate harms to the physical integrity of any person are universally condemned and are not characterized by the same degree of 'diagnostic controversies' involved in the legal regulation of emotional harms.[19] Discrimination and violence, as two categories of harm, are more straightforward targets for legal prohibition, when compared to incitement to hostility, since they are related to specific behaviour rather than attitudes.[20] Hostility, however, is related to discriminatory attitudes and not necessarily acts that are materially discriminatory. Through prohibition of incitement to hostility, Article 20(2) requires that states take legal action that goes beyond the issuance of discrimination laws, by taking the additional step of regulating discriminatory attitudes.

The hate element in the context of hate crime is different from that in the context of hate speech. Hate crime laws, widely endorsed across national legal systems, recognize the role of hate or prejudice towards an aspect (or presumed aspect) of a victim's identity as *motivation* to commit crimes. The punishment imposed on the perpetrators of these crimes is aggravated if the emotion of hatred has been proven or identified as a motivation for committing the crimes in question or, alternatively, an identity-based hostility has been proven before, during, or after the commission of the offence.[21] The concept of hate crime is, thus, a combination of an independent base offence plus a hate element.[22] However, the prohibition of hate speech is based on incitement to hatred as an effect, rather than motivation. This effect, in turn, justifies the imposition of liability on the speaker.[23] Thus, the element of 'hate' in 'hate speech' and 'hate crime' refers to different things: a specific kind of expression,

---

[15] Partsch, 'Freedom of conscience and expression', p. 228; Toby Mendel, 'Hate Speech under International Law', a paper available at www.law-democracy.org/wp-content/uploads/2010/07/10.02.hate-speech.Macedonia-book.pdf, p. 9.

[16] Mendel, 'Hate speech under international Law', p. 9.

[17] S. J. Roth, 'CSCE standards on incitement to hatred and discrimination on national, racial or religious grounds', in Sandra Coliver (ed.), *Striking a Balance: Hate Speech, Freedom of Expression, and Non-Discrimination* (Article 19, International Centre against Censorship, Human Rights Centre, University of Essex, 1992), p. 59.

[18] Teff, *Causing Psychiatric and Emotional Harm*, p. 2.

[19] Teff, *Causing Psychiatric and Emotional Harm*, p. 4.

[20] Bielefeldt et al., Joint Submission to OHCHR Expert Workshop on Africa; A/HRC/2/6, para. 38.

[21] Thomas Brudholm, 'Conceptualizing hatred globally: Is hate crime a human rights violation?', in Jennifer Schweppe and Mark Austin Walters (eds.), *The Globalization of Hate: Internationalizing Hate Crime?* (Oxford University Press, 2016), p. 34.

[22] Brudholm, 'Conceptualizing hatred globally', p. 35.

[23] Waldron, *The Harm in Hate Speech*, p. 35.

as well as harm that constitutes the offence itself, versus a particular kind of motivation that aggravates the punishment of a pre-existing offence.

In order to interpret the right to protection from incitement to hatred, or to develop universal standards for its implementation, an objective definition of hate needs to be formulated. However, hate defies objective legal definition given the problems of describing invisible and subjective emotions. The need to articulate legal definitions for 'hatred' and 'hostility' within the complicated context of restricting freedom of expression makes this task particularly complex. The emotional component of the right thus makes it challenging to clearly specify its exact definition or scope within an international legal framework.

The emotive component of the right not only poses an obvious definitional challenge but also represents a relativist challenge. The latter challenge becomes clearer in light of the organic relationship between emotions, on the one hand, and conceptions on morals, on the other. Extreme emotions, including hatred and hostility, are by-products of (and triggered by) moral conceptions, which, in turn, justify and rationalize them.[24] Emotional harms are thus morality-dependent harms, as they are mediated through the moral conceptions of the targeted listeners, in particular those central to the integrity of their identities.[25] The right to protection from incitement to hatred, through the prevention and prohibition of hostility, provides protection to specific sets of morals and values integral to national, racial, or religious identities.[26] The right obliges states to legally enforce 'norms of propriety in sensitive areas' within societies in relation to race, nationality, and religion.[27] Emotional harms caused by advocacy of hatred, in contrast to tangible harms, are to be identified and assessed in light of the moral standards and values that lie at the heart of particular identities. In other words, the assessment of emotional harms is to be informed by the moral unacceptability or indefensibility of the sentiments that certain expressions might communicate.[28] Given that the object of protection is feelings qua identities, such protection would indirectly cover the defining elements of the identities involved. The emotional aspect of the right indicates, or even presupposes, that the right is concerned with enforcing moral standards, and that hate speech laws come very close to legal moralism.[29] The latter is a philosophy of

---

[24]   Meital Pinto, 'What Are Offences to Feelings Really About? A New Regulative Principle for the Multicultural Era' (2010) 30(4) *Oxford Journal of Legal Studies*, 4, 6; Jeremy Waldron, *Liberal Rights: Collected Papers 1981–1991* (Cambridge University Press, 1993), p. 118; Christopher J. Nowlin, 'The Protection of Morals under the European Convention for the Protection of Human Rights and Fundamental Freedoms' (2002) 24(1) *Human Rights Quarterly*, 265–267.

[25]   Feinberg, *Harmless Wrongdoing*, p. 15.

[26]   Post, 'Hate speech', p. 130; Pinto, 'What Are Offences to Feelings Really About?', 6, 15.

[27]   Post, 'Hate speech', p. 136.

[28]   Michael Herz and Peter Molnar, 'Interview with Kenan Malik', in Michael Herz and Peter Molnar (eds.), *The Content and Context of Hate Speech: Rethinking Regulation and Responses* (Cambridge University Press, 2012), p. 81.

[29]   Feinberg, *Harmless Wrongdoing*, p. xiv.

law which holds that laws may be used to impose specific values, and to prohibit or regulate specific acts on the basis that they are immoral in the eyes of legislators.[30]

The cultural traditions and heritage of societies shape the regulation of rights in relation to matters liable to offend moral convictions.[31] Perceptions of morality encompass relativity and change; they shift across time and vary from place to place,[32] meaning that any legal regulation of emotional harms is directly affected by changing social values and morals.[33] Therefore, it is difficult to articulate detailed universal standards on issues of morality. The 'protection of morals' has been recognized in a number of provisions within IHRL instruments as an optional legitimate limitation on the exercise of freedoms.[34] However, these instruments do not indicate its content. The HRCttee has affirmed that the concept of morality is derived from different social, philosophical, and religious traditions and thus accords a wide margin of discretion to states in defining this concept for the purposes of limiting the exercise of freedoms.[35] Similarly, the ECtHR has accorded a wide margin of appreciation to state parties to the ECHR via the principle of protecting morals in order to legitimize restrictions on the exercise of freedoms, but without providing a definition of morals. The ECtHR justified this approach by acknowledging that differences exist between state parties when defining morals.[36] Thus, even countries in the same region do not necessarily share a uniform conception of morality. The acknowledgement of such varied and changing conceptions of morality allows individual states to apply the right to protection from incitement to hatred in a manner appropriate to their own national contexts.

Minimalist and maximalist approaches to the legal regulation of hate speech, which endorse, respectively, a narrower and a wider scope of limitations on the exercise of freedom of expression, offer different conceptions of the emotional aspect of the right. Most advocates of the minimalist approach do not recognize emotional harms that offend moral sensibilities, cause outrage, act as perceived insults, or evoke emotional distress, to be legally recognizable harms that justify restricting

---

[30] Pinto, 'What Are Offences to Feelings Really About?', 8.

[31] Vincenzo Zeno-Zencovich, *Freedom of Expression: A Critical and Comparative Analysis* (Routledge-Cavendish, 2008), pp. 83, 111; The Venice Commission, Report on the Relationship between Freedom of Expression and Freedom of Religion, CDL-AD(2008)026 (Strasbourg: Council of Europe, 2008), para. 79.

[32] Nowlin, 'The Protection of Morals', 268; Alexandre Charles Kiss, 'Permissible limitations on rights', in Louis Henkin (ed.), *The International Bill of Rights: The Covenant on Civil and Political Rights* (Columbia University Press, 1981), p. 304; Joel Feinberg, *Offense to Others* (Oxford University Press, 1985), p. 47.

[33] Teff, *Causing Psychiatric and Emotional Harm*, p. 7.

[34] Articles 12(2) on freedom of movement; 14(1) on right to publicity of court proceedings; 18(3) on the freedom to manifest religion or belief; 19(3b) on freedom of expression; 21 on freedom of peaceful assembly; 22(2) on freedom of association.

[35] CCPR, General Comment no. 22 (Art. 18), UN Doc. CCPR/C/21/Rev.1/Add.4 (30 July 1993), para. 8.

[36] See for example *Handyside v. United Kingdom*, Application no. 5493/72, ECtHR (7 December 1976), para. 49; Nowlin, 'The Protection of Morals', 279.

freedom of expression.[37] According to this standpoint, claims of emotional harm do not provide any basis for prohibiting expressions apart from particular moral views or the subjective aspects of feelings, including hurt, shock, and outrage, and accordingly such claims should not be legally validated. Furthermore, advocates of the minimalist approach to hate speech regulation consider emotional harms to be neither sufficient justifications for restricting freedom of expressions nor appropriate interests to support the existence of a right.[38] They argue that freedom to express emotions, including hate, is integral to freedom of expression; that the prohibition of hate speech on the basis of emotional harm violates the moral neutrality doctrine that states should abide by, and even represents the wielding of moral authoritarianism.[39] Post contends that the regulation of hate speech entails the enforcement of social norms that 'represent the well-socialized intuitions of the hegemonic class that controls the content of the law' and the use of the law to enforce 'hegemonic community norms'.[40]

The legislative moral neutrality doctrine, endorsed by most libertarians, runs counter to the principle of legal moralism. It requires the state not to interfere with individuals' evaluation of expressed views, nor punish their attitudes or control their thoughts.[41] This doctrine distinguishes between morally repugnant and hurtful expressions per se, regarded by many liberals as inappropriate objects of legislative concern, and other harmful expressions that might be legally regulated.[42]

According to the libertarian approach to rights, the prohibition of hate speech on the grounds of causing offence or causing insult to – or outrage in – others is incompatible with John Stuart Mill's harm principle. This principle is an important reference point for many libertarians in assessing the justifiability of imposing restrictions on the exercise of freedoms. According to this principle, 'the only purpose for which power can be rightfully exercised over any member of a civilized community, against his will, is to prevent harm to others'.[43] For example, Waldron argues that Mill's harm principle cannot be interpreted in a manner inclusive of moral harm or distress.[44] He further elaborates that outrage to feelings is 'something

---

[37]   Waldron, *Liberal Rights*, p. 116; Calvin R. Massey, 'Hate Speech, Cultural Diversity, and the Foundational Paradigms of Free Expression' (1992) 40 *UCLA Law Review*, 116–117.

[38]   David Norris, 'Note: A Communitarian Defense of Group Libel Laws' (1988) 101 *Harvard Law Review*, 687; Massey, 'Hate Speech and Cultural Diversity', 174.

[39]   Geoffrey R. Stone, 'Content-Neutral Restrictions' (1987) 54(1) *The University of Chicago Law Review*, 46–118; Geoffrey R. Stone, 'Content Regulation and the First Amendment' (1983) 25 *William and Mary Law Review*, 189–252.

[40]   Post, 'Hate speech', p. 132.

[41]   Ronald Dworkin, *A Matter of Principle* (Harvard University Press, 1985), pp. 353–354; Waldron, *Liberal Rights*, pp. 162–163, 165.

[42]   Evan Simpson, 'Responsibilities for Hateful Speech' (2006) 12(2) *Legal Theory*, 137; Feinberg, *Harmless Wrongdoing*, p. xiv.

[43]   John Stuart Mill, 'On liberty', in John Gray and G. W. Smith (eds.), *J. S. Mill, On Liberty in Focus* (Routledge, 1991), p. 30.

[44]   Waldron, *Liberal Rights*, pp. 118–126.

to be welcomed, nurtured, and encouraged in the free society that Mill is arguing for'[45] and adds that Mill conceives of moral distress as a positive outcome of exposure to competing accounts of 'the good life', which ultimately contributes to societal progress.[46] Additionally, Brink highlights that hurt feelings and injured sensitivities resulting from expressions do not constitute harm for the purposes of Mill's harm principle.[47] According to Simpson, Mill's harm principle submits hate speech to political, rather than legal, management that promotes tolerance and co-existence.[48] Sadurski contends that the criteria for harms are much more objective and neutral than those for morals. He understands harm as 'an intrusion into another person's autonomy' that hinders both this autonomy and the achievement of goals related to that person's 'own conception of the good'.[49] Similarly, Feinberg distinguishes between the type of morality that coincides with a tight formulation of Mill's harm principle, and legal moralism, on the basis that the former emphasizes the protection of personal autonomy as a basic principle of liberalism, and does not 'vindicate correct evaluative judgments of any and all kinds'.[50] This arguably makes Mill's harm principle much narrower than moralistic principles.[51] Feinberg distinguishes between Mill's harm principle and the 'offense principle', which legitimizes restrictions on liberties to prevent hurt or offence, as opposed to harm.[52] He defines harm as a 'setback to interests' that violates a person's rights,[53] and defines offence as 'any or all of a miscellany of disliked mental states' caused by the right-violating conduct of others.[54] Feinberg classifies expressions offensive to sensibilities as falling under the 'offense principle' rather than the 'harm principle'. He clarifies that 'extreme liberalism' endorses only the harm principle as a justification for restricting freedoms.[55] Thus, the perceived incompatibility of Mill's harm principle with prohibition of hate speech that causes emotional distress is crucial to understanding the reluctance of many liberals to recognize emotional harm as a valid ground for restricting freedom of expression.

Inherent practical difficulties arise in translating subjective, ambiguous, and complex concepts, such as moral rectitude, offence to feelings, and other wrongs resulting from hate speech, into the language of legal rights.[56] Defining the exact

---

[45] Jeremy Waldron, 'Mill and the Value of Moral Distress' (1987) 35(3) *Political Studies*, 413.

[46] Waldron, 'Mill and the Value of Moral Distress', 413.

[47] David O. Brink, 'Millian Principles, Freedom of Expression, and Hate Speech' (2001) 7(2) *Legal Theory*, 120, 144.

[48] Simpson, 'Responsibilities for Hateful Speech', 159.

[49] Wojciech Sadurski, *Moral Pluralism and Legal Neutrality* (Academic Publishers, 1990), p. 99.

[50] Feinberg, *Harmless Wrongdoing*, p. 12.

[51] Feinberg, *Harmless Wrongdoing*, p. 12.

[52] Joel Feinberg, *Harm to Others* (Oxford University Press, 1984), p. 12.

[53] Feinberg, *Harmless Wrongdoing*, p. x.

[54] Feinberg, *Harmless Wrongdoing*, p. xii.

[55] Feinberg, *Harm to Others*, p. 13.

[56] Wiktor Osiatynski, *Human Rights and Their Limits* (Cambridge University Press, 2009), p. 204; Pinto, 'What Are Offences to Feelings Really About?', 15.

scope of prohibited hate speech on the basis of psychological harm involves produ-
cing a description of such harm's extent, an intractable dilemma confronting the
formulation of hate speech laws.[57] Laws that acknowledge emotional harms have to
deal with 'the complexity of psychological phenomena' or the phenomenology of a
wide range of possible reactions and to determine how to ' . . . separate out those
feelings that are not appropriate for legislative concern from those which are or from
those that accompany other phenomena that are'.[58] These laws pose challenges
when it comes to differentiating between the various types and gradations of
emotional harm, and justifying why they deserve legal protection.[59] Also, some
scholars contend that the exercise of freedom of expression in general carries the
potential to cause psycho-emotional harms,[60] suggesting that any legal rule articulated in this regard would be 'too open-ended'.[61]

Notably, the subjective perceptions and responses of members of targeted
groups largely inform the identification and measurement of emotional
harms.[62] Thus, providing legal protection to feelings and sensibilities poses ex
post facto liability on speakers, based largely on the effect of their expressions
on listeners' feelings rather than objective or predictable standards.[63] This
might encourage members of targeted groups to pretend that they suffer from
emotional harms, with the aim of restricting expressions that are unfavourable
to them.[64] Feinberg cautions that offence can arise because parts of the
audience hold 'bigoted prejudices'; in his view, this discredits the use of
emotional harms as grounds for limiting freedom of expression.[65] Providing
legal protection to feelings, Grimm argues, 'would put the public discourse at
the mercy of the sensitivity' of different groups, and 'particularly of the most
militant among them'.[66] According to Sadurski, laws should exist to 'protect

---

[57] David Kretzmer, 'Freedom of Speech and Racism' (1986–1987) 8 *Cardozo Law Review*, 488–489;
      Loren P. Beth, 'Group Libel and Free Speech' (1955) 39 *Minnesota Law Review*, 178–179; David
      Goldberger, 'Sources of Judicial Reluctance to Use Psychic Harm as a Basis for Suppressing Racist,
      Sexist and Ethnically Offensive Speech' (1990–1991) 56 *Brooklyn Law Review*, 1200.
[58] Waldron, *The Harm in Hate Speech*, p. 113.
[59] Teff, *Causing Psychiatric and Emotional Harm*, p. 10; Kwame Anthony Appiah, 'What's wrong with
      defamation of religion?', in Michael E. Herz and Péter Molnár (eds.), *The Content and Context of
      Hate Speech: Rethinking Regulation and Responses* (Cambridge University Press, 2012), p. 171;
      Reichman, 'Criminalizing religiously offensive satire', pp. 352–353.
[60] Toni M. Massaro, 'Equality and Freedom of Expression: The Hate Speech Dilemma' (1991) 32
      William and Mary Law Review, 229–230; Waldron, *Liberal Rights*, p. 139.
[61] Massaro, 'Equality and Freedom of Expression', 229.
[62] Appiah, 'What's wrong with defamation of religion?', p. 176; Goldberger, 'Sources of Judicial
      Reluctance', 1200.
[63] Puja Kapai and Anne S. Y. Cheung, 'Hanging in a Balance: Freedom of Expression and Religion'
      (2009) 15 *Buffalo Human Rights Law Review*, 67.
[64] Appiah, 'What's wrong with defamation of religion?', p. 176.
[65] Feinberg, *Harm to Others*, p. 25.
[66] Dieter Grimm, 'Freedom of speech in a globalized world', in Ivan Hare and James Weinstein (eds.),
      Extreme Speech and Democracy (Oxford University Press, 2009), p. 19.

speakers against intolerant audiences, not to protect audiences against unpopular and even offensive speakers'.[67]

Against the background of the difficulties in determining whether, how, and to what extent, speakers have caused emotional harm, advocates of the minimalist approach to hate speech legislation hold that protecting feelings against offence or hurt is not an appropriate aim for the law. They argue that unless an unlawful *action* is involved, the state should not violate the principle of content neutrality in regulating freedom of expression by privileging some moral values over others or by enforcing its own vision of what constitutes appropriate forms of expression.[68] Legal systems endorsing the libertarian conception of rights recognize only evidently material harm in their threshold criteria for the legitimate restriction of individual freedoms.[69]

Through the lens of the minimalist approach to hate speech regulation, hostility in the context of Article 20(2) of the ICCPR refers to 'a state of mind which is acted upon',[70] 'an attitude displayed externally',[71] or 'a manifestation of hatred beyond a mere state of mind'.[72] Temperman argues that Article 20(2) is only concerned with the adverse tangible actions flowing from the original act of hatred aimed at the target group, rather than the creation of a state of mind that copies the inciter's hatred.[73] According to advocates of the minimalist approach, hostility in the context of Article 20(2) is conceived of as less intense than violence but still refers to an overt or manifested action.[74] The non-governmental organization (NGO) Article 19 contends that the difference between hostile action and violence is only a matter of scale.[75] The opposition to defining the term 'hostility' as referring to a certain state of mind, or to attempts to upgrade hostility to the same level as violence, reflects the resistance to lowering the threshold for the exercise of freedom of expression. However, the inclusion of discrimination and violence within the text of Article 20 (2) as two categories of hostile conduct indicates that 'hostility', as a third category, does not refer to hostile acts but rather to hostile *attitudes*.[76] Additionally, the HRCttee has used the term 'hostility' to refer to a 'passive state of mind', rather

[67] Wojciech Sadurski, *Freedom of Speech and Its Limits* (Springer, 1999), p. 197.

[68] Massaro, 'Equality and Freedom of Expression', 222.

[69] Heinze, 'Toward a legal concept of hatred', p. 98.

[70] ARTICLE 19: Global Campaign for Free Expression, Policy Brief on *Prohibiting Incitement to Discrimination, Hostility, or Violence* (2009), available at www.article19.org/data/files/medialibrary/3548/ARTICLE-19-policy-on-prohibition-to-incitement.pdf.

[71] Partsch, 'Freedom of conscience and expression', p. 228.

[72] ARTICLE 19, Policy Brief on: *Prohibiting Incitement to Discrimination, Hostility, or Violence*.

[73] Temperman, *Religious Hatred*, p. 188.

[74] Nazila Ghanea, *Articles 19 and 20 of the ICCPR*, paper presented to the expert seminar on the links between Articles 19 and 20 of the International Covenant on Civil and Political Rights, available at www.ohchr.org/Documents/Issues/Expression/ICCPR/Seminar2008/CompilationConference RoomPapers.pdf, p. 61.

[75] ARTICLE 19, Policy Brief on: *Prohibiting Incitement to Discrimination, Hostility, or Violence*.

[76] James J. Seeley, 'Article Twenty of the International Covenant on Civil and Political Rights: First Amendment Comments and Questions' (1970) 10 *Virginia Journal of International Law*, 339.

than a particular act.[77] The right to be protected from incitement to discrimination, hostility, or violence is thus concerned with prohibiting the reinforcement of certain negative attitudes or emotions in society, in addition to violent and discriminatory acts.

Advocates of the maximalist approach to hate speech regulation recognize severe emotional distress or offence, and the arousal of hostility towards targets of hate speech, as justifiable grounds for restricting freedom of expression, even if these harms are difficult to measure.[78] They call for a broader legal concept of harm that makes room for a 'dignitarian' harm, which may not necessarily be empirically demonstrable.[79] Critical race theorists refer to the results of empirical studies demonstrating the emotional effects of hate speech on its targets, including feelings of degradation, segregation, extreme emotional distress, and even psychosis.[80] They seek to ensure that victims' perspectives, circumstances, and experiences adequately inform the law.[81] They advocate the prohibition of the intangible harms of hate speech that cause attitudinal change. Those in favour of this approach often refer to the correlations between hate speech, on the one hand, and the hostile attitudes, beliefs, and actions of listeners, on the other. They argue that incitement to hatred or hostility, by inducing or strengthening the feelings of prejudice towards targeted groups, precedes, causes, and accompanies the infringement of these groups' rights, in particular through their subjection to discrimination and violence.[82] They also refer specifically to theoretical work conducted in the areas of social psychology and sociology, affirming the role played by hate propaganda (through the creation of hostile beliefs and feelings) as prerequisites for the commission of acts of violence and discrimination.[83] Thus, the advocates of recognizing emotional harms as justifiable grounds for restricting hate speech criticize

---

[77] Mendel, 'Study on international standards', p. 40; A/HRC/2/6, para. 40.

[78] Thomas C. Grey, 'Civil Rights vs. Civil Liberties: The Case of Discriminatory Verbal Harassment' (1991) 8(2) *Social Philosophy and Policy*, 82; Kent Greenawalt, *Fighting Words: Individuals, Communities, and Liberties of Speech* (Princeton University Press, 1995), pp. 50–59; Parekh, 'Is there a case for banning hate speech?', p. 45; Katharine Gelber, 'Reconceptualizing counterspeech in hate speech policy (with a focus on Australia)', in Michael E. Herz and Péter Molnár (eds.), *The Content and Context of Hate Speech: Rethinking Regulation and Responses* (Cambridge University Press, 2012), p. 212.

[79] Heinze, 'Toward a legal concept of hatred', p. 103.

[80] Mari J. Matsuda, 'Public Response to Racist Speech: Considering the Victim's Story' (1989) 87(8) *Michigan Law Review*, 23–25; Richard Delgado, 'Words That Wound: A Tort Action for Racial Insults, Epithets, and Name-Calling' (1982) 17 *Harvard Civil Rights – Civil Liberties Law Review*, 133–184.

[81] McGonagle, *Minority Rights*, p. 14; see generally Richard Delgado and Jean Stefancic, 'Four Observations about Hate Speech' (2009) 44 *Wake Forest Law Review*, 353–370.

[82] Bhikhu Parekh, 'Group libel and freedom of expression: Thoughts on the Rushdie affair', in Sandra Coliver (ed.), *Striking a Balance: Hate Speech, Freedom of Expression and Non-Discrimination* (Article 19, International Centre against Censorship, Human Rights Centre University of Essex, 1992), p. 359; Alexander Tsesis, 'Dignity and Speech: The Regulation of Hate Speech in a Democracy' (2009) 44 *Wake Forest Law Review*, 505.

[83] Kretzmer, 'Freedom of Speech and Racism', 456, 462–463; see for example the works of Gordon W. Allport, *The Nature of Prejudice* (Addison-Wesley Pub. Co., 1954), pp. 14–15; Neil J. Smelser, *Theory of Collective Behavior* (Collier-Macmillan, 1962), p. 79.

the exclusive focus of some laws that deal with tangible discriminatory actions at the expense of the underlying discriminatory attitudes fuelling those actions.[84] Such critics emphasize that preventing the creation of hostile feelings or attitudes would eliminate one of the necessary conditions for physical attacks or discrimination against targeted victims.[85]

Many advocates of the maximalist approach to hate speech regulation argue that the principle of moral neutrality of the state should not, and perhaps even cannot, be absolute in nature.[86] Moreover, a perceived connection exists between immorality per se and the choice of harms that deserve prohibition by law. Both are even considered mutually constitutive, pointing to the infeasibility of making a conceptual distinction between legal moralism and legislative moral neutrality.[87] Furthermore, an element of 'moral subjectivity' exists in all human rights; they are based on 'a belief about the range of aspirations which it is proper or desirable for people to pursue'.[88] Thus, according to this standpoint, the principle of moral neutrality of the state is not a valid justification for rejecting emotional harm-based restrictions on hate speech.

The ambiguity of the emotive component of the right to protection from incitement and the conundrums associated with that component, mostly related to the notions of legal moralism and relativism, are by no means the only causes of confusion about the meaning of the right. The next sections will address problems in determining its normative scope and meaning which arise from the four other constitutive features of the right.

2.3 THE INCITEMENT COMPONENT

The right to protection from incitement to discrimination, hostility, or violence features a causal explanatory mechanism, as well as a likelihood-based mechanism. The inherent complexities involved in proving the causal relationship between advocacy of hatred and its actual or potential harms, or at least the likelihood-based connection between them, are the second important feature of the right. The right does not recognize advocacy of hatred as inherently harmful, but rather as potentially harmful if it amounts to incitement to discrimination, hostility, or violence. The norm aims to suppress the *inciting* effect of hatred whenever it is publicly expressed or advocated and recognizes three different consequences of hate advocacy that warrant its prohibition. The first is incitement to an illegal act, whether violent or discriminatory, that actually takes place. The

---

[84] Heinze, 'Toward a legal concept of hatred', p. 94.

[85] Kretzmer, 'Freedom of Speech and Racism', 463.

[86] Parekh, 'Is there a case for banning hate speech?', p. 50.

[87] Feinberg, *Harmless Wrongdoing*, pp. 10–11; Neil MacCormick, *Legal Right and Social Democracy: Essays in Legal and Political Philosophy* (Oxford University Press, 1982), p. 29.

[88] Feldman, *Civil Liberties and Human Rights*, p. 6.

second is incitement to commit an illegal act that did not ultimately take place. The third is incitement to hostility, as an emotion or state of mind. In all three cases, proving incitement, or determining its threshold, are essential prerequisites of enforcing and invoking the right.

Incitement is an inchoate offence that gives rise to liability without necessarily requiring the actual occurrence of an associated substantive offence.[89] Successful and unsuccessful incitement can be distinguished; in the case of the latter, the question of causality does not become relevant, but rather likelihood does.[90] The offence of incitement enables law enforcement officials to intervene before the possible occurrence of illegal harms.[91] Therefore, it allows the state to prevent particular harms or at least reduce the incidence of their occurrence.[92] The centrality of the notion of incitement colours the right to protection from incitement to hatred with a strongly preventive character. The right obliges states to undertake preventive measures in order to enhance the rights to life and equality by addressing the root causes of possible violations.[93] The right is thus grounded in the risk thesis of recognizing rights, which provides that 'we have claims against others that they not impose risks of harm on us'.[94]

The term 'incitement' is, in itself, another example of the problems involved in constructing the normative content of the right to protection from incitement. Incitement is a familiar concept in the contexts of international and domestic criminal law, although its definition varies significantly.[95] None of the international human rights instruments using this term, including the ICERD and ICCPR, define it.[96] Few efforts have been made to provide a concrete definition of 'incitement' for the purposes of Article 20(2). The CERD, in General Recommendation 35, addressed incitement within the context of racist hate speech:

> Incitement characteristically seeks to influence others to engage in certain forms of conduct, including the commission of crime, through advocacy or threats. Incitement may be express or implied, through actions such as displays of racist symbols or distribution of materials as well as words. The notion of incitement as an inchoate crime does not require that the incitement has been acted upon[97]

---

[89]   Wibke Kristin Timmermann, 'Incitement in International Criminal Law' (2006) 88 *International Review of the Red Cross*, 825.

[90]   Temperman, *Religious Hatred*, p. 182.

[91]   Timmermann, 'Incitement in International Criminal Law', 826–827.

[92]   David Nash and Chara Bakalis, 'Incitement to Religious Hatred and the "Symbolic": How Will the Racial and Religious Hatred Act 2006 Work?' (2007) 28(3) *Liverpool Law Review*, 366.

[93]   Nowak, *U.N. Covenant on Civil and Political Rights*, p. 468.

[94]   This definition of risk thesis was provided by Judith Jarvis Thomson, *The Realm of Rights* (Harvard University Press, 1990), p. 243.

[95]   Langer, *Religious Offence*, p. 114.

[96]   Langer, *Religious Offence*, p. 115.

[97]   General Recommendation no. 35, UN Doc. CERD/C/GC/35 (26 September 2013), para. 16.

Incitement may have various qualifiers within different legal instruments, depending on the subject of regulation or object of incitement.[98] Within national legal systems, incitement is subject to various, mostly underdeveloped, definitions.[99] There are uncertainties in distinguishing incitement from instigation, justification, or moral complicity.[100]

Proving harms is essential for ensuring the enforceability of legal rights.[101] In the case of the right codified in Article 20(2) of the ICCPR, it is enforced by proving incitement to discrimination, hostility, or violence. The general difficulties encountered in proving incitement are compounded in the context of proving the inciting effect upon those listening to advocacy of hatred.[102] The harms that the right to protection from incitement to hatred seeks to prevent are diverted harms[103] or two-step harms[104]; the causal route between expressive acts and their harms is divided into two levels. The first level is between the speaker's expression and the audience, and the second level is between the audience's reaction and the harm inflicted upon the targeted victim. Thus, inciting speech has a target group, but its audience consists of third persons whom the inciter seeks to influence in order to inflict harm on that target group (the indirect effect of inciting speech).[105] It involves a triangle of the inciter, the audience, and the target group.

An intricate nexus between language, thought, emotion, and conduct, whether active or passive, exists.[106] In most cases, the causal connection between advocacy of hatred and its harms is indirect, cumulative, invisible, and too speculative.[107] Moreover, those harms occur through the listeners' mental or emotional intermediation of the beliefs, values, or attitudes advocated, characterizing them as 'belief-mediated'.[108] Hate speech involves a 'mechanism of subtle and pervasive attitudinal change'.[109] Through the listeners' endorsement of, or subscription to, the hateful

---

[98] A/HRC/2/6, para. 36.

[99] Allison G. Belnap, 'Defamation of Religions: A Vague and Overbroad Theory That Threatens Basic Human Rights' (2010) 2 *Brigham Young University Law Review*, 651.

[100] Zeno-Zencovich, *Freedom of Expression*, p. 84; Herz and Molnár, 'Interview with Kenan Malik', p. 85; A/HRC/2/6, para. 5.

[101] Osiatynski, *Human Rights and Their Limits*, p. 105.

[102] *Joint Statement by UN Special Rapporteurs on Freedom of Expression and Incitement to Racial or Religious Hatred.*

[103] Feinberg uses the expression 'merely diverted harm' to describe a situation when 'C's harm caused directly by 'B' as a consequence of an idea suggested by 'A'. Feinberg, *Harm to Others*, p. 239.

[104] Larry Alexander, *Is There a Right of Freedom of Expression?* (Cambridge University Press, 2005), pp. 76–77.

[105] Temperman, *Religious Hatred*, pp. 180–181.

[106] Laraine R. Fergenson, 'Group defamation: From language to thought to action', in Monroe H. Freedman and Eric M. Freedman (eds.), *Group Defamation and Freedom of Speech: The Relationship between Language and Violence* (Greenwood Press, 1995), p. 71.

[107] Parekh, 'Is there a case for banning hate speech?', p. 41; Feinberg, *Harm to Others*, p. 240; Kent Greenawalt, 'Speech and Crime' (1980) 5(4) *Law & Social Inquiry*, 667–668; Sumner, 'Incitement and the regulation of hate speech', p. 210.

[108] See the definition of 'belief-mediated distress' in Thomson, *The Realm of Rights*, p. 250.

[109] Sumner, 'Incitement and the regulation of hate speech', p. 209.

attitudes being advocated, they either react behaviourally against the targeted victims, by conducting discriminatory or violent acts against them, or develop hostile attitudes towards them.[110]

As a general rule, incitement is prohibited by law when the incited act itself is unlawful. Thus, the prohibition of incitement to hostility disengages from the stricter and narrower prohibition of incitement to unlawful acts, given that hostility, as an emotion or attitude, is not in itself unlawful. Proving the causal connection between advocacy of hatred and incitement to hostility is more complex in comparison to incitement to unlawful acts (whether discriminatory or violent).[111] Firstly, it is more difficult to apply standard evidential techniques when seeking to prove psychological harms, given the absence of a tangible link in the causal chain from speech to harm.[112] Secondly, the targets of hatred themselves (and not only other listeners) might mentally or emotionally intermediate hostility as a harm.[113] This leads to serious interpretive difficulties with respect to defining and identifying incitement when the alleged harm is hostility, especially when the nature of incitement itself is qualified by what is being incited.[114]

Given the aforementioned qualities of the causal relationship between advocacy of hatred and its alleged harms and difficulties associated with establishing the likelihood occurrence of such harms, it is generally not possible to prove incitement caused by such advocacy through the normal methods of empirical or experimental evidence.[115] The involvement of intangible processes concerning states of mind makes establishing such causal relationships too speculative, and assessments of risk or likelihood too uncertain.

Determination of whether hate speech constitutes incitement to discrimination, hostility, or violence largely hinges on context. It is difficult to provide a definitive or universal answer to the question of how tightly the law must draw the causal relationship or likelihood-based connection between advocacy of hatred and its actual or potential harms before it restricts the exercise of freedom of expression. Assessment of the nature and strength of that causal relationship and the likelihood of harm occurring both depend on the wider social environment, given that the

---

[110]   C. Edwin Baker, 'Scope of the First Amendment Freedom of Speech' (1978) 25 *UCLA Law Review*, 992–993; Wojciech Sadurski, 'On Seeing Speech through an Equality Lens: A Critique of Egalitarian Arguments for Suppression of Hate Speech and Pornography' (1996) 16 *Oxford Journal of Legal Studies*, 715.

[111]   Nash and Bakalis, 'Incitement to Religious Hatred', 366; Noorloos, *Hate Speech Revisited*, p. 44.

[112]   A/HRC/2/6, para. 69.

[113]   Kretzmer, 'Freedom of Speech and Racism', 460.

[114]   McGonagle, *Minority Rights*, p. 273.

[115]   David Kretzmer and Frderick Schauer, 'Speech, behaviour and the interdependence of fact and value', in David Kretzmer, Francine Kerschman Hazan, and Friedrich Ebert Stiftung (eds.), *Freedom of Speech and Incitement against Democracy* (Kluwer Law International, 2000), pp. 43, 45; Fergenson, 'Group defamation', p. 83; Jean-Francois Gaudreault-DesBiens, 'From Sisyphus's Dilemma to Sisyphus's Duty – A Meditation on the Regulation of Hate Propaganda in Relation to Hate Crimes and Genocide' (2001) 46 *McGill Law Journal*, 121.

prevailing context shapes the meaning and impact of expressions.[116] As Post notes, 'the relationship between speech and action is always a contextual matter, never matter just of the content of speech' and 'audiences always evaluate communication on the basis of their understanding of its social context'.[117] The prevalent patterns of tension between different communities, the particular situations of vulnerable groups or minorities (and the general climate of public opinion about them), the contemporaneous socio-political context, the medium of communication, and the position and status of the inciter, are all direct factors influencing the tightness and strictness of how the approach towards establishing causation or likelihood-based connection should be assessed.[118] In 2013, the CERD's General Recommendation No. 35 on racist hate speech emphasized the relevance of contextual factors and locality in establishing the existence of incitement and, in particular, the role of the prevalent economic, social, and political climate at the time of dissemination.[119] It emphasized that 'discourses which in one context are innocuous or neutral may take on a dangerous significance in another'.[120] Thus, proving the inciting effect of advocacy of hatred hinges on a contextual test; context has to be taken into account in addition to content.[121] Moreover, the demarcation line between the content and context of inciting speech is often difficult to identify.[122]

Advocates of the minimalist approach to hate speech regulation highlight the complexities involved in proving the harms of hate speech.[123] Many of them contend that, since listeners determine the extent of harms caused by hate speech, then speakers should not be held liable for such harms.[124] Baker emphasizes that the listeners' decision-making or mental mediation 'is where the chain of harmful consequences is autonomously generated'.[125] According to this line of argument, respect for the speakers' autonomy of expression and recognition of listeners' responsibility for their own unlawful acts, through the mental or emotional

---

[116] Molnar Peter, 'Responding to hate speech with art, education, and the imminent danger test', in Michael Herz and Peter Molnar (eds.), *The Content and Context of Hate Speech: Rethinking Regulation and Responses* (Cambridge University Press, 2012), p. 193; Mendel, 'Consistent rules on hate speech', p. 423; Temperman, *Religious Hatred*, p. 182.

[117] Robert Post, 'Racist Speech, Democracy, and the First Amendment' (1991) 32 *William and Mary Law Review*, 307.

[118] Sumner, 'Incitement and the regulation of hate speech', p. 213; Temperman, *Religious Hatred*, p. 182.

[119] General Recommendation no. 35, para. 15.

[120] General Recommendation no. 35, para. 15.

[121] Temperman, *Religious Hatred*, p. 169.

[122] Temperman, *Religious Hatred*, p. 172.

[123] Kretzmer, 'Freedom of Speech and Racism', 460.

[124] Susan J. Brison, 'Speech, Harm, and the Mind-Body Problem in First Amendment Jurisprudence' (1998) 4(1) *Legal Theory*, 52; David Boonin, *Should Race Matter?: Unusual Answers to the Usual Questions* (Cambridge University Press, 2011), pp. 214–216; Randall Kennedy, *Nigger: The Strange Career of a Troublesome Word* (Pantheon Books, 2002), p. 69; Sadurski, 'On Seeing Speech through an Equality Lens', 715, 718.

[125] Edwin C. Baker, 'Harm, Liberty, and Free Speech' (1997) 70 *Southern California Law Review*, 992–993.

intermediation of hostile attitudes, dictates whether liability to the listeners arises.[126] A reluctance to grant an audience that exhibits hostile reactions a power of veto to silence speakers also underlies this argument.[127] According to Sumner, the legal prohibition of incitement to an unlawful act (discriminatory or violent) is 'too remotely and speculatively linked to harms' to satisfy Mill's harm principle.[128] The minimalist approach requires a tight, direct, demonstrable, and immediate causal relationship between advocacy of hatred and its harms, narrowly defined as tangible, behavioural, and lawless, in order to justify restricting freedom of expression.[129] In other words, it requires a 'quasi-photographic capturing' of the translation of the advocacy of hatred into actual harms.[130] This insistence on a strict and direct causal connection reflects fears that states might abuse a looser causal connection in order to impose a wide range of content-based restrictions on freedom of expression.[131]

Most advocates of the maximalist approach to hate speech regulation define the causal relationship between advocacy of hatred and its harms in an indirect and cumulative manner.[132] They challenge the strictly material model of causation. According to this approach, a 'rational correlation' between advocacy and related harms, or even the mere tendency to cause harm, is sufficient grounds for restricting advocacy of hatred.[133] Moreover, the harms of hate speech are often conceived of as 'constituted' by such speech, not just 'caused' by it.[134] The maximalist approach regards the harms of hate advocacy to largely be of long-term causality, slowly building up through the reinforcement of prejudices and stereotypes against targeted persons and their gradual progression towards acts of discrimination or violence.[135] Advocates of this approach criticize the argument that hate speech may be restricted only when there is an imminent danger of unlawful acts occurring. Parekh contends that this argument 'fails to probe further the idea of imminent danger'. He points out that 'no action occurs in a historical vacuum, and every action produces consequences not inherently but against a particular background ... imminent danger occurs against, and is imminent because of the prevailing social climate (which groups are subject to deeply rooted prejudices built up over time)'.[136]

---

[126]   Baker, 'Harm, Liberty, and Free Speech', 990, 992; Boonin, *Should Race Matter?*, p. 213; Sadurski, 'On Seeing Speech through an Equality Lens', 716.

[127]   Sadurski, *Freedom of Speech*, p. 197; Sadurski, 'On Seeing Speech through an Equality Lens', 716.

[128]   Sumner, 'Incitement and the regulation of hate speech', p. 220.

[129]   Gaudreault-DesBiens, 'A Meditation on the Regulation of Hate Propaganda', 123–124; Norris, 'Note: A Communitarian Defense of Group Libel Laws', 687; Kretzmer, 'Freedom of Speech and Racism', 457; Massey, 'Hate Speech and Cultural Diversity', 174.

[130]   Gaudreault-DesBiens, 'A Meditation on the Regulation of Hate Propaganda', 123.

[131]   Robert Post, 'Religion and Freedom of Speech: Portraits of Muhammad' (2007) 14(1) *Constellations*, 83.

[132]   Parekh, 'Is there a case for banning hate speech?', p. 41.

[133]   Gaudreault-DesBiens, 'A Meditation on the Regulation of Hate Propaganda', 123.

[134]   Waldron, *The Harm in Hate Speech*, pp. 166, 169, 171.

[135]   Waldron, *The Harm in Hate Speech*, p. 160; Rosenfeld, 'Hate speech in constitutional jurisprudence', p. 282; Parekh, 'Is there a case for banning hate speech?', p. 45.

[136]   Parekh, 'Is there a case for banning hate speech?', p. 45.

Thereby, he calls for the concentration of efforts 'not only on fighting the immediate source of danger, but also on changing the climate'.[137] Waldron draws an interesting analogy between hate speech harms and environmental harms in terms of their pace of causation in order to demonstrate that isolated utterances and actions constitute, in a cumulative manner, long-term harms. Accordingly, he contends that the law can legitimately target both kinds of harm.[138]

The conception of the causal relationship between advocacy of hatred and its harms as long-term and cumulative leads to an expanded legal regulation of hate speech that seeks to prevent a wide range of harms (both direct and indirect).[139] Gaudreault-DesBiens rightly describes this conception as reflective of 'a preventive logic of risk management', whereas he describes the tight and strict conception of the causal relationship as reflecting 'a curative logic of imputation'.[140]

On the whole, the right to protection from incitement to discrimination, hostility, or violence recognizes a suggestive, rather than a tightly dispositive, causal relationship or likelihood-based connection between advocacy of hatred and its actual or potential harms. The right embodies an onerous standard of harm that heuristic processes are unlikely to demonstrate empirically. In the legal field, there are many riddles of causation, including the lack of a presumption that its assessment must be undertaken in a purely objective manner at all times.[141] Nevertheless, this element of subjectivity in the principles of causation is compounded in the implementation of hate speech laws. The emotional component that lies behind hate speech, the belief-mediated nature of its alleged harms (which may not be material or tangible), and the long-term or cumulative causality involved between hate speech and its harms create wider zones of subjectivity. The complexities associated with identifying and proving incitement make the interpretation and enforcement of the right to protection from incitement to hatred problematical. Additionally, given the necessity of assessing incitement contextually, the right faces a relativist challenge, undermining the possibility of reaching a universal interpretation.

2.4 THE TENSIONS BETWEEN EQUALITY AND LIBERTY RIGHTS OF SPEAKERS AND MEMBERS OF TARGETED GROUPS

The regulation of incitement to hatred is commonly perceived as a setting in which the two values of liberty and equality are in tension or even conflict with each other.[142] The minimalist approach to hate speech regulation, which recognizes a very narrow range of harms justifying its prohibition, is perceived to prioritize liberty

---

[137] Parekh, 'Is there a case for banning hate speech?', p. 46.
[138] Waldron, *The Harm in Hate Speech*, p. 97.
[139] Gaudreault-DesBiens, 'A Meditation on the Regulation of Hate Propaganda', 125.
[140] Gaudreault-DesBiens, 'A Meditation on the Regulation of Hate Propaganda', 123.
[141] Gaudreault-DesBiens, 'A Meditation on the Regulation of Hate Propaganda', 125.
[142] Delgado and Stefancic, 'Four Observations about Hate Speech', 370; Herz and Molnar, 'Introduction', p. 6; Caroline West, 'Words that silence? Freedom of expression and racist hate

over equality, whereas the maximalist approach, which recognizes a wider range of harms for such prohibition, is regarded as prioritizing equality over liberty.[143] Article 20(2) of the ICCPR is commonly regarded as containing an inbuilt clash or inherent dichotomy between the prerogative of free expression and the principle of freedom from discrimination.

Although freedom of expression might appear, prima facie, as the normative obstacle and counterweight of the right to be protected from incitement to hatred, the involvement of notions of liberty and equality within the right is far more complex and multifaceted. The regulation of hate speech should not be mischaracterized or oversimplified as entailing a dichotomy between liberty and equality. A deeper analysis of the minimalist and maximalist approaches to hate speech regulation indicates that the values of liberty and equality are simultaneously central to the reasoning of both approaches. The minimalist approach places more emphasis on protecting the speakers' rights to freedom of expression and equality in exercising that freedom, whereas the maximalist approach places more emphasis on protecting the equality rights of the targeted listeners, including their right to exercise freedom of expression, as a fundamental liberty.[144] Therefore, it is not only the liberty of speakers and equality of targeted listeners that must be considered in debates on hate speech regulation, but also the converse. The right to protection from incitement takes effect through restricting the exercise of speakers' freedom of expression, a fundamental freedom that is an indispensable element of individual liberty and should thus be equally enjoyed. Enhancing the rights of targeted listeners to equality, including their equal right to freedom of expression, largely grounds and justifies the protection provided by the right to be protected against incitement. Thus, the minimalist and maximalist approaches to hate speech regulation do not reflect their predominant perception as opposing trade-offs between liberty and equality as abstract values but, rather, feature trade-offs between various conceptions of each value and the respective competing interests of speakers and members of targeted groups in enjoying both values.

Thus, the regulation of hate speech does not entail a choice between liberty and equality. Instead, it requires a balance to be struck between the speakers' and targeted listeners' interests in both of these values. The chosen balancing mode therefore determines the scope of limitations on freedom of expression imposed for the purposes of protecting against the harms of hate speech. Any legal system that

speech', in Ishani Maitra and Mary Kathryn McGowan (eds.), *Speech and Harm: Controversies over Free Speech* (Oxford University Press, 2012), p. 222; Yared Legesse Mengistu, 'Shielding marginalized groups from verbal assaults without abusing hate speech laws', in Michael E. Herz and Péter Molnár (eds.), *The Content and Context of Hate Speech: Rethinking Regulation and Responses* (Cambridge University Press, 2012), p. 355; Wayne Sumner, 'Hate speech and the law: A Canadian perspective', in Arend Soeteman (ed.), *Pluralism and Law* (Springer, 2011), p. 37.

[143] Gaudreault-DesBiens, 'A Meditation on the Regulation of Hate Propaganda', 125; Brink, 'Millian Principles', 119; Herz and Molnar, 'Introduction', p. 6.

[144] Abigail Levin, *The Cost of Free Speech: Pornography, Hate Speech and Their Challenge to Liberalism* (Palgrave Macmillan, 2010), pp. 2–3.

accords the right to be protected from incitement to discrimination, hostility, or violence will have to undertake this difficult balancing task; this is true at both national and international levels. The two values, liberty and equality, appear on both sides of the equation in any cost–benefit assessment of hate speech restrictions.

Debates over hate speech, as Brink rightly notes, 'have teased apart libertarian and egalitarian strands within the liberal tradition'.[145] The libertarian strand adopts very narrow and fixed limitations on freedom of expression, consistent with its strict adherence to the tenets of classical negative liberalism, which views state interference as undesirable.[146] In contrast, the egalitarian strand emphasizes the numerous, fluctuating boundaries of freedom of expression, which is consistent with this strand's preference for a more interventionist state that takes an active role in addressing inequalities.[147] Advocates of the libertarian and egalitarian notions of freedom of expression each have different views on the degree, nature, and significance of harms that result from the suppression of hate speech. Those advocating a libertarian view adopt a minimalist approach to hate speech legal regulation. Those advocating an egalitarian view of freedom of expression adopt a maximalist approach. As Feldman observes, in the field of hate speech 'even liberals committed to personal and political freedom may find their values leading them in several directions'. [148]

The libertarian notion of freedom of expression assumes that harms arising from the exercise of this freedom are qualitatively different from those caused by other types of conduct. Schauer refers to this assumption as the 'lesser harm hypothesis' and regards it as an implicit supposition of Mill's harm principle.[149] According to this assumption, the possible harms of expressive acts are 'minimal',[150] less immediately dangerous and much more speculative in nature than harms caused by other categories of act.[151] This arguably makes the exercise of freedom of expression less likely to infringe upon the rights of others.[152] The libertarian notion of freedom of expression posits that the threshold test the right to be protected from incitement must satisfy in order to restrict advocacy of hatred includes a very restricted definition of resulting harms; they must be imminent and represent clearly unlawful

---

[145] Brink, 'Millian Principles', 119.

[146] See generally on libertarianism: Tibor R. Machan, 'Considerations of the Libertarian Alternative' (1979) 2 *Harvard Journal of Law and Public Policy*, 104–124.

[147] Massey, 'Hate Speech and Cultural Diversity', 106.

[148] Feldman, *Civil Liberties and Human Rights*, pp. 954–955.

[149] Frderick Schauer, 'The Phenomenology of Speech and Harm' (1993) 103(4) *Ethics*, 640.

[150] Brison, 'Speech, Harm, and the Mind-Body Problem', 40; Ronald Dworkin, 'Forward', in Ivan Hare and James Weinstein (eds.), *Extreme Speech and Democracy* (Oxford University Press, 2009), p. vi; Waldron, *The Harm in Hate Speech*, p. 148.

[151] Martin H. Redish, *Freedom of Expression: A Critical Analysis* (Michie Co., 1984), p. 5; Ronald Dworkin, *Taking Rights Seriously* (Duckworth, 1977), pp. 200–203.

[152] Schauer, 'The Phenomenology of Speech', 640, 641; Brison, 'Speech, Harm, and the Mind-Body Problem', 51; Kretzmer, 'Freedom of Speech and Racism', 459.

actions targeting individuals.[153] Scholars have often described this rationale for hate speech restrictions as the 'fighting words'-based argument, only prohibiting expressions that generate a significant risk that they 'incite an immediate breach of the peace'.[154]

Advocates of the minimalist approach frequently warn against the abuse of hate speech laws through the contraction and expansion of the scope of freedom of expression, either to curtail the political liberties of vulnerable minority groups or in response to changing public sentiment.[155] They have faith in the capacity of individuals to engage in counter-expressions that redress the effects of hate speech with the state assuming a neutral role in this regard.[156] Various theorists and scholars have frequently described this argument as the 'free marketplace of ideas', where open exchange and free competition of ideas guarantee that the best ones will survive and the bad ones will be confronted and neutralized.[157] According to this argument, state neutrality enhances the speakers' right to express themselves equally.[158] Sadurski argues that each person has an equal right to decide how to shape his or her life and that 'to attribute to some members of the community the authority to decide what is good for others would inevitably deny equal moral sovereignty for these other people'.[159] He further argues that the state should not seek to filter expressions under the pretext that their hateful content might persuade listeners, as this presumes that listeners are 'thoughtless receivers of ideas imposed upon them by speakers'.[160]

Through a libertarian lens, states' obligations under Articles 19 and 20 conflict on the basis that some categories of expression prohibited under Article 20(2) belong to the protected zones of freedom of expression.[161] Article 20(2) is also perceived as

---

[153] Grey, 'Civil Rights vs. Civil Liberties', 82; Nowak, *U.N. Covenant on Civil and Political Rights*, p. 439; Massey, 'Hate Speech and Cultural Diversity', 106; Janis L. Judson and Donna M. Bertazzoni, *Law, Media, and Culture, the Landscape of Hate* (Peter Lang, 2002), p. 55.

[154] See Samuel Walker, *Hate Speech: The History of an American Controversy* (University of Nebraska Press, 1994), p. 71, quoting Justice Frank Murphy in the US Supreme Court ruling in 1942 in *Chaplinsky v. New Hampshire*.

[155] Frederick M. Lawrence, 'Violence-conducive speech: Punishable verbal assault or protected political speech', in David Kretzmer and Francine Kershman Hazan (eds.), *Freedom of Speech and Incitement against Democracy* (Kluwer Law International, 2000), pp. 11–12; Dworkin, 'Forward', p. v; Boonin, *Should Race Matter?*, p. 246; Kretzmer, 'Freedom of Speech and Racism', 457, 491; C. Edwin Baker, 'Autonomy and hate speech', in Ivan Hare and James Weinstein (eds.), *Extreme Speech and Democracy* (Oxford University Press, 2009), p. 154.

[156] Massaro, 'Equality and Freedom of Expression', 222; Gaudreault-DesBiens, 'A Meditation on the Regulation of Hate Propaganda', 129.

[157] Jacob Rowbottom, 'Media Freedom and Political Debate in the Digital Era' (2006) 68(4) *The Modern Law Review*, 69, 491; Judson and Bertazzoni, *Law, Media, and Culture*, p. 55; Brink, 'Millian Principles', 119.

[158] Levin, *The Cost of Free Speech*, p. 1, 3.

[159] Sadurski, *Moral Pluralism*, p. 93.

[160] Sadurski, 'On Seeing Speech through an Equality Lens', 717.

[161] Joshua Foster, 'Prophets, Cartoons, and Legal Norms: Rethinking the United Nations Defamation of Religion Provisions' (2009) 48 *Journal of Catholic Legal Studies*, 35–36; Friedrich Kubler, 'How

settling 'a priori' tensions between freedom of expression and non-discrimination in favour of the latter.[162]

On the other hand, advocates of the egalitarian notion of freedom of expression, who endorse a maximalist approach to hate speech regulation, consider prohibition of discrimination without prohibition of hate speech to be ineffective on the basis that they are causally tied, conceptually linked, or both.[163] MacKinnon considers hate speech as a form of discrimination or an 'expressive form of inequality' that constitutes, rather than simply causes, discrimination and thus warrants legal regulation similar to that of other forms of discriminatory action.[164] The silencing effect of hate speech on its targets is a central argument used by the advocates of the maximalist approach.[165] This argument is the logical antithesis of the 'free marketplace of ideas'. It emphasizes that hate speech violates the equal rights of targeted persons to exercise their freedom of expression, since they become silenced under the subordinating, disempowering, and marginalizing effect of hate speech.[166] According to the 'silencing effect' argument, even when the targets of hate speech engage in the public discourse, their contributions become devalued due to the perpetuation and reinforcement of hostile attitudes against them.[167] The advocates of the maximalist approach to hate speech regulation criticize

Much Freedom for Racist Speech?: Transnational Aspects of a Conflict of Human Rights' (1998) 27 *Hofstra Law Review*, 357; Sejal Parmar, 'The Challenge of "Defamation of Religion" to Freedom of Expression and the International Human Rights' (2009) 3 *European Human Rights Law Review*, 368; Wibke Kristin Timmermann, 'The Relationship between Hate Propaganda and Incitement to Genocide: A New Trend in International Law towards Criminalization of Hate Propaganda?' (2005) 18(2) *Leiden Journal of International Law*, 258; Catlin, 'Proposal for Regulating Hate Speech', 797; Javaid Rehman, *International Human Rights Law* (Longman/Pearson, 2010), p. 110; Anat Scolnicov, *The Right to Religious Freedom in International Law: Between Group Rights and Individual Rights* (Routledge, 2011), p. 206. Scolnicov also finds Article 20(2) in conflict with Article 18 on freedom of Religion.

[162] Temperman, *Religious Hatred*, p. 12.

[163] Kretzmer, 'Freedom of Speech and Racism', 456; Brink, 'Millian Principles', 119; Mendel, 'Study on international standards', p. 10; Gaudreault-DesBiens, 'A Meditation on the Regulation of Hate Propaganda', 130; Farrior, 'Molding the Matrix', 97; Dworkin, 'Forward', p. vi; Sumner, 'Hate speech and the law', p. 37; Tsesis, 'Dignity and Speech', 505.

[164] Catharine A. MacKinnon, *Only Words* (Harvard University Press, 1993), p. 72; The term 'verbal discrimination' was employed by social psychologists to indicate that words can not only cause discrimination, but also can themselves constitute discrimination; see for example Carl F. Graumann, 'Verbal Discrimination: A Neglected Chapter in the Social Psychology of Aggression' (1998) 28(1) *Journal for the Theory of Social Behaviour*, 41–61.

[165] Alexander Tsesis, 'Hate in Cyberspace: Regulating Hate Speech on the Internet' (2001) 38 *San Diego Law Review*, 852; Judson and Bertazzoni, *Law, Media, and Culture*, p. 55; Tsesis, 'Dignity and Speech', 501; Levin, *The Cost of Free Speech*, p. 1; Kubler, 'How Much Freedom for Racist Speech?', 367; Kathleen E. Mahoney, 'Speech, Equality, and Citizenship in Canada' (2010) 39(1) *Common Law World Review*, 1; Gelber, 'Reconceptualizing counterspeech', p. 208; MacKinnon, *Only Words*, pp. 72–73, 75–76; Matsuda, 'Public Response to Racist Speech'.

[166] Levin, *The Cost of Free Speech*, p. 2; MacKinnon, *Only Words*, pp. 72–73; Matsuda, 'Public Response to Racist Speech', 2337, 2358; Brink, 'Millian Principles', 141; Lawrence, Violence-conducive speech, p. 452; W. Bradley Wendel, 'Certain Fundamental Truths: A Dialectic on Negative and Positive Liberty in Hate-Speech Cases' (2002) 65(2) *Law and Contemporary Problems*, 64.

[167] Brink, 'Millian Principles', 141; Parekh, 'Is there a case for banning hate speech?', p. 48.

the argument of the 'free marketplace of ideas' for ignoring the inequality of access to that marketplace.[168] They argue that the marketplace 'operates against the background of prevailing prejudices'[169] and thus results in the survival of the ideas of the most powerful groups in society, perpetuating inequality.[170] According to the supporters of this maximalist approach, the relationship between the marketplace of ideas, equality, and neutrality is de facto 'in crisis' due to the malfunctioning of the marketplace of ideas.[171] Pursuant to the 'silencing effect' argument, state neutrality is 'tantamount to a myopic neglect of the fundamental reality of unequal distribution of power'.[172] This argument thus emphasizes that societies should not tolerate or remain passive towards speech that is inherently adversarial to equality and human dignity but should rather redress the systemic inequalities perpetuated by hate speech.[173]

In response to critics warning of the danger of abusing hate speech laws, the defenders of hate speech regulation contend that the same risk of abuse is applicable to all restrictions on liberties and thus does not justify the toleration of hate speech.[174] They also emphasize the symbolic significance of hate speech laws, given that these laws have the declaratory value of indicating the state and society's rejection of anti-egalitarian speech and commitment to promoting equality and maintaining social peace and cohesion.[175]

The 'silencing effect' argument for prohibiting hate speech appeals to the values of liberty and equality. According to this argument, the net effect of prohibiting hate speech would be to allow wider expression, as it guarantees the participation of marginalized or minority groups in public discourse.[176] Thus, it emphasizes the value of consolidating freedom of expression for listeners targeted by hate speech.[177] It 'equalizes the right and opportunity both to speak and to be heard'.[178] Therefore, the 'silencing effect' argument considers that the goals of ensuring legal protection

---

[168]   Owen M. Fiss, *The Irony of Free Speech* (Harvard University Press, 1996), p. 16; Rosenfeld, 'Hate speech in constitutional jurisprudence', pp. 282–283; Parekh, 'Is there a case for banning hate speech?', p. 48.

[169]   Parekh, 'Is there a case for banning hate speech?', p. 48.

[170]   Gelber, 'Reconceptualizing counterspeech', p. 209; Mengistu, 'Shielding marginalized groups', pp. 352, 358; Farrior, 'Molding the Matrix', 95; Parekh, 'Is there a case for banning hate speech?', p. 48.

[171]   Levin, *The Cost of Free Speech*, p. 1.

[172]   Mengistu, 'Shielding marginalized groups', p. 358.

[173]   Rhoda E. Howard-Hassmann, 'Canadians Discuss Freedom of Speech: Individual Rights Versus Group Protection' (2000) 7(2) *International Journal on Minority and Group Right*, 138; Mendel, 'Study on international standards', p. 40; Farrior, 'Molding the Matrix', 499; Rosenfeld, 'Hate speech in constitutional jurisprudence', pp. 284–285; Parekh, 'Is there a case for banning hate speech?', p. 50.

[174]   Parekh, 'Is there a case for banning hate speech?', p. 54; Farrior, 'Molding the Matrix', 97; Rosenfeld, 'Hate speech in constitutional jurisprudence', p. 287; Gaudreault-DesBiens, 'A Meditation on the Regulation of Hate Propaganda', 132; Mendel, 'Consistent rules on hate speech', p. 425.

[175]   Delgado, 'Words That Wound', 149; Waldron, *The Harm in Hate Speech*, p. 103; Parekh, 'Is there a case for banning hate speech?', p. 46.

[176]   Levin, *The Cost of Free Speech*; Gelber, 'Reconceptualizing counterspeech', p. 210.

[177]   West, 'Words that silence?', p. 222; Parekh, 'Is there a case for banning hate speech?', p. 56.

[178]   Levin, *The Cost of Free Speech*, p. 2.

against the harms of hate speech and enhancing freedom of expression are complementary rather than contradictory.[179]

The formal and substantive conceptions of equality align, respectively, with the libertarian and egalitarian notions of freedom of expression.[180] The formal conception of equality requires that every individual be treated equally before the law, while the substantive conception of equality requires measures by the state to guarantee the effective realization of equal rights for everyone.[181] In the context of freedom of expression, the formal conception of equality is more or less reducible to the capacity for autonomy, a situation in which everyone has unrestricted ability to express or access a full range of views. Moreover, in this conception, the state does not favour the substantive autonomy of some individuals over others.[182] This formal conception of equality corresponds to the minimalist approach to hate speech regulation.[183] The advocates of this approach argue that expanded hate speech restrictions are inconsistent with safeguarding formal equality.[184]

On the other hand, the substantive conception of equality, in the context of freedom of expression, necessitates the state's intervention in order to address the harms that might result from the exercise of that freedom, thus corresponding to the maximalist approach to hate speech regulation. It acknowledges the existence of patterns of disadvantage, and structural imbalances, in the distribution of social power, employing the law to redress these through the protection of the marginalized and oppressed from the harms of hate speech.[185] According to this line of argument, the exclusive endorsement of the formal conception of equality is unlikely to succeed in achieving equality, either of outcome or opportunity, in light of existing social structural imbalances.[186] Through an egalitarian lens, states' obligations under Articles 19 and 20(2) are coherent and complementary.

The right to protection from incitement seeks to create a bridge between the values of liberty and equality through the balancing of listeners' and speakers' rights pertaining to both values. The reference, in Article 19(3), to the respect of the rights of others being a legitimate justification for limiting freedom of expression solves the prima facie inconsistency with Article 20(2), given that the latter seeks to protect the

---

[179] Gelber, 'Reconceptualizing counterspeech', p. 216.

[180] Louis Henkin, 'International human rights and rights in the United States', in Theodor Meron (ed.), *Human Rights in International Law* (Clarendon press, 1992), p. 42.

[181] Noorloos, *Hate Speech Revisited*, p. 24.

[182] Robert Post, 'The Constitutional Concept of Public Discourse: Outrageous Opinion, Democratic Deliberation, and Hustler Magazine v. Falwell' (1990) 103(3) *Harvard Law Review*, 601–686; Baker, 'Autonomy and hate speech', pp. 142–143; Massey, 'Hate Speech and Cultural Diversity', 173–174.

[183] Feldman, *Civil Liberties and Human Rights*, p. 1052.

[184] Massey, 'Hate Speech and Cultural Diversity', 173–174; Mengistu, 'Shielding marginalized groups', p. 355.

[185] Noorloos, *Hate Speech Revisited*, p. 24; Massey, 'Hate Speech and Cultural Diversity', 173–174; Mengistu, 'Shielding marginalized groups', pp. 352, 355.

[186] James Weinstein, *Hate Speech, Pornography, and the Radical Attack on Free Speech Doctrine* (Westview Press, 1999), pp. 92–93.

rights of listeners, including their exercise of freedom of expression.[187] A similar connection may be made between the protection of public order being another legitimate justification for limiting freedom of expression under Article 19(3) and the underlying rationale of Article 20(2).[188] Once the threshold of Article 20(2) is met, the expressive acts described therein should be prohibited. These expressive acts become excluded from the legitimate zones of exercising freedom of expression. This freedom is not absolute in nature but may be subject to restrictions, provided that they pursue a legitimate aim and respect the principles of legality, proportionality, and necessity.[189] Also, the interpretation of Article 19(3) must respect the terms of Article 20(2).[190] The ICCPR, through the inclusion of Article 20(2), succeeds in striking a balance between the liberty and equality rights of speakers and members of targeted groups, placing freedom of expression within a relational context to other rights.[191]

The obligations of states pursuant to the right to protection from incitement to discrimination, hostility, or violence, as codified in IHRL, do not support the strict libertarian notion of freedom of expression or the minimalist approach to hate speech regulation. Rather, they come closer to the egalitarian notion of freedom of expression or the maximalist approach to hate speech regulation. The existence of the right itself indicates that the principles of state neutrality and 'free marketplace of ideas' are insufficient to address the potential or actual harms of hate speech. Consequently, a feature of the right is that it restricts the exercise of freedom of expression on the basis of a wide scope of harms, which include intangible emotional harms as well as immediate unlawful actions. Furthermore, the right endorses a substantive, rather than exclusively formal, conception of equality that advances equality of enjoyment in addition to equality of opportunity. It endorses the victim's perspective through balancing the speakers' freedom of expression against the rights of targeted listeners to equality, including their equal right to exercise freedom of expression.[192]

The interpretation and implementation of the right to protection from incitement to discrimination, hostility, or violence should not be reduced to solving perceived conflicts or tensions between equality and liberty by giving primacy to one value over the other. Instead, the right requires a difficult balance to be struck between the speakers' interests in enjoying both liberty and equality rights, on the one hand, and

---

[187]   Anges Callamard, 'Towards an Interpretation of Article 20 of the ICCPR: Thresholds for the Prohibition of Incitement to Hatred', available at www.ohchr.org/Documents/Issues/Expression/ICCPR/Vienna/CRP7Callamard.pdf, p. 8; Catlin, 'Proposal for Regulating Hate Speech', 797; Mendel, 'Study on international standards', p. 31.

[188]   Feldman, 'Freedom of expression', p. 431; Nowak, *U.N. Covenant on Civil and Political Rights*, p. 477.

[189]   CCPR, General Comment no. 34 (Art. 19), UN Doc. CCPR/C/GC/34 (12 September 2011), para. 50.

[190]   Parmar, 'The Challenge of Defamation of Religion', 369.

[191]   Farrior, 'Molding the Matrix', 6.

[192]   Catlin, 'Proposal for Regulating Hate Speech', 777, 779.

the interests of the members of targeted groups in enjoying these rights, on the other. As described above, the libertarian and egalitarian notions of freedom of expression delineate these interests differently. In the context of hate speech regulation, it is not accurate to assume that the relationship between freedom of expression and equality is mutually exclusive, such that any step towards greater equality necessarily involves diminishing freedom of expression. Regulation of hate speech may in fact help preserve freedom of expression for the targets of hate speech. The right to protection from incitement to hatred ensures that freedom of expression, among other rights, applies equally to all members of society. If hate speech is impeding this, then legal regulation must be employed to balance the scales.

2.5 THE GROUP IDENTITY COMPONENT

The right to protection from incitement to discrimination, hostility, or violence has a clear group identity aspect. Pursuant to the right, advocacy of hatred is prohibited if it targets any of three specific collective identities: national origin, race, or religion.[193] The right is thus accorded on a collective basis and is concerned with preventing identity-based harms. The norm providing protection against incitement supports a collective right to identity. It provides protection against incitement for people, both as individuals and as members of groups.

Hate speech characteristically expresses hatred, not just towards individuals, but also towards groups or communities defined by reference to their identities.[194] The exercise of freedom of expression, in comparison to other liberties, has a more direct and evident impact on the tension between individual interests and the collective rights of groups.[195] The level of recognition of, and respect for, group rights directly affects the acceptable scope of limitations to the exercise of freedom of expression.[196]

The collective dimension of the right to protection from incitement to hatred raises a number of conundrums relating to whether states should provide protection against the harms of hate speech only to individuals on the basis of their membership in particular racial, religious, or national groups or also to these groups in themselves. There is an evident difficulty in drawing a sharp dividing line between the two categories of protection, since hate speech targets people based on their group-defining characteristics.

The question of whether the right is exclusively individual in nature, or both individual and collective, has significant consequences for the scope of freedom of

---

[193] Foster, 'Prophets and Cartoons', 35–36; Farrior, 'Molding the Matrix', 8; Chaloka Beyani, 'Law and Judicial Practices', available at www.ohchr.org/Documents/Issues/Expression/ICCPR/Nairobi/ChalokaBeyani.pdf, p. 1.

[194] Gelber, 'Reconceptualizing counterspeech', p. 215.

[195] Alex Conte, 'Democratic and civil rights', in Alex Conte and Richard Burchill (eds.), *Defining Civil and Political Rights the Jurisprudence of the United Nations Human Rights Committee* (Ashgate, 2009), p. 76.

[196] Greenawalt, *Fighting Words*, pp. 8–9.

expression and its limitations. If groups, in addition to individuals, bear this right then states must recognize collective harms as legitimate grounds for prohibiting freedom of expression. Moreover, this raises the dilemma of differentiating between speech targeting a group (as a collective) and speech denigrating its group-defining characteristics, given that these two categories inextricably overlap.[197]

The framing of the right as a group right entails the expansion of the scope of limitations on freedom of expression for the purpose of protecting group identities. That the right is a fusion of individual and collective elements thus poses challenges to its definition and interpretation. Any legal system, whether at the national or international level, which endorses this norm, will have to strike a difficult and delicate balance between individual and group rights. The interpretation of the right is therefore shaped by biases towards either the individualist or communitarian approaches to rights.

The individualist account of human rights, which is integral to the liberal theory of rights, conceives of them as individuals' rights protecting autonomous self-government against state oppression, as well as against more general collective and utilitarian considerations.[198] It perceives the scope of IHRL as traditionally associated with the regulation of state authorities' treatment of individuals under their jurisdiction.[199] Dworkin, for instance, describes rights as 'political trumps held by individuals – trumps which protect individuals from the uninhibited pursuit of collective goals'.[200] Gray also notes that liberalism 'asserts the moral primacy of the person against the collectivity'.[201] According to the 'individualized rights' argument, if an individual liberty contradicts a communal goal, the former should not be compromised but, rather, prioritized.[202] The supporters of this argument do not attribute rights to groups, refusing to define communal goals or interests as group rights.[203] They consider group rights 'antithetical to the idea of rights as a limit to collective power'.[204] Donnelly argues that group affiliations are largely disconnected from the rights that individuals should enjoy.[205] According to

[197] Waldron, *The Harm in Hate Speech*, pp. 60–61, 123.

[198] Mathieu Deflem, *Sociology of Law: Visions of a Scholarly Tradition* (Cambridge University Press, 2008), p. 199; Scolnicov, *The Right to Religious Freedom in International Law*, pp. 25, 31; Attracta Ingram, A Political *Theory of Rights* (Oxford University Press, 1994), p. 9.

[199] Ingrid Nifosi-Sutton, *The Protection of Vulnerable Groups under International Human Rights Law* (Routledge, 2017), p. 19.

[200] Dworkin, *Taking Rights Seriously*, p. xi.

[201] John Gray, *Liberalism* (Open University Press, 1995), p. 86.

[202] Waldron, *Liberal Rights*, p. 367; Baker, 'Autonomy and hate speech', p. 142–146; Feinberg, *Harmless Wrongdoing*, p. 84.

[203] Scolnicov, *The Right to Religious Freedom in International Law*, p. 25; Waldron, *Liberal Rights*, pp. 364–365.

[204] Scolnicov, *The Right to Religious Freedom in International Law*, p. 31.

[205] Jack Donnelly, *Universal Human Rights in Theory and Practice* (Cornell University Press, 2002), p. 206; Bhikhu C. Parekh, *Rethinking Multiculturalism: Cultural Diversity and Political Theory* (Harvard University Press, 2000), p. 213.

this line of argument, group rights should merely be perceived as an aggregation of individual rights, rather than as superior to these rights.[206]

The individualist account of rights highlights a number of practical problems pertaining to the legal recognition of group rights – in particular, their use as a pretext for infringing upon individuals' rights,[207] an increase in the scope of conflicting rights,[208] and the dilemma of identifying which groups should hold rights.[209] According to this account of rights, only individual claims and harms directed against individuals should be legally recognized, eliminating claims for protecting group values, identities, or interests.[210] From an individualist perspective, the right not to be discriminated against on the basis of a certain group identity is an individual right that should not be conceived of as a group right, since this might infringe upon individual rights.[211] Equality, according to this individualist conception of rights, is individually rather than communally based.

The rationales of freedom of expression, according to the individualized-rights argument, are rooted within strongly individualistic premises: the pursuit of self-fulfilment and autonomy.[212] Restrictions on hate speech are only acceptable when the target is a specific individual, rather than the larger community to which they belong.[213] Consequently, the recognition of a group right to be protected from the harms of hate speech is inconsistent with the 'individualistic foundation of the self-governance rationale for free expression'.[214]

Advocates of the individualist approach to rights criticize the enactment of group libel or defamation laws and refuse to equate group and individual libel laws.[215] They emphasize that the two essential conditions for incurring liability under individual libel laws (that the expressions in question must be factual and false) do not apply to instances of group defamation.[216] They further elaborate that group

---

[206] Scolnicov, *The Right to Religious Freedom in International Law*, p. 28; Massey, 'Hate Speech and Cultural Diversity', 195; Feinberg, *Harmless Wrongdoing*, p. 84.

[207] Paul Sieghart, *The International Law of Human Rights* (Oxford University Press, 1983), p. 368; Scolnicov, *The Right to Religious Freedom in International Law*, p. 25.

[208] Donnelly, *Universal Human Rights*, p. 210.

[209] Donnelly, *Universal Human Rights*, pp. 209–210.

[210] Robert C. Post, 'Cultural Heterogeneity and Law: Pornography, Blasphemy, and the First Amendment' (1988) 76(2) *California Law Review*, 299.

[211] Scolnicov, *The Right to Religious Freedom in International Law*, pp. 33–34.

[212] Thomas I. Emerson, *The System of Freedom of Expression* (Random House, 1970), pp. 397–399; Tom Campbell, *Rights: A Critical Introduction* (Routledge, 2006), pp. 50, 147; McGoldrick and O'Donnell, 'Hate-Speech Laws', 454; Norman Dorsen, 'Is there a right to stop offensive speech? The case of the Nazis at Skokie', in Lawrence O. Gostin (ed.), *Civil Liberties in Conflict* (Routledge, 1988), p. 124; Kretzmer, 'Freedom of Speech and Racism', 481; Massey, 'Hate Speech and Cultural Diversity', 107, 116, 132, 162; Grimm, 'Freedom of speech in a globalized world', p. 11; Marin Scordato and Paula A. Monopoli, 'Free Speech Rationales after September 11th: The First Amendment in Post-World Trade Center America' (2002) 13 *Stanford Law & Policy Review*, 194.

[213] Massey, 'Hate Speech and Cultural Diversity', 110, 174.

[214] Massey, 'Hate Speech and Cultural Diversity', 164; see also Post, 'Racist Speech', 316.

[215] Boonin, *Should Race Matter?*, pp. 223, 225.

[216] Kretzmer, 'Freedom of Speech and Racism', 496; Boonin, *Should Race Matter?*, pp. 219–220.

defamation involves subjective opinions, rather than factual or empirical assertions, and is thus unverifiable, unlike libellous speech that harms the reputation of individuals.[217] Group libel laws, according to this view, represent an unacceptable interference with the exercise of freedom of expression, since they give states wide discretion to interfere with the exercise of this freedom in connection with group issues.[218] They emphasize that criticisms of groups' behaviour, and their roles within society, are integral to public debates and should thus fall under the legitimate scope of freedom of expression.[219] Opponents of group libel laws also highlight the problem of delimiting the groups that require protection, especially given the existence of multiple relevant identities, such as sexual orientation and gender. They fear that in large heterogeneous or multicultural societies featuring diverse groups, each with their own identities and sensibilities, and each claiming an equal right to legal protection, the scope of permitted speech could become significantly diminished.[220] Moreover, the issue of asymmetrical group protection has been raised; Heinz even argues that providing protection to particular groups and not others makes group defamation laws inherently discriminatory.[221] Critics of group vilification laws have, furthermore, criticized these laws for sending out 'a signal of victimization: a signal that the members of the protected minority groups are disadvantaged victims who need protection', thus reinforcing existing prejudices.[222]

The communitarian approach to rights challenges the individualist conception of rights as attributable only to individuals.[223] According to the former approach, human rights are 'not premised on the protection of an atomistic individual' but, rather, on 'the protection of and development of an individual situated within the context of a wider society'.[224] Communitarians resist sharply contrasting individual and group rights and emphasize the 'intimate nexus' between the individual and the groups that he or she is affiliated with.[225] In this sense, they regard individuals as having a social character or as 'communally embedded', with their personal and communal identities complementary and inextricably interwoven.[226] According to

[217]   Kretzmer, 'Freedom of Speech and Racism', 496; Boonin, *Should Race Matter?*, pp. 219–220.
[218]   David A. J. Richards, *Free Speech and the Politics of Identity* (Oxford University Press, 1999), pp. 135, 142.
[219]   Sadurski, *Freedom of Speech*, p. 217; Weinstein, *Hate Speech and Pornography*, p. 167.
[220]   Post, 'Racist Speech', 316; Kretzmer, 'Freedom of Speech and Racism', 467; Alex Brown, *Hate Speech Law: A Philosophical Examination* (Routledge, 2017), pp. 176–177.
[221]   Heinze, 'Viewpoint Absolutism', 566.
[222]   Noorloos, *Hate Speech Revisited*, p. 48.
[223]   Feinberg, *Harmless Wrongdoing*, p. 82; Gray, *Liberalism*, p. 59; Michael J. Sandel, *Liberalism and the Limits of Justice* (Cambridge University Press, 1982); on communitarian thinking in general see Michael Walzer, *Spheres of Justice: A Defense of Pluralism and Equality* (Basic Books, 1983).
[224]   Mark Freeman and Gibran van Ert, *International Human Rights Law* (Irwin Law, 2004), p. 29.
[225]   Parekh, *Rethinking Multiculturalism*, p. 216; Kenneth Lasson, 'Group Libel Versus Free Speech: When Big Brother Should Butt In' (1984) 23(1) *Duquesne University Law Review*, 23, 116.
[226]   Norris, 'Note: A Communitarian Defense of Group Libel Laws', 690; Ian Cram, 'The Danish cartoons, offensive expressions, and democratic legitimacy', in Ivan Hare and James Weinstein (eds.), *Extreme Speech and Democracy* (Oxford University Press, 2009), p. 329; Parekh, 'Group

the communitarian conception of rights, many individual rights are realized when exercised collectively or through the protection of group rights.[227] Communitarians do not regard group rights as a mere aggregation of individual rights but, rather, emphasize that their bearers are collectives.[228]

The integrity of identities is recognized by advocates of the idea of group rights as group concerns that merit legal protection.[229] The increasing diversity of many societies across the world has contributed to the growing significance of protecting group identities and has revived calls to recognize and respect group rights.[230] The communitarian approach to rights contends that the protection of vulnerable groups and their members is an integral and central component of IHRL.[231] Its supporters have identified a number of vulnerable groups who are disproportionately affected by violations of rights and thus require special protection, for example, women, children, racial and ethnic groups, persons with disabilities, migrant workers and their family members, and internally displaced persons.[232]

Freedom of expression, from a communitarian standpoint, should align with the 'moral' and 'cultural' interests of the community and should protect the latter's 'deeply held beliefs, values and practices'.[233] Many advocates of the maximalist approach to hate speech regulation are concerned primarily with protecting the rights, status, and identities of groups from the harms of hate speech.[234] They seek to prevent hostile or derogatory statements against, negative stereotyping about, moral injury to, or discriminatory conduct against groups as collectives and not only their individual members.[235] A number of national legal systems use the terms 'group libel' and 'group defamation' to describe restrictions on hateful forms of expression

libel and freedom of expression', p. 359; Feinberg, *Harmless Wrongdoing*, pp. 85–86; Sandel, *Liberalism*, p. 179; Massey, 'Hate Speech and Cultural Diversity', 165.

[227] Koen De. Feyter, 'In defence of a multidisciplinary approach to human rights', in K. de Feyter and George Pavlakos (eds.), *The Tension between Group Rights and Human Rights: A Multidisciplinary Approach* (Hart Publications, 2008), pp. 35–36; Freeman and Ert, *International Human Rights Law*, p. 29; Louis B. Sohn, 'New International Law: Protection of the Rights of Individuals Rather than States' (1982) 32 *American University Law Review*, 48.

[228] Michael Freeman, 'Are there collective human rights?' in David Beetham (ed.), *Politics and Human Rights* (Wiley-Blackwell, 1995), p. 38.

[229] G. Nettheim, '"Peoples" and "Populations": Indigenous peoples and the rights of peoples', in James Crawford (ed.), *The Rights of Peoples* (Oxford University Press, 1988), p. 107.

[230] Danilo Turk, 'Introduction: Group rights and human rights', in K. de Feyter and George Pavlakos (eds.), *The Tension between Group Rights and Human Rights: A Multidisciplinary Approach* (Hart Publications, 2008), p. 8 ; Parekh, *Rethinking Multiculturalism*, p. 213.

[231] Nifosi-Sutton, *The Protection of Vulnerable Groups*, p. 19.

[232] Nifosi-Sutton, *The Protection of Vulnerable Groups*, p. 267.

[233] Parekh, 'Group libel and freedom of expression', p. 362.

[234] Greenawalt, *Fighting Words*, pp. 152–153; Norris, 'Note: A Communitarian Defense of Group Libel Laws', 691; Lerner, 'Freedom of Expression and Incitement to Group Hatred', pp. 90–91; Massaro, 'Equality and Freedom of Expression', 237.

[235] Louis Henkin, 'Group defamation and international law', in Monroe H. Freedman and Eric M. Freedman (eds.), *Group Defamation and Freedom of Speech: The Relationship between Language and Violence* (Greenwood Press, 1995), p. 125; Massey, 'Hate Speech and Cultural Diversity', 156–157; Sumner, 'Hate speech and the law, p. 37.

that constitute incitement to particular harms.[236] Supporters of group defamation laws have assimilated these laws into hate speech laws in general.[237] They highlight the negative effects that an atmosphere of group hatred or contempt has on the equality rights of groups – in particular, the vulnerable groups, the integrity of their identities, and social peace.[238] MacKinnon emphasizes that incidences of group hate propaganda, which stereotype and stigmatize groups, are 'the attitudinal engines of the exclusion, denigration, and subordination that make up and propel social inequality'.[239] Though she recognizes that defamation and discrimination address two different types of harm (reputational harms and status harms, respectively), she nevertheless describes group defamation as a 'verbal form' of discrimination, given the overlapping nature of both harms.[240] Furthermore, she highlights that 'the key element of a discrimination claim is group-based harm'.[241] According to this line of reasoning, group defamation laws promote equality.[242] Through this communitarian lens, equality on the basis of group identities is not just individually based: it is also group based.[243]

Advocates of group libel laws contend that it is illogical to accept libellous speech, which causes harm to an individual's reputation, as a legitimate subject of legal constraint, while denying the same protection to groups.[244] According to this view, acts of group libel multiply the harms to reputation and social status recognized by individual libel laws and should therefore be treated similarly by the law.[245] MacKinnon considers such inequality of treatment to be 'discriminatory against harms done through discrimination, in favour of what are regarded by distinction as individual harms'.[246] Group libel laws, on this view, provide – to individuals whose group affiliations are central to their identities – protection against discrimination, hostility, vilification, or moral injury, all of which may inhibit their self-autonomy and self-realization.[247] Riesman asserts that protecting an individual's reputation is intrinsically linked to protecting the reputation of groups to which he or she

---

[236] Waldron, *The Harm in Hate Speech*, p. 40.
[237] Waldron, *The Harm in Hate Speech*, p. 122.
[238] Richards, *Free Speech*, p. 142; MacKinnon, *Only Words*, p. 84; Massaro, 'Equality and Freedom of Expression', 235; Pinto, 'What Are Offences to Feelings Really About?', 6; Noorloos, *Hate Speech Revisited*, p. 44.
[239] MacKinnon, *Only Words*, p. 99.
[240] MacKinnon, *Only Words*, p. 99.
[241] MacKinnon, 'Pornography as defamation and discrimination', p. 260.
[242] MacKinnon, *Only Words*, p. 99.
[243] Scolnicov, *The Right to Religious Freedom in International Law*, p. 43.
[244] Kretzmer, 'Freedom of Speech and Racism', 466.
[245] MacKinnon, *Only Words*, pp. 82, 99; Parekh, 'Group libel and freedom of expression', p. 359.
[246] MacKinnon, *Only Words*, p. 82.
[247] Sionaidh Douglas-Scott, 'Hatefulness of Protected Speech: A Comparison of the American and European Approaches' (1999) 7 *William & Mary Bill of Rights Journal*, 338; Norris, 'Note: A Communitarian Defense of Group Libel Laws', 691; Henkin, 'Group defamation and international law', p. 128; Parekh, 'Group libel and freedom of expression', p. 359.

belongs.[248] Similarly to individual libel, group libel might potentially take the form of a factual claim that is fundamentally defamatory. In delimiting the groups that the state should protect from group libel, advocates of group libel laws suggest that distinctions can be drawn between 'constitutive' and 'instrumental' groups. The former shape the identities of their individual members and thus should be protected by group libel laws, whereas the latter aim to achieve the common goals of their members, whose identities are separable from their group membership and thus should not be protected.[249] Cross-national differences in the group characteristics that are legally protected reflect a number of contextual factors: local conditions, history, and the groups which are most successful in their campaigns for recognition.[250]

Support for group defamation laws might, alternatively, be based on a purely individualistic conception of rights. For example, Waldron supports such laws on the basis of protecting the dignity of individual members of the group, i.e. protecting individuals by reason of the characteristics they acquire from being part of a group and not on the basis of protecting the dignity of groups as such.[251] Waldron describes his argument as the 'dignitarian rationale' for group defamation laws; he conceives of dignity as referring to the 'objective or social aspects of a person's standing in society', rather than the collective dignity of the group. The latter, he suggests, should not be the concern of hate speech laws.[252]

The right to be protected from incitement to discrimination, hostility, or violence, as recognized in IHRL, is largely congruent with the essential thrust of the communitarian, rather than strict individualist, conception of rights. The right does not simply protect individuals' interests but is also integral to the promotion of collective goals, the prevention of communal harms, and the protection of groups' identities.[253] Through the lens of an individualist conception of rights that aligns with the libertarian conception of freedom of expression, Article 20(2) is biased towards the protection of group identities at the expense of individuals' rights, particularly the right to freedom of expression.[254] Through the communitarian lens, the right to protection from incitement to hatred is both an individual and group right[255] that obliges states to enact group defamation laws prohibiting hate speech that targets

---

[248] David Riesman, 'Democracy and Defamation: Control of Group Libel' (1942) 42(5) *Columbia Law Review*, 731.

[249] Douglas-Scott, 'Hatefulness of Protected Speech', 339; see for example Norris, 'Note: A Communitarian Defense of Group Libel Laws', 689–694.

[250] Garland and Funnell, 'Defining hate crime internationally', p. 25.

[251] Waldron, *The Harm in Hate Speech*, pp. 56–57, 123.

[252] Waldron, *The Harm in Hate Speech*, pp. 56–57, 123.

[253] Foster, 'Prophets and Cartoons', 35–36; Beyani, 'Law and Judicial Practices', p. 1; Farrior, 'Molding the Matrix', 8; Mohamed Saeed M. Eltayeb, 'The Limitations on Critical Thinking on Religious Issues under Article 20 of ICCPR and Its Relation to Freedom of Expression' (2010) 5 *Religion and Human Rights*, 128.

[254] Scolnicov, *The Right to Religious Freedom in International Law*, p. 32.

[255] Farrior, 'Molding the Matrix', 8.

groups and their members.[256] Moreover, the right is considered to be part of the 'international law on group defamation', together with the ICERD, the Genocide Convention, and the Apartheid Convention.[257] Advocates of group libel laws also cite Article 19(3), which allows restrictions on freedom of expression that are 'necessary for respect for the rights or reputations of others', to emphasize the consistency of these laws with IHRL, interpreting 'others' as referring to groups as well as individuals.[258]

The group identity component of the norm prohibiting incitement to hatred undoubtedly complicates its legal regulation. Group-based hatred refers to hatred defined by reference to (or centred around) group identities, which raises doubts about whether clear lines can be drawn between the provision of protection against incitement to individual members of groups, to groups themselves, and to collective identities or group-defining characteristics per se (in terms of shielding them from denigration or defamation).[259] Many groups consider contempt towards – or ridicule of – their identities as tantamount to incitement to hatred against them as groups (group defamation) as well as to their individual members, since they identify themselves primarily by their group identities. This is borne out by the fact that expressions that denigrate particular group identities frequently do have the effect of inciting hatred, discrimination, or violence against group members. Even if the three categories of expression specified above represent three distinct analytic categories, the inherent overlaps between them make distinguishing between them very complex in practice. While the communitarian conception of rights highlights the links, commonalities, and blurred lines between these three categories and includes them all under the ambit of the right to be protected from incitement to hatred, the individualist conception of rights cautions against their conflation and recognizes only harms against individuals. Different levels of commitment to the advancement of group rights thus lead to different conceptions of the scope and meaning of the right to protection from incitement. Other practical quandaries associated with the collective nature of incitement to hatred relate, firstly, to the determination of victim status and, secondly, to proving that specific statements have had harmful consequences for particular alleged victims. These conundrums, associated with the group identity component of the right, add still more complexity to the precise determination of its normative content.

---

[256] Henkin, 'Group defamation and international law', pp. 124, 128, 132; Peter Danchin, 'Defaming Muhammad: Dignity, Harm, and Incitement to Religious Hatred' (2010) 2 *Duke Forum for Law & Social Change*, 16; Parekh, *Rethinking Multiculturalism*, p. 314.

[257] Henkin, 'Group defamation and international law', pp. 124, 128, 132.

[258] Henkin, 'Group defamation and international law', p. 129.

[259] Waldron, *The Harm in Hate Speech*, pp. 122–123.

2.6 THE 'RELIGION' COMPONENT

Religion-based incitement is prohibited pursuant to the right to be protected from incitement to discrimination, hostility, or violence. This right to be protected from religious incitement is intrinsically related to freedom of religion – in particular, the expressive as well as collective aspects of this freedom. The expressive aspect involves the right to manifest religion and express religious ideas and mostly appears in worship, teaching, practice, and observance.[260] Another important facet of religion is 'religion as identity', which emphasizes affiliation with a group that shares theological beliefs as well as histories, cultures, and traditions.[261] This collective aspect is manifested in the fact that the exercise of freedom of religion can be either individual or communal. It protects the group identity of religious adherents, which is usually the basis for religious discrimination.[262] Article 18 of the ICCPR acknowledges both the collective and expressive aspects of freedom of religion. It states that the freedom to manifest one's religion may be exercised either 'alone' or 'in community with others'.

The right to protection from religious incitement limits the expressive aspect of freedom of religion; it sets a limit for religious manifestations, which must not amount to incitement to discrimination, hostility, or violence. The right recognizes the causal relationship between religious hate speech and infringement upon the freedom to express and manifest religion in relation to targeted religious groups. Incitement, once established in relation to any incident of religious hatred, constitutes not only a violation of the right to protection from religious incitement, but also a violation of freedom of religion, as it encroaches upon the right of members of targeted groups to practice and express their religion. The right to protection from religious incitement thus seeks to protect both the collective and expressive aspects of target groups' freedom of religion. While enhancing equality is the main rationale for providing protection against the harms of incitement, the prohibition of religion-based incitement is buttressed by an additional justification: safeguarding the religious freedoms of members of targeted groups. This additional justification, however, creates further complexity in the determination of the normative content of the right to protection from incitement to hatred.

When it comes to the regulation of religious hate speech, a delicate, and often very difficult, balance has to be struck between freedom of religion for those who express religious views, on the one hand, and religious followers targeted by those

---

[260]   Tseming Yang, 'Race, Religion, and Cultural Identity: Reconciling the Jurisprudence of Race and Religion' (1997) 73 *Indiana Law Journal*, 138; Scolnicov, *The Right to Religious Freedom in International Law*, p. 208.

[261]   T. Jeremy Gunn, 'The Complexity of Religion and the Definition of Religion in International Law' (2003) 16 *Harvard Human Rights Journal*, 200.

[262]   Eltayeb, 'Limitations on Critical Thinking on Religious Issues', 122; Gunn, 'Complexity of Religion', 203–204; A/HRC/2/6, para. 38; Rex Adhar and Ian Leigh, *Religious Freedom in the Liberal State* (Oxford University Press, 2013), p. 376.

speakers, on the other. There are inherent tensions between the expressive and collective identity aspects of freedom of religion, in the context of the right to protection from religious incitement. These tensions complicate determining the threshold for establishing religion-based incitement that should be prohibited pursuant to the right. The implications that legal regulation of religion-based incitement has for freedom of religion provoke enduring controversies pertaining to the right's exact normative definition.

Freedom of religion is a 'unique' freedom within the edifice of IHRL.[263] Its uniqueness is derived mainly from the fact that religions harbour their own value systems or normative regimes, and their adherents hold deep convictions about the meaning of human life and how best to regulate its relation to the world.[264] International standards addressing matters related to religions create another competing normative system that might not be consistent with particular religions. Religions' statuses within the structures of societies and states vary significantly.[265] In some societies, both the entire social structure and the sense of national identity are strongly rooted within the highest authority of a specific religion. Constitutions and national legislations address the relationship between state and religion in a variety of ways. Whether there is complete or partial separation or union between state and religion is crucial to the 'state's self-definition'.[266] Variations between states in this regard create difficult areas of contention among them when negotiating international standards on the exact nature and contours of freedom of religion.[267] This is particularly true as those standards go directly to 'the heart of constitutional structure and state identity'[268] and could 'infringe upon sacred dogmas or dominant traditions of different faiths'.[269] These areas of contention explain the normative paucity on freedom of religion within IHRL; its contours remain largely underdeveloped despite the expansion of international human rights standards over the last half century.[270]

Furthermore, a number of factors make the regulation of religion-based incitement more contentious compared to other grounds of incitement. The challenges encountered in determining the threshold for establishing religion-based incitement, and thus for imposing limitations on the right to express opinions on religious matters, further complicate the precise delimitation of the norm prohibiting incitement to religious hatred. Firstly, the conditions in which certain expressions might

---

[263] Scolnicov, *The Right to Religious Freedom in International Law*, p. 1.
[264] Herz and Molnár, 'Interview with Kenan Malik', p. 82; Scolnicov, *The Right to Religious Freedom in International Law*, p. 1.
[265] Scolnicov, *The Right to Religious Freedom in International Law*, p. 23.
[266] Scolnicov, *The Right to Religious Freedom in International Law*, p. 2.
[267] Foster, 'Prophets and Cartoons', 20.
[268] Scolnicov, *The Right to Religious Freedom in International Law*, p. 114.
[269] Jose A. Lindgren Alves, 'Race and Religion in the United Nations Committee on the Elimination of Racial Discrimination' (2008) 42 *University of San Francisco Law Review*, 945.
[270] E/CN.4./2006/17, para. 33; Richards, *Free Speech*, p. 179; Foster, 'Prophets and Cartoons', 20.

be tantamount to incitement to religious hatred vary between different religions.[271] Religious sensibilities might even be contradictory, given that religions are 'fundamentally opposed belief systems'[272] and 'are in a competitive position with regard to one another'.[273] Expressions that promote the superiority of one religion might have the effect of offending – or even inciting hatred against – adherents of another religion.[274] Certain instances of incitement to religious hatred could be justifiable on the basis of the speakers' understanding of the theological tenets or sacred texts of their religion or other religions, which causes problems in the interpretation and implementation of offences concerned with incitement to religious hatred.[275] Secondly, religious sensitivities are not fixed but vary across time and place; they evolve as the attitudes of religious communities develop, which opens the door to competing interpretations of offences on blasphemy, religious insult, and incitement to religious hatred.[276] Thirdly, in increasingly multi-religious societies, there is 'a standing danger' that religious adherents will be attacked, stigmatized, stereotyped, or denigrated on the basis of their religion.[277] Fourthly, religious perspectives are often closely entangled with political debates, for example, in connection with criticisms of government policies on religious grounds.[278] In many instances, religious leaders enter the public sphere and contribute to debates on matters of public controversy such as abortion, homosexuality, and the status of women in society.[279] Also, debates on governmental reactions to acts of terrorism allegedly committed in the name of religion, and public discussion of religious fundamentalism, in many instances complicate the separation between socio-political critiques of religion, political speech, and religious speech.[280] Fifthly, freedom of religion involves the freedom to change one's religion, which requires open and critical debate about

---

[271] Paul M. Taylor, *Freedom of Religion: UN and European Human Rights Law and Practice* (Cambridge University Press, 2005), p. 106; Anthony W. Jeremy, 'Religious Offences' (2003) 7(3) *Ecclesiastical Law Journal*, 138.

[272] Susannah C. Vance, 'Permissibility of Incitement to Religious Hatred Offenses under European Convention Principles' (2004) 14 *Transnational Law & Contemporary Problems*, 244.

[273] Ivan Hare, 'Blasphemy and incitement to religious hatred: Free speech dogma and doctrine', in Ivan Hare and James Weinstein (eds.), *Extreme Speech and Democracy* (Oxford University Press, 2009), p. 308.

[274] Michael Herz and Peter Molnar, 'Interview with Robert Post', in Michael Herz and Peter Molnar (eds.), *The Content and Context of Hate Speech: Rethinking Regulation and Responses*(Cambridge University Press, 2012), p. 36; Waldron, *Liberal Rights*, p. 138.

[275] Peter Cumper, 'Outlawing Incitement to Religious Hatred—a British Perspective' (2006) 1(3) *Religion and Human Rights*, 263.

[276] The Venice Commission Report, paras. 51, 79.

[277] Waldron, *The Harm in Hate Speech*, p. 130.

[278] Vance, 'Permissibility of Incitement to Religious Hatred Offenses', 246; Hare, 'Blasphemy and incitement to religious hatred', p. 300; Post, 'Religion and Freedom of Speech', 77.

[279] Hare, 'Blasphemy and incitement to religious hatred', p. 308; Cram, 'The Danish cartoons and offensive expressions', p. 324.

[280] Richard Moon, *Putting Faith in Hate: When Religion Is the Source or Target of Hate Speech* (Cambridge University Press, 2018), p. 62; Vance, 'Permissibility of Incitement to Religious Hatred Offences', 245.

religions and beliefs. Categorizing expressions that are offensive to the religious feelings of others as incitement to religious hatred might risk undermining freedom of religion itself. Sixthly, it is difficult to distinguish clearly between incitement to hatred against religious believers and beliefs as such or to distinguish between defamation of religious groups and defamation of religions themselves. As Waldron notes, 'defaming the group that comprises all Christians, as opposed to defaming Christians as members of that group, means defaming the creeds, Christ, and the saints. Defaming the group that comprises all Muslims, may mean defaming the Koran and the prophet Muhammad'.[281] The boundaries between the two categories of defamation are not always easy to draw.[282] Such difficulties are related to the conception of religion as both a personal choice and a cultural identity. These two aspects of religion create challenges in integrating religious freedoms within the realm of law in the first place. Individual choices are protected as a matter of liberty whereas group identities are protected as a matter of equality.[283] Many religious groups consider contempt towards – or defamation of – their most sacred religious principles or symbols as tantamount to incitement to religious hatred against them, and to group defamation, since they identify themselves primarily by their religious beliefs.[284]

Moreover, in reality, expressions that defame religions are often construed as inciting hatred against religious groups and are frequently used as a pretext to such incitement in an indirect manner.[285] Rosenfeld rightly notes that it is more difficult to 'exclude slippage from antireligion speech to hate speech in the case of minority religions'.[286] He clarifies: 'anti-Islam attitudes [in Europe] can easily and imperceptibly slip into anti-Muslim sentiments in a way that anti-Catholicism is not at all likely to denigrate into anti-French in France or anti-Italian in Italy'.[287] As Guerra suggests, 'in a predominantly religious society it is perfectly conceivable that an insult to religion may shock or offend, but it will in no way obstruct religious practice [for followers of the predominant religion]'.[288] Thus, comments or expressed opinions that defame religions could be perceived as 'threats or as actual impediments to the expression or practice of religious conviction', especially if the religion in question is not the predominant one, although this is not

---

[281] Waldron, *The Harm in Hate Speech*, p. 123.

[282] Eric Barendt, 'Religious Hatred Laws: Protecting Groups or Belief?' (2011) 17(1) *Res Publica*, 46.

[283] Moon, *Putting Faith in Hate*, pp. 20, 61.

[284] Cumper, 'Outlawing Incitement to Religious Hatred', 265.

[285] Noorloos, *Hate Speech Revisited*, p. 28; Eltayeb, 'Limitations on Critical Thinking on Religious Issues', 130; Pnina Werbner, 'Islamophobia: Incitement to Religious Hatred – Legislating for a New Fear?' (2005) 21(1) *Anthropology Today*, 9.

[286] Rosenfeld, 'Hate speech in constitutional jurisprudence', pp. 279–280.

[287] Rosenfeld, 'Hate speech in constitutional jurisprudence', pp. 279–280.

[288] Luis Lopez Guerra, 'Blasphemy and religious insult: Offenses to religious feelings or attacks on freedom?', in Josep Casadevall, Egbert Myjer, Michael O'Boyle, and Anna Austin (eds.), *Freedom of Expression: Essays in Honour of Nicolas Bratza President of the European Court of Human Rights* (Wolf Legal Publishers, 2012), p. 310.

inevitably the case.[289] A persistent campaign that amounts to incitement to violence, discrimination, or hostility targeting a specific religion can result in restrictions with regard to manifesting or practising religion (for example, the establishment of places of worship) and may therefore amount to a violation of freedom of religion. The challenge here also lies in proving the causal connection or establishing the likelihood-based connection between religious hate speech and the harm caused to the followers of the targeted religion (the dilemmas related to the second and fourth internal features of the norm prohibiting incitement to hatred).[290]

Defenders of the libertarian and individualist conceptions of rights criticize blasphemy or defamation laws that restrict expressions of opinion targeting religions or their symbols. They believe that these laws give primacy to protecting the religious identity of groups at the expense of individuals' freedom of expression.[291] According to the individualist account of rights, these laws amount to granting rights to religions themselves whereas abstractions, whether groups, ideologies, or religions, do not properly possess any rights.[292] Moreover, through the individualist lens, the denigration of religious objects or ideas does not constitute harm to individual members of religious groups.[293]

Although laws prohibiting defamation of religion and incitement to religious hatred have different ideological rationales and targets of protection (beliefs and believers), they both involve the protection of religious feelings. Given that religious sensibilities are defined by reference to religious beliefs, the protections provided by these two categories of law are extended to religious beliefs qua religious feelings. It is difficult to establish the presence of incitement to religious hatred while completely avoiding an assessment of the significance of the expressions in question in relation to the doctrinal tenets of the targeted groups. Additionally, the psychological harms resulting both from defamation of religion and expressions that clearly incite hatred against religious groups have similar effects in terms of the distress they cause to the members of targeted groups.[294] The distinction between incitement to hatred against religious *believers* and defamation of religions themselves can be made at the abstract level, as these two concepts represent separate analytical categories of expressive act. Nevertheless, it is complicated to establish empirically whether the level of incitement against religious believers has been reached in the case of religious defamation or anti-religious speech, thus justifying the legal prohibition of such expressions.[295]

---

[289] Guerra, 'Blasphemy and religious insult', pp. 309–310.
[290] Langer, *Religious Offence*, pp. 123–124.
[291] Richards, *Free Speech*, p. 210.
[292] Sieghart, *The International Law of Human Rights*, p. 368.
[293] Noorloos, *Hate Speech Revisited*, p. 54.
[294] Waldron, *The Harm in Hate Speech*, p. 122.
[295] Adhar and Leigh, *Religious Freedom in the Liberal State*, p. 434; Scolnicov, *The Right to Religious Freedom in International Law*, p. 33; Peter Cumper, 'Inciting religious hatred: Balancing free speech and religious sensibilities in a multi-faith society', in Nazila Ghanea-Hercock, Alan Stephens, and

2.7 CONCLUDING REMARKS

This chapter has explained how five internal features of the right to protection from incitement to discrimination, hostility, or violence have provoked enduring controversies pertaining to its exact normative definition, interpretation, and implementation. These five internal features each create challenges in reaching wide international agreement on the right's meaning and scope and explain the current underdeveloped state of the international legal framework on hate speech. Furthermore, this chapter has clarified the different arguments employed when considering the range of hate speech harms that justify imposing restrictions upon the exercise of freedom of expression. It has also grounded these arguments in different approaches to human rights in general.

The first internal feature of the right to protection from incitement to hatred is its 'emotional' component. Article 20(2) uses the term 'hatred' to describe the content of expressions that should be prohibited if they incite particular harms. It also recognizes incitement to hostility as a category of harm that justifies the prohibition of advocacy of hatred. The descriptive objects of the two terms, 'hatred' and 'hostility', belong to the realm of emotive states. The formulation of the right in emotive language renders its clear interpretation challenging within an international legal context. Furthermore, the right's emotional component makes its interpretation and implementation relative or contextual, as emotions are by-products of conceptions on morals, and morals are inherently relative and changeable.

Additionally, the interpretation and enforcement of the right both suffer from the difficulties inherent in proving the harms that it seeks to provide protection against. This factor relates to the second internal feature: the 'incitement' component. The prohibition of advocacy of hatred is justified only if that advocacy constitutes incitement to discrimination, hostility, or violence. In reality, proving sufficient causality to establish the existence of incitement is a complex exercise, and difficult to establish without contestation, given its indirect, cumulative, and mentally and emotionally mediated nature. The 'emotional' nature of both the content of the expressions involved and one particular category of their possible harms (i.e. hostility) exacerbate the difficulties of proving incitement. This makes the first two features of the right interrelated. It is difficult to provide a definitive answer to the question of how tightly the causal connection between advocacy of hatred and its possible harms must be drawn before restricting the former, as context determines whether incitement exists. This adds another relativist challenge to the right's interpretation and implementation. The first two features of the right thus demonstrate the

Raphael Walden (eds.), *Does God Believe in Human Rights? Essays on Religion and Human Rights* (Martinus Nijhoff Publishers, 2007), pp. 238–239, 241; David Norris, 'Are Laws Proscribing Incitement to Religious Hatred Compatible with Freedom of Speech?' (2008) 1(1) *UCL Human Rights Review*, 110.

inherent difficulties in reaching wide international agreement on the definition and conditions of expressions prohibited pursuant to the right. These two features highlight the problematic nature of the shift from the moral denunciation of hate speech to its international legal prohibition.

The third important feature of the right is that it embodies tensions between the speakers' and targeted listeners' rights to liberty and equality and not, as frequently claimed in hate speech literature, between the values of liberty and equality in the abstract. Providing protection for targeted groups against the harms of hate speech enhances their equality rights as well as their rights to freely express their opinions. This has to be carefully balanced against the speakers' right to exercise freedom of expression without discrimination. The interpretation and enforcement of the right therefore require a delicate and difficult balance to be struck between the speakers' and targeted listeners' equality and liberty rights and not between the values of liberty and equality in the abstract.

The right also has a group identity aspect as both the hateful content itself, and the harms caused by expressions prohibited pursuant to the right, target three group identities: national origin, race, and religion. This fourth internal feature of the right, which is related to its collective dimension, makes it difficult to distinguish clearly between individualized and collective protection, especially given that hate speech targets people on the basis of their group identity. Furthermore, the group identity component of the right raises the complicated dilemma of how to distinguish between providing protection to groups per se and, alternatively, to their group-defining characteristics, and whether such a distinction is feasible in practice. The competing individual and group claims, in the context of interpreting and implementing the right, are clearly interrelated with the competing interests of speakers and targeted groups in equality and liberty rights. A heightened emphasis on speakers' rights to liberty and equality aligns with the individualist conception of the right, whereas a heightened emphasis on the targeted groups' rights to equality and liberty aligns largely with the communitarian conception of the right.

Religion-based incitement is prohibited pursuant to the right to protection from incitement to hatred. This fifth aspect of the right creates inherent tensions between the expressive and collective identity aspects of freedom of religion, both in relation to those who express offensive religious views, and the religious followers who are targeted by such instances of expression. These tensions complicate the precise determination of the threshold beyond which advocacy of religious hatred should be prohibited pursuant to the right.

Any regulatory regime that recognizes the right to protection from incitement to discrimination, hostility, or violence has to grapple with the definitional challenges and tensions underlying these five internal features. Although this chapter has introduced them as separate features, it has also emphasized that they are inextricably interconnected and mutually reinforced. On the one hand, the emotional component of the right and the uncertainty in proving incitement make striking the balance between the targeted audience and speakers' rights to liberty and equality, as well as between individual and group rights, more complex. On the other hand, addressing the definitional uncertainties of the right, in particular the emotive and incitement components, becomes more intractable under the effect of its underlying tensions (related, in particular, to the third, fourth, and fifth of the aforementioned internal features). Different approaches to the reconciliation of these tensions lead to different definitions of the right's key terms and to different delineations of the scope and range of harms that justify imposing restrictions on the exercise of freedom of expression.

The regulation of hate speech is beset by complexities relating to the accommodation and reconciliation of both individual autonomy and collective interests, as well as formal and substantive notions of equality. Thus, libertarian and egalitarian notions of freedom of expression, as well as individualist and communitarian approaches to rights, influence theoretical debates on hate speech regulation considerably. This chapter has shown that the divisions on addressing the issues and controversies underlying the right's five internal features correspond to biases to one or more of the aforementioned approaches to rights. These approaches provide different estimations of the degree and nature of harms caused by hate speech and thus different conceptualizations of hate speech. Their proponents adopt varied positions on the nature of the causal relationship or likelihood that needs to be established between hate speech and its alleged harms before restricting such speech. Furthermore, advocates of these different approaches to rights resolve differently the tensions associated with the regulation of hate speech, between the targeted listeners' and speakers' rights to equality and liberty, between individual and group rights, and between targeted listeners' and speakers' freedom of religion. Accordingly, these different approaches to rights favour either a minimalist or maximalist approach to hate speech regulation and adopt varied normative interpretations of the right to protection from incitement to hatred.

The five internal features of the right to protection from incitement to discrimination, hostility, or violence provide a useful explanatory tool to understand its problematic path within IHRL. The definitional dilemmas and underlying tensions set out in this chapter inform the subsequent chapters. The wide gaps between states' positions at the UN during the drafting of Article 20(2) of the ICCPR, and during the recent standard-setting attempts in the area of hate speech, can be better understood through the lens of these five features. These features also help to explain the state of development of the hate speech jurisprudence of supranational human rights–monitoring bodies. The following three chapters will address these three significant aspects of the norm's restricted evolution and how they correspond to the conundrums arising from its five identified internal features.

3

The Difficult Birth of the Right to Protection from Incitement to Hatred in International Human Rights Law

3.1 INTRODUCTION

This chapter provides an analytical account of the drafting history of Article 20(2) of the ICCPR, which codified the right to be protected from incitement to discrimination, hostility, or violence. Bossuyt rightly describes the task of tracing the legislative history of even one article of the ICCPR as an 'onerous task'.[1] The Covenant's long and complicated drafting process began in 1947 in the Commission on Human Rights and continued, from 1954, in the Third Committee of the GA, until the GA finally adopted the Covenant in 1966.[2] In analysing the right's historical origins, this chapter relies on records of UN meetings, documenting the travaux préparatoires of the ICCPR.

The drafting records of multilateral treaties serve as 'political records', since they connect the adopted texts to real-world politics, in which the prevailing international politics at the time of negotiations influences the positions of negotiating states.[3] This chapter begins with a description of the historical and political context in which the negotiations of Article 20(2) took place. It identifies the states that supported the introduction of a provision within the ICCPR, providing protection against the harms of advocacy of hatred, and those that opposed such an inclusion. It then presents a taxonomy of the divisions that arose among negotiating states during the drafting of the Article, both in the Commission on Human Rights and in the Third Committee of the GA. These divisions centred upon the scope of hate speech harms that justify imposing restrictions on the exercise of freedom of expression, the addition of an emotive component to the international norm prohibiting hate speech, recognition of group rights, and implications for religious freedoms. This chapter examines the different proposals and statements reflecting states' positions and concerns, with reference to the regulation of hate speech within IHRL. It

---

[1] Marc J. Bossuyt, *Guide to the 'Travaux Préparatoires' of the International Covenant on Civil and Political Rights* (Martinus Nijhoff Publishers, 1987), p. xvi.

[2] Bossuyt, *Guide to the 'Travaux Préparatoires'*, p. xvi.

[3] Jan Klabbers, 'International Legal Histories: The Declining Importance of Travaux Préparatoires in Treaty Interpretation?' (2003) 50(3) *Netherlands International Law Review*, 285, 286.

demonstrates how the internal features of the norm prohibiting incitement influenced and shaped the main areas of contention among states during early negotiations.

3.2 THE HISTORICAL AND POLITICAL CONTEXT OF NEGOTIATIONS

The drafting of an international legal provision addressing hate speech took place against the backdrop of the then-recent gross human rights violations which took place before and during the Second World War. These violations, in which millions of people were victimized on the basis of their race, religion, or nationality, were associated with Nazi and fascist hate propaganda. The post-war international community was primarily concerned with preventing the recurrence of such atrocities by addressing their root causes.

The highly charged and ideologically polarized geopolitical environment of the Cold War had a direct impact on the protracted and difficult negotiations of Article 20(2). The supporters of the Article, who pushed hard for its inclusion within the Covenant, belonged mainly to the Eastern bloc, including the USSR and its allies, as well as many Third World and newly independent states. The states which resisted its inclusion in the Covenant, and then tried to narrow its scope as much as possible, were mainly allied with the Western bloc, that is states allied with the United States and NATO. However, rare exceptions did occur; a few countries did not concur with the dominant arguments of their respective camps. In these rare instances, debates did not reflect divisions strictly along Cold War lines.

The Article's supporters perceived its inclusion in the text of the Covenant as indispensable for establishing a new post-war world order and enhancing the UN Charter's principles of international peace, promoting tolerance, and eliminating discrimination.[4] They argued that the Covenant 'must have a clear and explicit Article which would take account of the grievous experiences of the century and offer to coming generations a surer path towards peace'.[5] The Article's advocates emphasized the notion of duties and responsibilities in exercising rights and sought to provide protection against the abuse of these rights. Furthermore, they affirmed that protection from the denial of human rights is itself a right that states should guarantee to every human being.[6] According to its supporters, the Article establishes 'the right of society to protect itself against abuses of that freedom [of expression] aimed at undermining the bases of national and international life'.[7] In their view, the Article protected 'the right to life and the right to live in peace with one's neighbours'.[8]

---

[4] E/CN.4/SR.378, at 5–6; E/CN.4/SR.379, at 8, 11.
[5] A/C.3/SR.1078, para. 16.
[6] A/C.3/SR.1080, para. 14.
[7] A/C.3/SR.1078, para. 7.
[8] A/C.3/SR.1081, para. 23.

The tragic legacy of hate propaganda surrounding the Second World War provided a major impetus for the inclusion of a provision within the Covenant giving protection against the harms of hate advocacy. The bitter experiences of the USSR and Eastern European states, which witnessed extreme forms of horror both prior to and during the war, remained fresh during the ICCPR's drafting process. These harsh experiences significantly shaped these states' positions during negotiations on the regulation of hate speech. These states frequently underlined the direct causal relationship between Nazi and fascist ideologies; policies that propagated racial, national, and religious hatred; and the murders and gross human rights violations which took place before and during the Second World War.[9] Eastern bloc states contended that these grave violations were the direct result of failing to eliminate hate propaganda in time.[10] They warned that, unless a clear provision was inserted in the ICCPR prohibiting the proponents of authoritarian ideologies from disseminating hate propaganda, a revival of Nazism, fascist doctrines, or similar totalitarian ideologies in different parts of the world was possible.[11]

During the negotiations, countries in the Eastern camp frequently referred to the specific ordeals and sufferings of their populations, linked to dissemination of fascist propaganda, and Nazism. The USSR criticized the remaining manifestations of fascism and Nazism in many countries and called for the prohibition of all kinds of hate propaganda.[12] It argued that 'everyone to-day was aware of the appalling consequences of Fascist propaganda. Everyone knew how Hitler's Mein Kampf had poisoned peoples' minds, and what the cost of the dissemination of those insidious ideas has been in terms of suffering borne by the freedom-loving peoples. It was strange that lessons of history should be so quickly forgotten'.[13] Yugoslavia referred to the loss of two million Yugoslav lives that resulted from the dissemination of fascist and Nazi propaganda. It noted that 'it was probably necessary to have been a victim of such propaganda, as the people of Yugoslavia had been, to appreciate the importance' of including a provision in the Covenant that explicitly prohibits fascist and Nazi views as well as any incitement to racial or religious hatred.[14] The Ukrainian SSR also referred to the sufferings of Ukrainian people as a result of fascism during the Second World War.[15] It similarly proposed that the Covenant should prohibit propaganda for Nazism, fascism, or racism, along with incitement to war or enmity between nations.[16] Poland cautioned against the dangers of incitement to hatred in light of the deaths of six million Poles during the Second World War.[17] It emphasized that 'the constant repetition of the theory of racial domination had led not only to the

---

9   E/CN.4/AC.1/SR.28, at 3.
10   E/CN.4/AC.1/SR.28, at 3.
11   E/CN.4/AC.1/SR.26, at 6.
12   E/CN.4/SR.123, at 4–5.
13   E/CN.4/SR.377, at 9–10.
14   E/CN.4/SR.174, paras. 40–41; E/CN.4/SR.377, at 6; E/CN.4/SR.378, at 12.
15   E/CN.4/SR.378, at 5–6.
16   A/C.3/SR.291, para. 12.
17   A/C.3/SR.1079, para. 27; E/CN.4/SR.377, at 4.

curtailment of human rights, but to the destruction of entire peoples'.[18] It added that 'the Poles today were all the more entitled to sound the alarm as those same racial theories were now being reborn, not only in the Federal Republic of Germany but in many other countries'.[19] Chile also argued that the need for a provision in the Covenant on hateful propaganda was obvious in light of the atrocities committed in the name of Hitlerism, which exemplified the ability of propaganda to 'successfully nullify the effects or falsify the premises of education' and eventually lead to violence.[20] It considered the inclusion of an Article to restrict the advocacy of hatred to be a 'spearhead' against authoritarian ideologies, in particular Nazism and fascism.[21]

Consequently, the USSR and countries allied with the Eastern bloc presented a number of proposals in 1948, in the Covenant's early drafting phases, which specifically addressed the prohibition of fascist and Nazi propaganda.[22] The USSR proposed the following: '[T]he propaganda in whatever form of Fascist-Nazi views and the propaganda of racial and national superiority, hatred and contempt shall be prohibited by law.'[23] It also called for the scope of recognized limitations on freedom of expression to be widened by clearly referencing the prevention of propaganda by Nazis or fascists, or propaganda supporting their ideas, in the Article on freedom of expression.[24] Furthermore, it also suggested the inclusion of a similar provision in the non-discrimination Article.[25] The Byelorussian SSR suggested restricting the right of association if it was abused for the purpose of establishing fascist organizations.[26] The USSR supported this proposal as 'a powerful weapon' for combating the dissemination of Nazi–Fascist propaganda.[27]

In contrast to the frequent connections that countries belonging to the Eastern bloc made between hate propaganda and the atrocities of the Second World War, Western countries made few such references. They looked at these atrocities from a different perspective. States belonging to the Western bloc emphasized that the suppression of expressions opposing totalitarian ideologies played a significant role in the prevalence of Nazi and fascist ideologies.[28] Sweden doubted that the prohibition of advocacy of hatred would have prevented the 'fanatical persecution' that the world had endured.[29] It argued that 'effective prophylaxis lay in free discussion, information and education'.[30] The United Kingdom warned against governments'

---

[18]   E/CN.4/SR.377, at 4.
[19]   A/C.3/SR.1079, para. 27.
[20]   E/CN.4/SR.378, at 11; A/C.3/SR.1078, para. 14.
[21]   E/CN.4/AC.1/SR.28, at 3.
[22]   E/CN.4/AC.1/SR.26, at 6; E/SR.438, at 55, 59.
[23]   E/CN.4/223.
[24]   E/CN.4/AC.1/SR.26, at 6.
[25]   A/C.3/SR.289, para. 38.
[26]   A/C.3/SR.575, para. 8.
[27]   E/CN.4/AC.1/SR.28, at 3.
[28]   E/CN.4/SR.378, at 10.
[29]   E/CN.4/SR.378, at 10.
[30]   E/CN.4/SR.378, at 10.

abuse of moral justifications for their conduct. It referred to the example of Germany under Hitler by stating that 'Hitler had started out on a moral platform, posing as the champion of a Germany oppressed through the Treaty of Versailles'.[31] The United States criticized the inclusion, in post-war peace treaties with Hungary, Bulgaria, and Romania, of provisions permitting the restriction of hostile propaganda.[32] It argued that such provisions 'provided a loophole for those seeking to ignore their obligations', and could be abused by states.[33] Western states showed a clear resistance to any reference to Nazism and fascism in the Covenant's text.[34] Accordingly, the attempts made during the Covenant's early drafting phases by a number of Eastern states to have prohibitions of Fascist and Nazi propaganda incorporated did not succeed.

Given the historical background against which Article 20(2) was drafted, a number of commentators have argued that the Article's object and purpose should be understood to forbid state-instigated hate propaganda inciting large-scale violent acts and advocacy of hatred that is broadly comparable to the fascist and Nazi propaganda of the Second World War era.[35] Nowak contends that Article 20 reflects 'the response mandated by the horrors of National Socialism' more than any other provision in the ICCPR.[36] He indicates that the Article should be interpreted in light of its 'responsive character', that is as an Article that was intended to address the roots of large-scale violence.[37] Asma Jahangir, the former UN Special Rapporteur on freedom of religion and belief, similarly argues that the historical conditions surrounding the Article's drafting make the threshold for restricting freedom of expression pursuant to it 'relatively high'.[38] According to Ghanea, the travaux préparatoires of the Article suggest that 'the drafters anticipated that the need for measures mandated by Article 20 would arise in the context of extreme situations of a seriousness approximating that of resort to violence or war'.[39] The numerous references made in the travaux préparatoires to the Third Reich's hate propaganda might explain why a number of Western states have

---

[31] E/CN.4/SR.379, at 7.

[32] E/CN.4/SR.174, para. 29.

[33] E/CN.4/SR.174, para. 29.

[34] E/CN.4/SR.123, at 6, 7.

[35] Nowak, *U.N. Covenant on Civil and Political Rights*, p. 475; Feldman, *Civil Liberties and Human Rights*, p. 431.

[36] Nowak, *U.N. Covenant on Civil and Political Rights*, p. 468.

[37] Nowak, *U.N. Covenant on Civil and Political Rights*, p. 475.

[38] Asma Jahangir, 'References to "Incitement to Religious Hatred"', a paper presented to OHCHR expert workshop on the prohibition of incitement to national, racial or religious hatred (2008), available at www.ohchr.org/EN/Issues/FreedomOpinion/Articles19-20/2008Seminar/Pages/ExpertPapers.aspx, p. 67.

[39] The Jacob Blaustein Institute for the Advancement of Human Rights, a paper presented to OHCHR expert workshop on the prohibition of incitement to national, racial or religious hatred (2011), available at www.ohchr.org/Documents/Issues/Expression/ICCPR/NGOs2011/JacobBlausteinInstituteVienna Workshop.pdf, p. 3.

perceived Article 20(2) to be of limited relevance from a contemporary legal perspective.[40]

The drafting history of the ICCPR reveals that efforts to address advocacy of hatred within the Covenant were indeed triggered, to a large extent, by the bitter experiences caused by Nazi and fascist hate propaganda before and during the Second World War. However, the inference that the object and purpose of Article 20 relates to hate speech inciting large-scale and state-instigated violence provides a reductionist reading of its drafting history. As this chapter will reveal, many states made assertions during the Article's drafting process regarding the necessity of addressing incitement to hostility and the importance of this goal in combating incitement to violence. Eventually, proposals to restrict the Article's scope only to incitement to violence failed. In its adopted version, the Article recognizes the legitimacy of prohibiting advocacy of hatred on the grounds of incitement to hostility. Notably, when the Third Committee of the GA considered the draft Covenant in 1961, the countries allied with the Eastern bloc shifted their focus from wartime events to racism.[41] The USSR emphasized that Article 20(2) 'touched upon the very serious problem of the dissemination of racialism' for which both the 'prejudices of certain social groups' and 'the colonial system' were responsible. It added that 'despite the rapid elimination of colonialism, racialism was still wide-spread for instance in the Non-Self-Governing and Trust Territories'.[42] Czechoslovakia also highlighted that 'racial and national hatred was at present particularly evident in connexion with the growing national liber-ation movement of colonial peoples'.[43] The African delegates whose states had only recently gained independence particularly favoured the inclusion of a provision specifically prohibiting incitement to racial hatred.[44] Moreover, the travaux préparatoires reveal that the drafters were not solely preoccupied with state-instigated hate speech; a number of states emphasized that such provisions cover horizontal types of incitement, that is they provide protection against incite-ment by non-state or private actors against other individuals or groups.[45] These elements suggest that the Article's object and purpose is not only to prevent and prohibit speech that incites large-scale violent acts or state-instigated hate propa-ganda. Moreover, the Article still enjoys direct contemporary relevance. In the post-Cold War era, hate speech acted as a catalyst for mass atrocities and large-scale human rights violations in a number of instances, for example in Rwanda and the former Yugoslavia and, more recently, in Kenya, Cote d'Ivoire, and Myanmar. As Chapter 1 illustrated, the scope and nature of hate speech harms have changed

---

[40]   Temperman, *Religious Hatred*, p. 33.
[41]   A/C.3/SR.1078, paras. 15–18; Farrior, 'Molding the Matrix', 35.
[42]   A/C.3/SR.1078, para. 17.
[43]   A/C.3/SR.1080, para. 11.
[44]   Timmermann, *Incitement in International Law*, p. 115.
[45]   E/CN.4/SR.160, at 13; E/CN.4/SR.160, at 12; E/CN.4/SR.163, at 11.

with the ongoing processes of globalization, and new challenges are constantly being posed. IHRL provisions do not apply exclusively to situations precisely analogous to the historic experiences that triggered their drafting. Rather, they should be interpreted as living instruments, in a dynamic manner that corresponds to contemporary circumstances and challenges.

3.3 FREEDOM OF EXPRESSION: THE DUAL USE OF THE LOGIC OF ABUSE

The exponents of Article 20(2) perceived it as a preventive tool offering protection against the abuse of freedom of expression, whereas its opponents perceived it as an abusive tool that would be detrimental to freedom of expression. The concern about the impact that prohibiting advocacy of hatred might have on the exercise of freedom of expression was the major source of controversy between the opposing camps during the Article's drafting phase. In advancing their arguments, parties both for and against the Article employed the logic of abuse.

The debates on the advocacy of hatred provision correlate closely with those over the Article on freedom of expression and, to a lesser degree, the Article on non-discrimination. During the drafting of Article 19, on freedom of expression, a number of Eastern bloc countries introduced proposals that aimed to recognize incitement to hatred as a legitimate limitation on that freedom. The USSR presented a proposal stipulating that freedom of expression should not be 'used for war propaganda, for inciting enmity among nations, racial discrimination and the dissemination of slanderous rumors'.[46] The Ukrainian SSR, Byelorussian SSR, and Poland all supported this proposal.[47] Poland also suggested adding that 'no one might exercise his right of freedom of expression in defiance of the principles of the United Nations, especially to engage in war propaganda, to arouse hostility between the nations, [or] to encourage racial discrimination ... '.[48] India proposed adding a reference that restricted 'expressions inciting to war or to national, racial, or religious hatred; attacks on founders of religions; incitement to violence and crime'.[49] Saudi Arabia supported the Indian proposal and asserted that it was consistent with protecting freedom of expression.[50] Brazil also suggested adding restrictions necessary 'for preventing any manifestations of racial, religious or class prejudices'.[51] Yugoslavia proposed adding a reference to 'the suppression of

---

[46] A/2929, p. 52.
[47] A/C.3/SR.289, para. 36.
[48] A/C.3/SR.571, para. 26.
[49] A/C.3/SR.1072, para. 2.
[50] A/C.3/SR.1070, paras. 30, 32.
[51] A/C.3/L.920.

propaganda in favour of national, racial or other discrimination, the fermenting of hatred between peoples … ' to the limitation clause within Article 19.[52]

Such proposals proved controversial. Western states took the stance that a general clause on limitations within Article 19 was sufficient to deal with the possible harms of hate propaganda, and strongly resisted the widening of the scope of limitations on freedom of expression through a specific reference to incitement to hatred.[53] Australia and the United Kingdom raised objections on the basis that a specific reference to the prohibition of incitement to hatred might constitute grounds for prior censorship.[54] Eventually, states agreed that the list of permissible limitations within Article 19 should be kept short.[55] Accordingly, the proposals to include references to hateful propaganda and incitement to hatred within Article 19 were withdrawn on the understanding that these proposals would be considered for inclusion in a separate Article.[56] Notably, however, at a later stage in the ICCPR negotiations, a number of Western countries, including the United States, the United Kingdom, and Australia, took the position that, if hate propaganda constituted a threat to a peaceful society, then Article 19(3) would be sufficient to address it, without the need for a separate Article on hate propaganda.[57]

The United States, Norway, Denmark, Finland, Sweden, and Japan argued that the prohibition of incitement to hatred was susceptible to governmental abuse and would enable authoritarian control over the exercise of freedom of expression in a manner detrimental, or even destructive, to that freedom.[58] The United States warned that it would be 'dangerous to permit such prohibitions' since 'any criticism of public or religious authorities might all too easily be described as incitement to hatred' and consequently governments could prohibit such criticism under the pretext of fulfilling their obligations under Article 20.[59] The United States stated that it is 'better to err on the side of too great freedom of speech' than to impose additional restrictions on that freedom and de facto undermine it.[60] Japan cautioned that restrictions on freedom of expression 'represented a far greater threat to lasting world peace than did propaganda for war and hostility'.[61] Australia and the United Kingdom also contended that legal prohibition would constitute a remedy worse than the problem it sought to address.[62] Scandinavian countries affirmed that the proposed Article 20 was 'so easy to misconstrue that those whom the provision was supposedly designed to protect might very well find

---

[52] E/1992, Annex III, A.
[53] A/5000; A/2929, at 64, 129.
[54] E/CN.4/SR.377, at 6, 8.
[55] A/5000.
[56] A/5000, para. 30; A/C.3/SR.1081, at 108; A/C.3/SR.1080, para. 1.
[57] E/CN.4/SR.174, paras. 24, 29, 42; E/CN.4/SR.377, at 6–7.
[58] A/C.3/SR.568, para. 15; A/C.3/SR.1078, para. 6; A/C.3/SR.1084, para. 4; A/C.3/SR.1082, para. 23.
[59] E/CN.4/SR.174, para. 24.
[60] E/CN.4/AC.1/SR.28, at 2–3.
[61] A/C.3/SR.1082, para. 25.
[62] E/CN.4/SR.377, at 7–8; E/CN.4/SR.379, at 6.

themselves its victims'.[63] France highlighted the difficulties associated with distinguishing between the abuse of freedom of expression and its legitimate exercise.[64]

A number of states opposing the inclusion of Article 20 employed the logic of the free marketplace of ideas to justify their resistance to prohibiting a wide range of harms associated with the advocacy of hatred. The United Kingdom opined that addressing advocacy of contempt or exclusiveness should be done through a 'safe remedy' which allows individuals to express themselves freely and that the state should trust people's 'good sense'.[65] It added that 'the power of democracy to combat propaganda lay in the last resort in the ability of its citizens to arrive at reasoned decisions in the face of conflicting appeals'.[66] The United States argued that 'the utmost freedom of speech is a better safeguard against hostility and violence than general laws giving increased powers to suppress freedom of speech'[67] and that 'propaganda and prejudice could be overcome only by the freest possible flow of information'.[68] It held the view that individual 'self-discipline' best addressed the issue of incitement, and not 'the enactment of laws which played into the hands of those who would attempt to restrict freedom of speech entirely'.[69] The United States added that, when people are allowed to listen to all views concerning a particular issue, they will be able to reach a 'wise conclusion'.[70] Uruguay also argued that respecting freedom of expression would allow people to 'discover the truth' regardless of any attempts to hide it.[71]

On the other hand, Article 20's supporters emphasized that freedom of expression comes with concomitant duties and responsibilities, in order to safeguard against its abuse. In their view, such abuse could eventually lead to the elimination of all freedoms.[72] They conceived of freedom of expression as both a precious and a dangerous instrument.[73] Czechoslovakia argued that 'it seemed inconceivable that freedom of expression should be used as pretext for allowing dissemination of views which insulted human dignity and led to physical violence and bloodshed'.[74] Indonesia also affirmed that 'the principle of freedom of information could not be regarded as so untouchable as to make it, possibly, immoral'.[75] The Philippines asked 'what would be the use of guaranteeing fundamental rights if nobody was to be there to enjoy them?'.[76] A number of states emphasized Article 20's direct relation

---

[63] A/C.3/SR.1084, para. 5.
[64] E/CN.4/SR.123, at 6.
[65] E/CN.4/AC.1/SR.28, at 3.
[66] E/CN.4/SR.377, at 9.
[67] E/CN.4/82.
[68] A/C.3/SR.1071, para. 12.
[69] E/CN.4/AC.1/SR.28, at 2–3.
[70] E/CN.4/AC.1/SR.28, at 2–3.
[71] A/C.3/SR.1083, para. 24.
[72] A/2929, at 51–52; A/C.3/SR.1073, para. 28.
[73] E/CN.4/SR.320, at 4.
[74] A/C.3/SR.1081, para. 14.
[75] A/C.3/SR.1081, para. 2.
[76] A/C.3/SR.1081, para. 23.

not only to Article 19 on freedom of expression, but also to the Articles on non-discrimination and minority rights, and suggested that the four Articles 'formed a harmonious and integrated whole', of which the Covenant should strive to maintain the balance.[77]

Article 20's supporters did not regard the logic of the free marketplace of ideas as sufficient protection against the harms of hate advocacy, given the inequality of access to that market. Venezuela argued that 'some people were powerless to make their views known'[78] and doubted that different groups could express their opinions 'on an equal footing with the most powerful interest groups'.[79] Saudi Arabia argued that 'only the privileged class' was capable of resisting certain kinds of propaganda disseminated through the media, while 'the masses' were not necessarily capable of 'arriving at a genuinely informed opinion: they were conditioned by the big press agencies which told them what to think'.[80] It cautioned against 'excessive' confidence in 'human intelligence'.[81] Similarly, Chile expressed concern that social methods like mutual respect and education were insufficient to curb incitement to hatred or to deal with the problems associated with specific forms of speech.[82] It criticized the laissez-faire logic that other countries used, and called for the adoption of legal methods at both national and international levels, to prohibit incitement to hatred.[83] In its response to the UK's assertion that the only way to protect democracy was the absolute protection of freedom of expression, Chile argued that the UK had not experienced the hazards associated with 'totalitarian ideologies' and, thus, would not appreciate their real dangers.[84]

The Article's supporters also used protection against discrimination as a fundamental rationale, as they perceived hate propaganda to be a violation of the principle of non-discrimination.[85] The USSR introduced the first version of the Article in 1947, as a clause within the Article on non-discrimination within the UDHR.[86] It provided that 'any advocacy of national, racial and religious hostility or of national exclusiveness, or hatred and contempt, as well as any action establishing a privilege or a distinction or race, nationality or religion, constitute a crime and shall be punishable under the law of the State'.[87] Despite the defeat of this proposal, that same year the Sub-Commission on Prevention of Discrimination and Protection of Minorities recommended that the Human Rights Commission should adopt provisions in the International Bill of Human Rights 'condemning incitement

---

[77] A/C.3/SR.1081, para. 24.
[78] A/C.3/SR.1083, para. 42.
[79] A/C.3/SR.1083, para. 42
[80] A/C.3/SR.1083, para. 36.
[81] A/C.3/SR.1083, para. 36.
[82] E/CN.4/SR.378, at 12.
[83] E/CN.4/SR.378, at 12.
[84] E/CN.4/AC.1/SR.28, at 3.
[85] E/CN.4/AC.1/SR.28, at 2.
[86] E/CN.4/Sub.2/21.
[87] E/CN.4/Sub.2/21.

to violence against religious groups, nations, races, or minorities'.[88] In the Covenant's early drafting phase, a number of states considered the possibility of incorporating a clause providing protection against incitement to discrimination in the Article on non-discrimination.[89] Despite the inclusion of such a clause in the non-discrimination provisions of the UDHR (Article 7), the United States and United Kingdom objected to its inclusion in the Article on non-discrimination within the ICCPR (Article 2) on the basis of its vagueness.[90] The UK and Australia held the view that Article 2 of the ICCPR was sufficient to provide comprehensive protection for individuals against discrimination and incitement to discrimination.[91]

Establishing a universal legislative policy for all state parties to the ICCPR, by prescribing elements of offences which were to be reflected at the level of national laws, presented a challenge to the drafting of Article 20(2). It is the only Article in the entire Covenant that stipulates that a certain conduct 'shall be prohibited by law'. The different stances of parties during the Article's negotiations reflected the challenges inherent in reaching consensus among states with different histories, cultures, and legal traditions, on the parameters of national hate speech regulation.[92]

A number of Western countries expressed the opinion that legislation was not necessarily the most effective means by which to address advocacy of hatred. Additionally, they highlighted the existence of different national approaches to this phenomenon which were not necessarily legal in nature.[93] They emphasized that states should enjoy a margin of appreciation in choosing an approach appropriate to their histories, legal traditions, and political cultures.[94] The UK, in objecting to an international obligation to enact hate speech laws, emphasized the logic of relativism in the context of human rights protection. It considered Article 20(2) to be alien to its legal tradition and mentioned that 'every state enjoyed the prerogative of passing any law that it liked, but it was another matter to impose on the society of states a requirement to enact legislation of a repressive character'.[95] The UK argued that 'it was for every government to deal with that sort of propaganda under its domestic law and it did not need the authority of an international obligation to do so'.[96] Australia claimed that nations could achieve tolerance through non-legislative means, such as policies and administrative actions or decisions.[97] Cyprus pointed out that what constitutes incitement to hatred differs from one country to another.[98]

---

[88]   E/CN.4/52, para. 4f.
[89]   E/CN.4/AC.1/SR.28, at 2.
[90]   E/CN.4/AC.1/SR.28, at 2.
[91]   A/C.3/SR.1084, paras. 10, 24.
[92]   Farrior, 'Molding the Matrix', 5.
[93]   E/CN.4/SR.174, paras. 24, 29.
[94]   Farrior, 'Molding the Matrix', 7–8.
[95]   E/CN.4/SR.379, at 6–7.
[96]   E/CN.4/AC.1/SR.28, at 6.
[97]   E/CN.4/SR.377, at 7.
[98]   A/C.3/SR.1082, para. 18.

France referred to the difficulties associated with extending conceptions that had their origin in national experiences to the international sphere.[99] It cautioned that 'no good would come on the international level of supporting a text which although its usefulness in certain areas was evident, could not be applied universally'.[100]

The states that opposed the inclusion of a separate provision on hate speech in the Covenant perceived it as not setting forth any individual human right, but rather, excessively restricting freedom of expression in a manner that jeopardized the core principles of that freedom.[101] Accordingly, these states contended that Article 20(2) did not fall strictly under the Covenant's substantive scope, since the Covenant was an instrument that should codify only individual rights entailing the non-interference of states.[102] The United States opined that the Article 'did not fit with the system of the Covenant'.[103] Ireland, Australia, Greece, Norway, Denmark, Finland, Iceland, and Sweden similarly considered the Article to be out of place in the Covenant.[104] New Zealand stated that the Article did not conform to 'the general pattern of the rest of the Covenant'.[105] Australia expressed its reservations about 'including an essentially negative Article in a draft Covenant consisting primarily of a positive statement of the rights of the individual'.[106] Similarly, the United Kingdom considered it 'unwise to insert a purely negative provision in a text which should be of a positivist nature',[107] a view endorsed by New Zealand.[108] Italy went so far as to contend that the Article endangered the Covenant's structural balance.[109] It also opined that the Article did not belong to the ICCPR, whose essential purpose was 'to safeguard human rights, and not to legislate against crime'.[110] During the drafting process, these countries repeatedly called for its deletion from the Covenant's text.[111]

The Article's opponents emphasized the arguments underlying the libertarian notion of freedom of expression, in particular the rationale of the free marketplace of ideas, and the 'slippery slope' argument, both of which call for a minimalist approach to hate speech regulation. They asserted that freedom of expression was such a fundamental and important pillar of democracy that states should take the risks involved in its exercise and that state intervention in its regulation should be minimal, so as to minimize the scope for abuse. This purely libertarian position was,

---

99   E/CN.4/SR.379, at 10.
100   E/CN.4/SR.379, at 10.
101   A/C.3/SR.1084, paras. 4, 20, 22–23; A/C.3/SR.1081, para. 70; A/C.3/SR.1083, para. 59.
102   A/C.3/SR.1084, paras. 4, 20, 22–23; A/C.3/SR.1083, para. 59; A/C.3/SR.1078, para. 6.
103   E/CN.4/SR.174, para. 24.
104   A/C.3/SR.1081, paras. 70–71; A/C.3/SR.1078, para. 17; A/C.3/SR.1084, paras. 4, 7, 11.
105   E/CN.4/82/Add.12, at 20–21.
106   A/C.3/SR.1084, para. 7.
107   A/C.3/SR.1079, para. 47.
108   A/C.3/SR.1084, para. 11.
109   A/C.3/SR.1084, para. 14.
110   A/C.3/SR.1084, para. 14.
111   A/C.3/SR.1079, paras. 23, 46; A/C.3/SR.1078, para. 6.

however, questioned by the Article's supporters in the light of lessons drawn from their actual experiences. Their conception of freedom of expression centred around the notion of duties and responsibilities to safeguard against its abuse, and their arguments aligned considerably with the egalitarian notion of freedom of expression and the communitarian approach to rights.

3.4 THE EMOTIVE COMPONENT: A MAJOR DIVIDING LINE

The issue of whether IHRL should recognize a right of protection from the emotional harms of hate advocacy proved very controversial during negotiations. The debates over the inclusion in Article 20(2) of protection from incitement to hostility brought into question the appropriateness of legislating morality, and this became a prominent issue during the Article's drafting.

Western states, driven by their desire to narrow the scope of limitations on freedom of expression as much as possible, insisted on the recognition of incitement to violence as the sole category of harm justifying the prohibition of advocacy of hatred.[112] They were willing to accept a formulation of the Article prohibiting advocacy of hatred that leads *only* to incitement to violence. They viewed violence as a tangible and narrowly defined harm that could, and should, lend itself to legal action, contrasting sharply in this respect with incitement to hatred and hostility.[113] Accordingly, Western states resisted the restriction of freedom of expression on the grounds of emotional harm and opposed the inclusion of references to incitement to hatred or hostility in the Covenant's text. The Article's opponents were frequently eager to express their sympathy with the spirit of the Article;[114] they condemned advocacy of hatred[115] and supported the moral and social principles that inspired the proposal of the Article.[116] Nevertheless, many of these states, including the United States, the United Kingdom, Ireland, Japan, Australia, Italy, the Netherlands, and Belgium, conceived the goal of addressing advocacy of hatred to be untranslatable into strictly legal terms in an international legal instrument.[117] The terms 'hatred' and 'hostility' were characterized as vague and subjective terms, defying objective legal definition or measurement, and potentially opening the door for abuse of the proposed Article.[118] Italy and the United States argued that there should be a minimum level of clarity, precision, and legal soundness in the terms used in an international legal instrument.[119]

---

[112] A/C.3/SR.1082, para. 18; A/C.3/SR.1080, para. 19.
[113] A/C.3/SR.1084, para. 20; A/C.3/SR.1078, para. 6; E/CN.4/SR.174, para. 67.
[114] A/C.3/SR.1082, para. 18; A/C.3/SR.1081, para. 67; A/C.3/SR.1078, para. 6; E/CN.4/SR.379, at 14.
[115] A/C.3/SR.1082, paras. 22–23; A/C.3/SR.1084, para. 5; A/C.3/SR.568, para. 15; E/CN.4/SR.377, at 8.
[116] A/C.3/SR.1082, para. 23; A/C.3/SR.1081, para. 65; A/C.3/SR.1083, para. 27.
[117] A/C.3/SR.1078, para. 17; A/C.3/SR.1081, para. 15; A/C.3/SR.1084, para. 8.
[118] E/CN.4/SR.174, para. 26; A/C.3/SR.1078, para. 17; E/CN.4/SR.377, at 8–9; E/CN.4/SR.379, at 5–6; A/C.3/SR.1082, para. 38; A/C.3/SR.1083, para. 30; A/C.3/SR.1084, at 8, 14, 20, 23.
[119] A/C.3/SR.1084, para. 13; A/C.3/SR.568, para. 15.

Resorting to legal prohibitions in order to combat advocacy of hatred was objected to by some states on the grounds that it amounted to legal moralism.[120] According to those that were against the inclusion of the terms 'hatred' and 'hostility' in the Article, hatred was a moral concept with no legal connotations, and its legal definition could be based only on the idea of incitement to violence. Australia emphasized that 'people could not be legislated into morality' and that 'tolerance could be achieved through means other than legislation'.[121] Uruguay questioned whether 'it was not altogether too ambitious to attempt to prohibit by means of a legal instrument ills which were inherent in human nature'.[122] It called for distinguishing between 'the aims or principles that were to be expressed and the legal forms that they should assume'.[123] Belgium similarly emphasized that 'it was not the committee's task to draw up a list of social or moral principles, but to draft an international legal instrument'.[124] France opined that 'to transform the state of mind of a nation was a laborious task and, moreover, not solely a matter for the legislator, since what was required was a revolution not merely in legislation but also in national ways of thought'.[125]

These assertions of the unsuitability of addressing emotional harms did not convince the Article's supporters; they also remained unconvinced by the calls made for a distinction between moral and juridical terms. They emphasized the overlap between law and morals, and the evolution of legal standards from moral concepts. Syria argued that 'in an instrument like the Covenant it seemed difficult to separate moral concepts from strictly juridical concepts'.[126] Iraq noted that, although the term 'hatred' 'might at present time be very difficult to define in legal terms, it had a moral validity' and that 'any Article dealing with human rights must out of necessity embody elements which belonged to the moral sphere rather than the legal'.[127] The USSR responded to criticism by Western states on the grounds of legal moralism by noting that 'the next logical step would be to deny the usefulness of legislation as a means of ensuring law and order in society'.[128] Poland contended that the Covenant's principles should be part of the 'national morality of . . . states' and that states should implement it as required, through the adoption of new legislation.[129] It refuted the argument that legislation could not combat advocacy of hatred by

---

[120]   A/C.3/SR.1081, para. 67; A/C.3/SR.1082, paras. 22–23; A/C.3/SR.1084, paras. 8, 15; A/C.3/SR.1083, paras. 13, 27; A/C.3/SR.568, para. 15.
[121]   E/CN.4/SR.377, at 7.
[122]   A/C.3/SR.1083, para. 24.
[123]   A/C.3/SR.1083, para. 18.
[124]   A/C.3/SR.1083, para. 27.
[125]   E/CN.4/SR.377, at 12.
[126]   A/C.3/SR.1081, para. 83.
[127]   A/C.3/SR.1081, para. 54.
[128]   E/CN .4/SR.377, at 10.
[129]   E/CN.4/SR.378, at 9–10.

arguing that penal law is not only a tool for punishment, but also contains 'elements of educative character'.[130] It added that

> just as certain iniquitous laws, such as the former 'Nuremberg Laws' of Nazi Germany, and the discrimination laws at present operative in South Africa and elsewhere undoubtedly promoted sentiments of exclusiveness and hostility in one section of the population against another, so it was possible for right sentiments to be fostered and wrong sentiments to be eradicated by the action of law.[131]

Although Chile recognized the difficulties of legally regulating the issues raised by the proposed Article 20(2), it did not consider this an impossible task and underlined the increasing need for legislation on such issues.[132] Romania also defended the addition of the phrase 'shall be prohibited by law' and argued that it was vital that the Article 'provided for positive legal sanction to deal with any manifestations directed against peace, human dignity, equality of rights or freedom of opinion'.[133] A number of countries, including the USSR, Yugoslavia, and Czechoslovakia, referred to provisions in their national laws that prohibited incitement to hatred as examples of the feasibility of its legal regulation.[134]

A significant number of states, including Lebanon, Greece, Japan, the United Kingdom, and Congo-Léopoldville, referred to the multiple difficulties inherent in the legal interpretation of the term 'hatred'.[135] The United States, supported by Belgium, referred to the difficulty of distinguishing between the numerous shades of feeling, and therefore meaning, that exist along a continuum from hatred, to ill-feeling, to mere dislike.[136] Greece affirmed that 'hatred was too abstract a concept – a feeling which meant something too different to each individual – for incitement to it to be defined in any way that was legally satisfactory'.[137] The United Kingdom asserted that the term 'hostility' was entirely 'out of place in a legal document' since it was a subjective term that could not be legally defined or measured.[138] Japan also doubted the feasibility of reaching an objective definition of the term 'hostility'.[139]

Different states perceived the relationship between the terms 'hatred' and 'hostility' differently. France held the view that hatred is stronger and wider than hostility; it was therefore illogical to prohibit advocacy of hatred constituting incitement to hostility, since 'hatred always resulted in hostility'.[140] A number of countries treated

---

[130]   E/CN.4/SR.378, at 9–10.
[131]   E/CN.4/SR.378, at 9–10.
[132]   A/C.3/SR.1078, para. 13.
[133]   A/C.3/SR.1083, at 25.
[134]   E/CN.4/SR.379, at 11; A/C.3/SR.1079, para. 8; A/C.3/SR.1080, para. 13.
[135]   E/CN.4/SR.174, paras. 38, 63; A/C.3/SR.1079, paras. 22, 41; A/C.3/SR.1081, para. 72.
[136]   E/CN.4/SR.174, para. 26.
[137]   A/C.3/SR.1081, para. 72.
[138]   A/C.3/SR.1084, paras. 22–23.
[139]   A/C.3/SR.1079, para. 22.
[140]   A/C.3/SR.1083, para. 9.

the two words as synonymous.[141] Pakistan, the United Kingdom, and Uruguay considered hostility to be wider than hatred.[142] The United Kingdom argued that the term 'incitement to hostility' was 'broader' than 'incitement to hatred'.[143] Poland considered hostility to have three different forms: hatred, violence, and discrimination.[144] It noted that discrimination stood 'halfway between hatred and violence' and was the 'most widespread form of national, racial or religious hostility'.[145] According to Saudi Arabia, hatred was 'far more specific than hostility' as two groups 'might be hostile to each other without coming to blows or closing the door to a settlement of differences, but hatred was a deep-seated emotion with fairly definite causes and effects'.[146]

A number of countries frequently expressed fears that the terms 'hatred' and 'hostility' might be abused. The United States warned that the use of these terms would render other Articles, specifically those dealing with freedoms of expression and association, 'null and void'.[147] The United Kingdom, the United States, and Greece considered the incorporation of the word 'hatred' within the Article to represent censorship of thought and a threat to freedom of expression.[148] China and Pakistan also expressed worries that use of the term 'hatred' would confer excessive authority upon governments.[149] The United Kingdom warned that using vague terms or criteria in the Article would give governments 'the power to take a subjective decision on whether an opinion offended against an accepted canon' and added that 'no more useful weapon could be handed to a government disposed to abolish free discussion'.[150]

Australia pointed out that the dictionary definition of 'hostility' included not only 'enmity and a state of warfare but also unfriendliness, antagonism and, even, contrariness'.[151] Thus, it cautioned against interpreting the legal prohibition of hostility in a manner inclusive of 'a mere difference of view'.[152] The use of the term 'hostility' in association with particular group identities presented a problem for some states. Lebanon criticized the use of the term in association with nationality on the ground that states could abuse it to prohibit freedom of expression in relation to the 'ideology and traditions of a nation'.[153] Chile concurred with Lebanon that

---

[141] Saudi Arabia, the Philippines, Lebanon, Thailand, Brazil, Cambodia, Ghana, Guinea, Iraq, Mali, Morocco, United Arab Republic, Yugoslavia, Congo (Leopoldville), Indonesia, and Poland A/C.3/SR.1082, para. 4.
[142] E/CN.4/SR.379, at 8, 13; E/CN.4/SR.378, at 6–7.
[143] A/C.3/SR.1084, paras. 22–23; E/CN.4/SR.174, para. 63.
[144] A/C.3/SR.1081, para. 34.
[145] A/C.3/SR.1082, para. 33.
[146] A/C.3/SR.1082, para. 31.
[147] E/CN.4/SR.174, para. 26.
[148] E/CN.4/SR.379, at 6, 14; A/C.3/SR.1081, para. 72.
[149] E/CN.4/SR.379, at 12, 14.
[150] E/CN.4/SR.377, at 8.
[151] A/C.3/SR.1084, para. 10.
[152] A/C.3/SR.1084, para. 10.
[153] E/CN.4/SR.174, para. 34–35.

objective expressions on ethnic issues can easily be read as hostile propaganda.[154] Ecuador also believed that 'while the term "racial or religious hostility" was definable in practice, the term "national hostility" had no specific meaning'.[155]

A number of countries, including Belgium, Canada, the United Kingdom, Japan, and Chile, also drew attention to the difficulty of objectively defining the term 'incitement' and distinguishing it from 'advocacy'.[156]

Some states highlighted the practical challenges associated with the Article's implementation and interpretation, being of the view that its vague and subjective terms resisted precise definition within an international treaty. Ireland pointed out that the Article's terms would create difficulties for national authorities trying to incorporate it into their national laws.[157] Similarly, Japan asserted that the Article's vagueness would make it impossible to implement, given that criminal legislation requires a precise definition of the criminal act.[158] The United States asserted that it could not easily define the term 'incitement to hatred' as a penal offence.[159] Italy also argued that states should define activities labelled offences under national laws precisely, to avoid any infringement of fundamental freedoms.[160] New Zealand pointed out the practical difficulties of identifying the line between legitimate expressions of opinion on religious and racial issues and other forms of expression that would amount to advocacy of racial or religious hatred.[161] With regard to the terms 'hostility', 'discrimination', and 'violence', Ireland argued that only 'violence' could be clearly proved in court by evidence.[162]

On the other hand, the Article's supporters objected to Western calls to restrict the protection offered by the Article against incitement to violence. According to these states, advocacy of hatred would create real risks which fell short of direct incitement to imminent violence. They underlined the causal relationship between the advocacy of hatred, on the one hand, and discrimination and the creation of an *atmosphere* which might be conducive to violence in the longer term, on the other.[163] Thus, they did not consider incitement to hatred to be any less serious than incitement to violence and argued that the Article should prohibit both.[164] Since most national legal systems already provided protection against incitement to violence, it was argued that restricting the protection the Article provided would inhibit its potential to act as a 'catalyst for progress'.[165] Ghana and Iraq argued that the

---

[154] E/CN.4/SR.174, para. 59.

[155] A/C.3/SR.1081, para. 43.

[156] E/CN.4/SR.174, paras. 31, 61; A/C.3/SR.570, para. 14; E/CN.4/SR.379, at 6; A/C.3/SR.1079, para. 22.

[157] A/C.3/SR.1081, para. 69.

[158] A/C.3/SR.1082, para. 23.

[159] A/C.3/SR.1078, para. 6.

[160] A/C.3/SR.1084, para. 13.

[161] E/CN.4/82/Add.12, at 20–21.

[162] A/C.3/SR.1081, para. 69.

[163] E/CN.4/SR.377, at 5, 8.

[164] E/CN.4/SR.377, at 5–6.

[165] A/C.3/SR.1081, paras. 57, 78; A/C.3/SR.1082, para. 11.

prohibition of incitement to violence 'did not represent any progress in international legislation. It was hatred and discrimination, which were the factors leading to violence, that must be prohibited'.[166]

Yugoslavia perceived manifestations of hatred, whether they led to violence or not, as representations of a 'degradation of human dignity and a violation of human rights'.[167] It argued that the Covenant should tackle 'all propaganda that constituted incitement to hatred and intolerance in every sphere', and not only incitement to violence.[168] Uruguay believed that 'it was obvious that the indulgence of hatred must inevitably lead to violence'.[169] Chile contended that hatred 'was at the root of violence'[170] and that 'some forms of propaganda', even if they do not constitute direct incitement to violence, 'were so insidious as to constitute a very real danger in the long run'[171] by justifying violence.[172] In its view, racial hatred 'once aroused, unleashed the worst instincts and succeeded in making racial extermination or the use of cremation ovens appear logical and natural'.[173] It described hate propaganda as 'a weapon of mass psychological penetration that could arouse national, racial or religious enmity'.[174] Chile explained that

> [since] modern technical facilities for dissemination of ideas, such as the press and wireless, were accessible to the young, they too were exposed to propaganda campaigns, which might be cleverly enough conducted to induce in the masses an attitude toward a nation, a race or a church that might end in an explosion of violence.[175]

Furthermore, Chile asserted that prohibiting incitement to violence alone would leave 'the door open to all other forms of intolerance' and 'render no service to the cause of tolerance'.[176] It supported undertaking preventive measures by attacking 'the evil at its roots'.[177] Poland shared this view, which held that restricting the Article's scope to the prohibition of incitement to violence alone did not go to 'the root of the evil' but 'merely tackled its consequences, and ... would only serve to hide the real nature of the problem'.[178] Poland argued that, in practice, it is very difficult to differentiate between propaganda leading to an environment conducive to violence and speech directly inciting listeners to violence.[179] The Article's supporters

---

[166] A/C.3/SR.1081, para. 57.
[167] A/C.3/SR.1079, para. 9.
[168] E/CN.4/SR.377, at 6.
[169] E/CN.4/SR.379.
[170] E/CN.4/SR.378, at 11.
[171] E/CN.4/L.269, at 5.
[172] E/CN.4/SR.378, at 12.
[173] E/CN.4/SR.378, at 12.
[174] E/CN.4/SR.378, at 12.
[175] E/CN.4/SR.377, at 4.
[176] E/CN.4/SR.377, at 14.
[177] E/CN.4/SR.378, at 11.
[178] E/CN.4/SR.377, at 4.
[179] E/CN.4/L.269.

contended that the Covenant should also prohibit incitement to hostility – in a similar fashion to its treatment of the protection of public morals – as an acceptable limitation on freedom of expression.[180] They also insisted on the inclusion of an explicit reference to 'incitement to discrimination'. They affirmed that the inclusion of the word 'discrimination' did not involve duplicating the Article on non-discrimination in the Covenant 'since the latter concerned a different matter, equality before the law'.[181] Poland elaborated further that discrimination might not necessarily be accompanied by violence, referring to the example of laws allowing racial segregation without necessarily involving violence.[182] On the other hand, France, although it accepted the reference to 'discrimination' in the Article, held that it was nevertheless 'unnecessary, since advocacy of national, racial or religious hatred could in fact be nothing else than advocacy of discrimination'.[183]

The states that supported Article 20(2) considered their opponents' arguments pertaining to the definitional problem of its key terms to be a pretext justifying their opposition.[184] These states downplayed, and even sometimes denied altogether, this definitional problem and argued that the Article contained definable legal concepts. They mentioned that other Articles within the Covenant contained terms that lent themselves to various interpretations in different countries and legal systems.[185] Cambodia argued that if the Article's terms were vague then, by the same token, terms such as freedom, justice, or equality would be vague as well.[186] Yugoslavia added that no word existed which had a single meaning[187] and Chile pointed out that many countries' domestic legislation used words like 'honour' and 'reputation', despite their definitional difficulties.[188] Chile also argued that the lack of a common agreement on the definitions of the terms used in the Article should not lead to the challenges that the Article aimed to address being ignored.[189] According to India and Iraq, the goals of the Article were clear enough, and the responsibility of delimiting the meaning of its key terms should be left to national courts.[190]

Yugoslavia denied the existence of a definitional problem for 'hatred', arguing that the inclusion of the phrase 'that constitutes incitement to discrimination, hostility or violence' settled the definition of 'hatred'.[191] It added that the ideas or elements underlying incitement to hatred 'had been the cause of the death of two million Yugoslavs … [The Yugoslav] people know what was meant by incitement to

[180] E/CN.4/SR.378, at 13; E/CN.4/SR.377, at 4; E/CN.4/SR.379, para. 8.
[181] A/C.3/SR.1082, para. 12.
[182] A/C.3/SR.1081, para. 33.
[183] A/C.3/SR.1083, para. 8.
[184] E/CN.4/SR.378, at 9.
[185] Farrior, 'Molding the Matrix', 37.
[186] A/C.3/SR.1081, para. 64.
[187] E/CN.4/SR.174, paras. 40–41.
[188] E/CN.4/SR.377, at 13–14.
[189] A/C.3/SR.1078, para. 13.
[190] A/C.3/SR.1081, para. 54; A/C.3/SR.1078, para. 34.
[191] A/C.3/SR.1082, para. 12.

hatred'.[192] Cambodia affirmed that 'hatred could not perhaps be defined, but it made itself understood and felt'. It added that the manifestations of hatred 'had always been recognized and no one could deny that it should be banished in the relations between human beings and above all between racial and religious groups'.[193] Pakistan perceived incitement to hatred as 'the arousing of the sentiment from which violence sprang'.[194]

Despite these protracted debates over the precise definitions of Article 20(2)'s key terms, and the ultimate inclusion of Article 20(2) within the Convention, the various parties never reached consensus on the meaning of these terms or the criteria for their identification.

3.5 GROUP RIGHTS AND RELIGIOUS FREEDOMS: ANOTHER DIVIDING LINE

The negotiations over Article 20(2) also raised the issue, explored more generally in the previous chapter, of recognizing groups as bearers of international human rights. The Article's supporters criticized the efforts of Western states to individualize the Article and the Covenant in general. Even at an early stage of drafting the Covenant, Czechoslovakia expressed its deep regret that the general drafting efforts 'had been guided by a spirit of individualism which was divorced from reality and had forgotten that human society was not composed of inanimate Articles and that individual freedom could exist only within the framework of society'.[195] Furthermore, the Byelorussian SSR criticized the assertion, by a number of Western countries such as France, the United Kingdom, Belgium, and Australia, that collective (as opposed to individual) rights had no place in the Covenant.[196] In its view, the Western countries sought to create a 'purely artificial division' between individual and group human rights.[197] On this basis, the Byelorussian SSR supported the inclusion of a provision on the prohibition of advocacy of hatred.[198]

The Article's supporters emphasized the repercussions of hate advocacy on the rights of groups as well as individuals, and the causal relationship between hate propaganda and discrimination against groups.[199] Ghana, for example, considered Article 19 to protect individual rights and Article 20 to protect 'collective rights'.[200] A statement submitted by the Preparatory Commission for the International Refugee Organization to the second session of the Commission on Human Rights in 1947[201]

---

[192] E/CN.4/SR.379, at 9.
[193] A/C.3/SR.1081, para. 64.
[194] E/CN.4/SR.378, para. 10.
[195] E/CN.4/SR.377, para. 55.
[196] A/C.3/SR.575, para. 3.
[197] A/C.3/SR.575, para. 3.
[198] A/C.3/SR.575, paras. 3, 8.
[199] Farrior, 'Molding the Matrix', 8–9, 22.
[200] A/C.3/SR.1079, para. 53.
[201] E/CN.4/41, at 1.

mentioned that it was 'desirable that municipal laws should contain adequate safeguards against discrimination, incitement to, and advocacy of, discrimination against individuals or groups of individuals'.[202] It stated the following:

> [I]ncitement to discrimination is frequently directed against national, religious and racial groups. Civil proceedings and criminal prosecutions against instigators of discrimination, or even violence, against such groups have sometimes failed in the past because the law provided only for the protection of individuals, but not of groups.[203]

In a statement submitted to the seventh session of the Commission on Human Rights in 1952, the World Jewish Congress also called for the Article on freedom of expression to include a reference to the prevention of dissemination of racial or religious hatred and intolerance. It argued that, although the Article protects the rights and reputations of others, it should also provide protection against incitement to such hatred targeting groups, as the latter are even more dangerous than attacks on the rights and reputation of individuals.[204]

Some countries called for a wider range of grounds for protection from incitement than those which were finally incorporated into the Article. Brazil called for the inclusion of class; it considered class hatred to be 'the scourge of modern times'.[205] China also criticized the lack of references to class hatred and warned against its dangerous repercussions in terms of 'social unrest and bloody civil wars'.[206] The Philippines proposed adding several categories, including sex, as a basis for prohibiting the advocacy of hatred and discrimination.[207]

The dilemma of how to differentiate between protected expressions addressing religious matters, and religious hate speech, was also raised during the debates. There were fears that the Article might negatively impact the enjoyment of religious freedoms. Chile foresaw problems in the area of religious discourse: 'all the religions based on the dogma of revelation believed they had an absolute and unquestionable monopoly of the truth: their propaganda was accordingly unfavourable or positively towards other religions'. It warned against precluding all religious discussions.[208] The United States also affirmed that the term 'religious hostility' was too ambiguous.[209] Lebanon raised the issue of whether addressing religious hostility should allow states to prevent persons from preaching a religion not yet practised in their territories.[210] The United Kingdom also presented a similar argument:

---

202 E/CN.4/41, at 2.
203 E/CN.4/41, at 2.
204 E/CN.4/NGO/39, at 5.
205 A/C.3/SR.580, at 11.
206 A/C.3/SR.1082, para. 27.
207 E/CN.4/365, at 365.
208 E/CN.4/SR.174, at 13.
209 E/CN.4/SR.174, para. 27.
210 E/CN.4/SR.174, at 8.

[I]n a country where a minority practised a religion different from that of the majority, there was room for a great deal of controversy. Supposing the religious leader of the minority put the case for his faith in violent and perhaps bitter words, the Government would then be able, on the strength of the proposed article, to evade its obligations to protect the minority.[211]

The UK also stated that 'hatred of what was sincerely believed to be false doctrine might be a legitimate objective of religious propaganda'.[212] Chile and Lebanon expressed their concerns about the use of the term 'hostility' regarding religion, as it might result in the curtailing of religious debates.[213]

3.6 THE DRAFTS LEADING TO THE ADOPTION OF ARTICLE 20(2)

During the ninth session of the Human Rights Commission in 1953, the following draft was presented as an attempt to reach a compromise on the Article: 'Any advocacy of national, racial or religious hostility that constitutes an incitement to hatred and violence shall be prohibited by the law of the State.'[214] The USSR considered the text 'too weak', since it prohibited advocacy of hostility only when it constituted an actual incitement to hatred *and* violence in contrast to their own favoured position that incitement to hatred be prohibited even if not associated with violence.[215] Yugoslavia suggested replacing the phrase 'hatred and violence' with the phrase 'hatred *or* violence' in order not to restrict the Article's application to situations in which advocacy of hostility incites violence alone.[216] It affirmed that 'it was just as important to suppress manifestations of hatred which, even without leading to violence, constituted a degradation of human dignity and a violation of human rights'.[217]

In another attempt to reach a compromise, Saudi Arabia, the Philippines, Lebanon, and Thailand presented a joint amendment that came to be known as the 'four-power amendment'. It read: 'Any propaganda for war and any advocacy of national, racial and religious hatred inciting to violence shall be prohibited by law.'[218]

The four sponsors of the proposed amendment shared the view that the law could not define hatred 'so long as it was passive' and not translated into tangible action(s).[219] They added that inserting the phrase 'inciting to violence' after the word 'hatred' solved the latter's definitional problem since 'hatred was easy to detect as soon as it lead to acts of violence'.[220] Saudi Arabia explained that the term 'inciting

---

[211]   E/CN.4/SR.379, at 5.
[212]   E/CN.4/SR.174, para. 63.
[213]   E/CN.4/SR.379, at 13; E/CN.4/SR.174, para. 35.
[214]   E/CN.4/SR.379, at 14.
[215]   A/C.3/SR.1079, para. 20.
[216]   A/C.3/SR.1079, para. 9.
[217]   A/C.3/SR.1079, para. 9.
[218]   A/C.3/L.932.
[219]   A/C.3/SR.1079, para. 61.
[220]   A/C.3/SR.1079, para. 61.

to violence' would apply to advocacy that incites to violence without necessarily actually causing violence.[221] The Philippines also affirmed that 'it was not necessary that violence itself should take place; any propaganda likely to lead to violence was prohibited'.[222] Both Saudi Arabia and the Philippines justified the lack of reference to discrimination by reference to the existence of a specific Article on non-discrimination.[223] A number of countries expressed their support for the four-power amendment, including India, Indonesia, Chile, Congo-Léopoldville, Pakistan, New Zealand, and Canada.[224] However, the USSR considered the amendment to be 'a step backwards' compared to earlier drafts and most existing national legislation, since it 'was not enough to prohibit everything that constituted incitement to violence'.[225] It added that 'discrimination, racial hatred and any form of racialism did not necessarily lead to violence; but they had all been very rightly condemned by the Nuremberg Tribunal in the name of the community of nations'.[226] The USSR warned that the amendment 'would enable certain quarters to avoid condemning propaganda for war and advocacy of national, racial and religious hatred on the pretext that they did not constitute incitement to violence'.[227] Yugoslavia concurred with the USSR.[228] Poland criticized the fact that 'only a combination of hatred and violence came within the prohibition' of the four-power amendment and 'if one of those two elements were lacking, the prohibition could no longer apply'. It considered this to be a significant defect in the proposal.[229]

Brazil, Cambodia, Ghana, Guinea, Iraq, Mali, Morocco, the United Arab Republic, and Yugoslavia then submitted another joint amendment known as 'the nine-power amendment'. It read: 'Any advocacy of national, racial or religious hostility that constitutes an incitement to hatred, discrimination and violence, as well as war propaganda, shall be incorporated in the law of the State.'[230]

The USSR and a number of states allied with the Eastern camp supported the nine-power amendment on the basis that it dealt with the root causes of the problem and not simply its consequences.[231] Poland asserted that the nine-power amendment 'was free from the defects' of the four-power amendment since 'it mentioned discrimination and, in enumerating the several elements, it employed the conjunction "or"'.[232] It added that 'the existence of any single one[element], all of which

[221] A/C.3/SR.1080, para. 20.
[222] A/C.3/SR.1081, para. 21.
[223] A/C.3/SR.1080, para. 21.
[224] A/C.3/SR.1081, paras. 3–4, 11, 16, 20, 40, 48.
[225] A/C.3/SR.1081, para. 78.
[226] A/C.3/SR.1081, para. 78.
[227] A/C.3/SR.1081, para. 78.
[228] A/C.3/SR.1082, para. 11.
[229] A/C.3/SR.1081, para. 35.
[230] A/C.3/L.930/Rev.2.
[231] A/C.3/SR.1081, paras. 31, 57, 78–79; A/C.3/SR.1080, para. 15.
[232] A/C.3/SR.1081, para. 36.

were very serious, would bring into play the ban on propaganda inciting to national, racial or religious hostility'.[233]

The competing four-power and nine-power amendments represented the two competing schools of thought on the scope of restrictions on hate advocacy under IHRL. The four-power amendment, which sought to prohibit advocacy of hatred only if it incites violence, was more acceptable to the states allied with the Western camp. However, most states allied with the Eastern camp supported the nine-power amendment, which sought to address a wider range of harms related to advocacy of hatred, including incitement to discrimination and hostility in addition to violence. In light of the impasse in negotiations, a working group was established from the membership of countries that presented each of these amendments, along with three additional states.[234] After prolonged discussions, this larger group drafted the 'sixteen-power amendment' as an attempted compromise. This amendment, ultimately adopted as Article 20(2), reads: 'Any advocacy of national, racial or religious hatred that constitutes incitement to discrimination, hostility or violence shall be prohibited by law.'[235]

According to the sixteen states that sponsored this final version, the meaning of 'national hatred' referred to hostility directed against specific ethnic groups within a state, including minority groups, while 'racial or religious hatred' was related to particular forms of hostility 'which might be independent of the national features of the peoples concerned'.[236] They regarded the term 'hatred' as the 'point of departure' and 'the prime cause of violence'.[237] They recognized that the Covenant 'could not deal with the subjective aspects of hatred but must condemn incitement to hatred only when it was externalized, at which point it was quite readily determined by courts'.[238] These states recognized the 'gradation' involved in the harms of hostility, discrimination, and violence and described the latter as the 'climax' of harms resulting from advocacy of hatred.[239] They clarified that 'prohibited by law' meant that 'the actions covered by the Article would be prohibited by the domestic law of the countries acceding to the Covenant'.[240] Yugoslavia affirmed that the sixteen-power amendment represented a compromise between the states which believed that 'hatred could not be legally defined and that the nine-power text might lead to the suppression of freedom of information', and those states that 'felt that an Article mentioning incitement to violence alone would be no innovation, since such incitement was already prohibited by most national legislations'.[241]

---

[233] A/C.3/SR.1081, para. 36.
[234] Brazil, Cambodia, Congo, Ghana, Guinea, Indonesia, Iraq, Lebanon, Mali, Morocco, Philippines, Poland, Saudi Arabia, Thailand, United Arab Republic, and Yugoslavia A/C.3/SR.1082, para. 1.
[235] A/C.3/L.933.
[236] A/C.3/SR.1082, para. 4.
[237] A/C.3/SR.1082, para. 5.
[238] A/C.3/SR.1082, para. 5.
[239] A/C.3/SR.1082, paras. 5, 6.
[240] A/C.3/SR.1082, paras. 5, 7.
[241] A/C.3/SR.1082, para. 11.

Western countries, among others, did not support the sixteen-power amendment since it was not restricted to incitement to violence and included terms they deemed unsuitable for inclusion in an international legal instrument.[242] The United States did not consider it to be a compromise between the two earlier amendments but, rather, a 'revised version of the nine-power amendment'.[243] The United States was dissatisfied with the inclusion of the two categories of incitement to discrimination and hostility.[244] New Zealand expressed a similar view and opined that the 'sixteen-power amendment' was an 'untrue compromise' that 'accentuated the undesirable effects of the nine-power amendment'.[245] Belgium opposed the sixteen-power amendment because it 'lent itself to a far-reaching and arbitrary interpretation and, if adopted, might well lead to a negation of the freedoms set forth in Article 19'.[246] France was not able to support the sixteen-power amendment because of the amendment's phrasing and not because it rejected the amendment's underlying principle.[247] It added that 'the Articles of the draft Covenant should be considered dispassionately, from the standpoint of their intrinsic merits and not of the value attached to some of the words therein. They should enshrine universal rules and not be made to fit a particular region or country'.[248] Japan was also unable to support the sixteen-power amendment because 'its wording remained vague and imprecise and because it could be invoked to suppress freedom of information'.[249]

A separate vote was taken regarding the inclusion (or not) of the words 'to discrimination, hostility or', and this was approved with forty-three in favour, twenty-one against, and nineteen abstentions.[250] Therefore, nearly half of the UN member states were against the recognition of emotional harms as grounds for the prohibition of advocacy of hatred. On 25 October 1961, the Third Committee of the GA adopted

---

[242] A/C.3/SR.1083, paras. 6–13, 15.
[243] A/C.3/SR.1083, para. 14.
[244] A/C.3/SR.1083, para. 15.
[245] A/C.3/SR.1084, para. 11.
[246] A/C.3/SR.1083, para. 27.
[247] A/C.3/SR.1083, para. 13.
[248] A/C.3/SR.1083, para. 13.
[249] A/C.3/SR.1083, para. 30.
[250] In favour: Ghana, Guinea, Haiti, Hungary, India, Indonesia, Iraq, Liberia, Libya, Mali, Mexico, Morocco, Nicaragua, Niger, Nigeria, Poland, Romania, Saudi Arabia, Sudan, Togo, Ukrainian Soviet Socialist Republic, Union of Soviet Socialist Republic, Upper Volta, Venezuela, Yemen, Yugoslavia, Afghanistan, Albania, Brazil, Bulgaria, Burma, Byelorussian Soviet Socialist Republic, Cambodia, Cameroon, Central African Republic, Ceylon, Chad, Chile, Congo (Brazzaville), Congo (Leopoldville), Cuba, Czechoslovakia, and Ethiopia. Against: Federation of Malaya, Finland, France, Greece, Iceland, Ireland, Israel, Japan, Lebanon, Norway, Peru, Sweden, Turkey, United Kingdom, United States of America, Uruguay, Belgium, Canada, Chile, Colombia, and Denmark. Abstain: Iran, Italy, Netherlands, New Zealand, Pakistan, Panama, Philippines, Portugal, South Africa, Spain, Thailand, Tunisia, Argentina, Australia, Austria, China, Cyprus, Dominican Republic, and Ecuador. A/C.3/SR.1083, para. 57.

the sixteen-power amendment with fifty in favour, eighteen against, and fifteen abstentions.[251]

None of the member states of the Council of Europe voted in favour of Article 20(2). Indeed, ten of them voted against it. The countries that voted against, or abstained from voting on, the Article reiterated their previous concerns regarding its inclusion in the text of the Covenant. The Scandinavian countries intimated that they considered it inappropriate for the UN to 'formulate treaty provisions which lent themselves to conflicting interpretations and contradictory applications'.[252] The United Kingdom affirmed that 'it had voted, not in favour of war propaganda or racial discrimination, but against the inclusion in the draft Covenant of concepts so imprecise as to make the Article unworkable and to endanger the rights embodied in Article 19'.[253] France,[254] Australia,[255] Canada,[256] and the United States[257] clarified that they would have supported Article 20(2) if it had been limited to restrictions on incitement to violence and had omitted the terms 'hatred' and 'hostility'. The states that voted in favour of the Article included African, Eurasian Communist, Asian, and South American states.

Five state parties to the ICCPR entered reservations to Article 20(2): Australia, Malta, New Zealand, the United Kingdom, and the United States.[258] These reservations absolved them from the requirement to introduce legislative provisions in fulfilment of the Article. State parties to the ICCPR which expressed reservations to Article 20(2) emphasized that states must interpret the Article in conformity with the rights of political liberty (Articles 19, 21, and 22). Belgium and Luxembourg made interpretive declarations that the implementation of Article 20 should take into account the rights to freedom of thought, religion, opinion, assembly, and association guaranteed in Articles 18, 19, 21, and 22 of the Covenant.[259] These stances

---

[251]   In favour: Dominican Republic, Ethiopia, Ghana, Guinea, Haiti, Hungary, India, Indonesia, Iraq, Israel, Lebanon, Liberia, Libya, Mali, Mexico, Morocco, Nicaragua, Niger, Nigeria, Pakistan, Philippines, Poland, Romania, Saudi Arabia, Sudan, Thailand, Togo, Tunisia, Ukrainian Soviet Socialist Republic, Union of Soviet Socialist Republic, Upper Volta, Venezuela, Yemen, Yugoslavia, Afghanistan, Albania, Brazil, Bulgaria, Burma, Byelorussian Soviet Socialist Republic, Cambodia, Cameroon, Central African Republic, Ceylon, Chad, Congo (Brazzaville), Congo (Leopoldville), Cuba, and Czechoslovakia. Against: Canada, Colombia, Denmark, Ecuador, Federation of Malaya, Finland, Iceland, Ireland, Japan, Netherlands, New Zealand, Norway, Sweden, Turkey, United Kingdom, United States, Uruguay, and Belgium. Abstaining: France, Greece, Iran, Italy, Panama, Peru, Portugal, South Africa, Spain, Argentina, Australia, Austria, Chile, China, and Cyprus. A/C.3/SR.1083, para. 58.

[252]   A/C.3/SR.1084, para. 5.

[253]   A/C.3/SR.1084, para. 24.

[254]   A/C.3/SR.1083, paras. 6–13.

[255]   A/C.3/SR.1084, para. 8–9.

[256]   A/C.3/SR.1084, para. 16.

[257]   E/CN.4/SR.379, at 14.

[258]   United Nations Treaty Series, Volume 4 International Covenant on Civil and Political Rights, available at http://treaties.un.org/doc/Publication/MTDSG/Volume%20I/Chapter%20IV/IV-4 .en.pdf, pp. 3, 9, 11, 13, 14.

[259]   United Nations Treaty Series, Volume 4, pp. 5, 8.

demonstrate that a number of states perceived a prima facie conflict, or at least tension, between freedom of expression and states' obligations under Article 20(2).

3.7 CONCLUDING REMARKS

This chapter analysed in detail the travaux préparatoires of Article 20(2) of the ICCPR, which codified the right to protection from incitement to discrimination, hostility, or violence. The Article's drafting history reveals that efforts to address advocacy of hatred within the ICCPR were, to a large extent, triggered by the bitter experiences caused by Nazi and fascist hate propaganda before and during the Second World War. The highly charged and ideologically polarized geopolitical environment of the cold war in the 1950s and 1960s significantly influenced the Article's negotiations. Those states which advocated its inclusion in the Covenant were mainly part of, or allied with, the Eastern bloc. Many of those countries had recent memories of Nazi and fascist propaganda and were convinced that this hateful propaganda had played a significant role in causing the crimes against humanity which characterized that period. They also argued that a lack of proper safeguards against hate propaganda could lead to the revival of extreme ideologies. On the other hand, the states with opposing views belonged mainly to the Western bloc. They considered human rights violations in Europe during the Second World War era in a different light. These countries argued that the suppression of opinions that might otherwise have countered hate propaganda constituted a major contributory factor to the consequences of such propaganda. Western states first resisted the incorporation of Article 20(2) within the Covenant and then advocated to narrow its scope as much as possible.

Although it is generally recognized that Western states largely dominated the drafting of the ICCPR, the codification of the right to protection from incitement to discrimination, hostility, or violence does not stem from Western influence or the libertarian theory of rights. Instead, states allied with the Eastern bloc were instrumental in securing the inclusion of Article 20(2) within the Covenant. The positions taken by the Article's supporters were aligned with the egalitarian notion of freedom of expression and the communitarian approach to rights.

The travaux préparatoires reveal that inclusion of the norm prohibiting incitement to discrimination, hostility, or violence within the ICCPR was highly controversial. The issues that caused profound controversies between the supporters and opponents of Article 20(2) relate directly to the five internal features of the norm identified in this book, which can be regarded as key thematic threads running through the debates. Concerns about the perceived tensions between freedom of expression and the prohibition of hate advocacy were prominent throughout the Article's drafting history. Both sides of the argument over the Article's incorporation in the Covenant frequently raised the prospect of rights and prohibitions being abused to advance their arguments, using this logic to justify calls for the narrowing or widening of restrictions on freedom of expression, depending on their viewpoint. The Article's advocates feared the abuse of the exercise of freedom of expression and viewed the Article as a preventive tool to provide protection to individuals and groups against discrimination. Conversely, the states that opposed the Article feared that legal prohibitions of hate speech could be abused in a manner that could jeopardize freedom of expression; they viewed the Article as an abusive tool in itself. The Article's drafting history presents a narrative of fear from abuse.

Furthermore, the emotional component of the right caused lengthy controversies during the Article's drafting and raised debates about the desirability of legislating morality. The question of whether IHRL should protect against emotional harms caused by advocacy of hatred, by prohibiting incitement to hostility, featured prominently during negotiations. There were strong objections, mainly from Western states, to the inclusion of the terms 'hatred' and 'hostility', on the basis that they defied objective legal definition, and so might be readily abused by states in order to infringe upon the legitimate exercise of freedom of expression. Such states sought to restrict the Article's scope to the prohibition of incitement to violence only as a definable legal concept. They affirmed that particularities of national context – especially histories, legal traditions, and political cultures – shape national approaches to addressing hate speech and that these approaches might not necessarily be legal in nature.

Some states allied with the Eastern bloc took the contrary view, which held that the Article should provide protection against a broader range of harms resulting from advocacy of hatred. Such states were keen to include a reference within the Article to incitement to hatred or hostility, in addition to violence, arguing that hatred and hostility were usually precursors of violence. They believed that incitement to hatred had serious repercussions, which justified its legal prohibition in all UN member states. While the Article's opponents believed that there would be practical difficulties in proving incitement and enforcing the right, its supporters minimized, and even denied, these difficulties, emphasizing the Article's preventive role.

The travaux préparatoires of IHRL instruments, in theory, have the potential to be a supplementary interpretive tool providing insights into, and elucidating the intended meaning of, the rights codified therein.[260] However, the travaux préparatoires of Article 20(2) do not provide conclusive guidance for determining the precise definition of its constituent terms, nor the Article's precise legal threshold, as the extensive debates on the meaning of these terms proved inconclusive. It is difficult to reconcile the multiplicity of intentions and understandings among the negotiators and drafters regarding the Article's terms and objectives into a coherent whole. The drafting history, thus, leaves many questions concerning the exact meaning of the norm prohibiting incitement to hatred unanswered.

---

[260]   Yogesh Tyagi, *The UN Human Rights Committee: Practice and Procedure* (New York, 2011), p. 9.

The final wording of Article 20(2) was the product of significant disagreements among states on both the Article's desired objectives and the means of achieving them. States were unable to fully resolve their differences, as shown by the voting record in the GA. The codification of the right to protection from incitement to discrimination, hostility, or violence in IHRL was the product of fragile international agreement; not only was the formulation of Article 20(2) controversial, but so was its very inclusion in the Covenant. Many states had argued that the norm prohibiting incitement to hatred was unsusceptible to translation into strictly legal terms in an international legal instrument.

The next chapter analyses how the jurisprudence of supranational human rights–monitoring bodies has addressed the definitional challenges and tensions that underlie the international norm prohibiting incitement to discrimination, hostility, or violence.

4

The Norm Prohibiting Incitement to Hatred through the Lens of Supranational Monitoring and Adjudicatory Bodies

4.1 INTRODUCTION

The language used to codify human rights in international legal instruments is mostly very abstract and generalized in its scope. This is usually the result of attempts to achieve the necessary reconciliation between the different cultures and legal traditions of negotiating states.[1] Consequently, a number of international human rights norms suffer from uncertainties regarding their exact meanings. In many instances, this makes them difficult to implement on a practical level.[2] The application of human rights norms requires an interpretative process.[3] The body of 'jurisprudence'[4] generated by supranational monitoring and adjudicatory bodies with the authority to interpret international human rights therefore plays an important role in addressing any inherent normative ambiguities and in developing, to varying degrees, our understanding of the scope of these rights.[5]

States' determinations of the meaning and scope of human rights are expected to be assessed, and at times even challenged, by these supranational monitoring and

---

[1] Nowak, *U.N. Covenant on Civil and Political Rights*, p. xxvi; Tobin, *The Right to Health*, pp. 75, 97; Besson, 'Human rights', p. 242; Parvez Hassan, 'International Covenants on Human Rights: An Approach to Interpretation' (1969–1970) 19 *Buffalo Law Review*, 42.

[2] Feldman, *Civil Liberties and Human Rights*, p. 38.

[3] Langer, 'Religious Offence', p. 372.

[4] 'Jurisprudence' in the proper sense of the word is 'the science of law, namely, that science which has for its function to ascertain the principles on which legal rules are based, so as not only to classify those rules in their proper order, and show the relation in which they stand to one another, but also to settle the manner in which new or doubtful cases should be brought under the appropriate rules'. Black, *Black's Law Dictionary*. For the purpose of this study, 'jurisprudence' refers to views, decisions, case-law of international and regional human rights bodies.

[5] Yvonne Donders, *Towards a Right to Cultural Identity?* (Intersentia, 2002), p. 7; Brems, 'Introduction', p. 2; Sarah Joseph, 'A Rights Analysis of the Covenant on Civil and Political Rights' (1999) 5 *International Legal Studies*, 80; Alex Conte and Richard Burchill, 'Introduction' in Alex Conte and Richard Burchill (eds.), *Defining Civil and Political Rights the Jurisprudence of the United Nations Human Rights Committee* (Ashgate, 2009), p. 14; Myres S. McDougal, Harold D. Lasswell, and Lung-chu Chen, 'Human Rights and World Public Order: A Framework for Policy-Oriented Inquiry' (1969) 63(2) *The American Journal of International Law*; Clapham, *Human Rights*, p. 52.

adjudicatory bodies.[6] Their jurisprudence carries the potential to generate soft law principles or benchmarks guiding the interpretation of rights. Moreover, supranational human rights jurisprudence has the potential to guide the possible evolution of rights.[7]

As discussed in Chapter 2, despite the absolute and mandatory nature of states' obligations under Article 20(2) of the ICCPR, the norm prohibiting incitement to discrimination, hostility, or violence embodies many definitional ambiguities and inherent tensions, giving rise to a multitude of interpretive dilemmas.[8] A purely textual analysis of the norm adds little to our understanding. Moreover, as described in the preceding chapter, the drafting history of Article 20(2) offers limited guidance in this regard. Thus, the norm prohibiting incitement to hatred seems in particular need of definitional refinement and interpretational determinacy from supranational monitoring and adjudicatory bodies. This would help dispel the confusion about its meaning and elaborate upon the legal benchmarks against which states' adherence to the norm could be determined. Such bodies are required to provide answers to numerous questions of implementation, including: what characterizes speech that constitutes prohibited incitement? How can such prohibited speech be distinguished from protected speech? And how can the causal connection between advocacy of hatred and prohibited incitement be proved? This chapter explores the extent to which monitoring and adjudicatory human rights bodies have addressed the interpretive dilemmas underlying the five internal features of the norm and to what extent they have answered these fundamental questions.

Firstly, the chapter provides an account of how the HRCttee, as the body responsible for interpreting the ICCPR and monitoring its implementation, has developed its jurisprudence on Article 20(2). It then moves on to analyse the racist hate speech jurisprudence of the CERD, as the body responsible for interpreting the ICERD and monitoring its implementation. It then examines the hate speech jurisprudence of the ECtHR, the only regional monitoring and adjudicatory body that has generated hate speech jurisprudence. Analysis of the ECtHR's jurisprudence provides insights into the prospects of addressing the inherent complexities of hate speech regulation at a regional level, where legal traditions and cultures among neighbouring states share some proximity.

---

[6] Louis Henkin, 'Introduction', in Louis Henkin (ed.), *The International Bill of Rights: The Covenant on Civil and Political Rights* (Columbia University Press, 1981), p. 25.

[7] Langer, 'Religious Offence', p. 372.

[8] Nowak, *U.N. Covenant on Civil and Political Rights*, p. 474; Partsch, 'Freedom of conscience and expression', p. 228; Theodor Meron, *Human Rights in International Law* (Clarendon press, 1992), p. 185; Seeley, 'Article Twenty', 332.

4.2 THE JURISPRUDENCE OF THE UN HUMAN RIGHTS COMMITTEE

The UN human rights treaty bodies are established by their respective international treaties and are composed of independent experts charged with monitoring state parties' implementation of their obligations under those treaties. These bodies have generated jurisprudence clarifying the normative content and scope of many human rights, while adapting them to address new challenges. This has occurred at different paces and, to varying depths, between different rights.[9]

The UN HRCttee is the body of independent experts established by the ICCPR to monitor the Covenant's implementation. According to the HRCttee's self-assessment of its role under Article 40 of the Covenant and the First Optional Protocol of the ICCPR, it interprets the provisions of the Covenant and the development of a jurisprudence.[10] The committee has affirmed, however, that it is 'neither a court nor a body with a quasi-judicial mandate'.[11]

The ICCPR has supplied the committee with three main tools enabling it to elaborate the meaning and scope of rights codified therein. These tools consist, firstly, of its decisions under the individual communications procedure; secondly, its General Comments on the Covenant's Articles; and, thirdly, its concluding observations and recommendations, adopted following the consideration of states' periodic reports on their implementation of the Covenant's provisions. Through its employment of these three tools, the committee has developed a body of jurisprudence. Academic literature variously describes this body as semi-authoritative,[12] authoritative,[13] or even the most[14] or only[15] authoritative interpretation of the ICCPR's provisions. The committee's body of jurisprudence has contributed to clarifying the normative content of many rights codified in the ICCPR.[16] However, some of the rights have received more attention and clarification from the committee than others.[17] The HRCttee's body of jurisprudence therefore varies in quality, particularly in terms of specific and clear legal reasoning.

[9] Helen Keller and Geir Ulfstein, 'Conclusions', in Helen Keller and Geir Ulfstein (eds.), *UN Human Rights Treaty Bodies: Law and Legitimacy* (Cambridge University Press, 2012), p. 415.

[10] CCPR, General Comment no. 24 (Art. 41), UN Doc. CCPR/C/21/Rev.1/Add.6 (4 November 1994), para. 11.

[11] HRCttee, 'Selected Decisions of the Human Rights Committee under the Optional Protocol', CCPR/C/OP/3, para. 7.

[12] Abram Chayes and Antonia Handler Chayes, *The New Sovereignty: Compliance with International Regulatory Agreements* (Harvard University Press, 1995), p. 209.

[13] Nowak, *U.N. Covenant on Civil and Political Rights*, p. xxvii.

[14] Yogesh Tyagi, *The UN Human Rights Committee: Practice and Procedure* (Cambridge University Press, 2011), p. 302.

[15] Conte and Burchill, 'Introduction', p. 9.

[16] Conte and Burchill, 'Introduction', pp. 16–18.

[17] Conte and Burchill, 'Introduction', p. 14. For example, the HRCttee has been reasonably active in the development of its jurisprudence concerning issues of discrimination. Also in the area of minority rights, while the committee has not been particularly radical in its interpretation of Article 27, its work in this area remains unique as it represents the only established legal framework that directly addresses the promotion and protection of minority rights.

Under the First Optional Protocol to the ICCPR, the committee can receive and decide upon communications from individuals claiming to have had their Covenant-guaranteed rights violated. The committee's decisions in this regard are not legally binding for state parties to the First Optional Protocol and do not serve as legal precedents in the strictest sense. Nevertheless, they are important references for interpreting the ICCPR.

The committee has been called upon to address Article 20(2) in very few of the individual communications submitted under the First Optional Protocol.[18] *JRT and the WG Party* v. *Canada*[19] (the first case in which Article 20 was invoked) concerned the Canadian Western Guard Party, which promoted its policies through the use of tape-recorded messages. Anyone could listen to these messages by dialling a specific telephone number. These messages warned diallers of 'the dangers of international finance and international Jewry leading the world into wars, unemployment and inflation and the collapse of world values and principles',[20] The Canadian Human Rights Commission investigated complaints in connection with these messages and found that they were 'likely to expose a person or persons to hatred or contempt' on the basis of race or religion.[21] The commission subsequently applied a provision of the Canadian Human Rights Act of 1978, declaring it illegal to communicate telephonically 'any matter that is likely to expose a person or persons to hatred or contempt by reason of the fact that the person or those persons are identifiable on the basis of a prohibited ground of discrimination'.[22] Accordingly, it ordered the termination of the party's telephone service.[23] The party then applied to the HRCttee, alleging that the Canadian authorities had violated Article 19 of the ICCPR on freedom of expression, which Canada defended by arguing that the applicable provision of the Canadian Human Rights Act was consistent with Article 20(2) of the Covenant.[24] The committee held the party's communication to be inadmissible, stating that the messages disseminated through the telephone system 'clearly constitute[d] the advocacy of racial or religious hatred which Canada has an obligation under Article 20 (2) of the Covenant to prohibit'.[25] The committee considered the statements in question to fall within the ambit of Article 20(2) and that there was no need for substantive scrutiny under Article 19. The committee's decision did not indicate the basis on which it classified the content of the telephone messages as advocacy of hatred that amounted to incitement to discrimination, hostility, or violence. Instead, the committee endorsed the Canadian authorities'

---

[18] Feldman, 'Freedom of expression', p. 435; Nowak, *U.N. Covenant on Civil and Political Rights*, p. 476.
[19] *J. R. T. and the W. G. Party* v. *Canada*, Communication no. 104/1981, CCPR (6 April 1983).
[20] *J. R. T. and the W. G. Party* v. *Canada*, para. 2.1.
[21] *J. R. T. and the W. G. Party* v. *Canada*, para. 2.4.
[22] *J. R. T. and the W. G. Party* v. *Canada*, para. 2.2.
[23] *J. R. T. and the W. G. Party* v. *Canada*, para. 2.4.
[24] *J. R. T. and the W. G. Party* v. *Canada*, para. 6.2.
[25] *J. R. T. and the W. G. Party* v. *Canada*, para. 8(b).

assessment of the content and effects of the restricted expressions (i.e. that they were 'likely to expose a person or persons to hatred or contempt' on the basis of race or religion),[26] without providing its own assessment.

In another communication, *Faurisson* v. *France*,[27] the applicant was a professor of literature who had, in a magazine interview, expressed personal convictions that the gas chambers used for extermination in Nazi concentration camps were a 'myth' and 'dishonest fabrication'.[28] A private criminal prosecution was filed in France against both the professor himself and the editor of the magazine. They were both convicted under the Gayssot Act of 1990, which made it a criminal offence 'to contest the existence of the category of crimes against humanity . . . on the basis of which Nazi leaders were tried and convicted by the International Military Tribunal at Nuremberg in 1945–1946'.[29] In his communication to the HRCttee, the applicant claimed that the government had violated his right to freedom of expression.[30] However, France invoked Articles 20(2), 19(3), and 5 of the ICCPR, and Article 4 of ICERD, to justify both the Gayssot Act and the applicant's conviction thereunder.[31] France called for the application of the committee's reasoning in the case of *JRT and the WG Party* v. *Canada* to this communication.[32] The HRCttee decided the communication on its merits and declared it admissible. In its reasoning, the committee considered whether the restrictions imposed on the applicant's freedom of expression satisfied the three necessary conditions for lawful restriction of this right, as per Article 19; that they are provided by law, address one of the aims set out in paragraphs 3(a) and (b) of Article 19, and are necessary to achieve a legitimate purpose.[33]

The HRCttee found that the first condition had been met and that the Gayssot Act itself, as well as its interpretation and application, were consistent with the Covenant's provisions.[34] The committee expressed the view that the applicant's statements '*were of a nature as to raise or strengthen* anti-Semitic *feelings*' and that the restriction of the applicant's right to freedom of expression 'served the respect of the Jewish *community* to live free from fear of an *atmosphere* of anti-Semitism [my emphasis]'.[35] Accordingly, the committee held that the applicant's statements infringed upon the rights of others, and so there were legitimate grounds for restricting freedom of expression under Article 19(3). In this case, the committee interpreted 'others' as referring to 'the community as a whole' and not only

---

[26] *J. R. T. and the W. G. Party* v. *Canada*, para. 2.4.
[27] *Faurisson* v. *France*, Communication no. 550/1993, CCPR (8 November 1996).
[28] *Faurisson* v. *France*, paras. 2.5, 2.6.
[29] *Faurisson* v. *France*, para. 2.3.
[30] *Faurisson* v. *France*, para. 3.1.
[31] *Faurisson* v. *France*, para. 7.7.
[32] *Faurisson* v. *France*, para. 7.8.
[33] *Faurisson* v. *France*, paras. 9.3, 9.4.
[34] *Faurisson* v. *France*, para. 9.5.
[35] *Faurisson* v. *France*, para. 9.6.

individuals.[36] Regarding the condition of necessity, the committee endorsed France's argument that the Gayssot Act 'intended to serve the struggle against racism and anti-Semitism' and that the 'denial of the existence of the Holocaust [is] the principle vehicle for anti-Semitism', The committee thus found that the restriction of the applicant's exercise of freedom of expression was necessary pursuant to Article 19(3).[37] It concluded that all three conditions for restricting the applicant's exercise of freedom of expression had been satisfied, finding no violation of Article 19.[38]

The HRCttee's reasoning also offered indirect insights into the interpretation of Article 20(2) without explicitly referring to that Article in its reasoning. Notably, in the subsequent case of *Ross v. Canada*,[39] the committee linked its decision in *Faurisson* to 'the principles reflected' in Article 20(2).[40] Such a reference appeared to be an attempt by the committee to rectify its earlier disregard of Article 20(2) in its reasoning on *Faurisson*, despite the Article's obvious relevance to that communication and France's invocation of it before the committee.

The concurring opinions in the *Faurisson* communication provided important insights into the committee members' positions on hate speech regulation. In a concurring individual opinion, committee member Lallah argued that the committee ought to have based its decision on Article 20(2) rather than Article 19(3).[41] He emphasized that 'the statements of the author amounted to the advocacy of racial or religious hatred constituting incitement, at the very least, to hostility and discrimination towards people of the Jewish faith'.[42] Another concurring individual opinion by committee members Evatt and Kretzmer highlighted that there might be circumstances in which the right to be free from incitement 'cannot be fully protected by a narrow, explicit law on incitement that falls precisely within the boundaries of Article 20, paragraph 2'. They contended that, in particular contexts:

> [expressions that] do not meet the strict legal criteria of incitement can be shown to constitute part of *a pattern* of incitement against a given racial, religious or national group, or where those interested in spreading hostility and hatred adopt sophisticated forms of speech that are not punishable under the law against racial incitement, even though their effect may be as pernicious as explicit incitement, if not more.[43]

Furthermore, Evatt and Kretzmer emphasized that the right to be free from racial, national, or religious incitement involves protecting the interests of the community as a whole. They also noted, however, that Article 19(3) should not be interpreted in

---

[36] *Faurisson v. France*, para. 9.6.
[37] *Faurisson v. France*, paras. 9.6, 9.7.
[38] *Faurisson v. France*, para. 10.
[39] *Ross v. Canada*, Communication no. 736/1997, CCPR (26 October 2000).
[40] *Faurisson v. France*, para. 11.5.
[41] *Faurisson v. France*, para. 11, individual opinion of Rajsoomer Lallah.
[42] *Faurisson v. France*, para. 9, individual opinion of Rajsoomer Lallah.
[43] *Faurisson v. France*, para. 4, individual opinion of Evatt and Kretzmer.

a manner that allows states to prohibit speech that was merely 'unpopular' or 'offensive'.[44] In the last of the individual opinions, committee member Bhagwati also emphasized the group identity aspect of the right to protection from incitement to hatred, stressing the right of the Jewish community as a whole to be protected from hostility, contempt, antagonism, and ill will.[45]

In the aforementioned *Ross* v. *Canada*, the Canadian Human Rights Board of Inquiry removed the applicant, who worked as a schoolteacher, from his position, based on some of his public statements and writings. The board had found these to 'denigrate the faith and beliefs of Jews and call upon true Christians to not merely question the faith and beliefs of Jewish beliefs and teachings but to hold those of the Jewish faith and ancestry in contempt as undermining freedom, democracy and Christian beliefs, and values'.[46] They noted that the applicant 'identifies Judaism as the enemy and calls on all Christians to join the battle'.[47] The board held that Ross's public statements and writings created a 'poisoned environment' within the school, which 'greatly interfered with the educational services' provided therein'.[48] The Canadian Supreme Court upheld the board's decision, affirming that 'the reason that it is possible to reasonably anticipate the causal relationship in this appeal is because of the significant influence teachers exert on their students'.[49] The court added that it was 'necessary to remove [the author] from his teaching position to ensure that no influence of this kind is exerted by him upon his students and to ensure that educational services are discrimination-free'.[50]

In his communication to the HRCttee, Ross alleged a violation of his rights under Articles 18 and 19 of the ICCPR. Canada asserted that Ross's publications fell within the scope of Article 20(2) and that measures taken against him were consistent with Canada's obligations under that Article.[51] Canada further argued that interpreting Articles 18 and 19 as protecting anti-Semitic expressions would deprive Jews of the freedom to exercise their religion, instil fear in them and other religious minorities, and degrade Christianity.[52] Furthermore, Canada described Ross's views as expressing 'hatred and suspicion of the Jewish people and their religion'.[53]

The HRCttee, as in *Faurisson* v. *France*, examined whether the conditions in Article 19(3) for restricting freedom of expression had been satisfied. In contrast to its decision in *Faurisson*, the committee made an explicit reference to Article 20(2) in its decision. It affirmed that restrictions on freedom of expression that might fall

[44] *Faurisson* v. *France*, para. 8, individual opinion of Evatt and Kretzmer.
[45] *Faurisson* v. *France*, individual opinion of Bhagwati.
[46] *Ross* v. *Canada*, para. 4.2.
[47] *Ross* v. *Canada*, para. 4.2
[48] *Ross* v. *Canada*, para. 4.3.
[49] *Ross* v. *Canada*, para. 4.6.
[50] *Ross* v. *Canada*, para. 4.6.
[51] *Ross* v. *Canada*, paras. 6.2–6.3.
[52] *Ross* v. *Canada*, para. 6.3.
[53] *Ross* v. *Canada*, para. 6.5.

under the scope of Article 20(2) must also be consistent with the requirements of Article 19(3).[54] The HRCttee found that the restrictions Canada had imposed on Ross's expressions were for the purpose of protecting the rights or reputations of persons of Jewish faith, including 'the right to have an education in the public school system free from bias, prejudice and intolerance'.[55] The committee reiterated its position from *Faurisson v. France* that the term 'others' in Article 19(3) referred to individuals or to a community as a whole.[56] It posited that 'restrictions may be permitted on statements which are of a nature as to raise or strengthen anti-Semitic feeling, in order to uphold the Jewish communities' *right to be protected from religious hatred*. Such restrictions also derive support from the principles reflected in Article 20(2) of the Covenant [my emphasis]'.[57] The committee found that Canada had met the condition of necessity in its actions, given the particular relevance of observing the special duties and responsibilities of freedom of expression in the context of the school system.[58] It affirmed that 'the influence exerted by school teachers may justify restraints in order to ensure that legitimacy is not given by the school system to the expression of views which are discriminatory'.[59] The committee noted that the Canadian Supreme Court had found that 'it was reasonable to anticipate that there was a causal link between the expressions of the author and the "poisoned school environment" experienced by Jewish children in the School district'.[60] As with its decision in *JRT and the WG Party* v. *Canada*, the committee's reasoning in *Ross* v. *Canada* did not elaborate further, however, on the question of when specific expressions constitute advocacy of hatred under Article 20(2).

It can be noted from the HRCttee's reasoning in all three of these communications that it analysed hate speech primarily through the lens or filter of Article 19(3), which sets forth the conditions for permitted limitations on freedom of expression. The committee affirmed that states' obligations under Articles 19 and 20 are fully compatible; taking measures that comply with Article 20(2) cannot be in violation of Article 19 and, similarly, a violation of Article 19 cannot be in compliance with Article 20(2). In each of the three communications, the committee examined the compliance of state parties with the Covenant through an examination of whether the measures undertaken conformed with Article 19, rather than Article 20(2). The committee employed Article 20(2) only as an additional or supplementary element to reinforce 'the protection of the rights and reputation of others' and 'necessity' as two legitimate conditions for restricting freedom of expression under Article 19. It did not attempt to define the exact threshold of Article 20(2). The committee's

---

54 *Ross* v. *Canada*, para. 10.6.
55 *Ross* v. *Canada*, para. 11.5.
56 *Ross* v. *Canada*, para. 11.5.
57 *Ross* v. *Canada*, para. 11.5.
58 *Ross* v. *Canada*, para. 11.6.
59 *Ross* v. *Canada*, para. 11.6.
60 *Ross* v. *Canada*, para. 11.6.

approach might be justifiable in light of the fact that the central issue in each of these communications was whether freedom of expression had been violated. However, given that state parties invoked Article 20(2) in their arguments, it might be argued that the committee missed the opportunity to delineate a more comprehensive interpretation of that Article.

The case of *Mohamed Rabbae, ABS and NA. v. Netherlands* enjoys particular significance in the jurisprudence of the HRCttee on hate speech. Prior to this case, the committee had not considered any communication alleging failure to implement national laws as required by Article 20(2) (i.e. failure to implement the positive obligation to investigate and prosecute advocacy of hatred, prohibited pursuant to the Article). The aforementioned three communications considered Article 20(2) in circumstances where applicants alleged that their national authorities had violated their right to freedom of expression, rather than failed to respect their right to protection from hate speech. The state parties had invoked Article 20(2) to justify restrictions imposed on freedom of expression when they had categorized the prohibited expressions as falling under the Article's scope. State parties in these cases considered themselves 'the main beneficiaries of Article 20(2)'.[61] In these three cases, the expressions under consideration were of unambiguously anti-Semitic nature and racist in character. However, *Rabbae* was the first communication submitted by alleged incitement victims and the first involving incitement on religious grounds.

The applicants in the *Rabbae* case claimed to be victims of violations by the Netherlands of their rights under a number of Articles of the ICCPR, including Article 20(2). The applicants (along with several other Muslim and migrant individuals and organizations in the Netherlands) lodged a complaint with a national court against a decision not to prosecute Geert Wilders, the founder of an extreme right-wing political party, for incitement to discrimination, violence, and hatred against Muslims, Moroccans, and non-Western immigrants. As a result, the Amsterdam Court of Appeal ordered the prosecution of Mr Wilders before the Amsterdam District Court on charges of insulting a group for reasons of race or religion and incitement to hatred and discrimination on grounds of religion or race.[62] The Amsterdam District Court decided that the necessary elements of the indictment could not be proven and acquitted Mr Wilders of all charges.[63]

The applicants to the HRCttee subsequently claimed that Mr Wilders's statements went beyond insults and amounted to incitement to hatred, discrimination, and violence.[64] They further averred that these statements caused harm to society as a whole, to ethnic and religious minorities, and to the applicants personally in their daily lives (since they, as Muslims and Moroccan nationals, had been subjected to

[61]   Temperman, *Religious Hatred*, p. 93.
[62]   *Mohamed Rabbae, A.B.S and N.A. v. Netherlands*, paras. 2.1, 2.2.
[63]   *Mohamed Rabbae, A.B.S and N.A. v. Netherlands*, para. 2.6.
[64]   *Mohamed Rabbae, A.B.S and N.A. v. Netherlands*, para. 2.7.

hate speech such as threatening messages).[65] The applicants claimed that Mr Wilders's statements were not directed against Islam as a religion but against Muslims, emphasizing that it is difficult to distinguish between attacking Islam and attacking Muslims.[66]

In this communication, the applicants sought to 'establish the practical meaning of their right to protection from incitement to discrimination, hostility, or violence'.[67] They argued that, despite Article 20 of the Covenant being drafted in terms of the state's obligations rather than the rights of individuals, this does not indicate that those matters are left to the internal jurisdiction of states.[68] Furthermore, they argued that the prosecutorial and judicial authorities' application of the existing incitement legislation was defective. The applicants averred that Article 20(2) not only imposed an obligation on states to outlaw incitement to hatred, but also gave individuals the right to protection from it.[69] Thus, the applicants did not challenge the manner in which the state party chose to legislatively implement Article 20(2) but argued that the prosecution was ineffective due to prosecutorial and judicial deficiencies.[70] They claimed that Mr Wilders's acquittal was contrary to Article 20(2) for a number of reasons: firstly, the court treated the different statements separately and disregarded their cumulative effect; secondly, the court emphasized 'the artificial distinction' between attacking Islam and inciting hatred against Muslims; thirdly, the court had refused to consider the case as incitement on racial grounds because 'Moroccans and non-Western migrants' do not represent any particular race.[71]

In response, the Netherlands disputed the admissibility of the communication on the basis of failure to exhaust domestic remedies, lack of victim status (that the communication was in essence an *actio popularis* since the authors failed to establish that Mr Wilders's statements personally affected them), and *ratione materiae*.[72] It argued that Article 20 does not codify individual rights and is not cast in terms of a justiciable right[73] (it is interesting to note how closely the views expressed by the Netherlands on Article 20(2) of the Covenant resembled those which were expressed by Western states during the drafting of the Article. The Netherlands added that Article 20(2) 'has been highly controversial among States, resulting in very different forms of implementation'.[74] It expressed the view that it is for national courts to decide whether incitement to hatred has occurred and that such courts are best

[65] *Mohamed Rabbae, A.B.S and N.A. v. Netherlands*, para. 2.4.
[66] *Mohamed Rabbae, A.B.S and N.A. v. Netherlands*, para. 2.7.
[67] *Mohamed Rabbae, A.B.S and N.A. v. Netherlands*, para. 2.7.
[68] *Mohamed Rabbae, A.B.S and N.A. v. Netherlands*, para. 3.2.
[69] *Mohamed Rabbae, A.B.S and N.A. v. Netherlands*, para. 5.4.
[70] *Mohamed Rabbae, A.B.S and N.A. v. Netherlands*, para. 10.5.
[71] *Mohamed Rabbae, A.B.S and N.A. v. Netherlands*, para. 3.1.
[72] *Mohamed Rabbae, A.B.S and N.A. v. Netherlands*, para. 4.1.
[73] *Mohamed Rabbae, A.B.S and N.A. v. Netherlands*, para. 6.5.
[74] *Mohamed Rabbae, A.B.S and N.A. v. Netherlands*, para. 6.5.

placed to assess the particularities of each case.[75] Moreover, it interpreted the HRCttee's case law as suggesting that Article 20(2) could not be invoked under the Optional Protocol.[76]

The Netherlands argued that the applicants had not demonstrated that the statements in question had specific imminent consequences that would personally affect them.[77] It explained that the concept of 'incitement' within the context of the Dutch criminal code referred to 'inflammatory behaviour that incites the commission of criminal offences or acts of violence'.[78] It added that the committee should not re-evaluate the national court's ruling on whether Mr Wilders's statements should be punished under domestic criminal law.[79] Furthermore, the Netherlands emphasized that its criminal code criminalized incitement to hatred, discrimination, or violence against persons, not religions.[80] It highlighted the differences between race and religion as two distinct grounds for incitement: 'An insulting attack on a belief does not automatically constitute an attack on those who adhere to that belief; under the law an insulting description of a belief is only insulting to persons if it involves drawing conclusions about those persons. That distinction applies only with respect to the grounds of religion or belief, not race or ethnic origin.'[81]

On the issue of victim status, the committee noted that the applicants were members of the group targeted by Mr Wilders's statements and that these statements had specific harmful consequences for them, such as 'creating discriminatory social attitudes against the group and against them as members of the group'. It further noted that they fell under the category of persons whom Article 20(2) was intended to protect and that they had adequately proved, for the purposes of admissibility, that their claims were not merely hypothetical.[82]

It is particularly interesting to note the committee's response to the Netherlands' argument that Article 20(2) is not cast in terms of a justiciable right. The committee affirmed that the Article provides protection for people as individuals, and as members of groups, against incitement to discrimination, hostility, or violence.[83] This represents clear confirmation of the right-declaratory nature of Article 20(2). The committee also clarified that the Article does not merely oblige states to adopt legislation prohibiting such incitement, but also to provide procedures for complaints and appropriate sanctions.[84]

---

[75] *Mohamed Rabbae, A.B.S and N.A. v. Netherlands*, para. 6.5.
[76] *Mohamed Rabbae, A.B.S and N.A. v. Netherlands*, para. 4.3.
[77] *Mohamed Rabbae, A.B.S and N.A. v. Netherlands*, para. 4.5.
[78] *Mohamed Rabbae, A.B.S and N.A. v. Netherlands*, para. 10.5.
[79] *Mohamed Rabbae, A.B.S and N.A. v. Netherlands*, para. 6.5.
[80] *Mohamed Rabbae, A.B.S and N.A. v. Netherlands*, para. 6.9.
[81] *Mohamed Rabbae, A.B.S and N.A. v. Netherlands*, para. 6.9.
[82] *Mohamed Rabbae, A.B.S and N.A. v. Netherlands*, para. 9.6.
[83] *Mohamed Rabbae, A.B.S and N.A. v. Netherlands*, para. 9.7.
[84] *Mohamed Rabbae, A.B.S and N.A. v. Netherlands*, para. 9.7.

The committee affirmed that the Netherlands had adopted a legislative framework through which statements described in Article 20(2) were prohibited under criminal law and which allowed victims to initiate, and participate in, a prosecution. It added that the court had issued a detailed judgement assessing Mr Wilders's statements in light of the applicable law.[85] It concluded that the Netherlands had taken the necessary measures to 'prohibit' statements made in violation of Article 20(2) and to guarantee the applicants' rights to an effective remedy protecting them against the harms of such statements. The committee added that 'the obligation under Article 20(2), however, does not extend to an obligation for the State party to ensure that a person who is charged with incitement to discrimination, hostility or violence will invariably be convicted by an independent and impartial court of law'.[86] It noted the Netherlands' argument that 'in the difficult area of hate speech, each set of facts is particular and must be assessed by a court or impartial decision maker on a case-by-case basis, according to its own circumstances and taking into account the specific context'.[87] The committee endorsed this view, which emphasizes the heightened significance of context in assessing whether the threshold for incitement to hatred has been breached. The committee concluded, on the facts before it, that there had not been a breach of any Covenant provisions.[88] Accordingly, despite the committee's recognition in *Rabbae* of the right-declaratory nature of Article 20(2), the committee has never, to date, found a breach of Article 20(2) to have been established.

Further analysis of the HRCttee's few decisions on Article 20(2) indicates that it has recognized intangible emotional harms creating an *atmosphere* of hatred and the provocation of hateful *feelings* as valid grounds for restricting freedom of expression. However, the committee has not provided standards or employed clear legal tests for how to determine whether specific expressions amount to 'advocacy of hatred' constituting incitement to hostility. It has tended to endorse the responding state parties' arguments that the restricted speech advocated hatred.[89] The committee has employed a causality standard that is indirect, cumulative, and non-imminent in nature. For example, it has used the qualifier 'possible to reasonably anticipate',[90] to describe the expressions in question and their potential or actual harms. The committee has not laid out a requirement for direct causality in this regard; a likelihood of the occurrence of such harms has been deemed sufficient to justify the prohibition of advocacy of hatred.

The HRCttee has endorsed the findings of national authorities on both the nature and effects of restricted expressions and has not provided its own autonomous

---

[85]　*Mohamed Rabbae, A.B.S and N.A.* v. *Netherlands*, para. 10.7.
[86]　*Mohamed Rabbae, A.B.S and N.A.* v. *Netherlands*, para. 10.7.
[87]　*Mohamed Rabbae, A.B.S and N.A.* v. *Netherlands*, para. 10.5.
[88]　*Mohamed Rabbae, A.B.S and N.A.* v. *Netherlands*, para. 11.
[89]　*J. R. T. and the W. G. Party* v. *Canada*, para. 8 (b); *Ross* v. *Canada*, para. 11.5.
[90]　*J. R. T. and the W. G. Party* v. *Canada*, para. 8 (b); *Ross* v. *Canada*, para. 11.5.

assessment. This reflects the committee's recognition of the importance of national contexts in implementing and enforcing the right to protection from incitement to discrimination, hostility, or violence. Similarly, the committee has recognized the right of groups themselves to be protected from the harms of hate speech, yet it has not addressed the delicate issue of how to distinguish between groups and their defining characteristics.

In summary, the HRCttee has not, so far, developed clear principles on the definitional complexities and tensions underlying the five internal features of the right to protection from incitement to discrimination, hostility, or violence in its decisions on individual communications.

The second interpretive tool available to the HRCttee is the issuing of General Comments[91] on the Articles of the ICCPR. These should, ideally, give substantive content to those Articles and delineate the scope of states' obligations pursuant to them.[92] Even though the committee's General Comments lack formal legal force and are non-binding for states, they have significant interpretive value.[93] In fact, they represent 'a new species of soft law' that 'enrich[es] and expand[s] the jurisprudence of human rights' and contributes to the evolution of international norms.[94] The quality of General Comments issued from the HRCttee has been variable. Some General Comments have been very clear, detailed, and instructive and have provided valuable guidance on the interpretation of certain Articles, such as those regarding the right to a fair hearing (Article 14) and the right to life (Article 6). On the other hand, some General Comments have been vague and of little value in elucidating the exact meaning and scope of the relevant Articles; this is true of those concerning Articles 20 and 27 (on the rights of minorities).[95]

The HRCttee has affirmed the special status of states' obligations under Article 20(2) in its General Comment No. 24 on 'issues relating to reservations made upon ratification or accession to the Covenant or the optional protocols thereto, or in relation to declarations under Article 41 of the Covenant' and also General Comment No. 29 on 'derogations during a state of emergency'. The committee has identified Article 20(2) as part of customary international law,[96] meaning that states are obliged to comply with the Article even when they are not parties to the ICCPR. Furthermore, it has affirmed that state parties to the Covenant cannot reserve the right to permit advocacy of national, racial, or religious hatred constituting incitement to discrimination, hostility, or

---

[91] Article 40(4) of the ICCPR.

[92] Conte and Burchill, 'Introduction', p. 11; Chayes and Chayes, *The New Sovereignty*, p. 216.

[93] Conte and Burchill, 'Introduction', p. 11; Helen Keller and Leena Grover, 'General comments of the Human Rights Committee and their legitimacy', in Helen Keller and Geir Ulfstein (eds.), *UN Human Rights Treaty Bodies: Law and Legitimacy* (Cambridge University Press, 2012), pp. 117–118; Tyagi, *The UN Human Rights Committee*, p. 306.

[94] Tyagi, *The UN Human Rights Committee*, pp. 294, 301.

[95] Rehman, *International Human Rights Law*, p. 119; Conte and Burchill, 'Introduction', pp. 11, 14.

[96] CCPR, General Comment no. 24, para. 8.

violence.[97] The committee has also held that states' obligations under the Article cannot be subject to lawful derogation during states of emergency.[98] Therefore, General Comments 24 and 29 indicate that Article 20(2) enjoys an unconditional and heightened importance within the ICCPR.[99]

The HRCttee issued General Comment No. 11 on Article 20 in 1983. In this General Comment, the committee emphasized that Article 20 is 'fully compatible' with the right of freedom of expression.[100] It indicated that the 'special duties and responsibilities' upon which the exercise of freedom of expression is contingent should reflect the prohibitions pursuant to Article 20.[101] It stated that 'for Article 20 to become fully effective there ought to be a law making it clear that propaganda and advocacy as described therein are contrary to public policy and providing for an appropriate sanction in case of violation'.[102] It added that Article 20 covers advocacy of hatred whether it 'has aims which are internal or external to the State concerned'.[103] However, General Comment No. 11 lacks any real interpretive weight, as it does not elucidate the meaning of key Article 20(2) terms (advocacy, hatred, hostility, and incitement), or the threshold of the Article's implementation. The implications on freedom of expression were a controversial issue during the drafting of General Comment No. 11 and even appeared to jeopardize the adoption of the General Comment by consensus.[104]

In 2011, the HRCttee issued General Comment No. 34 on Article 19, in which it reiterated that Articles 19 and 20 are 'compatible with and complement each other' and that 'the acts that are addressed in Article 20 are all subject to restriction pursuant to Article 19, paragraph 3'.[105] The committee considered Article 20 '*lex specialis* with regard to Article 19', in the sense that it requires from state parties a particular response in relation to the forms of expressions prohibited therein; it requires them to enact laws.[106] It also affirmed that displays of lack of respect for a religion or other belief system should be prohibited pursuant to Article 20(2) of the Covenant if they fall under the category of advocacy of religious hatred that incites discrimination, hostility, or violence.[107] Yet the committee did not provide guidance on the criteria for when displays of lack of respect for a religion would amount to

---

[97] Heinze, 'Viewpoint Absolutism', 544.

[98] CCPR, General Comment no. 29 (Art. 4), UN Doc. CCPR/C/21/Rev.1/Add.11 (31 August 2001), para. 13(e).

[99] Alex Conte, 'Limitations to and derogations from covenant rights', in Alex Conte and Richard Burchill (eds.), *Defining Civil and Political Rights: The Jurisprudence of the United Nations Human Rights Committee* (Ashgate Publishing Limited, 2009), p. 41.

[100] CCPR, General Comment no. 11, para. 2.

[101] CCPR, General Comment no. 11, para. 2.

[102] CCPR, General Comment no. 11, para. 2.

[103] CCPR, General Comment no. 11, para. 2.

[104] McGonagle, *Minority Rights*, p. 274.

[105] CCPR, General Comment no. 34, para. 50.

[106] CCPR, General Comment no. 34, para. 51.

[107] CCPR, General Comment no. 34, para. 48.

religious hate speech. General Comment No. 34 does not, therefore, facilitate any greater understanding of Article 20(2). Previously, in its General Comment No. 22 on the right to freedom of thought, conscience, and religion, the HRCttee affirmed that freedom of religion, in particular the freedom to manifest religion, did not include advocacy of hatred constituting incitement to discrimination, hostility, or violence.[108]

Against the backdrop of the General Comment No. 11's deficiencies, and more recent polarized debates at the UN on states' obligations under Article 20(2), several recent calls have been made for the HRCttee to issue a revised General Comment on Article 20(2). A number of UN Special Rapporteurs recommended that the committee draft a new General Comment focusing on the correlations between freedom of expression, freedom of religion, and non-discrimination.[109] The Office of the High Commissioner for Human Rights (OHCHR) has also requested that the committee, together with the CERD, develop a General Comment on incitement to hatred.[110] A number of academics and NGOs have made similar calls.[111] Moreover, a considerable number of states have requested that the committee elaborate, through a General Comment, on the content and exact scope of Article 20(2).[112] To date, this has not happened; this reflects clear resistance by the committee to addressing the complex definitional challenges and interpretive conundrums associated with the right to protection from incitement to discrimination, hostility, or violence.

The third interpretive tool available to the HRCttee is to issue concluding observations and recommendations after examining state parties' periodic reports on their implementation of the Covenant. Article 20(2) has not, however, been among the main issues addressed by the committee in such periodic reports.[113] The committee has focused more on compliance with Article 19[114] and has not carefully assessed the content or application of hate speech laws, nor has it considered their compliance with the requirements of Article 20(2). It is not enough to prohibit by law the categories of expressions included in Article 20(2) of the ICCPR; the Article must

---

[108]   CCPR, General Comment no. 22, paras. 25, 30, 33.
[109]   A/HRC/2/3, para. 61; A/67/537, para. 83.
[110]   A/HRC/2/6, para. 84.
[111]   Eltayeb, 'Limitations on Critical Thinking on Religious Issues'; 'Submission of ECLJ to OHCHR.'
[112]   A/HRC/13/58 Annex IV; Statement of Pakistan on behalf of OIC Member States Delivered at the UN Human Rights Council (September 25, 2007, available at http://portal.ohchr.org/portal/page/portal/HRCExtranet/6thSession/DraftResolutions/AHRC6L.8Rev.1/Pakistan(OIC).pdf; A/CONF.211/PC.3/4, paras. 16, 17.
[113]   Z. Majodina. 'Prohibition of Incitement to National, Racial and Religious Hatred in Accordance with International Human Rights Law: Some Aspects of the Work of the UN Human Rights Committee', 2011. www.ohchr.org/Documents/Issues/Expression/ICCPR/Nairobi/ZonkeMajodina.pdf.
[114]   Kevin Boyle, 'Religious intolerance and the incitement of hatred', in Sandra Coliver (ed.), *Striking a Balance: Hate Speech, Freedom of Expression and Non-discrimination* (Article 19, International Centre Against Censorship, Human Rights Centre University of Essex, 1992), p. 65.

also be effectively implemented through the investigation of relevant offences and, where appropriate, the prosecution of alleged offenders. The committee has not reflected upon the appropriateness of states' applications of this aspect of their obligations. A previous chairman of the committee has noted that states' reports have failed to give information on national legislation adopted in compliance with Article 20(2), thereby hampering the committee's work and blocking it from documenting many violations of the Article.[115] However, the monitoring of governments' compliance with their treaty obligations does not depend only on self-reporting by states, but also on 'shadow reporting' by civil society and reports of UN Special Rapporteurs. The state of implementation of Article 20(2) also appears not to have been among the main issues brought to the attention of the committee in such shadow reports.

In its concluding observations, the HRCttee has expressed general concerns regarding incidents of incitement to discrimination, hostility, or violence without providing precise descriptions of the nature of expressions prohibited by Article 20(2).[116] The committee has, however, condemned the use of ethnic, racial, and religious hatred; xenophobic statements in political discourse;[117] racial profiling by law enforcement personnel;[118] and the failure of law enforcement officials to investigate, prosecute, and punish hate crimes and hate speech incidents.[119]

In this sense, the committee's recommendations have been of a very general nature. They have called upon state parties to undertake steps to adequately investigate allegations of incitement to hatred and prosecute those responsible for them,[120] conduct awareness-raising campaigns, promote tolerance and diversity, and reduce tensions between different groups.[121] Only in a very few instances has the committee been specific in its observations and recommendations to states regarding their implementation of Article 20(2). For example, with reference to Hungary, the committee has expressed concern about 'the Constitutional Court's restrictive interpretation of Article 269 of the Penal Code on incitement to violence, which may be incompatible with the State party's obligations under Article 20'.[122] While it recommended legislative reforms to ensure compliance with Article 20(2), the committee failed to specify the precise nature of these legal reforms needed, nor did it indicate the exact criteria that hate speech laws must meet. Another example is

---

[115] Report of the OHCHR Expert Workshop for Asia and the Pacific on the Prohibition of Incitement to National, Racial or Religious Hatred, 6–7 July 2011, available at www.ohchr.org/Documents/Issues/ Expression/ICCPR/Bangkok/MeetingReportBangkok.pdf, para. 19.

[116] CCPR/C/79/Add.41, para. 11; CCPR/C/BEL/CO/5, para. 22; CCPR/CO/84/SVN, para. 3.

[117] CCPR/C/79/Add.118, para. 18; CCPR/C/AUT/CO/4, para. 20; CCPR/CO/79/RUS, para. 24.

[118] CCPR/CO/79/RUS, para. 24; CCPR/C/HUN/CO/5, para. 18.

[119] CCPR/CO/72/CZE, para. 11; CCPR/C/POL/CO/6, para. 6; CCPR/C/SWE/CO/6, para. 19.

[120] CCPR/C/AUT/CO/4, 20; CCPR/C/BEL/CO/5, para. 22; CCPR/CO/72/CZE, para. 11; CCPR/C/ HUN/CO/5, para. 18; CCPR/C/ESP/CO/5, para. 20; Doc. CCPR/CO/79/RUS, para. 24; CCPR/C/ 79/Add.118, para. 18; CCPR/CO/84/SVN, para. 3.

[121] CCPR/C/AUT/CO/4, para. 20; CCPR/C/HUN/CO/5, para. 18; CCPR/C/CHE/CO/3, para. 10.

[122] CCPR/C/HUN/CO/5, para. 18.

the case of Togo, where the committee simply recommended the adoption of legislative reforms needed to criminalize any advocacy of national, racial, or religious hatred constituting incitement to discrimination, hostility, or violence, and impose criminal penalties on any person making statements whose effect is the incitement to such acts, in violation of Article 20 of the Covenant.[123] In general, the approach that the committee has followed in drafting concluding observations and recommendations in connection with Article 20(2) has provided neither useful interpretive insights into the Article's exact content and scope nor useful guidance to states on how to ensure that their national legislation complies with its requirements.[124]

Notably, the HRCttee has recently made links between Articles 20, 24, and 26 of the ICCPR in the context of addressing discrimination against lesbian, gay, bisexual, and transgender persons.[125] The committee has expressed its concern regarding the increase in hate speech against these groups and has criticized the lack of provisions within national penal codes to address hate speech and hate crimes involving sexual orientation or gender identity.[126] Consequently, it has recommended the amendment of Poland's penal code in order to 'define hate speech and hate crimes based on sexual orientation or gender identity among the categories of punishable offences'.[127] The committee also recently cited Article 20 in relation to people with disabilities.[128] The inclusion of groups other than racial, religious, or national groups under the ambit of Article 20(2) indicates the committee's willingness to expand the range of groups that should be protected from the harms of hate speech. However, the committee has not shown any similar dynamic or expansive interpretive approach beyond the textual confines of Article 20(2) in connection with the right to be free from the harms of hate speech.

An overview of the HRCttee's jurisprudence on Article 20(2) indicates that it has developed slowly and is limited both quantitatively and qualitatively.[129] The committee has been largely ineffective in performing its interpretive role in relation to the Article. It has not addressed the definitional uncertainties and ambiguities of the right to protection from incitement to discrimination, hostility, or violence; nor has it developed principles to guide states in determining the application threshold of Article 20(2).[130] The committee has not developed clear definitions of the Article's

---

[123] CCPR/C/TGO/CO/4, para. 9.
[124] Majodina, Prohibition of Incitement.
[125] CCPR/C/MNG/CO/5, para. 9.
[126] CCPR/C/POL/CO/6, para. 8; CCPR/C/USA/CO/3, para. 25.
[127] CCPR/C/POL/CO/6, para. 8.
[128] CCPR/C/MNG/CO/5, para. 10.
[129] Nowak, *U.N. Covenant on Civil and Political Rights*, p. 476; Ghanea, 'Articles 19 and 20 of the ICCPR', 61; Feldman, 'Freedom of expression', p. 435; A/HRC/2/3, para. 61.
[130] Mendel, 'Study on international standards', p. 25, 27, 56; A/HRC/2/6, para. 36; Toby Mendel, 'Hate Speech Rules under International Law', 2010. www.law-democracy.org/wp-content/uploads/2010/07/10.02.hate-speech.Macedonia-book.pdf,7; A/HRC/2/3, para. 67; Temperman, *Religious Hatred*, p. 168.

key terms, particularly 'hatred', 'hostility', and 'incitement'. The first term describes the substantive content of expressions that fall under the Article's scope, the second describes one category of the harms that justify prohibiting these expressions, and the third is crucial to the enforcement of the right via proof of causation between expressions and alleged harms. The committee has also not set out a definition of the '*actus reus* of the incitement offence within the meaning of Article 20(2) of the ICCPR'.[131] Consequently, states have been left without guidance as to the exact nature and scope of their obligations under the Article.

There are multiple contributory factors to the deficiencies characterizing the HRCttee's body of jurisprudence on Article 20(2). The definitional challenges and inherent tensions underlying the five internal features of the right to protection from incitement to hatred have compounded the difficulties of reaching consensus among committee members on the interpretation of the Article. In particular, elements of legal moralism in hate speech regulation have hindered the committee's ability to provide specific universal standards for the Article's implementation. The committee has traditionally held the position that the concept of morals 'derives from many social, philosophical, and religious traditions' and has consequently held that limitations on freedoms for the purposes of protecting morals 'must be based on principles not deriving exclusively from a single tradition'.[132] The committee has thus accorded a wide margin of appreciation to states to determine the contours of the principle of protecting morals in the context of limitations on freedoms. The indeterminacy of the committee's approach to Article 20(2) reflects its tendency to secure flexibility in states' implementations of their obligations under the Article in a context-based manner.

The travaux préparatoires of the Covenant's Articles have, in some instances, facilitated the committee's interpretive tasks.[133] It has occasionally used them to elucidate the precise scope of rights when issuing decisions on individual communications.[134] However, the limited interpretive utility of Article 20(2)'s travaux préparatoires, as explored in the previous chapter, may also have contributed to the weakness of the HRCttee jurisprudence on the Article.

Furthermore, the weaknesses of the jurisprudence on Article 20(2) produced with each of the committee's interpretive tools negatively affect the quality of the jurisprudence it produces with the others, given that the outcomes of all three tools are closely connected and interdependent. For example, the committee has not accumulated sufficient experience through its monitoring procedures – whether concluding observations or decisions on individual communications – to allow it to update General Comment 11. In turn, General Comment 11 itself does not assist the committee with the task of drafting more practical or detailed concluding

---

[131] Temperman, *Religious Hatred*, p. 168.
[132] CCPR, General Comment no. 22, para. 8.
[133] Tyagi, *The UN Human Rights Committee*, pp. 8, 10.
[134] Conte and Burchill, Introduction, p. 15.

observations and recommendations on the implementation of Article 20(2). General Comment 11 has also been of little use to the committee in interpreting Article 20(2) when drafting its decisions on individual communications.

Political factors have also influenced the HRCttee's approach to addressing hate speech. The committee has not been immune to national political influences. States have been keen to ensure that treaty bodies do not exercise their interpretive functions in a manner beyond the boundaries of the treaty obligations to which the states themselves have consented or in a manner which diverges from their own interpretations of the Covenant's Articles.[135] In recent years, states have taken an increased involvement in the drafting process of General Comments, particularly when compared to the early years of the HRCttee.[136] Some states have expressed their dissatisfaction with certain of the committee's drafts.[137] Feedback received from both state and non-state actors has, lately, begun to directly affect the committee's drafting of General Comments.[138] Interestingly, Pakistan has expressed fears that a revised General Comment on Article 20 might be shaped by Western influences on the HRCttee.[139] On the other hand, Western states fear that a possible updating of that General Comment might restrict the scope of the legitimate exercise of freedom of expression.[140] If the existence of a reasonable level of consensus among states regarding the content of a right can be achieved, this might legitimize an evolutionary interpretation by the committee.[141] However, as the previous chapter detailed, and as the following chapter will demonstrate, there is currently a lack of widespread agreement among states on the exact meaning of Article 20(2). A former UN Special Rapporteur on Freedom of Expression has indicated that the committee's members are wary of expanding its jurisprudence on Article 20(2), given the political sensitivities and divisions among UN member states, particularly in debates over religious hate speech.[142]

The influence of the body of jurisprudence developed by HRCttee on the Covenant's rights reaches beyond its own domain; it also influences the jurisprudence of other international, regional, and national human rights–monitoring and adjudicatory bodies. The deficiencies of the committee's jurisprudence on Article 20(2) hampers its ability to assume a guiding role in the hate speech jurisprudence of

---

[135] Keller and Ulfstein, 'Conclusions', p. 422.

[136] Keller and Grover, 'General comments', p. 186.

[137] Keller and Ulfstein, 'Conclusions', p. 422.

[138] Keller and Grover, 'General comments', p. 186.

[139] John Cerone, 'Inappropriate Renderings: The Danger of Reductionist Resolutions' (2008) 33 *Brooklyn Journal of International Law*, 375–376.

[140] L. Bennett Graham, 'Defamation of Religions: The End of Pluralism' (2009) 23 *Emory International Law Review*, 82.

[141] Birgit Schlutter, 'Aspects of human rights interpretation by the UN treaty bodies', in Helen Keller and Geir Ulfstein (eds.), *UN Human Rights Treaty Bodies: Law and Legitimacy* (Cambridge University Press, 2012), p. 318.

[142] Interview with Former UN Special Rapporteur on the promotion and protection of the right to freedom of opinion and expression, Geneva, 13 January 2011.

these different bodies. The lack of a concrete, comprehensive definition of the right to protection from incitement to hatred in the work of the HRCttee negatively impacts the prospects of its normative development within both supranational and national contexts. The following sections of this chapter explore to what extent the hate speech jurisprudence of other supranational monitoring and adjudicatory bodies has been able to illuminate the meaning and scope of the norm prohibiting incitement to hatred.

4.3 THE JURISPRUDENCE OF THE UN COMMITTEE ON ELIMINATION OF RACIAL DISCRIMINATION

The CERD, as the body responsible for interpreting ICERD and monitoring its implementation, has developed jurisprudence on racist hate speech. Most of the decisions of the CERD on individual communications related to Article 4 have dealt with the compliance of state parties with their positive obligations concerning the investigation and prosecution of racist hate speech.[143] This contrasts with the few decisions issued by the HRCttee on hate speech, in which applicants have mainly alleged that national authorities had interfered in their right to freedom of expression.

In *Mohammed Hassan Gelle v. Denmark*[144] a daily newspaper published a letter to the editor criticizing the Minister of Justice's consultations with a number of organizations, including the Danish Somali Association, about a draft law on female genital mutilation. The letter stated: 'To me, this corresponds to asking the association of paedophiles whether they have any objections to a prohibition against child sex or asking rapists whether they have any objections to an increase in the sentence for rape.'[145] This communication's applicant filed a complaint with the public prosecutor alleging a violation of the Danish criminal code's provisions criminalizing public statements in which a group of people are threatened, insulted, or degraded on account of their race, colour, national or ethnic origin, religion, or sexual inclination.[146] However, the prosecutor dismissed this complaint on the grounds that the letter 'did not refer to all Somalis as criminals or otherwise as equal to paedophiles or rapists, but only argued against the fact that a Somali association is to be consulted about a bill criminalizing offences committed particularly in the country of origin of Somalis'.[147] The applicant claimed, among other things, that Denmark had violated Article 4 of the ICERD by failing to carry out a proper investigation into this incident.[148] In its decision on admissibility, the

---

[143] Noorloos, *Hate Speech Revisited*, pp. 170–171.
[144] *Mohammed Hassan Gelle* v. *Denmark*, Communication no. 034/2004, CERD (6 March 2006).
[145] *Mohammed Hassan Gelle* v. *Denmark*, para. 2.1.
[146] *Mohammed Hassan Gelle* v. *Denmark*, para. 2.2.
[147] *Mohammed Hassan Gelle* v. *Denmark*, para. 7.4.
[148] *Mohammed Hassan Gelle* v. *Denmark*, para 3.4

CERD noted that the content of the letter was 'not of such an inoffensive character as to *ab initio* fall outside the scope of Articles 2, paragraph 1 (d), 4, and 6 of the Convention'.[149] It found the content of the letter to be '*degrading or insulting to an entire group of people*' (i.e. persons of Somali descent) and to '*generalize negatively*' about them on the basis of their national or ethnic origin, not their views or actions related to female genital mutilation.[150] It held that the use of the words 'paedophiles' and 'rapists' was '*offensive*' and '*deepen[ed] the hurt experienced*' by the targeted group.[151] The committee found that the failure of the public prosecutor and the police to carry out an effective investigation into the applicant's complaint violated Article 2, paragraph 1(d), and Article 4 of the ICERD.[152]

In *LK v. The Netherlands*[153] a Moroccan citizen residing in the Netherlands had visited a house for which he had been offered a lease. While there, the man heard shouts of 'no more foreigners' from a group of people gathered outside. Others warned him that if he moved into the house, they would set fire to it and damage his car.[154] Local residents signed a petition that noted that the applicant would not be accepted on their street and urged Utrecht's housing department to allocate a different house to the applicant and his family.[155] The applicant filed a complaint with the police, stating that he had been the victim of racial discrimination.[156] However, the state did not initiate a prosecution. Furthermore, on appeal, a Dutch court dismissed the applicant's request for a prosecution.[157] The CERD held that the comments and threats against the applicant constituted 'incitement to racial discrimination and to acts of violence against persons of another colour or ethnic origin'.[158] The CERD thus overruled the Dutch authorities' judgement in this regard. It found a violation of Article 4(a), holding the Netherlands responsible for its failure to investigate the complaint of the applicant 'with due diligence and expedition'.[159]

In *Jewish Community of Oslo et al.* v. *Norway*[160] a group calling themselves the 'Bootboys' organized and participated in a march commemorating the Nazi leader Rudolf Hess. The leader of the group delivered a speech claiming, inter alia, that 'our people and country are being plundered and destroyed by Jews, who suck our country empty of wealth and replace it with immoral and un-Norwegian thoughts'.

---

[149]   *Mohammed Hassan Gelle* v. *Denmark*, para. 6.2.
[150]   *Mohammed Hassan Gelle* v. *Denmark*, para. 7.4.
[151]   *Mohammed Hassan Gelle* v. *Denmark*, para. 7.4.
[152]   *Mohammed Hassan Gelle* v. *Denmark*, para. 7.6.
[153]   *L. K.* v. *The Netherlands*, Communication no. 4/1991, CERD 16 March 1993.
[154]   *L. K.* v. *The Netherlands*, paras. 2.1, 6.3.
[155]   *L. K.* v. *The Netherlands*, para. 2.1.
[156]   *L. K.* v. *The Netherlands*, para. 2.2.
[157]   *L. K.* v. *The Netherlands*, paras. 2.5–2.8.
[158]   *L. K.* v. *The Netherlands*, para. 6.3.
[159]   *L. K.* v. *The Netherlands*, para. 6.6.
[160]   *The Jewish Community of Oslo et al.* v. *Norway*, Communication no. 30/2003, CERD (15 August 2005).

He added that his group would 'follow in [Hitler's and Hess's] footsteps' and 'fight for what [it] believe[s] in'.[161] Furthermore, he accused immigrants of robbing, raping, and killing Norwegians. The leader of the group was charged with extreme speech offences under the Norwegian criminal code. The Norwegian Supreme Court held that punishing the approval of Nazism and prohibiting Nazi organizations was incompatible with freedom of expression. The court held that 'the speech contained derogatory and offensive remarks, but … no actual threats were made, nor any instructions to carry out any particular actions'.[162] The applicants to the CERD contended that they were victims of a violation of Article 4 of the ICERD, given that the Supreme Court's judgement deprived them from protection against the dissemination of ideas of racial discrimination and hatred, as well as incitement to such acts.[163] Norway contended that states should be given a margin of appreciation in balancing their obligations under the ICERD with freedom of expression. Nevertheless, the CERD held the communication to be admissible on the basis that the applicants belonged to a group of potential victims, although they were not confronted directly by the participants of the march. It made its own assessment of the statements made by the leader of the group and categorized these statements as clearly constituting 'incitement at least to racial discrimination, if not to violence'.[164] The CERD held that the statements 'were of exceptionally/manifestly *offensive* character'.[165] It noted that it had fully taken into account the Supreme Court's decision and the analysis contained therein, but that '[the CERD] has the responsibility to ensure the coherence of the interpretation of the provisions of Article 4 of the Convention as reflected in its general recommendation No. 15'.[166] The CERD concluded that the Norwegian Supreme Court's acquittal of the leader of the group constituted a violation of Article 4 of ICERD.[167] Thus, the CERD overruled a national court's ruling on a complaint about racist incitement.

Thus, it can be seen that the CERD has taken a strong stance on states' duties to fulfil their obligations under Article 4 of ICERD. Furthermore, it has submitted its own characterizations of expressions under review, departing, in a number of its communications, from the assessments submitted by the domestic authorities of state parties.

The CERD has issued a General Recommendation No. 15 on Article 4 (in 1993) and a General Recommendation No. 35 (in 2013) to provide guidance on the requirements of the Convention in the area of racist hate speech. General Recommendation No. 15 affirmed that the prohibition of dissemination of all ideas based upon racial superiority or hatred is compatible with freedom of

---

[161] *The Jewish Community of Oslo et al.* v. *Norway*, para. 2.1.
[162] *The Jewish Community of Oslo et Al.* v. *Norway*, para. 2.7
[163] *The Jewish Community of Oslo et Al.* v. *Norway*, para. 7.3.
[164] *The Jewish Community of Oslo et Al.* v. *Norway*, para. 10.4.
[165] *The Jewish Community of Oslo et Al.* v. *Norway*, para. 10.5.
[166] *The Jewish Community of Oslo et Al.* v. *Norway*, para. 10.3.
[167] *The Jewish Community of Oslo et Al.* v. *Norway*, para. 10.5.

expression as a fundamental freedom.[168] It described the relationship between prohibiting racist hate speech and respecting freedom of expression as complementary and 'not the expression of a zero sum game'.[169] General Recommendation No. 15 did not provide a detailed interpretation of Article 4, but General Recommendation No. 35 offered more detailed guidance on the forms of conduct to be regarded as criminal offences in terms of the Article. On the issue of whether incitement qualifies as an offence punishable by law, the committee presented a number of factors that it considered to be 'contextual'. These factors were the content and form of speech; the economic, social, and political climate; the position or status of the speaker; the reach of the speech; and the objectives of the speech.[170] General Recommendation No. 35 further affirmed that 'it is not its function to review the interpretation of facts and national law made by domestic authorities, unless the decisions are manifestly absurd or unreasonable'.[171]

In its various concluding observations on state parties' periodic reports, the CERD has closely scrutinized compliance with the requirements of Article 4, especially in comparison with the HRCttee's approach to Article 20(2). The CERD closely monitors national legislative frameworks to assess whether they are fully in accordance with the requirements of Article 4. For example, it has expressed concern about the restrictive nature of Austria's legal provision regarding the offence of incitement to racial discrimination, on the basis that it is 'limited to acts that endanger public order and which are committed against individuals who are members of ethnic groups'.[172] It issued a recommendation to Austria that its legal provision ought to 'cover all acts of racial discrimination against persons belonging to all vulnerable groups, including ethnic minorities, migrants, asylum-seekers and foreigners, without limiting them to public order, in order to give full effect to provisions of Article 4 of the Convention'.[173] It has also criticized Article 130(1) of the German penal code for making the prohibition of incitement to racial hatred subject to a condition not forming part of Article 4: the disturbance of peace.[174] On similar grounds, the CERD raised objections to the UK's Race Relations Act 1976, which required that 'incitement to racial hatred' must be 'threatening, abusive or insulting'.[175] CERD has also assessed whether state parties have combated racist hate speech effectively by means of prosecuting relevant incidents, i.e. an evaluation of state parties' enforcement policies with respect to Article 4. For example, the committee urged Ukraine to consider relaxing the strict requirement of intent in its legal provision on incitement to racial discrimination

[168]   General Recommendation No. 15 (Art. 4), UN Doc. A/48/18 (23 March 1993), para. 4.
[169]   General Recommendation No. 35, para. 45.
[170]   General Recommendation No. 35, para. 15.
[171]   General Recommendation No. 35, para. 17.
[172]   CERD/C/AUT/CO/17, para. 15.
[173]   CERD/C/AUT/CO/17, para. 15.
[174]   A/32/18, paras. 84, 87.
[175]   A/33/18, para. 339.

in order to facilitate successful prosecutions.[176] It has observed that Denmark's incitement laws have resulted in alarmingly few convictions.[177] It has also expressed concern that the number of charges and convictions for expressions of racial hatred and acts of violence in Hungary is low relative to the number of abuses reported.[178] On the other hand, the CERD has praised some state parties' active prosecution of racist hate speech incidents.[179]

Evidently, the CERD has conceptualized Article 4 of the ICERD to a far greater extent than the HRCttee has done with regard to Article 20(2) of the ICCPR.[180] According to Article 4 of the ICERD, the mere acts of dissemination and promotion of racist ideas constitute legitimate grounds for their prohibition. The two criteria of advocacy and incitement to specific harms, which Article 20(2) of ICCPR stipulates for the prohibition of hateful expressions, are not necessarily required as qualifiers for determining racist hate speech under the ICERD,[181] which imposes wider restrictions on racist speech than the ICCPR. The lower threshold for prohibiting racist hate speech under Article 4 of ICERD, in comparison to Article 20(2) of ICCPR, has made the CERD's task in assessing whether state parties have violated Article 4 less problematic than the HRCttee's equivalent task. In particular, the CERD does not necessarily need to delve into the complexities of proving incitement, which is largely contingent upon context. This helps explain the CERD's more proactive interpretive approach.

Furthermore, the bolder and more proactive role taken by the CERD on racist hate speech in comparison to the jurisprudence of HRCttee on prohibited incitement can be partially explained by the narrower grounds of prohibition under the ICERD. Article 4 of the ICERD focuses exclusively on racist hate speech, whereas the prohibited grounds for incitement under Article 20(2) include national origin, race, and religion. The conundrums associated with the religious component of the norm prohibiting incitement pursuant to Article 20(2) make the HRCttee's task of interpretation more complicated. The CERD, in its General Recommendation No. 35, affirmed that, in light of the principle of intersectionality, 'the committee's attention has also been engaged by hate speech targeting persons belonging to certain ethnic groups who profess or practice a religion different from the majority, including expressions of Islamophobia, anti-Semitism and other similar manifestations of hatred against ethno-religious groups'.[182] However, the jurisprudence of the CERD itself betrays its reluctance to delve deeply into matters of religious incitement or the interface between race and religion in relation to hate speech; it has declared a number of communications inadmissible on the basis of lack of

---

[176] CERD/C/UKR/CO/18, para. 9.

[177] A/51/18, 17, para. 63.

[178] A/51/18, 22, para. 116.

[179] A/58/18, 19, para. 23.

[180] Temperman, *Religious Hatred*, p. 132

[181] A/CONF.119/10, para. 83.

[182] General Recommendation No. 35, para. 6

intersectionality between religious and racial grounds of incitement.[183] Temperman even contends that although 'CERD has paid lip-service to the problem of "double discrimination", in practice it is often reluctant to accept the full ramifications of the phenomenon of intersectionality'.[184]

4.4 REGIONAL JURISPRUDENCE: THE HATE SPEECH JURISPRUDENCE OF THE EUROPEAN COURT OF HUMAN RIGHTS

Neither the ECHR nor the African Charter for Human and People's Rights (ACHPR) includes an explicit hate speech provision that obliges state parties to introduce laws prohibiting incitement to hatred. However, the American Convention on Human Rights (ACHR) includes a provision with terminology close to that of Article 20(2) of the ICCPR. Article 13(5) of the ACHR provides:

> Any propaganda for war and any advocacy of national, racial, or religious hatred that constitute incitements to lawless violence or to any other similar illegal action against any person or group of persons on any grounds including those of race, colour, religion, language, or national origin shall be considered as offences punishable by law.

Article 13(5) of ACHR and Article 20(2) of ICCPR are the only provisions in their respective instruments that oblige state parties to declare a specific type of conduct to be an offence punishable by law. However, Article 13(5) prohibits a narrower range of expressions. Under the ACHR, advocacy of hatred should be prohibited only if it incites others to 'lawless violence' or 'other similar illegal action'; the intangible or emotional harms of advocacy of hatred constitute invalid grounds for its prohibition. Thus, the ACHR's threshold for prohibiting advocacy of hatred is considerably higher than ICCPR's. Nevertheless, ACHR protects a wider range of groups from the harms of advocacy of hatred than ICCPR. Article 13(5) refers to 'any grounds' and mentions the grounds of race, religion, national origin, language, and colour as examples, rather than setting out an exhaustive list. The ACHR's approach to the regulation of hate speech is closer to that taken by the United States.[185] Its drafting history reveals that the United States objected to the first draft of Article 13(5), which included a reference to incitement to 'discrimination, hostility, crime or violence'. The United States presented an alternative draft, which was more consistent with the First Amendment to the US Constitution and less restrictive to freedom of expression. This draft was finally incorporated in the ACHR.[186]

---

[183]   Temperman, *Religious Hatred*, pp. 132–134.
[184]   Temperman, *Religious Hatred*, pp. 158–159.
[185]   Defeis, 'Freedom of Speech and International Norms', 112; Eduardo Bertoni, 'A Study on the Prohibition of Incitement to Hatred in the Americas', available at www.ohchr.org/Documents/Issues/Expression/ICCPR/Santiago/SantiagoStudy_en.pdf, 16.
[186]   Farrior, 'Molding the Matrix', 1–98; J. Oyediran, 'Article 13(5) of the American Convention on Human Rights', in Sandra Coliver (ed.), *Striking a Balance: Hate Speech, Freedom of Expression, and*

Neither the Inter-American Court on Human Rights, nor its predecessor, the Inter-American Commission on Human Rights, has provided a definitive interpretation of Article 13(5) in their jurisprudence.[187] Thus, no standards have been developed within the inter-American human rights system for assessing the consistency of hate speech legislation among state parties to the ACHR. Similarly, the African Commission on Human and Peoples' Rights (ACommHPR) has not generated hate speech jurisprudence, with the exception of one decision, which did not provide useful criteria for analysing whether particular expressions amount to hate speech.[188] Given their absence of hate speech jurisprudence, it cannot be said that either of these two regional human rights systems has developed guiding principles for hate speech regulation.

The situation in the European human rights protection system is quite different from the other two regional systems. The ECtHR and the former European Commission of Human Rights generated hate speech jurisprudence. Their jurisprudence on Articles 10 and 17 of the ECHR demonstrates their recognition that the right to protection from hate speech is implied by these two Articles.[189] Article 10 of the ECHR, on freedom of expression, stipulates that the exercise of this freedom carries with it 'special duties and responsibilities'. It specifies the grounds that justify imposing restrictions on the exercise of freedom of expression, including the protection of national security, social and public order, morals, and the reputations and rights of others. The limitations on freedom of expression specified in the ICCPR and the ECHR are thus very similar. Article 17 of the ECHR (the abuse of rights clause) stipulates: 'nothing in this Convention may be interpreted as implying for any State, group or person any right to engage in any activity or perform any act aimed at the destruction of any of the rights and freedoms set forth herein or at their limitation to a greater extent than is provided for in the Convention'. In a number of cases, the ECtHR and the former commission have held that hate speech restrictions are consistent with state parties' obligations under Articles 10 and 17 of the ECHR.[190]

While the ECtHR introduced the term 'hate speech' into its jurisprudential lexicon in 1999, the term remains undefined by its case law.[191] This reflects the

---

Non-discrimination (Article 19, International Centre Against Censorship, Human Rights Centre, University of Essex, 1992), p. 34.

[187] Eduardo Bertoni, 'Hate Speech under the American Convention on Human Rights' (2006) 12 *ILSA Journal of International & Comparative Law*, 571, 574.

[188] Institute for Human Rights and Development in Africa (on behalf of Sierra Leonean refugees in Guinea) v. Republic of Guinea, African Commission on Human and People's Rights, Communication no. 249/02 (2004).

[189] Adhar and Leigh, *Religious Freedom in the Liberal State*, p. 453; Defeis, 'Freedom of Speech and International Norms', 103; Mendel, 'Consistent rules on hate speech', p. 421; Farrior, 'Molding the Matrix', 3.

[190] Farrior, 'Molding the Matrix', 62–66.

[191] Tarlach McGonagle, 'A survey and critical analysis of Council of Europe Strategies for countering "hate speech"', in Michael E. Herz and Péter Molnár (eds.), *The Content and Context of Hate Speech: Rethinking Regulation and Responses* (Cambridge University Press, 2012); Stefan Sottiaux,

court's preference for a case-by-case approach which prevents it from being constrained by definitions which might restrict its power of action in future cases.[192] Prior to 1999, the ECtHR had been reluctant to use the term 'hate speech' but had dealt with forms of expressions similar to those that it later characterized as such. This reluctance is indicative of the court's unease with integrating the term into its jurisprudence, given the definitional difficulties involved.[193] In some hate speech cases, the ECtHR has relied on Article 10 to uphold hate speech restrictions without invoking Article 17. To justify this reliance, it has used the rationale of 'the protection of the reputation or rights of others' and applied the three tests for upholding restrictions on freedom of expression as provided in Article 10: that they must (i) be prescribed by law, (ii) serve a legitimate purpose, and (iii) be necessary in a democratic society.[194] In another category of hate speech cases, prohibited expressions aimed at the destruction of the rights and freedoms of others have been deemed by the ECtHR to fall under Article 17 and disqualified outright from substantive assessment under Article 10.[195] A third category of hate speech cases invokes both Articles in its legal reasoning, interpreting Article 10 in the context of Article 17.[196] In a few hate speech cases, the ECtHR, in interpreting Article 10 of the ECHR, has also taken into account state parties' obligations under Article 4 of the ICERD and Article 20(2) of the ICCPR.[197]

Despite the fact that state parties to the ECHR are not specifically required to impose restrictions on incitement to hatred, discrimination, or violence, the ECtHR has permitted and even encouraged them to do so.[198] The court has explicitly held that expressions that 'spread, incite, promote, or justify hatred based on intolerance' are unprotected forms of expressions under the Convention.[199] Either sanctioning or preventing these expressions, according to the ECtHR, 'may be considered necessary in certain democratic societies' provided that 'any "formalities", "conditions",

---

'Bad Tendencies in the ECtHR's "Hate Speech" Jurisprudence' (2011) 7(1) *European Constitutional Law Review*, 53.

[192] Mario Oetheimer, 'Protecting Freedom of Expression: The Challenge of Hate Speech in the European Court of Human Rights Case Law' (2009) 17 *Cardozo Journal of International and Comparative Law*, 428–429.

[193] McGonagle, 'A survey and critical analysis', pp. 463–464.

[194] See for example *Jersild* v. *Denmark*, Application no. 15890/89, ECtHR (23 September 1994).

[195] Callamard, 'Towards an Interpretation of Article 20 of the ICCPR', p. 6; Parmar, 'The Challenge of Defamation of Religion', 371; McGonagle, 'A survey and critical analysis', p. 461; *Norwood* v. *United Kingdom*, Application no. 23131/03, ECtHR (16 November 2004); *Glimmerveen and Hagenbeck* v. *Netherlands*, Application nos. 8348/78, 8406/78, ECommHR (11 October 1979); *Witzsch* v. *Germany*, Application no. 7485/03, ECtHR (13 December 2005).

[196] *Kuhnen* v. *Federal Republic of Germany*, Application no. 12194/86, ECommHR (12 May 1988); *Schimanek* v. *Austria*, Application no. 32307/96 (1 February 2000).

[197] Noorloos, *Hate Speech Revisited*, p. 64; Feldman, 'Civil liberties and human rights', p. 760. See for example *Jersild* v. *Denmark*, para. 30.

[198] Defeis, 'Freedom of Speech and International Norms', 103, 106; A/HRC/2/6, para. 28.

[199] *Erbakan* v. *Turkey*, Application no. 59405/00, ECtHR (6 June 2006), para. 56.

"restrictions" or "penalties" imposed are proportionate to the legitimate aim pursued'.[200]

The ECtHR has adopted an 'instrumentalist view' of freedom of expression.[201] While it attaches particular importance to political speech or expressions on matters of public interest and is reluctant to allow restrictions on this category of speech,[202] it also gives state parties wider zones of discretion to impose restrictions on non-political speech or expressions which do not positively contribute to a democratic society.[203]

In its reasoning in hate speech cases, the ECtHR has relied heavily on the doctrine of 'margin of appreciation', which grants state parties flexibility or discretionary power to take into account national contexts when implementing the ECHR.[204] The court has noted that

> [i]t is not for [the ECtHR] to determine what evidence was required under [national] law to demonstrate the existence of the constituent elements of the offence of inciting to ... hatred. It is in the first place for the national authorities, notably the courts, to interpret and apply domestic law. The Court's task is merely to review under Article 10 the decisions they delivered pursuant to their power of appreciation.[205]

The court has held that 'a wider margin of appreciation is generally available to the Contracting States when regulating freedom of expression in relation to matters liable to offend intimate personal convictions within the sphere of morals or, especially, religion'.[206] In a number of cases, the court has gone so far as to recognize 'the right to be free from offence of different kinds'.[207] This is particularly evident in cases regarding religious offence.

Despite the notable fact of the ECtHR affirming that freedom of expression applies not only to information and ideas 'that are favourably received or regarded as inoffensive or as a matter of indifference', but also to those that 'offend, shock, or disturb the State or any sector of the population',[208] this principle has not always been observed in practice, particularly in cases involving speech which may be regarded as offensive to religious beliefs.[209]

---

[200]   *Gunduz* v. *Turkey*, Application no. 4870/02, ECtHR (4 December 2003), para. 40.

[201]   Vance, 'Permissibility of Incitement to Religious Hatred Offences', 207.

[202]   *Erbakan* v. *Turkey*, para. 55; *Wingrove* v. *United Kingdom*, Application no. 17419/90, ECtHR (25 November 1996), paras. 57–58; Paul Mahoney, 'Universality Versus Subsidiarity in the Strasbourg Case Law on Free Speech' (1997) 4 *European Human Rights Law Review*, 372.

[203]   Vance, 'Permissibility of Incitement to Religious Hatred Offences', 206; Mahoney, 'Universality Versus Subsidiarity', 371, 375; Cumper, 'Inciting religious hatred', p. 257.

[204]   Vance, 'Permissibility of Incitement to Religious Hatred Offences', 206, 212.

[205]   *Pavel Ivanov* v. *Russia*, Application no. 35222/04, ECommHR (20 February 2007), para. 1.

[206]   *Wingrove* v. *United Kingdom*, para. 58; *Gunduz* v. *Turkey*, para. 37.

[207]   Feldman, *Civil Liberties and Human Rights*, p. 905.

[208]   *Handyside* v. *United Kingdom*, para. 48.

[209]   Noorloos, *Hate Speech Revisited*, p. 87; Anthony Lester, 'The right to offend', in *Freedom of Expression: Essays in Honour of Nicolas Bratza President of the European Court of Human Rights* (Wolf Legal Publishers, 2012), pp. 298–299.

On the subject of religious hate speech, the ECtHR has held that 'as in the field of morals, and perhaps to an even greater degree, there is no uniform European conception of the requirements of "the protection of the rights of others" in relation to attacks on their religious convictions'.[210] It has also deemed it impossible 'to discern throughout Europe a uniform conception of the significance of religion in society'.[211] In the same case, the court affirmed that it was not possible to provide a precise definition of the scope of permissible interference with speech that might offend the religious feelings of others.[212] The court has also emphasized that 'what is likely to cause substantial offence to persons of a particular religious persuasion' will differ considerably at different times and in different places, especially with the widening range of faiths and beliefs.[213] Thus, it has indicated that national author-ities, with 'their direct and continuous contact with the vital forces of their coun-tries', are better positioned than judges in international courts to assess the necessity and extent of any related interference.[214] It has also elaborated that nation states are better positioned to define 'the protection of the rights of others' and 'necessity' when assessing whether speech ought to be restricted for the purposes of protecting 'those whose deepest [religious] feelings and convictions would be seriously offended'.[215]

It is also clear that the ECtHR has given a particularly wide margin of appreci-ation to state parties in cases involving the balancing of the freedoms of expression and religion.[216] According to the court, anti-religious expressions that are 'gratuit-ously offensive to others' do not contribute to 'any form of public debate capable of furthering progress in human affairs'.[217] The court has evidently recognized the particular capacity of this category of expression to cause public disorder.[218] In the context of religious opinions and beliefs, the ECtHR has held that expressions that are gratuitously offensive to religious adherents violate those adherents' right to express and exercise their religion.[219] It has emphasized that 'in extreme cases the effect of particular methods of opposing or denying religious beliefs can be such as to inhibit those who hold such beliefs from exercising their freedom to hold and express them'.[220] Furthermore, it has held that 'the respect for the religious feelings of believers as guaranteed by Article 9 can legitimately be thought to have been

---

[210] *Wingrove* v. *United Kingdom*, para. 58.
[211] *Otto-Preminger-Institut* v. *Austria*, Application no. 13470/87, ECtHR (20 September 1994), para. 50.
[212] *Otto-Preminger-Institut* v. *Austria*, para. 50.
[213] *Wingrove* v. *United Kingdom*, para. 58.
[214] *Otto-Preminger-Institut* v. *Austria*, para. 50.
[215] *Otto-Preminger-Institut* v. *Austria*, para. 50; see also *Murphy* v. *Ireland*, Application no. 44179/98, ECtHR (10 July 2003), para. 67.
[216] *Giniewski* v. *France*, Application no. 64016/00, ECtHR (31 January 2006), para. 44; *Aydin Tatlav* v. *Turkey*, para. 25–27; *Wingrove* v. *United Kingdom*, para. 58; The Venice Commission Report, para. 51; Mahoney, 'Universality Versus Subsidiarity', 368.
[217] *Otto-Preminger-Institut* v. *Austria*, para. 56; see also *Gunduz* v. *Turkey*, para. 37.
[218] Cumper, 'Inciting religious hatred', p. 257.
[219] *Otto-Preminger-Institut* v. *Austria*, para. 56.
[220] *Otto-Preminger-Institut* v. *Austria*, paras. 47–48.

violated by provocative portrayals of objects of religious veneration'.[221] Nevertheless, the ECtHR has left the question of how to distinguish between 'gratuitously offensive' religious expressions and other protected forms of expression largely unanswered, especially when it is considered that the term 'gratuitously offensive' is highly subjective and vague.

In *Otto-Preminger-Institut* v. *Austria*, the ECtHR characterized the case as entailing 'the conflicting interests of the exercise of two fundamental freedoms guaranteed under the Convention, namely the right of the applicant association to impart to the public controversial views ... on the one hand, and the right of other persons to proper respect for their freedom of thought, conscience and religion, on the other hand'.[222] In *IA* v. *Turkey*,[223] the court found the applicant's conviction for publishing a novel containing disparaging remarks about Islam and the Prophet Mohamed not to be a violation of his freedom of expression, on the basis that 'the present case concerns not only comments that offend or shock, or a "provocative" opinion, but also an abusive attack on the Prophet of Islam' and 'believers may legitimately feel themselves to be the object of unwarranted and offensive attacks'.[224] Thus, the court accepted the right to protection of one's religious feelings, or the right not to be offended in one's religious belief, either as an implied right under Article 9 of the ECHR or derived from – or integral to – the right to freedom of religion. This conclusion with regard to freedom of religion is informed by the fact that certain expressions inhibit those who hold such beliefs from exercising their freedom to hold or express them.[225] One commentator even considers that the ECtHR jurisprudence on offensive religious expressions 'undoubtedly' grants 'protection from offence' to religious beliefs.[226] The religious hate speech jurisprudence of the ECtHR has therefore been criticized in some quarters for endorsing 'low-threshold blasphemy or religious insult restrictions'.[227]

The ECtHR has referred to a relatively wide range of hate speech harms as justifying the imposition of restrictions on freedom of expression. These harms include offence to 'intimate personal convictions within the sphere of morals',[228] 'feelings of distrust, rejection or hatred',[229] 'feelings of hostility',[230] 'injuring or

---

[221] *Otto-Preminger-Institut* v. *Austria*, para. 47.

[222] *Otto-Preminger-Institut* v. *Austria*, para. 55.

[223] *I.A.* v. *Turkey*, Application no. 42571/98, ECtHR (13 September 2005).

[224] *I.A.* v. *Turkey*, para. 29.

[225] Jeroen Temperman, 'Blasphemy, Defamation of Religions & Human Rights Law' (2008) 26 (4) *Netherlands Quarterly of Human Rights*, 534; Scolnicov, *The Right to Religious Freedom in International Law*, p. 203; Noorloos, *Hate Speech Revisited*, p. 80; Feldman, *Civil Liberties and Human Rights*, p. 905; Kapai and Cheung, 'Hanging in a Balance', 63; Robert Post, 'Religion and Freedom of Speech', 79.

[226] Cram, 'The Danish cartoons and offensive expressions', p. 319.

[227] Temperman, *Religious Hatred*, p. 148.

[228] *Wingrove* v. *United Kingdom*, para. 58.

[229] *Feret* v. *Belgium*, Application no. 15615/07, ECtHR (16 July 2009).

[230] *Feret* v. *Belgium*, para. 69.

defaming targets of hate speech',[231] 'serious offence to the religious feelings and convictions',[232] 'outrage and insult the feelings' of religious believers,[233] 'offensive attacks on matters regarded as sacred',[234] reactions that are 'incompatible with a serene social climate',[235] '[an] insulting tone directed against believers',[236] 'incitement to, as well as promotion of, hatred',[237] and 'danger for social peace and political stability'.[238] It is clear from this wide range of harms that the ECtHR has recognized intangible or emotional harms as valid grounds for upholding restrictions on hate speech. In a recent judgement, the ECtHR stated that

> inciting to hatred does not necessarily entail a call for an act of violence. Attacks on persons committed by insulting or slandering specific groups of the population can be sufficient for the authorities to favour combating racist speech in the face of freedom of expression exercised in an irresponsible manner.[239]

The ECtHR has, however, refrained from defining the main concepts it has employed in its hate speech jurisprudence concerning states of minds or emotions, such as 'hatred', 'insult', or 'offence', and, as mentioned above, has avoided defining the term 'hate speech' itself.[240] In most inadmissibility decisions based on the absence of ECHR violations, the court (as with the former commission) has provided limited reasoning on the substantiation of harms that justify the upholding of hate speech restrictions.[241] Moreover, limited analysis has been provided on the content of the instances of speech or expression that have fallen under its consideration.[242]

The ECtHR has endorsed accumulative and indirect, rather than tight, direct, or immediate, causality standards between hateful expressions and their harms.[243] According to the ECtHR, the likelihood, tendency, and the risk or probability of the occurrence of harms all constitute sufficient grounds for restricting hate speech.[244] The court has used causality standards such as 'susceptible to instil' or 'of such a nature as to arouse'.[245] It has considered the 'tendency' of expressions to

---

[231] *Le Pen v. France*, Application no. 18788/09, ECtHR (20 April 2010), para. 73.
[232] *Otto-Preminger-Institut v. Austria*, para. 50; *Wingrove v. United Kingdom*, para. 58; *Murphy v. Ireland*, para. 67.
[233] *Wingrove v. United Kingdom*.
[234] *I.A. v. Turkey*, paras. 29–30.
[235] *Le Pen v. France*, para. 77.
[236] *Aydin Tatlav v. Turkey*, Application no. 50692/99, ECtHR (2 May 2006), para. 28.
[237] *Giniewski v. France*.
[238] *Le Pen v. France*, para. 73.
[239] *Vejdeland and Others v. Sweden*, Application no. 1813/07, ECtHR (9 February 2012), para. 55.
[240] Sottiaux, 'Bad Tendencies', 54.
[241] See for example *Kuhnen v. Federal Republic of Germany*; *Glimmverveen and Hagenbeck v. Netherlands*; McGoldrick and O'Donnell, 'Hate-speech Laws', 465–469; Mendel, 'Hate speech rules under international law', p. 7.
[242] Mendel, 'Consistent rules on hate speech', p. 422.
[243] Noorloos, *Hate Speech Revisited*, p. 78.
[244] Mendel, 'Hate speech', p. 7.
[245] *Feret v. Belgium*, para. 77.

convince others to adopt hateful or discriminatory attitudes to be indicative of incitement to hatred and discrimination.[246] At other times, the court has equated expressions 'susceptible to cause' feelings of hatred with 'intentional incitement to hatred'.[247] Thus, in establishing incitement, the ECtHR has found the potential for hateful expressions to cause harms, including the elicitation of the mental state of hatred in others, to be sufficient.

The ECtHR has also recognized the harms of hate speech targeting groups, and not just their individual members, as justifying restrictions on hate speech.[248] It has held that attacks against ethnic or religious groups, including linking groups as a whole with terrorism, are incompatible with the ECHR's underlying values (in particular tolerance, social peace, and non-discrimination), and therefore that these fall outside the legitimate scope of freedom of expression.[249] The court has also held that 'attacks on persons' can be committed by 'insulting, holding up to ridicule or slandering specific groups of the population'.[250] It has also upheld restrictions on freedom of expression in order to protect groups as such from defamation.[251] In a case related to neo-Nazi bullying of Roma and Jews, the court referred to the 'right to live without intimidation of the members of the target groups'.[252] Applying reasoning similar to that used by the HRCttee, the court considered the protection of 'the reputation or rights of others' as grounds for restricting freedom of expression to include the protection of groups as such.[253] The negative stereotyping of groups and the creation of feelings of hostility among them can be identified as rationales shaping the ECtHR's hate speech jurisprudence.[254] Therefore, the court has recognized the group identity aspect of the right to protection from incitement to hatred and has recognized groups as bearers of this right. Nevertheless, the court has not provided an explanation on how to differentiate between hate speech targeting groups and hate speech directed against a group characteristic.[255] This delicate issue, one of the main difficulties in confronting the interpretation and implementation of the right to protection from incitement, has not been addressed in the court's hate speech jurisprudence to date.

In its reasoning on hate speech cases, the ECtHR has looked at a number of factors. In particular, it has considered the intent of speaker, the speaker's status in society (which feeds directly into the possible impact of their speech), the medium of speech (which determines the scope of its dissemination), and the impact and

---

[246] *Feret* v. *Belgium*, paras. 70–71, 78.

[247] Sottiaux, 'Bad Tendencies', 54.

[248] *Feret* v. *Belgium*, para. 69; *Le Pen* v. *France*, para. 73.

[249] *Norwood* v. *United Kingdom*.

[250] *Vejdeland and Others* v. *Sweden*, para. 55.

[251] X v. *Federal Republic of Germany*, Application no. 9235/81, ECommHR (16 July 1982).

[252] *Vona* v. *Hungary*, Application no. 35943/10, ECtHR (9 December 2013), para. 66.

[253] *Giniewski* v. *France*, para. 40.

[254] *Feret* v. *Belgium*, para. 76; *Soulas and Others* v. *France*, Application no. 15948/03, ECtHR (10 July 2008); Noorloos, *Hate Speech Revisited*, pp. 74–75.

[255] Noorloos, *Hate Speech Revisited*, p. 118.

tone or form of expression.[256] Nevertheless, the court has employed the margin of appreciation doctrine in a manner affirming its conviction that the assessment of these different factors hinges upon historic, cultural, and demographic contexts. In determining hate speech harms, the court has mostly endorsed the reasoning of national authorities on the content and effects of the expressions under consideration, as well as on the necessity of imposing restrictions upon these expressions.[257] In most cases, the ECtHR has not placed its own substantive assessment to the fore. It has neither required nor recognized the feasibility of applying a uniform legal approach to hate speech across European states. Rather, the court has remained cognizant of the relevance of context and national sensitivities when determining the extent of hate speech's harmfulness, as well as the nature of the required response.[258] The court has justified its heavy reliance on the margin of appreciation doctrine by referencing the absence of Europe-wide consensus on the conception of morals in general and religious issues in particular. The court's approach indicates its limited capacity, as a supranational body, to provide a substantiated assessment of the content of particular expressions and their possible consequences within varied national contexts. It has viewed national authorities as better equipped to distinguish between permitted and prohibited hateful expressions.

The ECtHR has, nevertheless, developed the most extensive corpus of supranational hate speech jurisprudence despite the ECHR (in contrast to the ICCPR and ICERD) not obliging states to adopt anti-incitement laws. Accordingly, this jurisprudence does not scrutinize the quality of incitement laws applied by state parties.[259] Almost all of the hate speech cases considered by the court have been brought by convicted hate speech offenders as claims that their freedom of expression had been violated, rather than by victims of hate speech offences. The court has either considered whether the restrictions imposed on specific expressions satisfied the tripartite test under Article 10 (that such restriction was prescribed by law, served a legitimate purpose, and was necessary) or classified the restriction as consistent with Article 17 (the abuse of rights clause) without substantive assessment of the free speech complaint. The latter approach, which prevents claims of violations of freedom of expression from being assessed on their merits, has been described as the 'guillotine approach'.[260]

The ECtHR has legitimized the imposition of restrictions on freedom of expression in order to provide protection from the harms of hate speech, which implies that it recognizes the right to protection from hate speech harms, despite the absence of

---

[256]   Tulkens, 'When to Say Is to Do', 15; Guerra, 'Blasphemy and religious insult', p. 316.

[257]   McGonagle, *Minority Rights*, p. 349.

[258]   The Venice Commission Report, para. 51; Sottiaux, 'Bad Tendencies', 54; Tulkens, 'When to Say Is to Do', 12.

[259]   Temperman, *Religious Hatred*, p. 147.

[260]   Hannes Cannie and Dirk Voorhoof, 'The Abuse Clause and Freedom of Expression in the European Human Rights Convention: An Added Value for Democracy and Human Rights Protection?' (2011) 29(1) *Netherlands Quarterly of Human Rights*, 58.

an explicit reference to such a right in the ECHR's text. However, the court's hate speech jurisprudence has been subjected to a broad range of criticisms.[261] Critics have pointed out its definitional and interpretive deficiencies,[262] including the court's refusal to define the term 'hate speech'[263] and the allocation of an 'excessive' degree of discretion to national authorities in their regulation of offensive expressions, in particular those of a religious nature.[264] The classification in some cases of restrictions on the exercise of freedom of expression as consistent with the abuse of rights clause without substantive assessment under Article 10 has been criticized for amounting to a type of 'content discrimination' given that the court has decided that certain expressions are ipso facto excluded from the protection of the Convention.[265] Temperman argues that 'the reasons that move the Court to apply Article 17 at the expense of a robust Article 10 assessment are quite obscure, leaving extreme speech cases quite unpredictable'.[266]

Furthermore, the court has been criticized for its reluctance to exercise 'much control' over state parties' approaches to imposing restrictions on religion-based hate speech.[267] The court's 'more relaxed form of supranational scrutiny in religious offences'[268] has not provided clear guidance to states regarding the conditions that they must meet in order to ensure that their hate speech laws comply with the ECHR.[269] Feldman goes as far as to contend that the court's approach to religion-based hate speech is 'potentially dangerous as it could sometimes serve simply to legitimate, rather than test rigorously, a regime of stringent censorship'.[270] Leigh describes the nexus drawn in the anti-religious hate speech jurisprudence of the court between religious hate speech and freedom of religion as a 'fallacy'; he argues that religious offence caused by certain expressions does not prevent or deter any person from choosing, practising, or manifesting their belief. Furthermore, he describes the court's references to states' obligations to respect religious feelings, and the right not to be offended, as creating 'illusory' rights.[271]

In conclusion, the ECtHR's hate speech jurisprudence is not as helpful as it might be in guiding national authorities through the complexities and tensions that beset

---

[261]   Cumper, 'Inciting religious hatred', p. 255; Lester, 'The right to offend', p. 306.
[262]   McGonagle, 'A survey and critical analysis', p. 498.
[263]   McGonagle, 'A survey and critical analysis', pp. 464–465.
[264]   Cram, 'The Danish cartoons and offensive expressions', p. 314.
[265]   Temperman, *Religious Hatred*, p. 151.
[266]   Temperman, *Religious Hatred*, p. 151.
[267]   Feldman, *Civil Liberties and Human Rights*, p. 906.
[268]   Cram, 'The Danish cartoons and offensive expressions', p. 317.
[269]   Niraj Nathwani, 'Religious Cartoons and Human Rights: A Critical Legal Analysis of the Case Law of the European Court of Human Rights on the Protection of Religious Feeling and Its Implications in the Danish Affair Concerning Cartoons of the Prophet Muhammed' (2008) 4 *European Human Rights Law Review* 4, 488; Vance, 'Permissibility of Incitement to Religious Hatred Offences', 211.
[270]   Feldman, *Civil Liberties and Human Rights*, p. 906.
[271]   Ian Leigh, 'Damned If They Do, Damned If They Don't: The European Court of Human Rights and the Protection of Religion from Attack' (2011) 17(1) *Res Publica*, 72.

hate speech regulation.[272] The interpretative challenges underlying the five internal features of the right to protection from incitement to hatred have not been sufficiently overcome at a regional level, even where the cultures and legal traditions of states are relatively homogenous. This is particularly true when it is considered that this task has been assigned to a court with a long and rich tradition of human rights adjudication.

4.5 CONCLUDING REMARKS

This chapter has examined the utility of hate speech jurisprudence generated by supra-national monitoring and adjudicatory bodies in elucidating the parameters of the norm prohibiting incitement to discrimination, hostility, or violence. The HRCttee, as the designated interpretive body of the ICCPR, assumes an important responsibility in clarifying the meaning of the norm codified in Article 20(2) of the ICCPR. However, analysis of the HRCttee's hate speech jurisprudence reveals quantitative and qualitative limitations in clarifying the two thresholds for invocation of the right to protection from incitement to hatred; firstly, that certain expressions amount to advocacy to hatred and, secondly, that such advocacy constitutes prohibited incitement.

Despite the HRCttee's competence to provide qualitative assessment of national incitement laws and their compatibility with Article 20(2), it has provided guidance to neither states nor their national prosecutorial or judicial authorities on the application of such laws. This significantly undermines the potential of Article 20(2) to shape the regulation of hate speech at national levels.[273] Also, the applicable legal benchmarks for protection against the harms of hate speech remain a grey area within the HRCttee's jurisprudence. Overall, the right to be free from incitement to hatred remains ill-defined and vague (both with respect to its normative core, and consequently, as to what constitutes a violation) within the HRCttee's jurisprudence.

In light of the HRCttee's limited and unsatisfactory contribution to the elucidation of the exact scope of the norm prohibiting incitement to hatred, this chapter has sought guidance from the hate speech jurisprudence of other supranational human rights–monitoring and adjudicatory bodies. Specifically, it has examined the jurisprudence of the CERD and the ECtHR. The CERD and ECtHR have followed a more proactive interpretive approach in comparison to the HRCttee. However, none of these three human rights bodies have yet developed, in their hate speech jurisprudence, clear and well-established sets of principles demarcating precisely the boundaries between hate speech and free speech.[274] They have avoided

---

[272] Leigh, 'Damned If They Do', 907.
[273] Seeley, 'Article Twenty', 331–332.
[274] Ghanea, 'Articles 19 and 20 of the ICCPR', 62; A/HRC/2/6, para. 84; Martins, 'Freedom of Expression and Equality', 2; A/HRC/15/53, 17.

articulating the essential definitional elements of the key terms integral to hate speech adjudication, making these terms open to over or under inclusiveness. They have not developed the constitutive elements of the threshold of hatred for the purposes of international law. Furthermore, they lack a systematic method of identifying incitement.[275] Clarity on the precise obligations of states pursuant to the norm prohibiting incitement is therefore difficult to locate within existing jurisprudence.

Supranational human rights bodies, while addressing the norm prohibiting incitement, have been required to enter into an interpretative dialectic that must reconcile not only several freedoms (freedom of expression, freedom of religion, and freedom from discrimination), but also competing approaches to rights (the individualist, communitarian, egalitarian, and libertarian). The analysis presented in this chapter indicates that the difficulties in grappling with the inherent definitional complexities and tensions associated with the five internal features of the norm have contributed to the paucity of consolidated, consistent, and comprehensive supranational hate speech jurisprudence.

The inability of supranational monitoring and adjudicatory bodies to formulate objective legal definitions for the key terms involved in hate speech regulation is largely attributable to the inherent emotional component of the norm prohibiting incitement. Notably, these bodies have validated intangible emotional harms as grounds for restricting freedom of expression. This emotional component has informed their relaxed scrutiny approach in the monitoring of states' own formulation and implementation of hate speech laws. As Chapter 2 illustrated, the emotional component introduces elements of legal moralism into the regulation of hate speech, since any legal regulation of emotional harms is directly affected by changing social values and morals. Traditionally, supranational adjudicatory bodies have avoided giving clear directions to states on the meaning and scope of the protection of public morals as a liberty-limiting principle on the basis that the notion of public morals should be contextually interpreted.[276] Even at a regional level, the ECtHR has held that it is not possible to find a uniform conception of morals in the domestic legislation of state parties and that national authorities are in a better position than the international judiciary to adjudicate upon questions of morals and the necessity of any legal restrictions to protect them.[277]

The absence, within supranational hate speech jurisprudence, of clear tests of causality between hate speech and its alleged harms, or the likelihood of such harms, is largely attributable to the challenging nature of this task. In most cases, the causal connection between advocacy of hatred and its harms, and the likelihood of the occurrence of such harms, is indirect, cumulative, invisible, overly speculative, and

---

[275] Mendel, 'Does international law Provide for consistent rules on hate speech?', p. 428; A/HRC/2/6, para. 69.
[276] CCPR, General Comment no. 22, para. 8.
[277] *Handyside* v. *United Kingdom*, para. 49.

belief-mediated by listeners. Moreover, the assessment of whether certain expressions constitute incitement is highly contingent upon context, further explaining the tendency of supranational monitoring bodies to adopt national authorities' assessments in this regard.

The analysis of supranational hate speech jurisprudence presented here indicates that monitoring bodies endorse an egalitarian notion of freedom of expression, rather than a strict libertarian notion. They have recognized a wide range of harms, including intangible emotional harms, as justifying the restriction of hate speech, thereby safeguarding the equality rights of those subjected to hate speech. Moreover, they have endorsed indirect and cumulative causality standards to prove the inciting nature of the expressions in question, rather than tight, direct, demonstrable, and immediate causality standards. However, none of these bodies have articulated strictly defined parameters or stringent tests to distinguish between free expression and prohibited hate speech. The multifaceted and complex interrelationship of liberty and equality in the right to protection from incitement and the underlying tensions between speakers' and listeners' interests in both values have prompted supranational bodies to adopt an almost entirely case-by-case approach in their hate speech jurisprudence. The interaction of the liberty and equality rights of speakers and listeners presents complications so rich and diverse that it is difficult to devise a catch-all formula that can be judiciously applied across all situations to resolve the tensions involved. The body of supranational hate speech jurisprudence indicates that only through a case-based or contextualized consideration of the value of speech and the 'harm' caused by it, can an appropriate balance be struck between the competing interests of speakers and listeners in these two fundamental values.

Moreover, supranational human rights–monitoring bodies have not endorsed a strictly individualist approach to protection against hate speech. Instead, they have recognized group rights to such protection and validated collective harms as a ground for restricting advocacy of hatred. However, they have been unable to address the delicate issue of how to distinguish between attacks on groups as such and attacks on groups' defining characteristics, especially in the context of religious hate speech, despite the increasing relevance of this issue.

Close analysis of supranational hate speech jurisprudence reveals that the norm prohibiting incitement to hatred suffers from serious interpretational gaps and lacks definitional specificity. The norm's definition, both with respect to its normative core and to what constitutes its violation, remains ambiguous. Despite the considerable challenges facing judges, legislators, and policymakers in the area of hate speech, supranational monitoring bodies have failed to consolidate principles to guide the drafting, interpretation, and implementation of national hate speech laws. As long as non-enforcement at the national level is not subject to consistent scrutiny at supranational level, vigorous implementation at national levels will be jeopardized.[278]

The gaps and weaknesses in the legal interpretation of the right to protection from incitement to discrimination, hostility, or violence leave the right open to charges that it is intrinsically indeterminate and unsusceptible to a concrete binding definition at supranational level. Supranational hate speech jurisprudence has, in a number of instances, utilized the terminology of rights, e.g. the right to protection from incitement. However, the interest in being protected from the harms of hate speech has largely been presented in this jurisprudence as a legitimate additional limitation upon freedom of expression. The granting of legal standing to alleged incitement victims by judicial and quasi-judicial supranational human rights bodies is likely to contribute to the development of jurisprudence that is focused on the right to be free from incitement, rather than the legitimization (or otherwise) of the restrictions imposed on freedom of expression.[279] It appears that the right to freedom from incitement has received insufficient attention from civil society organizations providing legal counsel to alleged victims of human rights breaches and submitting complaints on their behalf to supranational human rights bodies.

The need to clarify states' obligations in the area of hate speech is becoming ever more pressing and pertinent, given that new problems pertaining to legal regulation of this phenomenon are constantly arising. Unfortunately, however, the norm prohibiting incitement has not benefited from the interpretive development that is normally achieved when supranational human rights–monitoring bodies have continuous monitoring responsibilities, involving the issuance of adjudicative decisions.

---

[278] Temperman, *Religious Hatred*, p. 32.
[279] Temperman, *Religious Hatred*, p. 163.

5

Recent Normative Battles within the UN on Hate Speech

5.1 INTRODUCTION

This chapter examines the more recent attempts to further develop international standards providing protection against hate speech. Between 1999 and 2010, the UN adopted annual resolutions aimed at combating the defamation of religions. These non-binding resolutions endeavoured to prohibit defamation of religions on human rights grounds on the basis that such defamation is a form of incitement to religious hatred, discrimination, and violence. In 2006, the UN Ad Hoc Committee on the Elaboration of Complementary Standards (Ad Hoc Committee) was established, and took as its mandate the development of new binding international standards on incitement to hatred. Efforts to develop new international standards on hate speech, whether as non-binding recommendations on norms of conduct and policy, in the form of UN resolutions, or as legally binding obligations on states, ultimately failed. This chapter will examine how and why this happened.

Firstly, it will outline the content of the proposed standards and the major players who either spearheaded or resisted the standard-setting efforts. It will then examine states' polarized positions on the meaning of the international norm prohibiting incitement to discrimination, hostility, or violence and the need for new international standards on hate speech. It will also examine how the standard-setting agenda's focus on the religious grounds of hate speech complicated the process of reaching international consensus on the further development or refinement of that norm. More specifically, it will analyse how the interaction of the proposed standards with the scope of freedom of religion, and their conflation of racism and advocacy of religious hatred, further increased opposition to their introduction. Finally, the chapter will examine how certain actions and characteristics of both supporters and opponents of the standard-setting agenda contributed to the failure of that agenda.

5.2 UN RESOLUTIONS ON DEFAMATION OF RELIGIONS

For more than a decade, from 1999 onwards, the Commission on Human Rights and its successor, the HRC, endorsed resolutions on defamation of religion. From 2005 onwards, the GA began to adopt similar resolutions.[1] These resolutions were presented by member states of the Organization of Islamic Cooperation (OIC). Islamic states have traditionally regarded the situation of Muslim minorities in the West (and, more particularly, the protection of their religious freedoms, sensibilities, and identities) as the pre-eminent issue of their collective diplomatic agenda. According to the OIC Charter, the organization's objectives include 'to protect and defend the true image of Islam, to combat defamation of Islam and encourage dialogue among civilisations and religions'[2] and 'to safeguard the rights, dignity and religious and cultural identity of Muslim communities and minorities in non-Member States'.[3] Following the post-9/11 intensification of Islamophobia,[4] Islamic states have become particularly concerned by the defamation and negative stereotyping of Islam and its sacred persons, as well as the profiling and stigmatization of Muslims in the Western media.[5] The upsurge in anti-Muslim prejudice in the West gave Islamic states significant political impetus to campaign for the development of new international standards on religious hate speech.[6] They sought to bring the repercussions which religious hate speech has upon the rights of Muslim individuals and communities in the West to the attention of the international community and to have them recognized as violations of IHRL. The Danish cartoon crisis in 2005, which sparked outrage in the Muslim world, injected additional urgency into Islamic states' efforts in the area of religious hate speech at the multilateral level and contributed to a more focused and legally driven approach to these efforts.[7] The crisis also represented a flashpoint, bringing more attention and publicity to such efforts.[8] Subsequent similar cases, such as the 'Innocence of Muslims' video clip, were

---

[1] Every year, since 1999, the Commission on Human Rights adopted a resolution on the topic of defamation of religions (E/CN.4/Res/1999/82, E/CN.4/Res/2000/84, E/CN.4/Res/2001/4, E/CN.4/Res/2002/9, E/CN.4/Res/2003/4, E/CN.4/Res/2004/6 and E/CN.4/Res/2005/3). In December 2005, the UN General Assembly followed suit by adopting an identically titled resolution. It has continued to adopt these resolutions on an annual basis (A/Res/60/150, A/Res/61/164, A/Res/62/154, A/Res/63/171, A/Res/64/156, A/Res/65/224). Starting from March 2007, the UN Human Rights Council, adopted these resolutions (A/HRC/Res/4/9, A/HRC/Res/7/19, A/HRC/Res/10/22, A/HRC/Res/13/16).

[2] Charter of the Organisation of the Islamic Conference (OIC Charter (2008)), 14 March 2008, OIC Doc. OIC-CHARTER-FINAL-miscdoc-ah-08, Art. 1(12).

[3] Art. 1(16) OIC Charter (2008).

[4] Islamophobia is a term that has been widely used since the 1990s to refer to the hatred of Islam and Muslims with the consequences of discrimination against Muslim individuals and communities.

[5] OIC, Final Communiqué, Islamic Summit Conference, 11th sess., OIC/SUMMIT-11/2008/FC/Final (14 March 2008), para. 176.

[6] Rebecca J. Dobras, 'Is the United Nations Endorsing Human Rights Violations?: An Analysis of the United Nations' Combating Defamation of Religions Resolutions and Pakistan's Blasphemy Laws' (2008–) 37 *Georgia Journal of International and Comparative Law*, 379; Parmar, 'The Challenge of Defamation of Religion', 355; Foster, 'Prophets and Cartoons', 39.

[7] Graham, 'Defamation of Religions', 71; Floyd Abrams, 'On American hate speech law', in Michael E. Herz and Péter Molnár (eds.), *The Content and Context of Hate Speech: Rethinking Regulation and Responses* (Cambridge University Press, 2012), p. 122; Waldron, *The Harm in Hate Speech*, p. 125; Langer, *Religious Offence*, p. 18; OIC Member States started to present resolutions on defamation of religions to UN GA since 2005.

[8] Foster, 'Prophets and Cartoons', 23.

seen by Islamic states as part of a continuous pattern of defamation of Islam, rather than isolated incidents.

Although the UN resolutions did not attempt to define defamation of religion, they did refer to specific manifestations and incidents that, from the perspective of Islamic states, represented the main elements of this phenomenon. These elements included the negative stereotyping of religions, religious adherents, symbols, and sacred persons; the profiling of religious groups; and the use of the media as a vehicle for inciting acts of violence, discrimination, xenophobia, and related intolerance. The resolutions referred specifically to Islam and its association with human rights violations and terrorism, as well as the circumstances of Muslim minority communities.

According to these resolutions, defamation of religion was 'a serious affront to human dignity'[9] and the 'worst form' of incitement to religious and racial hatred and discrimination that consequently restricts religious freedoms.[10] The resolutions strongly deplored 'all acts of psychological and physical violence and assaults, and incitement thereto, against persons on the basis of their religion or belief'.[11] They resolved that the 'respect of religions and their protection from contempt' were 'essential' for the exercise of freedom of religion[12] and constituted legitimate restrictions to the exercise of freedom of expression.[13] Furthermore, the resolutions urged states to undertake constitutional and legal measures against 'acts of hatred, discrimination, intimidation and coercion resulting from defamation of religions', as well as to ensure the full respect and protection of religious symbols.[14]

Islamic states expressed a view that negative stereotyping or defamation of religions was a 'modern expression' of religious hatred and that the latter covers not only individuals, but also 'religions and belief systems'.[15] They emphasized 'the inapplicability of using freedom of expression as a pretext to defame religions'.[16] Through the UN's ongoing adoption of these resolutions, Islamic states sought to move gradually towards making the prohibition of religious defamation an international human rights norm with significant political and legal weight.[17] However, the non-binding nature of these resolutions made them insufficient, in the eyes of these states, to fully address their concerns. At OIC Summit level, they explicitly expressed their

---

[9]   A/HRC/Res/10/22, para. pmbl.
[10] A/HRC/Res/10/22, paras. 5, 6, 13, 14, 15. pmbl. A/HRC/Res/10/88, para. 70.
[11] A/HRC/Res/13/16, para. 3.
[12] A/HRC/Res/7/19, para. 10.
[13] A/HRC/Res/4/9, para. 10.
[14] A/HRC/Res/4/9, para. 13; A/HRC/Res/13/16, para. 16.
[15] Statement of Pakistan on behalf of OIC Member States delivered at UN Human Rights Council (2 October 2009) available at www.unhchr.ch/huricane/huricane.nsf/view01/6A69FF0F95283CE7C1257 6430046793B?opendocument.
[16] OIC, Final Communiqué, Islamic Summit Conference, 3rd extr. sess. (7–8 December 2005), part II, para. 3.
[17] OIC, Second OIC Observatory Report on Islamophobia (June 2008 to April 2009), OIC-CS-2ndOBS-REP-FINAL-May 10, 2009 (Damscas, 2009), 4.

intention to draft a legally binding international instrument to 'prevent intolerance, discrimination, prejudice, and hatred on the grounds of religion and defamation of religions and to promote and ensure the respect of all religions'.[18] Resolutions on defamation of religion were thus intended only to be the first step in a long journey towards binding international standards on religious hate speech.

However, Western countries criticized the general approach and conceptual framework of these resolutions on the basis of their incompatibility with IHRL. They repeatedly emphasized that the concept of religious defamation had no basis in IHRL, which should not grant protection to religions, entities, or ideologies.[19] They did not view defamation of religion as meeting the threshold for incitement prohibited under Article 20(2) of the ICCPR. EU member states called for distinctions to be drawn between 'advocacy of religious hatred' and 'questioning others' religions and beliefs'.[20] Western states criticized the resolutions' overall emphasis on one religion: Islam. The resolutions, in their view, gave precedence to Muslims, as a particular religious community.[21] Furthermore, the resolutions were regarded as having the potential to diminish the scope of legitimate exercise of freedom of expression under IHRL.[22] A number of Latin American and Asian countries increasingly came to share a similar opposition to the resolutions.

[18]   OIC, Final Communiqué 2008, para. 180.

[19]   Statement on behalf of the European Union Delivered at the UN Human Rights Council (30 March 2007), available at http://portal.ohchr.org/portal/page/portal/HRCExtranet/4thSession/DraftResolutions/AHRC4L.12; Statement of Canada delivered at the UN Human Rights Council (30 June 2006), available at http://portal.ohchr.org/portal/page/portal/HRCExtranet/1stSession/OralStatements/300606/Tab7; Statement of Brazil delivered at the UN Human Rights Council (25 March 2010), available at http://portal.ohchr.org/portal/page/portal/HRCExtranet/13thSession/DraftResolutions/AHRC13L.1; Statement of Chile delivered at the UN Human Rights Council (25 March 2010), available at www.un.org/webcast/unhrc/archive.asp?go=100325; Statement of the United States delivered at the UN Human Rights Council (24 March 2011), available at http://portal.ohchr.org/portal/page/portal/HRCExtranet/16thSession/DraftResolutions/AHRC16L.38/L-38-United%20States.pdf.

[20]   Statement on behalf of the European Union Member States at UN Human Rights Council (2011), available at www.un.org/webcast/unhrc/archive.asp?go=110324.

[21]   Statement of Canada delivered at UN Commission on Human Rights (15 April 2002), available at http://daccess-dds-ny.un.org/doc/UNDOC/GEN/G02/127/56/PDF/G0212756.pdf?OpenElement; Statement of Spain on behalf of European Union Member States Delivered to UN Commission on Human Rights (15 April 2002), available at http://daccess-dds-ny.un.org/doc/UNDOC/GEN/G02/127/56/PDF/G0212756.pdf?OpenElement; Statement of India delivered at UN Commission on Human Rights (25 April 2003), available at http://daccess-dds-ny.un.org/doc/UNDOC/GEN/G03/133/76/PDF/G0313376.pdf?OpenElement; Statement of the US to UN Commission on Human Rights (April 2003), available at http://daccess-dds-ny.un.org/doc/UNDOC/GEN/G03/133/76/PDF/G0313376.pdf?OpenElement; Statement of Dominican Republic delivered at UN Commission on Human Rights (13 April 2004), available at http://daccess-ods.un.org/access.nsf/Get?Open&DS=E/CN.4/2004/SR.45&Lang=E; Statement of Japan delivered at UN Human Rights Council (30 March 2007), available at www.un.org/webcast/unhrc/archive.asp?go=070330.

[22]   Statement on behalf of European Union Member States delivered at the UN Human Rights Council (30 June 2006), available at http://portal.ohchr.org/portal/page/portal/HRCExtranet/1stSession/OralStatements/300606/Tab7; Statement on behalf of European Union Member States Delivered at the UN Human Rights Council (27 March 2008), available at www.un.org/webcast/unhrc/archive

The four rapporteurs on freedom of expression within the UN, the Organization for Security and Co-operation in Europe, the Organization of American States (OAS), and the (ACommHPR), all rejected the incorporation of the religious defamation concept within the lexicon of IHRL.[23] Given the difficulties in objectively defining the concept at international level, a number of UN Special Rapporteurs affirmed that the concept is 'open to abuse'.[24] Asma Jahangir, the former UN Special Rapporteur on Freedom of Religion or Belief, referred to the incompatibility of laws on religious defamation with Article 20(2) of the ICCPR. She called for the replacement of these laws with laws providing protection to individuals in accordance with Article 20(2).[25] Jahangir also warned against the possible creation of an atmosphere of religious intolerance as a result of attempts to lower the threshold of Article 20(2).[26] A number of UN Special Rapporteurs affirmed that 'freedom of religion or belief covers the rights to search for meaning by comparing different religions or belief systems, to exchange personal views on questions of religion or belief, and to exercise public criticism in such matters'.[27] CERD, in its General Recommendation No. 35, also affirmed that 'criticism of religious leaders or commentary on religious doctrine or tenets of faith' should not be prohibited or punished.[28] Furthermore, a wide range of international, Western, and Southern NGOs criticized the resolutions on defamation of religion and expressed similar concerns to the opposing states.[29] Such NGOs repeatedly refused to categorize defamation of religion and blasphemy laws as incitement laws in terms of Article 20(2).[30]

.asp?go=080327; Statement of Canada delivered at the UN Human Rights Council (2009), available at www.un.org/webcast/unhrc/archive.asp?go=090326; Statement of Brazil delivered at the UN Human Rights Council (30 March 2007), available at http://portal.ohchr.org/portal/page/portal/HRCExtranet/4thSession/DraftResolutions/AHRC4L.12.

[23] E/CN.4/2001/64 (Annex V).

[24] Githu Muigai et al., 'Joint Statement on "Freedom of Expression and Incitement to Racial or Religious Hatred"', OHCHR side event during the Durban Review Conference, Geneva, 22 April 2009; A/HRC/9/25, para. 39; A/HRC/12/38, para. 2.

[25] A/62/280, para. 76.

[26] A/HRC/2/3 para. 50.

[27] Heiner Bielefeldt et al., Joint Submission to OHCHR Expert Workshop on Africa.

[28] General Recommendation No. 35, para. 6.

[29] A Joint Open Letter of 113 NGOs to 16th Session of the UN Human Rights Council, available at http://sacw.net/article1974.html; Joint NGO Statement on Danger of U.N. 'Defamation of Religions' Campaign, available at https://norskpen.no/en_GB/2009/03/25/joint-ngo-statement-on-danger-of-u-n-defamation-of-religions-campaign; United States Commission on International Religious Freedom, 'Policy focus on the Dangerous Idea of Protecting Religions from Defamation'; ECLJ, 'Combating Defamation of Religions', 2, 6, 8, 13; International Humanist and Ethical Union, 'Speaking Freely about Religion: Religious Freedom, Defamation and Blasphemy', 2009 available at http://iheu.org/content/speaking-freely-about-religion-religious-freedom-defamation-and-blasphemy; Article 19, 'Article 19 Calls on Human Rights Council Members to Vote against Proposed Resolution on Defamation of Religions', 2009, available at www.Article19.org/pdfs/press/human-rights-council-pr-Article-19-calls-on-hrc-members-to-vote-against-prop.pdf.

[30] ECLJ, 'Combating Defamation of Religions', 8, 9; United States Commission on International Religious Freedom, 'Policy focus on the Dangerous Idea of Protecting Religions from Defamation'; International Humanist and Ethical Union, 'Speaking Freely about Religion'.

Thus, a variety of stakeholders mounted widespread resistance to mainstreaming the concept of defamation of religions in IHRL and to categorizing incidents of religious defamation under the ambit of the international norm prohibiting incitement to discrimination, hostility, or violence. This resistance sprang from the firm conviction that IHRL provides protection to religious adherents only against incitement and not against contempt, defamation, or insult of religions, their symbols, or venerated religious figures. The EU member states,[31] some Latin American states,[32] a number of UN Special Rapporteurs,[33] and the OHCHR[34] repeatedly called for the use of Article 20(2)'s exact terminology, instead of the concept of defamation of religion, when addressing religious hate speech within the UN human rights machinery.

Notably, however, Doudou Diène, the former UN Special Rapporteur on contemporary forms of racism, racial discrimination, xenophobia and related intolerance, supported the adoption of legal measures to combat defamation of religion.[35] He emphasized the close nexus between combating religious defamation and addressing discrimination against religious adherents, by positing that defamation of religion legitimizes discriminatory and racist discourse.[36] According to Diène, defamation of religions and incitement to religious hatred are interrelated. He argued that 'political and ideological polarization on the question of the defamation of religions is artificial. Indeed, analysis of international, regional and national human rights instruments shows that provisions against inducement to national, racial or religious hatred are almost universal'.[37] Islamic states welcomed Diène's reports to the HRC on the issue of defamation of religion as his views supported, or perhaps even strengthened, the arguments they had used in defence of the resolutions.[38]

The resolution on combating defamation of religions, which was successfully adopted within the UN for eleven consecutive years, was last submitted by OIC member states to the UN in 2010. The circumstances that caused the OIC member states' standard-setting circumstances to be abandoned will be examined in depth later in this chapter.

---

[31] Statement on behalf of the European Union Member States at UN Human Rights Council (2011), available at www.un.org/webcast/unhrc/archive.asp?go=110324.

[32] Statement of Brazil delivered at the UN Human Rights Council (25 March 2010), available at http://portal.ohchr.org/portal/page/portal/HRCExtranet/13thSession/DraftResolutions/AHRC13L.1; Statement of Chile delivered at the UN Human Rights Council (2009), available at www.un.org/webcast/unhrc/archive.asp?go=090326.

[33] Githu Muigai et al., 'Joint Statement on "Freedom of Expression and Incitement to Racial or Religious Hatred'; A/HRC/9/25, para. 39; A/HRC/12/38, 2.

[34] A/CONF.211/PC.4/5, para. 10.

[35] A/HRC/12/38, 21.

[36] A/HRC/12/38, 7.

[37] A/HRC/9/12, para. 13.

[38] See for example A/HRC/4/9.

5.3 POLARIZED POSITIONS ON THE NEED FOR COMPLEMENTARY STANDARDS TO ARTICLE 20(2) OF THE ICCPR

Islamic states undertook two main steps in their efforts to establish standards in the area of religious hate speech. Their first step was the presentation of the aforementioned annual resolutions to the UN. Their second step was to argue that the existing international legal framework needed to be complemented by the addition of new standards. Islamic states initiated a standard-setting process within the HRC in order to develop international binding standards on incitement to hatred. In 2006, the HRC passed a resolution, initiated by Islamic and African states, establishing the Ad Hoc Committee with a specific mandate to

> elaborate, *as a matter of priority and necessity*, complementary standards in the form of either a convention or additional protocol(s) to the International Convention on the Elimination of All Forms of Racial Discrimination, filling the existing gaps in the Convention and also providing new normative standards aimed at combating all forms of contemporary racism, including *incitement to racial and religious hatred* [my emphasis].[39]

The African and OIC groups agreed on the need to create new international binding standards on incitement to racial and religious hatred. The African group had traditionally made combating all forms and manifestations of racism a priority. It recognized the existence of normative gaps in existing international instruments on racism, racial discrimination, xenophobia, and intolerance and believed that these gaps warranted the setting of additional standards.[40] Thus, the African group's interest in the establishment of the Ad Hoc Committee can be viewed in the context of its wider interest in the normative expansion of IHRL standards to address contemporary forms of racism and xenophobia. Islamic and African states therefore injected unprecedented momentum into standard-setting efforts on incitement to hatred by establishing a new institutional mechanism with a clear mandate.

These states identified the existence of multiple gaps within Article 20(2), not only with regard to its interpretation and application, but also with regard to standards.[41] Islamic states endorsed a wide perception of normative gaps within IHRL; they interpreted such gaps as a lack of precision or sufficient focus to comprehensively address new human rights challenges. They argued that the proliferation of IHRL instruments on specific rights and the rights of particular vulnerable groups would not have been possible other than with a wide perception

---

[39] A/HRC/3/103, para. a.

[40] Statement of Nigeria on behalf of African Group Delivered at the UN Human Rights Council (25 March 2010), available at http://portal.ohchr.org/portal/page/portal/HRCExtranet/13thSession/OralStatements/230310/Tab1/Tab4/9%20GD%20-%20Nigeria%20for%20African%20Group.pdf.

[41] A/HRC/10/88; Statement of Pakistan on behalf of OIC Member States Delivered at the UN Human Rights Council (25 September 2007), available at http://portal.ohchr.org/portal/page/portal/HRCExtranet/6thSession/DraftResolutions/AHRC6L.8Rev.1/Pakistan(OIC).pdf.

of normative gaps.[42] Islamic states contended that the 'evolutionary' and 'non-static' nature of IHRL would necessitate the adoption of new international stand-ards in response to contemporary manifestations of religious discrimination, xeno-phobia, and related intolerance.[43] They considered the employment of non-legal measures, such as advancing intercultural and inter-religious dialogue and pro-moting tolerance, to be insufficient to address contemporary hate speech challenges.[44] Moreover, Islamic states emphasized that these non-legal measures should not be used as a pretext for resisting the development of new international standards on hate speech.[45]

The standards proposed by Islamic states to the Ad Hoc Committee, and sup-ported by the African group,[46] focused on religious hate speech. They sought to oblige states to legally prohibit several categories of expression, including expres-sions that defame and negatively stereotype religions and their followers.[47] Other suggested prohibitions concerned 'the uttering of matters that are grossly abusive or insulting in relation to matters held sacred by any religion thereby causing outrage among a substantial number of the adherents to that religion';[48] 'public expressions with racist aims, or of an ideology which claims the superiority of, or which deprecates or denigrates, a grouping of persons on the grounds of their race, colour, language, religion, nationality, or national or ethnic origin';[49] and 'racio-religious profiling or profiling based on any grounds of discrimination recognized under international human rights law'.[50] Furthermore, the standards proposed by Islamic states aimed to achieve legal prohibition of organizations 'based on ideas or theories of superiority of one race or group of persons of one colour or ethnic origin, or which attempt to justify or promote national, racial and religious hatred and discrimination in any form'.[51]

The African group proposed a similar set of standards to the Ad Hoc Committee. These standards sought to oblige states to prohibit by law the following expressive acts: 'profiling based on stereotypes founded on grounds of discrimination prohib-ited by international law, including on racial, ethnic and/or religious grounds';[52] 'all dissemination of ideas aimed at discrimination or hatred, as well as all acts of

---

[42] 'Presentation of the Report of the Adhoc Committee on the Elaboration of Complementary Standards by Chairperson-Rapporteur Idriss Jazairy at the UN HRC', March 2010, available at http://portal .ohchr.org/portal/page/portal/HRCExtranet/13thSession/OralStatements/230310/Tab1/Ad%20Hoc% 20Com%20Elab%20Compl%20Standarts.pdf.

[43] A/HRC/13/58, Annex I.

[44] A/HRC/13/58, Annex I.

[45] A/HRC/18/36, paras. 65, 71.

[46] A/HRC/10/88, para. 72.

[47] A/HRC/10/88, para. 72; A/HRC/13/58, Annex I.

[48] A/HRC/13/58, para. 38.

[49] A/HRC/13/58, para. 38.

[50] A/HRC/13/58, para. 103.

[51] A/HRC/13/58, para. 29.

[52] A/HRC/13/58, para. 100.

violence or incitement to such acts against any particular group of persons';[53] and 'insulting publicly, through a computer system, individuals or groups distinguished by race, colour, descent or national or ethnic origin, as well as religion'.[54]

All Western state members of the HRC, as well as South Korea and Japan, voted against the Council's decision to establish the Ad Hoc Committee in 2006; the decision was adopted with thirty-three in favour, thirteen against, and one abstention.[55] Western states considered the reference made, within the Ad Hoc Committee's mandate, to incitement to racial and religious hatred, as prejudging the identification of normative gaps in IHRL and predetermining in an arbitrary manner the content of possible standards.[56]

During the Ad Hoc Committee's sessions, European states averred that there was no consensus on the need to create complementary standards and, accordingly, resisted substantive discussions on the possible nature and form of any such standards.[57] They emphasized that 'any identification of gaps needed to be based on empirical data and not simply views' and should be 'evidence-based'.[58] European states also noted that complementary standards do not have to be binding but could take various forms, such as general comments, guidelines, and best practices.[59] The United States expressed firm opposition to the creation of new international standards on the basis that it did not acknowledge any normative gaps in the existing international legal framework.[60] Canada and Norway expressed the same view.[61] The United States even refused to discuss the issue of hate speech within the committee in accordance with the terminology of Article 20(2). It argued that a number of countries had reservations regarding the Article and that it would be impossible to have a fruitful discussion based on the language of the Article. Instead,

---

[53] A/HRC/13/58, para. 26(2)(a).

[54] A/HRC/13/58, para. 108.

[55] Countries that voted in favour were Algeria, Argentina, Azerbaijan, Bahrain, Bangladesh, Brazil, Cameroon, China, Cuba, Ecuador, Gabon, Ghana, Guatemala, India, Indonesia, Jordan, Malaysia, Mali, Mauritius, Mexico, Morocco, Nigeria, Pakistan, Peru, Philippines, Russian Federation, Saudi Arabia, Senegal, South Africa, Sri Lanka, Tunisia, Uruguay, and Zambia. Counties that voted against were Canada, Czech Republic, Finland, France, Germany, Japan, Netherlands, Poland, Republic of Korea, Romania, Switzerland, United Kingdom of Great Britain, and Northern Ireland. Ukraine abstained.

[56] Statement on behalf of European Union Member States delivered at the UN Human Rights Council (April 2007), available at http://portal.ohchr.org/portal/page/portal/HRCExtranet/3rdSession/ DraftResolutions/AHRC3L.3/Finland(EU).pdf; Statement of Switzerland delivered at the UN Human Rights Council (April 2007), available at www.un.org/webcast/unhrc/archive.asp? go=061208; Statement of Japan delivered at the UN Human Rights Council (April 2007), available at http://portal.ohchr.org/portal/page/portal/HRCExtranet/3rdSession/DraftResolutions/AHRC3L.3 /Japan.pdf.

[57] A/HRC/10/88, para. 75, Annex II; 'Statement of EU at HRC 2010', 25 March 2010.

[58] A/HRC/13/58, para. 12.

[59] A/HRC/13/58, paras. 117, 119.

[60] A/HRC/13/58, para. 14.

[61] A/HRC/13/58, para. 118.

the United States was in favour of discussing broader issues of discrimination and intolerance.[62]

Within the Ad Hoc Committee's sessions, a cross regional group was also formed in order to express a common position with a membership of twelve states drawn from different regions: Argentina, Armenia, Brazil, Chile, Colombia, Costa Rica, Guatemala, Japan, Mexico, Republic of Korea, Switzerland, and Uruguay.[63] The cross regional group emphasized the importance of adopting a consensual working basis.[64] It affirmed the need for further assessment, research, and empirical data to better evaluate the current challenges. It considered the development of a legally binding instrument to be premature.[65]

All Western states, in addition to the states of the cross regional group, shared the view that there were no normative gaps in IHRL in the area of incitement to racial and religious hatred.[66] They contended that international efforts in addressing the challenges of religious intolerance, xenophobia, and racial discrimination should focus on overcoming the implementation gaps of existing IHRL standards.[67] They highlighted the importance of policy measures such as advancing intercultural and inter-religious dialogue and promoting diversity to addressing the rise of incidents of advocacy of hatred, without resorting to legal restrictions on expression.[68]

Given the situation described above, the OIC and African groups were, unsurprisingly, the only two groups that submitted proposals for potential standards on incitement to hatred during the Ad Hoc Committee's sessions. The substantive contributions of other states to the work of the committee involved only recommendations on policy measures aimed at enhancing the implementation of states' obligations under existing IHRL non-discrimination standards.

It was readily apparent that the positions of Islamic and African states, on the one hand, and Western and cross regional group states, on the other, were significantly polarized on several issues, including the legitimacy of the Ad Hoc Committee's mandate, whether gaps in legal protection were normative or implementative in nature, and what the appropriate measures to address any such gaps might be.

---

[62] UN Watch, 'Controversial Durban Committee Meets in Geneva', 2001, available at https://unwatch .org/controversial-durban-committee-meets-in-geneva-day-3.

[63] The Cross Regional Group includes the following countries: Switzerland, Argentina, Brazil, Chile, Colombia, the Dominican Republic, Guatemala, Japan, Mexico, the Republic of Korea, and Uruguay.

[64] A/HRC/13/58, para. 117.

[65] Statement of the Cross Regional Group delivered at the UN Human Rights Council (March 2010), available at http://portal.ohchr.org/portal/page/portal/HRCExtranet/13thSession/OralStatements/ 230310/Tab1/Tab4/9%20GD%20-%20Switzerland.pdf.

[66] A/HRC/13/58, paras. 14, 30, 117–119, Annex III; A/HRC/10/88, paras. 17, 67, 123; A/HRC/18/36, paras. 74–75; Statement of the Cross Regional Group delivered at the UN Human Rights Council (March 2010).

[67] A/HRC/10/88, paras. 17, 67, 123; A/HRC/13/58, paras. 14, 31, 30(2), 118.

[68] U.S. Department of State, 'Remarks by Hillary Clinton US Secretary of State on the Release of the 2009 Annual Report on International Religious Freedoms' (26 October 2009), available at www .state.gov/secretary/rm/2009a/10/130937.htm; A/HRC/13/58, para. 31.

During the first two sessions of the committee, Islamic and African states wanted to expedite the execution of the committee's mandate even at the expense of achieving consensus.[69] They perceived other states' insistence on reaching consensus on the need for new standards as a pretext to paralyse the work of the committee.[70] They also accused Western states of lacking the political will necessary to advance the work of the committee.[71] Many states were reluctant even to discuss the issue of hate speech and believed that debates on the subject would cause irreconcilable divisions.[72] This polarization stalemated the committee's work during its first four years. Reaching agreement among states on the committee's agenda and the programme of work for its sessions consumed a considerable proportion of its time. As a consequence, the time allocated for substantive discussions on implementing the committee's mandate was minimal.

The position of Islamic and African states regarding normative gaps also failed to gain the support of UN Special Rapporteurs and other independent human rights experts consulted by the UN. The Special Rapporteurs on freedom of expression, freedom of religion, and racism all recognized the difficulty of defining the types of conduct that might trigger Article 20(2) and recommended the development of objective legal criteria on the Article's proper implementation.[73] However, they did not recommend any standard-setting exercises. Notably, the UN also consulted five independent experts on the possible creation of complementary international standards in a number of areas, including incitement to hatred.[74] In their report, these experts concluded that religious intolerance, combined with racial and xenophobic prejudice, was sufficiently protected under existing IHRL standards.[75] They did not identify any substantive gaps in existing international human rights standards on religion.[76] They found a protection gap only in the matter of implementation and affirmed that proper implementation of states' obligations under IHRL could effectively prevent and punish acts of incitement to racial and religious hatred.[77] They asked for 'further guidance' from treaty bodies on the scope and threshold of application of norms within Article 4 of the ICERD and Article 20(2) of the ICCPR.[78] The experts specifically recommended the adoption by CERD of a general recommendation on the nexus between racism

[69]   A/HRC/10/88, para. 11, 19; A/HRC/13/58, paras. 116, 120.

[70]   A/HRC/10/88, paras. 82, 108; A/HRC/13/58, paras. 17, 18.

[71]   Statement of Nigeria on behalf of African Group Delivered at the UN Human Rights Council (25 March 2010), available at http://portal.ohchr.org/portal/page/portal/HRCExtranet/13thSession/OralStatements/230310/Tab1/Tab4/9%20GD%20-%20Nigeria%20for%20African%20Group.pdf.

[72]   A/HRC/18/36, para. 23.

[73]   Githu Muigai et al., 'Joint Statement on "Freedom of Expression and Incitement to Racial or Religious Hatred"'.

[74]   A/HRC/4/WG.3/6.

[75]   A/HRC/4/WG.3/6, para. 130.

[76]   A/HRC/4/WG.3/6, paras. 150, 151.

[77]   A/HRC/4/WG.3/6, para. 152.

[78]   A/HRC/4/WG.3/6, paras. 145–146, 150, 152.

and religion.[79] They further recommended that states should adopt non-legal measures in the areas of education, public awareness, and self-regulatory govern-ance of the internet in order to combat harmful incitement.[80] The African and Islamic states criticized the conclusions and recommendations of the five inde-pendent experts, given that their testimony was unsupportive of their standard-setting agenda.[81]

Many NGOs also explicitly rejected the Islamic and African states' proposals. In a joint letter submitted to the Ad Hoc Committee, a number of international, Western, and Southern NGOs expressed the view that 'the proposals submitted by OIC and the African Group distort and undermine existing international human rights protection of both the right to freedom of expression and equality'.[82] Their main concern was the proposals' 'inclusion of religions, religious ideas, objects and personalities as subjects that warrant protection under international human rights law'.[83] They strongly recommended that the committee should reject the proposals on the grounds that they 'overstep ... the long-established limits of international human rights law, principles and values which protect individuals and groups, rather than religious ideas, objects and symbols'.[84] These organizations encouraged the committee to focus instead on 'measures that promote diversity and pluralism, promote equitable access to the means of communication, and guarantee the right of access to information and creating an enabling environment for both freedom of expression and equality'.[85] They recommended that the committee support 'the proper implementation by states of existing international human rights law on freedom of expression, as guaranteed by Articles 19 and 20 of the International Covenant on Civil and Political Rights'.[86] In addition, one of the leading inter-national NGOs in the area of freedom of expression – an organization named Article 19 – affirmed that existing international standards were 'sufficient' to address incite-ment to hatred and that the international human rights community should focus instead on 'the development of a clear international definition of incitement and a set of rigorous tests to determine its threshold'.[87] The committee did not receive any proposals from NGOs for new international standards on incitement to hatred.

---

[79] A/HRC/4/WG.3/6, paras. 48–49.
[80] A/HRC/4/WG.3/6, paras. 150, 151.
[81] A/HRC/6/21.
[82] 'A Joint Open Letter of 113 NGOs'.
[83] 'A Joint Open Letter of 113 NGOs'.
[84] 'A Joint Open Letter of 113 NGOs'.
[85] 'A Joint Open Letter of 113 NGOs'.
[86] 'A Joint Open Letter of 113 NGOs'.
[87] Sim Kok Eng Amy, 'Preventing Hatred or Silencing Voices: Making the Case for a Rigorous Threshold for the Incitement to National, Racial or Religious Hatred', a paper presented to OHCHR expert workshop on the prohibition of incitement to national, racial or religious hatred in Bangkok (2011), available at www.ohchr.org/Documents/Issues/Expression/ICCPR/Bangkok/AmySim.pdf, 19.

In summary, the consensus among the UN Special Rapporteurs, the five independent experts consulted by the UN, and human rights NGOs was that interpretive and implementative, rather than normative, gaps existed in the international human rights framework on hate speech.[88] This position aligned with that of the states of the West and the cross-regional group, all of whom opposed standard-setting attempts in the area of hate speech.

Following the suspension of the resolutions on defamation of religions, the Ad Hoc Committee's focus shifted to the *implementation* gaps of existing IHRL standards on discrimination and intolerance, and the topic of incitement to hatred was subsequently dropped altogether from the list of issues under the committee's consideration.[89]

The following sections of this chapter will analyse the factors that contributed to the ultimate failure of standard-setting efforts in the area of hate speech.

5.4 THE PROPOSED STANDARDS' INTERACTION WITH THE SCOPE OF FREEDOM OF RELIGION

The major focus of the standard-setting efforts led by Islamic states was religious hate speech or speech that incites hatred on the grounds of religion. Consequently, these efforts involved direct engagement with the scopes of both freedom of expression and freedom of religion. They reflected a view that religious hate speech deserved or required different or special protection. Islamic states considered defamation of religion, negative profiling of religious adherents, insult to religious feelings, and offensive attacks on matters regarded as sacred by religious followers not only as violations of the right to be protected from incitement to religious hatred, discrimination, and violence, but also as violations of freedom of religion.[90] OIC member states therefore sought to strike a new balance between the freedoms of religion and expression, as well as the right to be free from religious discrimination, a balance grounded in the right to be protected from the harm of religious hate speech.[91] This attempted rebalancing was based on Islamic states' conception of these rights and their precise scopes.

The direct interaction of Islamic states' proposed standards with the definition and scope of freedom of religion under IHRL added further complexities to their standard-setting attempts. National legal systems across the world take diverse approaches as to what constitutes prohibited forms of expression on religious matters at both normative and jurisprudential levels.[92] They reflect different views on whether, and to what extent, respect for religious beliefs and feelings should limit

---

[88] A/HRC/10/88, para. 122; A/HRC/2/3, para. 61; A/HRC/4/WG.3/6, para. 152.
[89] A/HRC/18/36, para. 67.
[90] A/HRC/7/19, para. 10.
[91] A/HRC/13/58, Annex I.
[92] A/HRC/9/7, para. 67.

freedom of expression. The varying status of religions in states' structures contributes to such differences; a clear distinction exists between states with a recognized state religion whose protection preserves national and state identity and those who do not, with the latter group including secular states in particular.[93] The creation of international standards on religious discrimination has proven to be a particularly challenging task. Although specific and elaborate international instruments on racial and gender discrimination have been adopted, the international community has failed to reach consensus on similar elaborate standards concerning religious discrimination. In the early 1960s, the GA adopted a resolution to draft a declaration in preparation for a convention on racial and religious discrimination. Member states later decided, however, that racial and religious discrimination should be addressed in separate instruments because of difficulties encountered while negotiating standards on religious discrimination.[94] The declaration on racism was adopted in 1963, followed by the ICERD in 1965. On the other hand, the Declaration on the Elimination of Religious Intolerance became the subject of difficult and prolonged debate for two decades among states on its content. It was finally adopted in 1981.[95]

The 1981 Declaration (composed of only eight Articles) does not include a provision prohibiting of incitement to religious discrimination comparable to Article 4 of the ICERD prohibiting racist speech. The declaration avoided addressing the interrelatedness between freedoms of religion and expression. The subcommission on what became the 1981 Declaration suggested a number of anti-incitement clauses in its drafts. These clauses obliged states to prohibit by law the 'promotion or incitement to religious intolerance or discrimination',[96] 'incitement to hatred or acts of violence whether by individuals or organizations against any religious group or persons belonging to a religious community', and 'organizations which promote and incite to religious discrimination'.[97] A number of Western states opposed the anti-incitement clauses on the basis that they constituted infringement upon freedom of expression. Eventually, these provisions were dropped from the final text of the declaration.[98] It has proven difficult to reach agreement at international level on the appropriate balance between the freedoms of religion and expression or the threshold for prohibiting freedom of expression in matters of religion.[99] Determining the range of protected manifestations of freedom of religion, including religious expression, has been among the most contentious areas

---

[93] Foster, 'Prophets and Cartoons', 56; Belnap, 'Defamation of Religions', 680.
[94] Taylor, *Freedom of Religion*, p. 9.
[95] Boyle and Baldaccini, 'A critical evaluation', pp. 148–149; Richards, *Free Speech*, p. 178; Natan Lerner, *The UN Convention on the Elimination of All Forms of Racial Discrimination* (Sijthoff & Noordhoff, 1980), p. 1.
[96] E/CN.4/920.
[97] E/3873.
[98] Boyle, 'Religious intolerance', p. 65.
[99] A/HRC/9/7, para. 67; Boyle, 'Religious intolerance', p. 65.

during international negotiations on the scope of freedom of religion and has long been an intractable issue within IHRL.[100]

Indeed, consensus on international binding standards against religious discrimination has proven much more challenging to achieve than consensus on standards against racism. This reflects the complexities and sensitivities of the issues involved and the lack of agreement on the exact scope of religious freedom that governments should respect. Agreement on a detailed binding instrument on religious discrimination and intolerance does not, therefore, appear likely in the near future.[101]

The difficulties associated with reaching broad agreement on the contours of freedom of religion have translated into difficulties in attempting to develop the normative content of the right to protection from religious incitement. There is a particularly wide gap between Islamic and Western states in this regard. Polarized conceptions of the rationales underpinning freedoms of religion and expression therefore lead not only to different positions on their boundaries and mutual relations, but also complicate standard-setting in the area of religious hate speech. Different approaches to balancing these freedoms lead directly to different conceptions of the meaning and scope of the right to protection from the harm of religious hate speech.

One major controversy that arose between supporters and opponents of standard-setting efforts was whether contempt of religion and offence to religious feelings constituted violations of freedom of religion. Islamic states believed that they did and went so far as to assume an automatic causal relationship between such categories of expressions and infringement of targeted adherents' religious freedoms that in turn justify their prohibition. The proposed standards expanded the normative scope of freedom of religion to include the right to protection from defamation of religion, negative profiling of religious groups, and offence or insult to religious feelings. When addressing freedom of religion, the proposed standards thus prioritized the protection of the targeted adherents' identity and expressive aspects of freedom of religion over the speakers' expressive aspect of the same freedom.

Conversely, Western states excluded any possible causal relationship between contempt of religions or offence to religious feelings and infringement upon freedom of religion. Along with a number of Latin American states, they firmly resisted the recognition of respect for religions as integral to the enjoyment of freedom of religion.[102] A number of UN Special Rapporteurs emphasized that freedom of

---

[100] Taylor, *Freedom of Religion*, pp. 2, 25.

[101] Robert F. Drinan, *Can God & Caesar Coexist?: Balancing Religious Freedom and International Law* (Yale University Press, 2004), p. 43.

[102] Statement on behalf of European Union Member States delivered at the UN Human Rights Council (30 June 2006), available at http://portal.ohchr.org/portal/page/portal/HRCExtranet/1stSession/ OralStatements/300606/Tab7; Statement of the United States delivered at the UN Human Rights Council (24 March 2011), available at http://portal.ohchr.org/portal/page/portal/HRCExtranet/ 16thSession/DraftResolutions/AHRC16L.38/L-38-United%20States.pdf; Statement of Canada delivered at the UN Human Rights Council (2009), available at www.un.org/webcast/unhrc/archive

religion or belief under IHRL does not include the right to have religions or beliefs protected from criticism or ridicule.[103] Asma Jahangir, the former UN Special Rapporteur on Freedom of Religion or Belief, held that freedom of religion 'primarily confers a right to act in accordance with one's religion but does not bestow a right for believers to have their religion itself protected from all adverse comment' and 'does not protect religions or beliefs per se'.[104] Jahangir further noted that 'any attempt to lower the threshold of Article 20 ... would not only shrink the frontiers of free expression, but also limit freedom of religion or belief itself. Such an attempt could be counterproductive and may promote an atmosphere of religious intolerance'.[105] She has rightly held that 'defamation of religions may offend people and hurt their religious feelings but *does not necessarily or at least directly* result in a violation of their rights, including their right to freedom of religion [my emphasis]'.[106] She has convincingly affirmed that

> [the question] as to whether criticism, derogatory statements, insults or ridicule of one religion may actually negatively affect an individual's right to freedom of religion or belief can only be determined objectively and, in particular, by examining whether the different aspects of the manifestation of one's right to freedom of religion are accordingly negatively affected.[107]

A number of UN Special Rapporteurs have recognized that 'the exercise of freedom of expression could *in some extreme cases* affect the right to manifest the religion or belief of certain identified individuals [emphasis added]'.[108] However, they considered it 'conceptually inaccurate' to 'present "defamation of religions" *in abstracto* as a conflict between the right to freedom of religion or belief and the right to freedom of opinion or expression'.[109]

The question of whether hate speech against a religion should be equated with hate speech against religious adherents proved to be the most controversial aspect of states' varying conceptions of the norm prohibiting incitement to religious hatred. As addressed in detail in Chapter 2 (Section 2.6), the issue of distinguishing between incitement to hatred against religious *ideas* and incitement to hatred against religious *adherents* is a complex one. The causal relationship between these expressive

---

.asp?go=090326; Statement of Brazil delivered at the UN Human Rights Council (30 March 2007), available at http://portal.ohchr.org/portal/page/portal/HRCExtranet/4thSession/DraftResolutions/ AHRC4L.12; Statement of Argentina delivered at the UN Human Rights Council (2007), available at www.un.org/webcast/unhrc/archive.asp?go=070330.

[103] Heiner Bielefeldt et al., Joint Submission to OHCHR Expert Workshop on Africa; A/67/537, para. 53.

[104] A/HRC/2/3, paras. 37–38.

[105] A/HRC/2/3, para. 50.

[106] A/HRC/2/3, para. 37.

[107] A/HRC/2/3, para. 39.

[108] Githu Muigai et al., 'Joint Statement on "Freedom of Expression and Incitement to Racial or Religious Hatred"'.

[109] Githu Muigai et al., 'Joint Statement on "Freedom of Expression and Incitement to Racial or Religious Hatred"'.

acts and violation of freedom of religion is not inevitable, inherent, or automatic, as Islamic states presumed; but neither is it impossible, as implied by Western states' positions. Many scholars rejected the standards proposed by Islamic states on the basis that they conflated defamation of religion and the incitement to religious hatred, thus advocating the protection of religions under IHRL while simultaneously lowering the threshold for prohibiting freedom of expression.[110] Such scholars endorsed a necessary distinction between these two categories of religious expression.[111]

Supranational hate speech jurisprudence has provided no definitive guidance on how to distinguish between expressions that defame, insult, or ridicule religions and expressions that constitute incitement against religious followers.[112] This testifies to the complexities involved. The jurisprudence of the ECtHR, as detailed in the previous chapter, embraced the right to have one's religious feelings protected against offence as an aspect of freedom of religion but accorded a wide margin of appreciation to states when imposing restrictions on offensive religious expressions.[113] The ECtHR has recognized that 'provocative portrayals of objects of religious veneration' and extreme cases of 'opposing or denying religious beliefs' both represent infringements upon the rights of religious adherents.[114] It is interesting to note that the court's line of reasoning in upholding restrictions on anti-religious expressions that are gratuitously offensive, insulting, or outraging to believers – that reasoning being that religious freedoms should not be inhibited – is not entirely divorced from the reasoning invoked by Islamic states in defending their suggested standards.[115]

The difficulties that arose prior to the enactment of the Racial and Religious Hatred Act 2006, which created an offence of incitement to religious hatred in England and Wales, exemplifies Western fears of conflating incitement to religious hatred with defamation of religion. The UK government had made two unsuccessful attempts to enact an offence of incitement to religious hatred within a four-year period.[116] Many commentators regarded these attempts as a governmental response

---

[110] Robert C. Blitt, 'The Bottom up Journey of 'Defamation of Religion' from Muslim States to the United Nations: A Case Study of the Migration of Anti-Constitutional Ideas' (2011) 56 *Studies in Law, Politics, and Society*, 31; Parmar, 'The Challenge of Defamation of Religion', 365; Dobras, 'Is the United Nations Endorsing Human Rights Violations?', 343; Maxim Grinberg, 'Defamation of Religions V. Freedom of Expression: Finding the Balance in a Democratic Society' (2006) 18 *Sri Lanka Journal of International Law*, 203–204; Graham, 'Defamation of Religions', 71.

[111] Vance, 'Permissibility of Incitement to Religious Hatred Offences', 244; Scolnicov, *The Right to Religious Freedom in International Law*, pp. 210–211; Waldron, *The Harm in Hate Speech*, pp. 120, 123; Temperman, 'Blasphemy', 531.

[112] Scolnicov, *The Right to Religious Freedom in International Law*, pp. 208, 210.

[113] Kapai and Cheung, 'Hanging in a Balance', 75.

[114] *Otto-Preminger-Institut v. Austria*, paras. 47–48.

[115] See for example *Otto-Preminger-Institut v. Austria*.

[116] Anthony Bradney, *Law and Faith in a Skeptical Age* (Routledge-Cavendish, 2009), p. 144; Cumper, 'Outlawing Incitement to Religious Hatred', 249–250, 253; Vance, 'Permissibility of Incitement to Religious Hatred Offences', 203.

to the post-9/11 demands of the UK Muslim community for protection against prejudice and hatred.[117] The issue of how to distinguish between incitement to hatred targeting religious *believers* and incitement to hatred targeting religious *beliefs* was at the heart of controversial discussions over the drafting of this law.[118] The enacted offence stipulates that '[a] person who publishes or distributes written material which is threatening is guilty of an offence if he intends thereby to stir up religious hatred'.[119] The confinement of the offence to threatening forms of expression narrowed its scope significantly; one commentator has gone so far as to consider its scope non-existent.[120] The offence includes a clause that draws a sharp distinction between incitement to hatred against religious believers and against the beliefs themselves, and prohibition is restricted to the former.[121] This clause stipulates that

> [n]othing in this Part shall be read or given effect in a way which prohibits or restricts discussion, criticism or expressions of antipathy, dislike, ridicule, insult or abuse of particular religions or the beliefs or practices of their adherents, or of any other belief system or the beliefs or practices of its adherents, or proselytizing or urging adherents of a different religion or belief system to cease practising their religion or belief system.[122]

The inclusion of this clause was widely perceived as limiting the prospects of successful prosecutions under the legislation, rendering it more or less symbolic.[123] In fact, the enactment of this legislation was one of the factors that justified abolishing the offence of blasphemy in England and Wales in 2008.[124]

Certain characteristics of the period during which Islamic states proposed their standards on religious hate speech at the UN are particularly relevant to understanding the resistance of Western states to those standards. Currently, blasphemy offences in the West are mostly being de jure abolished or de facto deactivated.[125] The legal protection of Christian religious beliefs, doctrine, and symbols has a long tradition in the West and originally evolved at a time when religion and the state were closely interwoven.[126] With the gradual decoupling of state and religion in

---

[117] Werbner, 'Islamophobia: Incitement to Religious Hatred', 5; Maleiha Malik, 'Extreme Speech and Liberalism', in Ivan Hare and James Weinstein (eds.), *Extreme Speech and Democracy* (Oxford University Press, 2009), p. 101.

[118] Cumper, 'Outlawing Incitement to Religious Hatred', 249–250, 253, 266; Vance, 'Permissibility of Incitement to Religious Hatred Offences', 203; Bradney, *Law and Faith*, p. 144.

[119] Racial and Religious Hatred Act 2006, c.1 (England and Wales).

[120] Hare, 'Blasphemy and incitement to religious hatred', p. 310.

[121] Adhar and Leigh, *Religious Freedom in the Liberal State*, p. 453.

[122] Racial and Religious Hatred Act 2006 (England and Wales), sch., s. 29J.

[123] Oliva, 'The Legal Protection of Believers', 83, 85–86; Hare, 'Blasphemy and incitement to religious hatred', p. 310; Adhar and Leigh, *Religious Freedom in the Liberal State*, p. 454.

[124] Hare, 'Blasphemy and incitement to religious hatred', p. 300.

[125] Blasphemy offences now exist in a small number of countries of Council of Europe Austria, Denmark, Finland, Greece, Ireland, Italy, Liechtenstein, Netherlands, and San Marino. See the Venice Commission Report, para. 19.

[126] Grimm, 'Freedom of speech in a globalized world', p. 17.

Western states, blasphemy offences have become increasingly irrelevant.[127] The change of religion's place in the secular state, where freedom of religion has become more dependent on the state's neutrality in religious issues, has changed the boundaries of protection accorded to religious speech in the West.[128] Blasphemy offences, the 'world's oldest hate speech provisions',[129] have become 'the most arcane and archaic pieces of European legislation'[130] and have 'waned to the point of near universally recognized obsolescence'.[131] The number of prosecutions pursuant to blasphemy laws has decreased to the point where the laws are rarely activated[132] and punishments thereunder have 'passed into history'.[133] In the past few years, EU institutions have issued recommendations calling upon European states to review their offences on blasphemy, religious insult, and insults to religious feelings.[134] These recommendations were justified by invoking 'the greater diversity of religious beliefs in Europe and the democratic principle of the separation of state and religion'.[135] Opponents to the introduction of the concept of defamation of religion perceived it to be 'blasphemy in new clothes'.[136] In their opinion, the concept mixes two normative systems, law, and religion, which should be kept separate, with the former's content not being influenced by the latter.[137] Accordingly, efforts to create new international standards obliging states to prohibit defamation of religions ran counter to contemporaneous trends in the West regarding blasphemy offences. The standard-setting efforts were therefore perceived as an attempt to turn the clock back in Western states.[138]

Moreover, the standard-setting efforts of Islamic states coincided temporally with the increasing delegitimization, by the UN human rights machinery, of domestic legislation restricting freedom of expression based on religious defamation, blasphemy, or insult to religious feelings. In the context of reviewing state parties' periodic reports, the HRCttee has expressed negative views on blasphemy laws and similar legal provisions on the basis that they discriminate against adherents

---

[127] Blitt, 'The Bottom up Journey of "Defamation of Religion"', 7.
[128] Grimm, 'Freedom of speech in a globalized world', p. 18.
[129] Haraszti, 'Forward', p. xvii.
[130] Cecile Laborde, 'The Danish Cartoon Controversy and the Challenges of Multicultural Politics: A Discussion of the Cartoons That Shook the World' (2011) 9(3) *Perspectives on Politics*, 603.
[131] Levey and Modood, 'Muhammad Cartoons', 436.
[132] Jytte Klausen, *The Cartoons That Shook the World* (Yale University Press, 2009), p. 144.
[133] Drinan, *Can God & Caesar Coexist?*, p. 220.
[134] The Venice Commission Report, para. 89.c; 'Recommendation of Parliamentary Assembly of Council of Europe Number 1805 on Blasphemy, Religious Insults and Hate Speech against Persons on Grounds of Their Religion' (2007), available at http://assembly.coe.int/Documents/AdoptedText/ta07/EREC1805.htm, paras. 10–11.
[135] Parliamentary Assembly, 'Report of the Blasphemy, Religious Insults and Hate Speech against Persons on Grounds of Their Religion', Doc. 11296 (8 June 2007), available at https://assembly.coe.int/nw/xml/XRef/X2H-Xref-ViewHTML.asp?FileID=11521&lang=EN.
[136] Langer, *Religious Offence*, p. 260.
[137] Langer, *Religious Offence*, p. 260.
[138] Grimm, 'Freedom of speech in a globalized world', p. 17.

of specific religions and thereby restrict religious expression. For example, it expressed alarm at the 'criminal prosecution, imprisonment and fining of authors and journalists in connection with their non-violent expression of opinion, and artistic expression, which in some cases has been deemed to be disrespectful of Islam' in Kuwait.[139] The committee also expressed regret that the law on defamation of religion in Indonesia, 'which prohibits the interpretations of religious doctrines considered divergent of the teachings of protected and recognised religions … unduly restricts the freedom of religion and expression of religious minorities'.[140] The committee held that this law 'is inconsistent with the provisions of the Covenant and that it should be repealed forthwith'. The committee, on the other hand, 'welcome[d] the adoption of the Criminal Justice and Immigration Act 2008 abolishing the common law offences of blasphemy in England and Wales'.[141]

A number of UN Special Rapporteurs have criticized blasphemy laws and other similar provisions for restricting the legitimate exercise of freedom of expression, especially inter-religious and intra-religious criticism. They have also condemned their frequent discriminatory application, which has infringed upon the rights of religious minorities and exacerbated religious intolerance.[142]

There are recognized links, commonalities, and blurred lines between expressions that are defamatory of religions and expressions that are likely to raise or strengthen hostile feelings vis-à-vis religious adherents. While the right to protection from religious hate speech clearly prohibits the latter, Islamic states also sought prohibition of the former under IHRL. Their proposed standards presumed an automatic causation between expressions that defame, contempt, or insult religions, on the one hand, and incitement to harms that infringe upon the rights of religious adherents, on the other, which was refuted absolutely by opponents to these standards. In fact, the correlation between defamation of religion and incitement to religious discrimination, hostility, or violence is neither automatic or inevitable, nor absolutely impossible. Instead, it should be empirically examined without holding predetermined assumptions.[143] Defamation of religion could (under certain circumstances and within specific contexts) overlap, in practical terms if not in strictly normative or conceptual terms, with such incitement against religious adherents, as examined more fully in Chapter 2 (Section 2.6).[144]

In its recently issued General Comment No. 34 on freedom of expression, the HRCttee recognized Article 20(2) as the benchmark for determining the consistency of blasphemy and defamation of religious laws with IHRL. The committee affirmed

[139] CCPR/CO/69/KWT, para. 20.
[140] CCPR/C/IDN/CO/1, para. 25.
[141] CCPR/C/GBR/CO/6, para. 4.
[142] Heiner Bielefeldt et al., Joint Submission to OHCHR Expert Workshop on Africa; Githu Muigai et al., 'Joint Statement on "Freedom of Expression and Incitement to Racial or Religious Hatred"'; E/CN.4/2001/64 (Annex V); A/HRC/2/3, para. 42.
[143] Levey and Modood, 'Muhammad Cartoons', 435.
[144] Rosenfeld, 'Hate speech in constitutional jurisprudence', p. 277.

that 'prohibitions of displays of lack of respect for a religion or other belief system, including blasphemy laws' are incompatible with the ICCPR, *except* under 'the specific circumstances' stipulated in Article 20(2).[145] The committee added that such prohibitions must comply with the strict requirements of Article 19(3), as well as Articles 2, 5, 17, 18, and 26 of the ICCPR.[146] It emphasized that such laws should not discriminate in favour of, or against, any particular religion or belief system, or in favour of religious believers over non-believers.[147] Furthermore, the committee added that laws prohibiting defamation of religion should not be employed to 'prevent or punish criticism of religious leaders or commentary on religious doctrine and tenets of faith'.[148] The committee's stance is therefore symptomatic of its recognition of possible overlaps between the prohibition of defamation of religion and states' obligations under Article 20(2). The committee has been eager to stipulate a number of safeguards to ensure states' compliance with IHRL and to underline the differences between incitement to religious discrimination, hostility, or violence, and commentary on religious matters or criticism of religious leaders. Similarly, Frank La Rue, the former UN Special Rapporteur on freedom of expression, emphasized that Article 20(2) is the benchmark for determining whether anti-religious expressions represent legitimate exercise of freedom of expression. He opined that

> the right to freedom of expression includes the right to scrutinize, debate openly, make statements that offend, shock and disturb, and criticize belief systems, opinions and institutions, including religious ones, *provided that they do not advocate hatred that incites hostility, discrimination or violence* [my emphasis].[149]

5.5 THE PROPOSED STANDARDS' INTERACTION WITH THE NOTION OF RACISM

The solutions on combating defamation of religion which Islamic states presented to the UN's HRC fell under the agenda item of racism. The resolutions advanced the argument that incitement to religious hatred and defamation of religions, especially the profiling of individuals based on their religion, represented contemporary manifestations of racism.[150] The resolutions also urged states to take action to prohibit 'the dissemination . . . of racist and xenophobic ideas and material aimed

[145] CCPR, General Comment no. 34.
[146] CCPR, General Comment no. 34, para. 48.
[147] CCPR, General Comment no. 34, para. 48.
[148] CCPR, General Comment no. 34, para. 48.
[149] A/67/537, para. 53.
[150] A/HRC/4/9, para. 7; A/HRC/7/19, para. 3; Statement of Pakistan on behalf of OIC Member States Delivered at the UN Human Rights Council (25 September 2007), available at http://portal .ohchr.org/portal/page/portal/HRCExtranet/6thSession/DraftResolutions/AHRC6L.8Rev.1 /Pakistan(OIC).pdf.

at any religion or its followers that constitute[s] incitement to racial and religious hatred, hostility and violence'.[151] The resolutions asserted that prohibition of religious defamation was consistent with freedom of expression, citing in support of this proposition the CERD's General Recommendation No. 15, which emphasized the compatibility between freedom of expression and the prohibition of expressions on racial superiority or hatred.[152] The resolutions declared this General Recommendation 'equally applicable to the question of incitement to religious hatred'.[153] Moreover, the resolutions called upon the UN Special Rapporteur on racism to report on the manifestations of defamation of religion.[154]

Within the Ad Hoc Committee, Islamic states contended that contemporary racism was focused on discrimination on the basis of religious identity.[155] The standards proposed by African and Islamic states considered defamatory religious expressions to be a manifestation of 'racio-religious' intolerance involving racial profiling against religious adherents.[156] They sought to extend the scope of racial hatred to include hatred against religious groups.[157] African and Islamic states' proposals sought to legally prohibit organizations that promote or justify religious hatred along the same lines that the ICERD currently prohibits organizations that promote racial hatred.[158] Islamic states wanted to extend the ban of racist speech under the ICERD, which includes the prohibition of racist ideas regardless of their potential or actual consequences, to cover defamation of religion.[159]

Islamic states also considered contempt of religion, negative profiling of religious adherents, and offence to religious feelings not only to be violations of the international norm prohibiting incitement, and violations of freedom of religion, but also to be contemporary forms of racism and forms of racio-religious intolerance. Their suggested standards conflated manifestations of religious hatred with racism. Islamic states considered defamation of religion to be a proxy for incitement to hatred, discrimination, or violence against religious adherents, not only on the basis of their religious identities but also on the basis of their racial and ethnic identities.[160]

The rising challenges of Islamophobia in the aftermath of 9/11 prompted Islamic states to call for the overlaps between racism and religious prejudice to be considered within the context of IHRL. They argued that existing international norms against racism did not sufficiently address the links between race and religion.[161] Islamic states drew an analogy between anti-Semitism and post-9/11 Islamophobia.

[151] A/HRC/7/19, para. 8.
[152] General Recommendation No. 15.
[153] A/HRC/7/19, para. 13; A/HRC/13/16, para. 12.
[154] A/HRC/4/9, para. 12.
[155] A/HRC/10/88, para. 9.
[156] A/HRC/10/88, paras. 10, 35, 65; A/HRC/13/58, para. 103.
[157] A/HRC/13/58, para. 26(1).
[158] A/HRC/13/58, paras. 26(2)(b), 29.
[159] A/HRC/10/88, para. 66; A/HRC/13/58, paras. 26, 29.
[160] A/HRC/10/88, para. 65.
[161] A/HRC/10/88, paras. 53–54.

They expressed their fears that defamation of Islam 'might become as widespread and endemic as anti-Semitism had been in the past'.[162] They considered the crime of incitement to racial hatred to encompass offences motivated by religious hatred against immigrant communities.[163] They framed Islamophobia as a multifaceted phenomenon that takes on racio-religious tones when expressed against migrants and also takes the form of racial profiling in the context of the war against terrorism.[164] OIC member states were cognizant that the recognition of Islamophobia as anti-Muslim racism would grant Muslims wider legal protection against religious hate speech, similar to the level of protection afforded to Jews, as a racial and religious group, against anti-Semitism in the West.

In the aftermath of 9/11, analogies have been drawn between Islamophobia and anti-Semitism as forms of racism in Europe.[165] Although Muslims do not all share the same ethnicity or race, much Islamophobia in Western states might be argued to take the form of racism, especially given that Muslims do not typically form the ethnic majority in these states.[166] Levey and Modood point out that 'cultural and religious groups also can be racialized; that Muslims can be the victims of racism qua Muslims as well as qua Asians or Arabs or Bosnians'.[167] For example, Bosnian Muslims were targeted as an ethnic group.[168] In many instances, hateful expressions of anti-Arab and anti-Muslim sentiment overlap with one another and the lines separating racial and religious identities get blurred, particularly given that Arab minorities are mostly Muslim.[169] In the context of the fight against terrorism in a post-9/11 world, manifestations of Islamophobia often assume both racial and religious components.[170] A number of academic writings refer to the subjection of Muslims in Europe to a discourse of racialization, involving the targeting of persons who are visually identifiable as Muslims, and governmental 'racial profiling' of Muslims on the basis of their visual appearance.[171] Overlaps between anti-Muslim and anti-Islamic prejudice have notably coloured Islamophobia with elements of racism.[172] Viljoen and Madlingozi have gone so far as to hold that the challenges of Islamophobia in the post-9/11 era indicate that religious intolerance and

[162] E/CN.4/1999/SR.61 19, para. 1; A/HRC/10/88, para. 32.

[163] A/HRC/10/88, Annex I.

[164] A/CONF.211/PC.3/10, 3.

[165] Modood, 'The place of muslims in british secular multiculturalism', p. 242.

[166] Adhar and Leigh, *Religious Freedom in the Liberal State*, p. 434.

[167] Levey and Modood, 'Muhammad Cartoons', 443.

[168] Tariq Modood, Randall Hansen, Erik Bleich, Brendan O'Leary, and Joseph H. Carens, 'The Danish Cartoon Affair: Free Speech, Racism, Islamism, and Integration' (2006) 44 (5) *International Migration*, 56; Rosenfeld, 'Hate speech in constitutional jurisprudence', pp. 276–277.

[169] Modood et al., 'The Danish Cartoon Affair', 17, 55, 58; Rosenfeld, 'Hate speech in constitutional jurisprudence', p. 277.

[170] Alves, 'Race and Religion', 942, 981.

[171] Nasar Meer and Tariq Modood, 'Refutations of Racism in the "Muslim Question"' (2009) 43 (3–4) *Patterns of Prejudice*, 339, 343; Levey and Modood, 'Muhammad Cartoons', 441.

[172] Fernne Brennan, 'Punishing Islamophobic Hostility: Are Any Lessons to Be Learned from Racially Hostile Crimes?' (2003) 8 *Journal of Civil Liberties*, 49; Werbner, 'Islamophobia: Incitement to

discrimination are tied to the substantive scope of the ICERD.[173] It is also worth noting that Doudou Diène, the former UN Special Rapporteur on racism, categorized anti-Semitism, Christophobia, and Islamophobia as manifestations of religious defamation as well as racial and religious hatred.[174]

Scepticism towards the existence of a racial aspect to Islamophobia has created resistance within Western legal systems to equating Islamophobia with anti-Semitism.[175] Anti-Semitism is considered to be unique in combining both racist and anti-religious hate.[176] Historically, Jews have been viewed as having distinct ethnic origins; Judaism is widely considered a mono-ethnic religion.[177] On the other hand, Islamophobia and Christophobia are less readily characterized as forms of anti-racial hatred since Muslims and Christians are not monoracial and thus the links between their religious and racial identities are less rigid.[178] Accordingly, it is controversial to consider the situations of Muslim and Jewish minorities comparable. On a terminological level, anti-Semitism clearly refers to discrimination against or persecution of people, not faith. The discrimination is directed towards a particular group and the individuals that belong to it.[179]

The categorization by Islamic states of religious hate speech as a contemporary manifestation of racism was an attempt to legitimize their proposed international standards and might potentially have provided a way through the impasse ultimately reached when negotiating the standards, which, as we have seen, lay at the intersection between three rights: freedom of religion, freedom of expression, and the right to protection from incitement to discrimination, hostility, or violence. Nevertheless, many states, including EU member states, Canada, India, and a number of UN Special Rapporteurs rejected any equivalence between religious intolerance and racism, or between religious defamation and racist speech.[180] Opponents of the

Religious Hatred', 5; Meer and Modood, 'Refutations of Racism', 339, 343; Modood et al., 'The Danish Cartoon Affair', 55, 58; Rosenfeld, 'Hate speech in constitutional jurisprudence', p. 227.

[173] E/CN.4/2006/WG.21/BP.2.

[174] A/HRC/4/19, 2.

[175] Meer and Modood, 'Refutations of Racism', 338.

[176] Nazila Ghanea-Hercock, '"Phobias" and "Isms": Recognition of difference or the slippery slope of particularisms?' in Nazila Ghanea-Hercock, Alan Stephens, and Raphael Walden (eds.), *Does God Believe in Human Rights? Essays on Religion and Human Rights* (Martinus Nijhoff Publishers, 2007), p. 222.

[177] Mari J. Matsuda, 'Outsider jurisprudence: Toward a victim's analysis of racial hate messages', in Monroe H. Freedman and Eric M. Freedman (eds.), *Group Defamation and Freedom of Speech: The Relationship between Language and Violence* (Greenwood Press, 1995), p. 93; Rosenfeld, 'Hate speech in constitutional jurisprudence', p. 276.

[178] Ghanea-Hercock, 'Phobias', p. 222; Bradney, *Law and Faith*, p. 84.

[179] Langer, *Religious Offence*, pp. 243–244.

[180] Statement on behalf of European Union Member States delivered at the Commission on Human Rights, 2001, http://daccess-dds-ny.un.org/doc/UNDOC/GEN/G01/132/47/PDF/G0113247.pdf?OpenElement; Statement of Canada delivered at the UN Commission on Human Rights (2001), available at http://daccess-dds-ny.un.org/doc/UNDOC/GEN/G01/132/47/PDF/G0113247.pdf?OpenElement; Statement of India delivered at the UN Human Rights Council (27 March 2008), available at http://portal.ohchr.org/portal/page/portal/HRCExtranet/

standards resisted the appeal made by Islamic states to the fight against racism. They refused to include religious hatred within the general compass of racism under IHRL.

As we have seen, Islamic states' attempt to extend the scope of racial hatred to include defamation of religions and to place race and religion on an equal footing as proscribed hate speech grounds under IHRL further fuelled the complexities of their standard-setting efforts. This section will shed light on the normative conundrums associated with their failed attempts.

The international norm prohibiting racist hate speech was itself the outcome of a difficult compromise among negotiating states during the drafting of the ICERD, given its interaction with the exercise of freedom of expression.[181] In particular, the inclusion of the clause 'all dissemination of ideas based on racial superiority or hatred' was very controversial due to fears, mainly expressed by Western states, of imposing excessive restrictions on freedoms of expression and association.[182] The 'due regard' clause was added to address these Western fears.[183] However, twenty state parties to the ICERD (again, mostly Western states)[184] submitted either reservations to, or interpretive statements in relation to, Article 4, based on concerns that it would interfere materially with the exercise of freedoms of expression and association. A number of scholars also shared the position, expressed by some states, that Article 4 is inherently problematic on the basis that it jeopardizes those two freedoms.[185] The fact that Article 4 imposes more restrictions on racist speech than Article 20(2) has even led some commentators to consider it inconsistent with Article 20(2).[186]

Article 1 of the ICERD recognizes only race, colour, descent, and national or ethnic origin as grounds of racism, with no reference to religion. Religion is mentioned in Article 5, in which the 'right to freedom of thought, conscience and religion' is listed among the civil rights that parties undertake to protect for their citizens regardless of their race. Although the CERD has addressed the religious freedoms of racial and ethnic groups,[187] it has nevertheless avoided directly

7th Session/DraftResolutions/AHRC7L.15/India.pdf; Heiner Bielefeldt et al., Joint Submission to OHCHR Expert Workshop on Africa; A/HRC/2/3, 12.

[181] Lerner, *The UN Convention*, p. 47; Noorloos, *Hate Speech Revisited*, p. 168.

[182] Noorloos, *Hate Speech Revisited*, p. 164.

[183] Farrior, 'Molding the Matrix', 49.

[184] Antigua and Barbuda, Australia, Austria, the Bahamas, Barbados, Belgium, Fiji, France, Ireland, Italy, Japan, Malta, Monaco, Nepal, Papua New Guinea, Switzerland, Thailand, Tonga, the United Kingdom, and the United States.

[185] Theodor Meron, *Human Rights Law-Making in the United Nations: A Critique of Instruments and Process* (Clarendon Press, Oxford University Press, 1986), 25; Mendel, 'Does international law provide for consistent rules on hate speech?', p. 419; Boyle and Baldaccini, 'A critical evaluation', p. 160; Richards, *Free Speech*, p. 180; Partsch, Racial Speech, pp. 27–28; Callamard, 'Towards an Interpretation of Article 20 of the ICCPR', 16.

[186] Parmar, 'The Challenge of Defamation of Religion', 369; Mendel, 'Does international law provide for consistent rules on hate speech?', p. 1.

[187] Alves, 'Race and Religion', 942.

addressing advocacy of religious hatred. In its General Recommendation No. 35, the CERD affirmed that it had addressed 'hate speech targeting persons belonging to certain ethnic groups who profess or practice a religion different from the majority, including expressions of Islamophobia, anti-Semitism and other similar manifest-ations of hatred against ethno-religious groups'.[188] It justified its approach in this regard by reference to the principle of intersectionality between different grounds of discrimination. In fact, racial discrimination impacts upon the enjoyment of reli-gious freedom. However, the committee was cautious, when exercising its mandate, not to conflate the racial and religious grounds of hate speech.[189] In the aftermath of the Danish cartoons affair, some members of the committee who came from Islamic countries suggested that the committee should adopt a general recommendation calling upon state parties to prohibit expressions defamatory to religion, in accord-ance with their obligations under Article 4 of the ICERD.[190] However, other members of the committee refused to issue a recommendation to that effect, claiming that it fell outside the committee's mandate.[191] The committee has expli-citly stated that it is not authorized to address discrimination based only on religious grounds in the absence of any nexus with the discrimination grounds recognized in the ICERD. In 2007, the committee declared a communication alleging a violation of Article 4 to be inadmissible on the basis that 'the impugned statements specifically refer to the Koran, to Islam and to Muslims in General'[192] and 'no specific national or ethnic groups were directly targeted'.[193] The committee elaborated that 'Islam is not a religion practiced solely by a particular group'[194] and that Muslims were of heterogeneous origin.[195]

The prospect of applying the criteria for restricting racist speech to the advocacy of religious hatred has also been resisted by number of scholars.[196] Such resistance is based on the following argumentative process; religion is widely considered to be a chosen, voluntary, acquired, and changeable system of ideas and values; race, on the other hand, is an innate, inherited, and immutable identity,[197] widely conceived

---

[188]   General Recommendation No. 35, para. 6.
[189]   Patrick Thornberry, 'Forms of Hate Speech and the Convention on the Elimination of All Forms of Racial Discrimination (ICERD)' (2010) 5(2) *Religion & Human Rights*, 114.
[190]   Alves, 'Race and Religion', 972.
[191]   Alves, 'Race and Religion', 972.
[192]   *P. S. N. v. Denmark*, Communication no. 36/2006, CERD (8 August 2007), para. 6.2.
[193]   *P. S. N. v. Denmark*, para. 6.2.
[194]   *P. S. N. v. Denmark*, para. 6.3.
[195]   *P. S. N. v. Denmark*, para. 6.2.
[196]   Modood et al., 'The Danish Cartoon Affair', 7, 12, 46; Heiner Bielefeldt et al., Joint Submission to OHCHR Expert Workshop on Africa; 'Report of Select Committee on Religious Offences in England and Wales' (June 2003), HL 95-I, available at www.parliament.the-stationery-office.co.uk/pa/ld200203/ldselect/ldrelof/95/95.pdf, 26; Ghanea, 'Nature and Means of Effective Remedies'; Scolnicov, *The Right to Religious Freedom in International Law*, pp. 195, 208.
[197]   Modood et al., 'The Danish Cartoon Affair', 42, 47; Heiner Bielefeldt et al., Joint Submission to OHCHR Expert Workshop on Africa, 10; A/HRC/2/3, 12; Kretzmer, 'Freedom of Speech and Racism', 467; Delgado, 'Words That Wound', 136; Cumper, 'Inciting religious hatred', p. 253.

as being 'without content, ideology, teachings, or dogma',[198] and 'not synonymous with a system of beliefs'.[199] The element of choice, a characteristic of religious identity which is absent from racial identity, arguably demands greater latitude to be given to the free discussion of religious matters.[200] It is necessary to consider the wider context of societal or political debates, or even disputes on religious matters, in order to affirm the principle of autonomy in the exercise of religious freedoms.[201] Religions may even be regarded as competing with one another; they make claims that might be incompatible. The same dynamics are not applicable to racial discourse.[202] The inseparability of race from an individual belonging to that particular race demands the prohibition of expressions targeting races as well as the members of racial groups.[203] By contrast, the perceived separation between religions per se and the dignity of believers requires the prohibition of expressions that target members of religious groups but not those that target the tenets of their religions.[204] Moreover, racist speech neither establishes nor facilitates the exercise of any human right; there are no racial freedoms that need to be safeguarded or enhanced.[205] By contrast, claims of religious superiority might, for example, be regarded as an aspect of religious freedom, and in particular the right to manifest religion.[206] Speech that is critical of race is categorically and absolutely unacceptable, whereas speech that is critical of religion is not necessarily so.[207] On a practical level, racist expressions are more easily identified and objectively assessed than anti-religious speech or claims of religious superiority.[208]

These differences between racist and religious hate advocacy have been used to justify different criteria for prohibitions on racist speech and the advocacy of

---

[198] 'Report of Select Committee on Religious Offences in England and Wales', Vol. II, 72.

[199] Cumper, 'Outlawing Incitement to Religious Hatred', 261.

[200] Hare, 'Blasphemy and incitement to religious hatred', p. 308.

[201] Bradney, *Law and Faith*, pp. 93–94; Cumper, 'Outlawing Incitement to Religious Hatred', 259; 'Report of Select Committee on Religious Offences in England and Wales', 28; Noorloos, *Hate Speech Revisited*, p. 27.

[202] Jogchum Vrielink, 'Islamophobia and the Law: Belgian Hate Speech Legislation and the Wilful Destruction of the Koran'(2014)14 (1) *International Journal of Discrimination and the Law*, 57; Hare, 'Blasphemy and incitement to religious hatred', p. 308.

[203] 'Report of Select Committee on Religious Offences in England and Wales', 27.

[204] 'Report of Select Committee on Religious Offences in England and Wales', 27.

[205] Githu Muigai et al., 'Joint Statement on "Freedom of Expression and Incitement to Racial or Religious Hatred"'; Heiner Bielefeldt et al., Joint Submission to OHCHR Expert Workshop on Africa; Ghanea, 'Nature and Means of Effective Remedies', 12–13; Scolnicov, *The Right to Religious Freedom in International Law*, pp. 32, 195, 206, 208.

[206] Githu Muigai et al., 'Joint Statement on "Freedom of Expression and Incitement to Racial or Religious Hatred"'; Heiner Bielefeldt et al., Joint Submission to OHCHR Expert Workshop on Africa; Ghanea, 'Nature and Means of Effective Remedies'; Scolnicov, *The Right to Religious Freedom in International Law*, pp. 32, 195, 206, 208.

[207] Temperman, *Religious Hatred*, p. 5.

[208] Githu Muigai et al., 'Joint Statement on "Freedom of Expression and Incitement to Racial or Religious Hatred"'; Waldron, *The Harm in Hate Speech*, p. 118.

religious hatred.[209] More precisely, they are used to justify the argument that the threshold for the latter prohibition should be kept higher than the former. A number of UN Special Rapporteurs have emphasized that 'the difficult question of what precisely constitutes religious hatred, at any rate, cannot be answered by simply applying definitions found in the area of racial hatred'.[210]

The United Kingdom's enactment of the Racial and Religious Hatred Act 2006, which incorporated an offence of incitement to religious hatred, exemplified Western resistance to legal regulation of advocacy of religious hatred on a similar basis to racist speech. The UK government initially sought to add a ground of religious hatred to the existing offence of incitement to racial hatred, thereby treating religion and race on an equal footing.[211] However, this was subject to considerable criticism from civil society organizations that feared excessive limitation of freedom of expression on religious matters.[212] Accordingly, the offence of incitement to religious hatred, as enacted in the 2006 Act, adopted a higher threshold for restricting freedom of expression.[213] This offence is limited to 'threatening words or behaviour', rather than the criteria of abusive and insulting words applicable to the offence of incitement to racial hatred.[214] The criteria used for identifying incitement to religious hatred restricts the offence's scope, in practice, to incidents 'where violence is incited or a fear of violence is reasonable apprehended'.[215] Moreover, a freedom of expression clause, which has no equivalent provision in the offence of incitement to racial hatred, was added to the Act in order to safeguard against possible infringement of freedom of expression on religious issues.

On a different view, the legal equation of religious hate speech with racist speech can be justified on a number of bases. Similarities between religion and race in terms of their functional importance and role in identity formation (for both individuals and groups) have been identified.[216] Religious identities might, for social purposes, be regarded as unchangeable or involuntary in a similar way to racial identities,[217] since they are 'instilled at an early age, transferred by family, and taught as part of a person's value and belief system' or may be imposed on this by a higher authority.[218] Thornberry contends that 'only in some cases is [religion] the product of deliberate choice' and that 'the voluntarist paradigm does not always fit the material of everyday life'.[219] Vrielink also argues that most adherents to a religion do not

---

[209] 'Report of Select Committee on Religious Offences in England and Wales', 27.

[210] Heiner Bielefeldt et al., Joint Submission to OHCHR Expert Workshop on Africa.

[211] Bradney, *Law and Faith*, p. 144; Malik, 'Extreme speech', p. 101.

[212] Cumper, 'Outlawing Incitement to Religious Hatred', 254; Noorloos, *Hate Speech Revisited*, p. 309.

[213] Bradney, *Law and Faith*, p. 81.

[214] Racial and Religious Hatred Act 2006, c.1 (England and Wales).

[215] Adhar and Leigh, *Religious Freedom in the Liberal State*, p. 452.

[216] Yang, 'Race, Religion and Cultural Identity', 123.

[217] Yang, 'Race, Religion and Cultural Identity', 132–133; Meer and Modood, 'Refutations of Racism', 345.

[218] Yang, 'Race, Religion and Cultural Identity', 132–133.

[219] Thornberry, 'Forms of Hate Speech', 114–115.

actively choose their beliefs but are instead 'born into them'.[220] Similarly, Cox contends that 'for many religious devotees their religion is immutable'.[221] Thus, the element of choice is not always a valid distinction between religion and race or a valid justification for imposing different limitations on racist and religious forms of hate speech.[222] Furthermore, religion has traditionally been one of the defining characteristics of ethnicity, and the latter is universally recognized as one of the grounds of racism.[223] As former UN Special Rapporteur on freedom of religion Abdelfattah Amor clarifies, 'religion shares something of the definition of ethnicity, just as ethnicity is basic to religious identity'.[224] Yang also argues that, within the context of legal regulation, 'the dichotomy of biology and belief through which race and religion is generally viewed is largely unjustified'.[225] Meer and Modood reject the characterization of racism as a form of 'inherentism' or 'biological determinism'. In response to the increasingly complex evolution of racism, they suggest using the concept of 'cultural racism' instead of the 'narrow' definition of racism. The former 'is not solely premised on conceptions of biology in a way that ignores religion, culture and so forth' but embraces ethno-cultural groups as well.[226] Furthermore, in response to the contention that racism, unlike religion, is 'content-free', Noorloos argues that racism embodies a set of 'biological and national-territorial ideas' and that 'while the former have lost ground, the coupling of normative differences to territory lives forth in culturalist discourse, through the idea that the dominant national culture is superior to other cultures'.[227] The identification of racist speech is not always a straightforward exercise; it can be as problematic as religious hate speech. Racist hate speech is often disguised as core political speech or criticism of government policies, in particular those concerning integration or migration.[228]

In addition to the aforementioned analogies between racial and religious identities, religious hatred might, in practice, entail hatred against the race to which most adherents of a certain religion belong.[229] In many communities, religion is closely bound to race or nationality, and religious groups are often constructed as racial groups.[230] Manifestations of religious hatred often overlap with racial or ethnic hatred.[231] Thus, in many instances, it is impossible to distinguish between racial

[220]   Jogchum Vrielink, 'Islamophobia and the Law: Belgian Hate Speech Legislation and the Wilful Destruction of the Koran' (2014) 14 (1) *International Journal of Discrimination and the Law*, 57.
[221]   Neville Cox, 'Blasphemy, Holocaust Denial, and the Control of Profoundly Unacceptable Speech' (2014) 62 *American Journal of Comparative Law*, 745.
[222]   Thornberry, 'Forms of Hate Speech', 114–115.
[223]   Alves, 'Race and Religion', 951; Yang, 'Race, Religion and Cultural Identity', 127.
[224]   A/CONF.189/PC.1/7, para. 122.
[225]   Yang, 'Race, Religion and Cultural Identity', 123.
[226]   Meer and Modood, 'Refutations of Racism', 344.
[227]   Noorloos, *Hate Speech Revisited*, p. 27.
[228]   Weinstein, *Hate Speech and Pornography*, p. 160.
[229]   Modood et al., 'The Danish Cartoon Affair', 12, 17.
[230]   Yang, 'Race, Religion and Cultural Identity', 121.
[231]   A/HRC/25/58, para. 17.

and religious discrimination.[232] As Gearty notes, some religions have a 'powerful ethnic tinge' and '[i]n such situations, the concept of religious intolerance must stand or fall apart from ethnicity in a way that is not altogether unproblematic'.[233] Rosenfeld also states, rightly, that racist and religious hate speech might have more similarities than differences in the context of religious minorities comprising immigrants of heterogeneous racial origin.[234]

Based on such correlations and overlaps, some scholars and human rights experts have recognized religious intolerance and negative stereotyping of religious groups as forms of anti-religious racism or contemporary manifestations of racism.[235] This position resembles Islamic states' position on their suggested hate speech standards. A number of scholars argue that there should be no element of discrimination in the levels of protection accorded to racial and religious groups against the harms of hate speech.[236] Lerner even considered the differences in legal treatment between racist speech and advocacy of religious hatred to be 'unfair' and 'illogical'.[237] In light of this, he contends that the protection provided by Article 4 of the ICERD to victims of racial hatred should similarly be extended to victims of religious hatred.[238] One commentator has even gone so far as to criticize Article 20(2) of the ICCPR for treating the religious and racial grounds of advocacy of hatred as equal and overlooking the distinctive character of expressions on religious issues as integral to the exercise of religious freedoms.[239] Viljoen and Madlingozi also criticized the definition of racial discrimination in the ICERD for omitting religion, especially as racism and religious intolerance have recently become more interwoven.[240] Doudou Diène, the former UN Special Rapporteur on racism, noted that the 'increasing trend in defamation of religions cannot be dissociated from a profound reflection on the ominous trends of racism, racial discrimination, xenophobia and related intolerance'.[241] He justified making such a connection by referencing the role of defamation of religion in 'legitimizing racist and discriminatory discourse'.[242] He considered religious hatred to be reflective of 'the resurgence of racism, racial discrimination and xenophobia'.[243]

---

[232] Yang, 'Race, Religion and Cultural Identity', 121.

[233] Conor A. Gearty, 'The internal and external "other" in the Union legal order: Racism, religious intolerance and xenophobia in Europe', in Philip Alston, Mara R. Bustelo, and James Heenan (eds.), *The EU and Human Rights* (Oxford University Press, 1999), p. 337.

[234] Rosenfeld, 'Hate speech in constitutional jurisprudence', p. 276.

[235] A/HRC/4/WG.3/6, para. 123; Modood et al., 'The Danish Cartoon Affair', 55.

[236] Rosenfeld, 'Hate speech in constitutional jurisprudence', p. 277; E/CN.4/2006/WG.21/BP.2; Lerner, 'Freedom of Expression and Incitement to Group Hatred', 4, 6.

[237] Lerner, 'Freedom of Expression and Incitement to Group Hatred', 92.

[238] Lerner, 'Freedom of Expression and Incitement to Group Hatred', 4, 6.

[239] Scolnicov, *The Right to Religious Freedom in International Law*, pp. 206, 208.

[240] E/CN.4/2006/WG.21/BP.2, para. 144.

[241] A/HRC/6/6, para. 5.

[242] A/HRC/6/6, para. 13.

[243] A/HRC/4/19, 2.

While recognizing that racism and religious prejudice are essentially two different phenomena and two distinct analytical categories, the analogies in motivations and repercussions which can be drawn between religious and racial grounds of incitement should not be overlooked.[244] The prohibition of racial and religious-based incitement protects the identity of groups, safeguards their rights of liberty and equality, and avoids the escalation of inter-group hostility. It cannot be ignored that racial characterization of religious groups and racially motivated religious hatred are both phenomena that have been identified in practice; certain incidences of incitement to hatred against religious adherents have been based on their racial or ethnic identities as well as their religious identities. Anti-religious hatred and anti-racial hatred may be conflated invisibly; hate speech targeting a religion can be a disguised form of hate speech targeting adherents of that religion on the basis of their racial, ethnic, or national origin.[245] However, this merely represents a possibility and is not inevitable.[246] Isolating religious prejudice from racial or ethnic prejudice in this context is often a difficult and complex exercise.[247] Accordingly, legal regulation of racially motivated religious hatred is far from straightforward, and such hatred is difficult to prove at the level of prosecution or adjudication.[248] Given the problems created by this complexity, it is remarkable neither IHRL nor its associated jurisprudence has satisfactorily addressed the issues located at the intersection between race and religion.[249]

Of course, the characteristics of the supporters and opponents of the aforementioned standard-setting attempts also played an important role in the eventual outcome of these attempts. These characteristics will be the focus of the next section.

5.6 THE CHARACTERISTICS OF SUPPORTERS AND OPPONENTS OF STANDARD-SETTING ATTEMPTS ON HATE SPEECH

New international human rights standards develop through multilateral diplomacy and negotiations between different states with competing national interests, cultures, and ideologies. States enjoy varied capacities to advance their normative human rights agendas at an international level.[250] Political and regional groups

---

[244] David Keane, 'Cartoon Violence and Freedom of Expression' (2008) 30(4) *Human Rights Quarterly*, 875; Modood et al., 'The Danish Cartoon Affair', 12; Lerner, 'Freedom of Expression and Incitement to Group Hatred', 89, 93; Yang, 'Race, Religion and Cultural Identity', 121.

[245] McGonagle, *Minority Rights*, p. 369; Rosenfeld, 'Hate speech in constitutional jurisprudence', p. 277.

[246] Kay Goodall, 'Incitement to Religious Hatred: All Talk and No Substance?' (2007) 70(1) *The Modern Law Review*, 99.

[247] Boyle, 'Religious intolerance', p. 62.

[248] Goodall, 'Incitement to Religious Hatred', 99.

[249] A/HRC/4/WG.3/6, para. 48; E/CN.4/2006/WG.21/BP.2.

[250] Upendra Baxi, *The Future of Human Rights* (Oxford University Press, 2002), p. 106; Makau Mutua, 'Standard Setting in Human Rights: Critique and Prognosis' (2007) 29(3) *Human Rights Quarterly*, 557.

within the UN often regard international human rights standard-setting processes as attempts at ideological impositions by other groups, so these usually prove politically contentious.

Such standard-setting processes expose the divisions between developing and developed states over the ideological and philosophical foundations of IHRL. Developing states seek to counter the ideological hegemony that Western and developed countries hold over these processes. Civil and political rights codified in IHRL instruments find their theoretical roots mostly in a liberal theory that conceives of rights as negatively defined: that is, as individually based and requiring either minimal or no interference from states.[251] These rights represent, as Brown notes, 'a contemporary, internationalised and universalised, version of the liberal position on rights'.[252] Developing states try to mitigate the influence of the Western libertarian paradigm on the codification of IHRL standards by presenting initiatives that are not solely informed by the liberal perception of rights. They give priority to addressing groups' rights; social, economic, and cultural rights; the right to development; duties in the exercise of rights; and combating contemporary manifestations of racism and intolerance. Their efforts in this regard usually meet resistance from Western countries on the basis that they are perceived to change the focus of IHRL and undermine its liberal and individualist character.

Standard-setting processes typically elicit opposing points of view among states when diagnosing the nature of protection gaps, i.e. whether these represent gaps in norms or in implementation.[253] This leads to polarized positions on whether or not there is a need to create new international human rights standards. Another source of tension is that suggested standards sometimes specifically target deficits in particular countries. The creation of international human rights standards is one way in which states can pursue an interest in the way that other states treat people within their jurisdiction. The supporters of new standards can use them as a mechanism for publicly criticizing other countries where deficiencies are particularly visible. This usually triggers resistance to the suggested standards from the targeted countries.[254]

These different sources of tension featured repeatedly in the failed standard-setting attempts pertaining to religious hate speech. Islamic states explicitly referred to the bias in international human rights standard-setting in favour of Western states' priorities.[255] They noted the unevenness in normative evolution between

---

[251] Steiner, Alston, and Goodman, *International Human Rights in Context*, pp. 517–539; Donnelly, *Universal Human Rights*, pp. 57–126; Griffin, *On Human Rights*, pp. 133–145; Mutua, 'Standard Setting in Human Rights', 550.

[252] Chris Brown, 'Universal human rights: A critique' in Timothy Dunne (ed.), *Human Rights in Global Politics* (Cambridge University Press, 1999), p. 105.

[253] International Council on Human Rights, *Human Rights Standards: Learning from Experience*, 8.

[254] Campbell, *Rights: A Critical Introduction*, p. 104.

[255] Idriss Jazairy Chairperson-Rapporteur of the Adhoc Committee on the Elaboration of Complementary Standards, 'Presentation of the Report of the Adhoc Committee on the Elaboration of Complementary Standards' (23 March 2010), available at http://portal.ohchr.org

international human rights instruments initiated by Western countries and those initiated by developing countries (specifically, on racism and the rights of migrants).[256] Moreover, Islamic states framed their proposed standards in response to their rising concern about the situation of Muslim minorities in the West.[257] They sought to exert political pressure on Western states to address the rising manifestations of Islamophobia in the aftermath of 9/11.[258] Resolutions on combating defamation of religion explicitly expressed concern regarding 'laws or administrative measures that have been specifically designed to control and monitor Muslim and Arab minorities, thereby stigmatizing them further and legitimating the discrimination that they experience'.[259] The accusatory tone used by Islamic states against the West has created a fraught political environment within the UN. Islamic states regarded Western states' opposition of the proposed standards as reflecting their desire to deflect the international community's attention away from Western states' deficits in the areas of minority rights, racism, Islamophobia, and xenophobia.[260] Furthermore, Islamic states also viewed such resistance as an attempt to impose Western values on the rest of the world.[261] Thus, polarized and heated debates between Islamic and Western states on the issue of religious hate speech dominated multilateral human rights diplomacy for a number of years. Such debates risked deepening pre-existing prejudices between the West and the Islamic world. The former US Assistant Secretary of State Esther Brimmer has even described the standard-setting efforts as a 'battleground' between the Islamic world and the West that has caused some 'wounds'.[262]

   The issue of how multiculturalism should inform human rights protection has been raised mainly in connection with societies that have received many immigrants over the last few decades. Many of these are Western societies. The option of developing a regional legal instrument on the issue of defamation of religion within the OIC was not even considered by Islamic states since, in their view, the problems of religious defamation and religious hate speech are rooted in the West.[263] Conversely, many opponents of the Islamic states' standard-setting efforts regarded

/portal/page/portal/HRCExtranet/13thSession/OralStatements/230310/Tab1/Ad%20Hoc%20Com%20Elab%20Compl%20Standarts.pdf.

[256] 'Presentation of the Report of the Adhoc Committee on the Elaboration of Complementary Standards'.

[257] 'Presentation of the Report of the Adhoc Committee on the Elaboration of Complementary Standards'.

[258] Interview with a diplomat from one of OIC Member States, Geneva, 20 April 2012.

[259] A/HRC/4/9, para. 5.

[260] 'Presentation of the Report of the Adhoc Committee on the Elaboration of Complementary Standards'.

[261] Statement of Pakistan on Behalf of OIC Member States Delivered at the UN Human Rights Council (2010), available at www.un.org/webcast/unhrc/archive.asp?go=100325.

[262] U.S. Department of State, 'U.S. Emphasizes Freedom of Expression at Human Rights Council' (15 September 2009), available at http://iipdigital.usembassy.gov/st/english/article/2009/09/20090915123614ajesromo.9471704.html#axzz2AdiwOgMP.

[263] Langer, *Religious Offence*, p. 250.

such efforts as clear attempts to export, globalize, and legitimize the widely criticized national laws of Islamic states on defamation of religion and to extend the religious rationale dominant in their national legal systems to the international level.[264] These opponents conceived of such domestic laws as existing legal implementations of the proposed international standards on religious hate speech.[265] Religious defamation offences within Islamic states are, indeed, 'very much alive'.[266] Western states, many NGOs, a number of UN Special Rapporteurs, and various academics have criticized the excessive legislation of religious defamation laws within Islamic states, and their overzealous implementation in a manner that leads to systematic violations of human rights.[267] Islamic states' track record in drafting and implementing such laws has negatively affected their ability to convince other states and stakeholders to support their suggested standards. In general, Islamic states are subjected to many criticisms with regard to the reconciliation of religious minorities' rights with those of their dominant religious communities.

The willingness of the standard-setting advocates to advance their normative agenda does not necessarily imply an ability to do so.[268] Certain factors are crucial to the success of such efforts. These include access to tools of political influence, effective persuasive and organizational skills, adequate funding, the capacity to build broad coalitions with national and international NGOs, credible reputations, and effective lobbying.[269] Developing states are generally at a disadvantage in these areas, limiting their contributions to standard-setting within IHRL in comparison to developed countries.[270] As this section will demonstrate, the characteristics of the

[264] Statement 'NGOs Oppose United Nations "Defamation of Religions" Resolution' (13 November 2009), available at http://erlc.com/Article/erlc-100-plus-groups-oppose-united-nations-defamation-of-religions-resoluti; United States Commission on International Religious Freedom, 'Policy focus on the Dangerous Idea of Protecting Religions from Defamation'; Human Rights First, 'Focus Paper on Defamation of Religions' (March 2010), available at www.humanrightsfirst.org/wp-content/uploads/pdf/3-2010-focus-paper-defamation-of-religions.pdf; ECLJ, 'Combating Defamation of Religions'; Blitt, 'The Bottom up Journey of "Defamation of Religion"', 8, 13; Dobras, 'Is the United Nations Endorsing Human Rights Violations?', 371, 380; Belnap, 'Defamation of Religions', 635; Langer, *Religious Offence*, p. 371.

[265] Githu Muigai et al., 'Joint Statement on "Freedom of Expression and Incitement to Racial or Religious Hatred"'; International Humanist and Ethical Union, 'Speaking Freely about Religion'; Dobras, 'Is the United Nations Endorsing Human Rights Violations?', 379; Belnap, 'Defamation of Religions', 670.

[266] Temperman, 'Blasphemy', 522, 525.

[267] Statement of the United States delivered at the UN Human Rights Council (24 March 2011), available at http://portal.ohchr.org/portal/page/portal/HRCExtranet/16thSession/DraftResolutions/AHRC16L.38/L-38-United%20States.pdf; Githu Muigai et al., 'Joint Statement on "Freedom of Expression and Incitement to Racial or Religious Hatred"'; European Centre for Law and Justice, report submitted to OHCHR expert workshop on the prohibition of incitement to national, racial, or religious hatred (29 September 2010), available at http://eclj.org/PDF/Submission-to-the-UN-on-ICCPR-Arts_20100929.pdf; Human Rights First, 'Focus Paper on Defamation of Religions'; Dobras, 'Is the United Nations Endorsing Human Rights Violations?', 345, 379; Belnap, 'Defamation of Religions', 664–665.

[268] Mutua, 'Standard Setting in Human Rights', 579–580.

[269] Mutua, 'Standard Setting in Human Rights', 584, 579.

[270] Mutua, 'Standard Setting in Human Rights', 581.

supporters (mainly Islamic states) and opponents (mainly Western states, with the support of some Asian and Latin American states, and a number of international, Western, and non-Western NGOs) of standard-setting attempts in the area of hate speech have contributed to the failure of those attempts.

During the attempted standard-setting process, the OIC group in the UN was internally effective in unifying the positions of its members in relation to the group's statements, initiatives, and voting patterns. The coherence and dynamism of the OIC group in the UN had strengthened since 9/11 as a reaction to the rising concerns of Islamic states about the situation of Muslims in the West.[271] Moreover, the numerical leverage within the HRC that Islamic, African, and Non-Aligned Movement (NAM) states enjoyed allowed them to influence the Council's agenda.[272] The successful adoption, over more than a decade, of resolutions on combating defamation of religion, and the establishment of the Ad Hoc Committee despite resistance from Western states bear witness to this capacity. However, OIC member states were ineffective in their ability to garner other states' support for the creation of new standards on hate speech. They were unable to convince a critical mass of states that their suggested standards were compatible with the normative framework of existing international human rights. They were also unable to convince either states, UN human rights experts, or influential NGOs of the existence of normative gaps in the area of hate speech regulation which would justify the adoption of new international binding standards. OIC member states not only failed to secure the support of Western states; they also gradually lost the support of some African, Asian, and Latin American states.

On the other hand, the opposition of Western states to the standard-setting efforts translated into mobilization of support for their position from other states, and the exertion of political pressure on Islamic states to abandon their efforts. Western opposition to these efforts gained significant traction in 2009 when the United States' policy towards the HRC shifted from isolationism to active engagement. The United States was one of only four countries[273] that voted against the GA resolution establishing the Council in March 2006.[274] It was highly sceptical about the Council's ability to perform its designated mandate, especially in light of

---

[271] Richard Gowan and Franziska Brantner, 'Policy Paper of the European Council on Foreign Relations: A Global Force for Human Rights? An Audit of European Power at the UN (September 2008), available at http://ecfr.eu/page/-/ECFR-08_A_GLOBAL_FORCE_FOR_HUMAN_RIGHTS, 30; Human Rights First, 'Focus Paper on Defamation of Religions'.

[272] Testimony of Brett D. Schaefer from the Heritage Foundation to the Subcommittee on International Operations and Organizations, Democracy and Human Rights Committee on Foreign Relations (United States Senate, July 2006), available at www.foreign.senate.gov/imo/media/doc/SchaeferTestimony070726p.pdf; Jan Wouters, Sudeshna Basu, and Nadia Bernaz, 'Study on the Role of the European Union in the Human Rights Council' (November 2008), available at https://eprints.mdx.ac.uk/4299/1/Bernaz-_Role_of_EU.in_Human_Rights_Council.pdf, 20.

[273] The three other states were Israel, Marshall Islands, and Palau.

[274] U.S. Department of State, 'The United States Will Not Seek Election to the UN Human Rights Council' (6 April 2006), available at http://2001-2009.state.gov/r/pa/prs/ps/2006/64182.htm.

membership criteria that, in its view, allowed states that it considered 'gross human rights abusers' to join.[275] The United States therefore took an isolationist stance towards the Council during its first three years. It was dissatisfied with the Council's performance and considered it a 'flawed' body[276] with a 'troubled history'.[277] One of the major reasons for its dissatisfaction was the Council's approach towards freedom of expression.[278] A former Deputy Assistant Secretary of State, Daniel Baer, described this freedom as being 'under assault' in the Council.[279] However, the United States decided to seek HRC membership in 2009. This decision was consistent with the Obama administration's 'new era of engagement', which placed more emphasis on conducting US foreign policy in a multilateral manner.[280] It also followed calls from a number of US NGOs for active US diplomacy within the Council in order to influence its dynamics in a manner consistent with the US values and thereby redress its perceived unsatisfactory outcomes.[281] The inability of the EU to assume a leadership role in combating HRC initiatives with which the United States was dissatisfied had also pressurized the United States to end its boycott of the Council.[282]

---

[275] Statement of Kristen Silverberg, Assistant Secretary for International Organization Affairs to the Senate Committee on Foreign Relations (Subcommittee on International Operations and Organizations, Democracy and Human Rights) (26 July 2007), available at www.foreign.senate.gov/imo/media/doc/SilverbergTestimony070726p.pdf.

[276] Written Testimony Submitted by Suzanne Nossel Deputy Assistant Secretary, Bureau of International Organization Affairs, to the Tom Lantos Human Rights Commission on 'The U.S. Government's Relationship with the Human Rights Council' (25 October 2011), available at http://tlhrc.house.gov/docs/transcripts/2011_10_25_Human%20Rights%20Council/25oct11_hearing_Suzanne%20Nossel%20-%20Oral%20Testimony.pdf. The United States was dissatisfied with the manner the Council dealt with human rights situation in specific countries, including Sri Lanka, Cuba, Sudan, Israel, and the Occupied Palestinian Territories.

[277] U.S. Department of State, 'U.S. Emphasizes Freedom of Expression'.

[278] 'Written Testimony Submitted by Suzanne Nossel'; 'Statement of Kristen Silverberg to the US Senate'; Testimony of Daniel Baer Deputy Assistant Secretary Bureau of Democracy, Human Rights, and Labor in the Tom Lantos Human Rights Commission, on 'The U.S. Government's Relationship with the Human Rights Council' (25 October 2011), available at http://tlhrc.house.gov/docs/tran scripts/2011_10_25_Human%20Rights%20Council/25oct11_hearing_Dan%20Baer%20-%20Oral%20Testimony.pdf.

[279] 'Testimony of Daniel Baer to the Tom Lantos Human Rights Commission'

[280] U.S. Department of State, 'Obama Administration Seeks Greater Involvement with U.N.' (14 April 2009), available at www.america.gov/st/democracyhr-english/2009/April/20090414111055ajes romo.7777979.html.

[281] Testimony of Thomas O. Melia Deputy Executive Director Freedom House to the Subcommittee on International Operations and Organizations, Democracy and Human Rights U.S. Senate Committee on Foreign Relations (26 July 2007), available at www.foreign.senate.gov/imo/media/doc/MeliaTestimony070726p.pdf; Testimony of Peggy Hicks Global Advocacy Director, Human Rights Watch to the Senate Foreign Relations Committee Subcommittee on International Operations and Organizations, Democracy and Human Rights (26 July 2007), available at www.foreign.senate.gov/imo/media/doc/HicksTestimony070726p.pdf.

[282] 'Testimony of Peggy Hicks to the Senate Foreign Relations Committee'; Karen E. Smith, 'The European Union at the Human Rights Council: Speaking with One Voice but Having Little Influence' (2010) 17(2) *Journal of European Public Policy*, 225; Gowan and Brantner, 'Policy Paper

Since gaining HRC membership in 2009, the United States has been able to exert influence on its political dynamics.[283] It has given special priority to changing the Council's approach to freedom of expression. This freedom is considered the cornerstone of American democracy and the 'central'[284] and 'most cherished'[285] human right protected by the US Constitution. 'American exceptionalism' is usually referred to in the context of freedom of expression, reflecting the special primacy given to this freedom and its unique protection within the United States.[286] The United States rejected the imposition of additional IHRL restrictions on the exercise of freedom of expression.[287] It considered resolutions on defamation of religion 'pernicious'.[288] Furthermore, it feared that these resolutions might represent an 'international opinion' on the interpretation of IHRL that could be abused to either justify infringement upon the exercise of freedom of expression or to criticize non-compliant countries in international human rights fora.[289] A former US ambassador to the UN, Jeane Kirkpatrick, warned that these resolutions might leak like 'groundwater' into international jurisprudence.[290] Accordingly, the United States was eager to prevent the gradual development of these resolutions into accepted international standards and the integration of religious defamation into internationally binding standards.

The United States played a vital role in suspending the resolutions on defamation of religion in 2011 and preventing the creation of new standards within the Ad Hoc Committee. It invested considerable political capital and intensive diplomatic efforts to prevent the creation of new international standards reconstituting the boundaries of legitimate expression.[291] Before joining the HRC, the US Department of State raised these issues, including the resolution on religious defamation, during bilateral talks with other countries.[292] Following its accession

---

of the European Council on Foreign Relations', 46; Wouters, Basu, and Bernaz, 'Study on the Role of the European Union in the Human Rights Council', 20.

[283] 'Written Testimony Submitted by Suzanne Nossel'.

[284] Richards, *Free Speech*, p. 239.

[285] Michel Rosenfeld. 'Hate Speech in Constitutional Jurisprudence: A Comparative Analysis' (2002) 24 *Cardozo Law Review*, 1529.

[286] C. Edwin Baker, 'Hate speech', in Michael E. Herz and Péter Molnár (eds.), *The Content and Context of Hate Speech: Rethinking Regulation and Responses* (Cambridge University Press, 2012), p. 58.

[287] U.S. Department of State, 'Remarks by Hillary Clinton US Secretary of State on the Release of the 2009 Annual Report on International Religious Freedoms'.

[288] 'Written Testimony Submitted by Suzanne Nossel'.

[289] 'Testimony of Daniel Baer to the Tom Lantos Human Rights Commission'.

[290] Nina Shea, 'An Anti-Blasphemy Measure Laid to Rest', *Assyrian International News Agency* (4 January 2011), available at www.aina.org/news/20110331211600.htm.

[291] U.S. Department of State, 'United States Working to Bridge Gaps in U.N. Human Rights Council' (2 October 2009), available at http://iipdigital.usembassy.gov/st/english/Article/2009/10/20091002162038esnamfuako.2326319.html#axzz1mCQaRbKn; 'Testimony of Daniel Baer to the Tom Lantos Human Rights Commission'; U.S. Department of State, 'Obama Administration Seeks Greater Involvement with U.N.'; 'Written Testimony Submitted by Suzanne Nossel'.

[292] 'Statement of Kristen Silverberg to the US Senate'.

to the HRC in 2009, the United States also directly influenced the positions of some state members of the Council towards reform. Former US Deputy Assistant Secretary of State Suzanne Nossel has affirmed that the United States followed an assertive 'global outreach' approach, with the aim of pushing members of the Council to reject the resolution on combating religious defamation, ultimately succeeding in lowering its margin of acceptance.[293] High-level diplomatic démarches were made by the United States towards other countries at ministerial level, calling upon them not to vote in favour of the resolutions.[294] The United States thereby diluted the cohesion of regional and political groups' voting patterns within the UN on these resolutions, in particular those of the African group.[295] In parallel with these American efforts, an increasing number of African and Latin American states withdrew support for the resolution, leading to a significant decrease in non-Islamic support. In 2007, the breakdown of the voting in the HRC was twenty-four states in favour, fourteen against, with eight abstentions.[296] In 2008, it was twenty-one in favour, ten against, with fourteen abstentions.[297] In 2009, it was twenty-three in favour, eleven against, with fifteen abstentions.[298] By 2010, it was twenty states in favour, seventeen against, with eight abstentions.[299] Thus, it can be seen that support for the resolution gradually diminished. From 2008 onwards, the number of states

---

[293] 'Written Testimony Submitted by Suzanne Nossel'.
[294] Interview with a diplomat from one of OIC Member States, Geneva, 24 April 2012.
[295] 'Written Testimony Submitted by Suzanne Nossel'.
[296] In favour: Algeria, Azerbaijan, Bahrain, Bangladesh, Cameroon, China, Cuba, Djibouti, Gabon, Indonesia, Jordan, Malaysia, Mali, Mauritius, Mexico, Morocco, Pakistan, Philippines, Russian Federation, Saudi Arabia, Senegal, South Africa, Sri Lanka, and Tunisia. Against: Canada, Czech Republic, Finland, France, Germany, Guatemala, Japan, Netherlands, Poland, Republic of Korea, Romania, Switzerland, Ukraine, United Kingdom of Great Britain, and Northern Ireland. Abstaining: Argentina, Brazil, Ecuador, Ghana, India, Nigeria, Peru, Uruguay, and Zambia (UN Doc. A/HRC/4/123).
[297] In favour: Azerbaijan, Bangladesh, Cameroon, China, Cuba, Djibouti, Egypt, Indonesia, Jordan, Malaysia, Mali, Nicaragua, Nigeria, Pakistan, Philippines, Qatar, Russian Federation, Saudi Arabia, Senegal, South Africa, and Sri Lanka. Against: Canada, France, Germany, Italy, Netherlands, Romania, Slovenia, Switzerland, Ukraine, United Kingdom of Great Britain and Northern Ireland. Abstaining: Bolivia, Brazil, Gabon, Ghana, Guatemala, India, Japan, Madagascar, Mauritius, Mexico, Peru, Republic of Korea, Uruguay, and Zambia (UN Doc. A/HRC/7/78).
[298] In favour: Angola, Azerbaijan, Bahrain, Bangladesh, Bolivia, Cameroon, China, Cuba, Djibouti, Egypt, Gabon, Indonesia, Jordan, Malaysia, Nicaragua, Nigeria, Pakistan, Philippines, Qatar, Russian Federation, Saudi Arabia, Senegal, and South Africa. Against: Canada, Chile, France, Germany, Italy, Netherlands, Slovakia, Slovenia, Switzerland, Ukraine, United Kingdom of Great Britain, and Northern Ireland. Abstaining: Argentina, Brazil, Bosnia and Herzegovina, Burkina Faso, Ghana, India, Japan, Madagascar, Mauritius, Mexico, Republic of Korea, Uruguay, and Zambia (UN Doc. A/HRC/10/29).
[299] In favour: Bahrain, Bangladesh, Bolivia (Plurinational State of), Burkina Faso, China, Cuba, Djibouti, Egypt, Indonesia, Jordan, Kyrgyzstan, Nicaragua, Nigeria, Pakistan, Philippines, Qatar, Russian Federation, Saudi Arabia, Senegal, and South Africa. Against: Argentina, Belgium, Chile, France, Hungary, Italy, Mexico, Netherlands, Norway, Republic of Korea, Slovakia, Slovenia, Ukraine, United Kingdom of Great Britain and Northern Ireland, United States of America, Uruguay, and Zambia. Abstaining: Bosnia and Herzegovina, Brazil, Cameroon, Ghana, India, Japan, Madagascar, and Mauritius (UN Doc. A/HRC/13/56).

that voted against or abstained from voting on the resolution exceeded the number of states that voted in its favour. The risk of its outright defeat even started to arise. In 2010, South Africa was the only non-Islamic state from the African group that supported the resolution. The support from Latin American and Asian countries also declined significantly over time. OIC member states publicly and explicitly expressed their dissatisfaction that 'pressure instead of reason' had been used by major powers 'to coerce countries to change their votes'. Islamic states described pressures exerted to influence the voting on these resolutions as reflecting an 'imperial' attitude.[300]

A number of diplomats from OIC member states affirmed in interviews that, in the aftermath of the assassination of Pakistan's Minister of Minorities Shahbaz Bhatti in 2011, the United States exerted intensive diplomatic pressure on Pakistan, the coordinator of the OIC group in Geneva, not to present the resolution to the HRC.[301] The assassination had been specifically linked to the minister's opposition to Pakistani laws prohibiting defamation of religion. This tragic event underscored the negative repercussions of such laws, and a number of Western NGOs perceived it to demonstrate the failure of such laws to effectuate social peace and safeguard minority rights.[302] It is widely believed within diplomatic circles that a deal was concluded at a high political level between Washington and Islamabad to the effect that attempts to create new religious defamation standards would cease, in exchange for non-escalation of the US reaction to the assassination and internal political developments in Pakistan in general.[303] Pakistan had traditionally played a leading role in coordinating and shaping the positions of the OIC group in the HRC and was a hardliner on preserving the concept of defamation of religion. Accordingly, its reaction to the pressure exerted by the United States played a major role in shifting the OIC group's position. The multilateral activism of the United States, both in Geneva and a number of Islamic capitals, sought to influence key OIC member states in order to secure the cessation of the group's religious hate speech initiatives.[304]

In 2011, OIC member states did not present their annual resolution on combating defamation of religion to the HRC. This was the first time since 1999 that the resolution had not been presented at the UN. The pressure from Washington on key Islamic states led to the abandonment of the OIC group's strongly held position

---

[300] Statement of Pakistan on Behalf of OIC Member States Delivered at the UN Human Rights Council (2010), available at www.un.org/webcast/unhrc/archive.asp?go=100325.

[301] Interview with a diplomat from one of OIC Member States, Geneva, 20 April 2012; Interview with a diplomat from one of OIC Member States, Geneva, 22 April 2012.

[302] Interview with a diplomat from one of OIC Member States, Geneva, 20 April 2012; Interview with a diplomat from one of OIC Member States, Geneva, 22 April 2012.

[303] Interview with a diplomat from one of OIC Member States, Geneva, 20 April 2012; Interview with a diplomat from one of OIC Member States, Geneva, 22 April 2012.

[304] Interview with a diplomat from one of OIC Member States, Geneva, 22 April 2012; Skorini, The OIC and freedom of expression, pp. 131–132.

on this issue.[305] The assassination of Shahbaz Bhatti has rightly been described as the *coup de grâce* for the resolution on combating religious defamation.[306] The significant erosion of support for the resolution after 2007 facilitated the successful application of political pressure on OIC member states. Moreover, the opposition of UN Special Rapporteurs and NGOs to the mainstreaming of the concept of religious defamation within IHRL further isolated the position of the OIC group in the HRC. Notably, the OIC group had to remove a reference to this concept in the outcome document of the Durban Review Conference of 2009 in order to reach a compromise on this document.[307] It replaced this concept with the phrase 'derogatory stereotyping and stigmatization of persons based on their religion or belief.'[308]

The United States not only utilized its tools of political influence to exert pressure on Islamic and other states, but it also used these tools to push forward alternative initiatives on the issue of religious intolerance. According to former US Assistant Secretary of State Esther Brimmer, the United States wanted to carve out the role of liaison between Western and Islamic States for itself.[309] This took place against the backdrop of President Obama's famous June 2009 Cairo speech to the Islamic world, in which he sought to foster a rapprochement between the United States and Islamic countries.[310] In this speech, President Obama characterized the fight against negative stereotyping of religions as a policy goal, not a legal commitment. He said, 'I consider it part of my responsibility as President of the United States to fight against negative stereotypes of Islam whenever they appear.'[311] After it joined the HRC in 2009, the United States sought to create broad partnerships within the Council, transcending the traditional geopolitical groups on controversial issues, particularly freedom of expression.[312]

The United States sought consensus on addressing the root concerns underlying the resolutions on religious defamation, which it believed to represent 'instrument[s] of division'.[313] The United States, in addition to EU countries and a number of Latin American states, repeatedly affirmed that manifestations of intolerance and discrimination in matters of religion should be addressed by a new approach consistent with

---

[305]   Interview with a diplomat from one of OIC Member States, Geneva, 24 April 2012.

[306]   Shea, 'An Anti-Blasphemy Measure Laid to Rest'.

[307]   Lorenz Langer, 'Recent Development: The Rise (and Fall?) of Defamation of Religions' (2010) 35 *Yale Journal of International Law*, 261.

[308]   Outcome Document of the Durban Review Conference, April 2009, available at www.un.org/en/durbanreview2009/pdf/Durban_Review_outcome_document_En.pdf, p. 12.

[309]   US Department of State, 'United States Working to Bridge Gaps in U.N. Human Rights Council'.

[310]   US Department of State, 'U.S. Emphasizes Freedom of Expression'.

[311]   President Obama's remarks to the Muslim world (4 June 2009), available at www.nytimes.com/2009/06/04/us/politics/04obama.text.html.

[312]   'Testimony of Daniel Baer to the Tom Lantos Human Rights Commission'; US Department of State, 'United States Working to Bridge Gaps in U.N. Human Rights Council'.

[313]   Statement of the US at HRC 2010.

existing IHRL.[314] Accordingly, the United States played a key role in drafting a replacement resolution (Resolution 16/18). OIC member states responded positively to the US initiative. The new resolution, entitled 'Combating intolerance, negative stereotyping and stigmatization of, and discrimination, incitement to violence, and violence around the world against persons based on religion or belief', was adopted by consensus in 2011. The United States played an instrumental role in achieving consensus on this resolution.[315] There was a discernible change of emphasis in the new resolution. It focused exclusively on the rights of individuals rather than religions by including references to 'the negative projection of the followers of religions'[316] and 'derogatory stereotyping, negative profiling and stigmatization of individuals based on their religion or belief'.[317] The resolution did not link incidents or phenomena related to religious intolerance or discrimination to any specific region or religion. In contrast to the previous focus within religious defamation resolutions on legal measures that states should adopt to address religious intolerance, the new resolution adopted the Western states' policy-driven approach. It focused on policies aimed at fostering a domestic environment of religious tolerance, peace, and respect, and emphasized the role of education, awareness-raising, building mutual understanding, and the promotion of interfaith dialogue. The resolution's only reference to legal measures was a narrowly drafted one, encouraging states to adopt 'measures to criminalize incitement to imminent violence based on religion or belief', thereby mirroring the US approach to addressing hate speech.[318]

The United States considered the new resolution 'ground-breaking'[319] and described it as marking a 'sea change' in international efforts to address religious hate speech, putting an end to the concept of defamation of religions, and imposing no further restrictions on freedom of expression.[320] In partnership with the OIC, the United States aims at fulfilling a leading role in implementing the new resolution.[321] Together they launched, in the presence of former US Secretary of State Hillary Clinton, and former Secretary General of the OIC Ekmeleddin Ihsanoglu, a series of meetings that came to be known as the 'Istanbul Process' as a follow-up

---

[314] Statement of EU at HRC 2010, 2010; Statement of the US at HRC 2010; Statement of Argentina at HRC 2010; Statement of Chile at HRC 2010.

[315] 'Written Testimony Submitted by Suzanne Nossel'.

[316] A/HRC/16/18, para. pmbl 9.

[317] A/HRC/16/18, para. 1.

[318] A/HRC/16/18, para. 5(f).

[319] 'Testimony of Daniel Baer to the Tom Lantos Human Rights Commission'.

[320] U.S. Department of State, 'Fact Sheet: U.S. Accomplishments at U.N. Human Rights Council' (30 March 2011), available at http://iipdigital.usembassy.gov/st/english/Article/2011/03/20110330121913suo.677879.html#axzz1mCQaRbKn; 'Written Testimony Submitted by Suzanne Nossel'.

[321] 'Statement of Ekmeleddin Ihsanoglu, the OIC Secretary General at the High Level Meeting on the Implementation of the Human Rights Council Resolution 16/18 on Combating Incitement to Violence, and Intolerance Based on Religion or Belief' (19 July 2011), available at www.oicun.org/oicus/oicusprojects/20110719042534728.html.

mechanism on the implementation of the new resolution. These meetings were attended by a number of experts from different countries.[322] The goal of the Istanbul Process, which was launched in 2011, is to exchange ideas and discuss best practice in the area of respecting religious diversities and combating discrimination, intolerance, and violence on the basis of religion or belief, while ensuring full respect for freedom of expression.[323] The former Secretary General of the OIC emphasized that Islamic States' endorsement of the new resolution reflected the fact that they were not wedded to a particular conceptual framework and that their ultimate goal was to address religious intolerance and discrimination.[324] The former US Secretary of State Hillary Clinton emphasized the importance of transcending 'the polarizing debates of the past' and evading 'the old patterns of divisions' on such issues.[325]

The United States is eager to ensure that the Istanbul Process does not focus exclusively on discrimination against Muslims in the West, or addressing religious intolerance in a specific region, but also tackles the situation of religious minorities elsewhere in the world, including in the Middle East and Asia.[326] The former OIC Secretary General emphasized during the first meeting of the Istanbul Process that the approach followed in Resolution 16/18 must tackle 'the vital concerns of all parties' and, in particular, clarify legal grey areas such as the 'exact nature and scope of the complementarities between freedom of opinion and expression and the prohibition of incitement ... as stipulated in Articles 19 and 20 of the ICCPR'.[327] Discussions within the Istanbul Process have revolved mainly around the exchange of national experiences on dealing with discrimination, incitement to hatred, and intolerance.[328] Meetings held during the Process have re-exposed the traditional areas of contention among states with regard to their respective interpretations of the international norm prohibiting incitement to hatred and more specifically with regard to determining at which point the exercise of freedom of expression crosses the threshold of incitement and becomes liable to legal proscription.[329] The euphoria surrounding the adoption of Resolution 16/18 artificially masked the gaps

---

[322] 'Statement of the OIC Secretary General to the Washington Meeting on the Istanbul Process' (14 December 2011), available at www.oicun.org/oicus/oicusprojects/20111215123907595.html.

[323] 'Remarks by Hillary Clinton US Secretary of State at the OIC High-Level Meeting on Combating Religious Intolerance' (15 July 2011), available at www.state.gov/secretary/rm/2011/07/168636.htm.

[324] 'Statement of Ekmeleddin Ihsanoglu, the OIC Secretary General at the High Level Meeting on the Implementation of the Human Rights Council Resolution 16/18'.

[325] 'Remarks by Hillary Clinton US Secretary of State at the OIC High-Level Meeting on Combating Religious Intolerance'.

[326] 'Remarks by Hillary Clinton US Secretary of State at the OIC High-Level Meeting on Combating Religious Intolerance'.

[327] 'Statement of the OIC Secretary General to the Washington Meeting on the Istanbul Process'.

[328] Interview with a Senior Official of the Secretariat of OHCHR, Geneva, 14 January 2015.

[329] Marc Limon, Nazila Ghanea and Hilary Power, 'Freedom of expression and religions, the United Nations and the "16/18 Process"', in Jeroen Temperman and András Koltay (eds.), Blasphemy and Freedom of Expression Comparative, Theoretical and Historical Reflections after the Charlie Hebdo Massacre (Cambridge University Press, 2018), p. 662; Skorini, 'The OIC and freedom of expression', p. 134.

between states' positions on the nature of incitement to hatred and how best to address it.[330] The adoption of Resolution 16/18 has not achieved the reconciliation of such differences. The Resolution represented an agreement among states not to bring their disagreements on the issue of incitement to hatred, in particular religious incitement, to the UN table. Accordingly, it is doubtful that the Istanbul Process is capable of articulating a concrete common position among states on how religious incitement should be legally addressed.

Following the 2011 suspension of the resolution on combating defamation of religion, the standard-setting agenda of the Ad Hoc Committee has been stalemated.[331] Previously, in 2010, the African group had responded to the United States' insistence on drafting the annual resolution of the Ad Hoc Committee presented to the HRC in a procedural manner, without envisioning a role for the committee in the area of standard-setting.[332] The following session of the committee, which concluded in April 2011, was a turning point. This session witnessed the success of the United States, supported by European and cross-regional group states, in putting discussions on standard-setting on hold. Since then, the work of the committee has become geared towards the discussion of implementation gaps in existing IHRL standards rather than execution of its standard-setting mandate.[333] The political will of Islamic and African states to create new international binding standards on hate speech has waned significantly and the whole process has lost its momentum. The African group has preferred to proceed with discussing issues related to contemporary forms of racism and xenophobia within the Ad Hoc Committee, rather than further stalemating its work because of polarized positions on the issue of religious hate speech.[334] The committee's work has therefore proceeded in the direction favoured by Western states, focusing on measures enhancing the implementation of existing international standards rather than embarking on a standard-setting exercise.

The composition of the supporters and opponents of international standard-setting efforts plays a significant role in the success or failure of such efforts.[335] No single constituency is capable of advancing a human rights standard-setting agenda at the international level alone; rather, the process requires a broad coalition of agents or advocates.[336] The presence of strong support from – or partnership with – international and national NGOs contributes to the success of standard-setting efforts in IHRL. NGOs play an important role in drawing attention to particular challenges to human dignity, providing information and analysis on these

---

[330]   Limon, Ghanea and Power, 'Freedom of expression and religions', p. 659.

[331]   A/HRC/18/36, para. 67.

[332]   UN Watch, 'Adhoc Committee on Complementary Standards' (14 April 2011), available at http://blog
        .unwatch.org/index.php/category/ad-hoc-ctte-on-complementary-standards.

[333]   A/HRC/18/36, para. 67.

[334]   Interview with a diplomat from one of African States, Geneva, 13 March 2012.

[335]   Mutua, 'Standard Setting in Human Rights', 584.

[336]   International Council on Human Rights, *Human Rights Standards: Learning from Experience*, 21.

challenges and technical assistance on specific proposals for new standards, and mobilizing support for proposed standards.[337] However, the supporters of standard-setting attempts on religious hate speech were exclusively composed of (mainly Islamic) nation states. There were no national or international NGOs complementing the standard-setting efforts of Islamic states with lobbying or advocacy efforts. Furthermore, no support for their efforts was forthcoming from UN Special Rapporteurs on human rights.

Moreover, no NGOs from Islamic or African states showed support for the standard-setting efforts. A number of NGOs from Islamic and African states even joined advocacy networks composed of Western and international NGOs that rejected the resolutions on religious defamation and opposed the proposed standards.[338] NGOs from OIC member states frequently criticized the excessive legal restrictions imposed in their countries on the exercise of freedom of expression through the implementation of laws prohibiting defamation of religion. These NGOs frequently accused Islamic states of abusing such laws in order to suppress political opposition and minority groups.[339] These laws closely resembled the content of the suggested standards on religious hate speech and thus did not acquire the necessary support from NGOs within Islamic states. These NGOs had concerns that new standards might legitimize further restrictions on freedom of expression in Islamic states. Since OIC member states, supported by African states, were the only supporters of these standard-setting attempts, other actors did not fill the vacuum in advocacy which resulted when standard-setting efforts were suspended. Accordingly, standard-setting efforts within international diplomatic fora petered out.

On the other hand, international and Western NGOs, which enjoy the expertise, resources, lobbying capacities, and influence needed to shape the international human rights normative agenda, strongly resisted standard-setting attempts. Most international NGOs advocate a minimal regulation of freedom of expression that is closer to the libertarian notion of that freedom.[340] A significant number of international and Western NGOs, and some Southern NGOs, coordinated their opposition to resolutions on religious defamation and formed a broad transnational network. This network, comprised of over 180 NGOs, delivered joint statements in the UN and issued joint press statements rejecting the imposition of new limitations on religious expression.[341] All submissions made by NGOs to the UN rejected the

---

[337]   See on the role of NGOs in human rights standard setting Peter R. Baehr, *Non-governmental Human Rights Organizations in International Relations* (Palgrave Macmillan, 2009), pp. 76, 128; Mutua, 'Standard Setting in Human Rights', 591.

[338]   UN Watch, 'NGOs Call for Rejection of "Defamation of Religions" Campaign' (25 March 2009), available at www.unwatch.org; Statement 'NGOs Oppose United Nations "Defamation of Religions" Resolution'; 'A Joint Open Letter of 113 NGOs'.

[339]   'A Joint Open Letter of 113 NGOs'.

[340]   Haraszti, Forward, p. xii.

[341]   UN Watch, 'NGOs Call for Rejection of 'Defamation of Religions' Campaign'; Statement 'NGOs Oppose United Nations "Defamation of Religions" Resolution'.

introduction of the concept of religious defamation and opposed national laws criminalizing expressions offensive to religions.[342] In response to these submissions, Islamic states accused these NGOs of being biased and of ignoring violations against Muslims in connection with defamatory campaigns against Islam and its adherents.[343]

Pressure from a number of US NGOs (particularly those working on issues of religious freedom and freedom of expression), as well as the US Committee on International Religious Freedom, influenced the key role that the United States played in thwarting the resolutions on defamation of religion.[344] Members of Congress also persistently lobbied the US Department of State to intensify its efforts against resolutions on defamation of religion and to make diplomatic démarches to OIC member states.[345] The Tom Lantos Human Rights Commission, a caucus of the US Congress, held a hearing on this issue.[346] In September 2009, a resolution was submitted to the House of Representatives, which was then referred to the Committee on Foreign Affairs; it emphasized that UN resolutions on defamation of religion were incompatible with the protection of individual rights. It called upon the Secretary of State to exert efforts to prevent the adoption of these resolutions within the UN and any other initiatives that would constitute a threat to the exercise of freedom of expression.[347] Moreover, a number of members of Congress raised concerns about the resolutions, especially the risk of their abuse, to a number of foreign leaders, politicians, and ambassadors.[348]

In summary, the supporters of the standard-setting agenda on religious hate speech failed to convince a majority of the international law-making community of the need to develop new international standards on hate speech. By contrast, the opponents of this agenda, with their diverse composition, possessed the capability to bring it to a halt. They employed political pressure and were able to convince other actors of the dangers of adopting the suggested standards and their incompatibility with the existing international normative framework of human rights.

---

[342] A/HRC/9/7.

[343] UN Commission on Human Rights, Summary Record of the 37th Meeting, 58th Session (2002), para. 88.

[344] Most significantly Becket Fund for Religious Liberty, Ethics and Religious Liberty Commission, American Center for Law and Justice, Hudson Institute.

[345] United States Commission on International Religious Freedom, 'Opposition to UN Anti-Blasphemy Resolution Grows' (22 December 2010), available at www.uscirf.gov/news-room/press-releases/3485.html; Shea, 'An Anti-Blasphemy Measure Laid to Rest'; United States Commission on International Religious Freedom, 'Policy focus on the Dangerous Idea of Protecting Religions from Defamation'.

[346] See www.house.gov/list/press/az02_franks/FranksUNReligFreed.html.

[347] Resolution of House of Representatives, 111th Congress 1st Session H. Res. 763 (22 September 2009), available at www.gpo.gov/fdsys/pkg/BILLS-111hres763ih/pdf/BILLS-111hres763ih.pdf.

[348] Hearing before the Tom Lantos Human Rights Commission, House of Representatives 111th Congress 2nd Session (25 February 2010), available at http://tlhrc.house.gov/docs/transcripts/2010_02_25_Iran/02-25-2010_The_current_status_of_human_rights_and_religious_freedom_in_Iran.pdf; United States Commission on International Religious Freedom, 'Opposition to UN Anti-Blasphemy Resolution Grows'; Shea, 'An Anti-Blasphemy Measure Laid to Rest'.

5.7 CONCLUDING REMARKS

For more than a decade, Islamic states led efforts to develop international standards on hate speech in a manner that clearly challenged the Western interpretation and application of norms on freedom of expression and freedom of religion. These efforts were fiercely resisted by Western states. Islamic states sought to legitimize their proposed standards, as embodied within the resolutions on defamation of religion and as presented to the Ad Hoc Committee with a mandate to create new binding standards on incitement to hatred, by appealing to the international norm prohibiting incitement to discrimination, hostility, or violence. They emphasized that their suggested standards were complementary to Article 20(2) of the ICCPR and were aimed at addressing its normative gaps. Accordingly, there has been extensive engagement with Article 20(2) at the level of multilateral human rights diplomacy after years of effective dormancy. The polarized debates at the UN surrounding these efforts revealed deep divisions among states' conceptions of the scope and regulative core of the international norm prohibiting incitement to hatred. The standard-setting attempts exposed a confrontational reading of Article 20(2) as a highly controversial Article within the edifice of the ICCPR. The historic definitional and threshold-related debates between states that arose during codification of this norm within the ICCPR were shown still to be relevant and alive during the course of the more recent debates on standard setting.

OIC member states, with the support of most African states, acted as the only advocates of standard-setting efforts in the area of religious hate speech. In the aftermath of 9/11, Islamic states were primarily concerned with the intensification of anti-Muslim and anti-Islam prejudices in the West. They aimed to bring the increasing defamation of Islam and its symbols and venerated personalities, and the derogatory profiling of Muslims in the West, to the attention of the international community and to characterize these as violations of IHRL.

With the rise in religious hate speech during the post-9/11 era, much discussion has centred on questions such as whether defamation of religion should be equated to hate speech against religious adherents; whether the full enjoyment of freedom of religion requires the prohibition of religious defamation and the negative profiling of religious adherents; and whether religious hate speech represents a manifestation of racism that should be regulated in a similar manner to racist speech. Islamic states responded affirmatively and formulated their suggested international standards on religious hate speech accordingly. On the other hand, Western states, together with a number of national and international NGOs and UN human rights experts, took the opposing view. Accordingly, they opposed the Islamic states' proposed standards and became counter-advocates of the standard-setting agenda.

The standard-setting efforts spearheaded by Islamic states eventually failed. This chapter showed how the content of the suggested standards – in particular their direct interaction with the scope of the freedoms of religion and expression and the right to freedom from racism – as well as the characteristics of their supporters and opponents, contributed to this failure. It appears inconceivable that any future standard-setting efforts in the area of hate speech possessing the same characteristics would garner the necessary support from a majority of the international law-making community.

Islamic states' proposed standards sought to align with the normative scope of the right to protection from incitement to hatred through direct engagement with the five internal features of that right, as identified earlier in this book. Firstly, they expanded the emotional component of the international norm prohibiting incitement to discrimination, hostility, or violence by protecting and respecting the feelings of religious adherents and recognizing offence, insult, or outrage to those feelings as legitimate grounds for restricting freedom of expression. Secondly, they presupposed an automatic and inherent causal relationship between religious defamation and offence to religious feelings, on the one hand, and the violation of the human rights of religious adherents via incitement to hatred against them, on the other. The suggested standards indicate that there is a right to protection from religious defamation which falls within the ambit of the right to protection from incitement to religious hatred. By implying this right, the suggested standards overlooked the difficulties in proving the causal relationship between advocacy of religious hatred and either its alleged harms or the inciting effect of advocating hatred, each an important criterion for enforcing this right. Thirdly, they sought to lower the threshold of the legitimate exercise of freedom of expression in relation to religion, through the prohibition under IHRL of expressions that insult, offend, negatively stereotype, or defame religions and their followers. The aim of this was to enhance the equality and liberty rights of the targeted groups. Fourthly, the proposed standards expanded the group identity aspect of the norm prohibiting incitement by enhancing the protection accorded to the identities of religious groups. They sought not only to protect individual religious adherents, but rather to extend that protection to religions, their symbols, and sacred personalities. This expansion of the group identity aspect of the right to be free from incitement to hatred reflects Islamic states' conviction on the inseparability of incitement targeting followers of religions and defamation of religions. Fifthly, the proposed standards framed the prohibition of religious defamation and the derogatory profiling of religious adherents as being integral to safeguarding freedom of religion for targeted individuals and groups, as well as to combating racism.

The analysis provided in this chapter exposes how states' polarized positions on standard-setting efforts were rooted in different perceptions of how to address the definitional uncertainties and tensions underlying the norm's five internal features. The suggested standards openly challenged the libertarian and individualist conceptions of rights. They were rooted in a communitarian and duty-based conception of rights and attempted to dilute the West's perceived monopoly over the human rights standard-setting agenda.

On the other hand, the states that opposed the standard-setting agenda decoupled the standards suggested by Islamic states from the scope of Article 20(2). They rejected the proposed standards' perceived interference with the normative content and scope of the right to protection from incitement to hatred under IHRL. In particular, they rejected the inclusion of the prohibition of defamation of religion under the ambit of that right, on the basis that this would infringe upon the legitimate exercise of freedom of expression. Opponents of the suggested standards emphasized that religions do not warrant protection under IHRL, which protects only the rights of individuals, and that those rights do not include the right to be free from insults or offence to religion. Furthermore, they believed that the Islamic states' proposals, if adopted, would negatively impact the international human rights system itself by distorting IHRL's focus on individuals. They contended that the current IHRL framework lacked any normative gaps and was sufficient to address contemporary hate speech challenges.

Islamic states assumed an inherent and automatic causal relationship between defamation of religion and numerous human rights violations. Such perceived violations included incitement to discrimination, hostility, or violence against religious adherents; infringement upon freedom of religion; and perpetuation of racism against themselves. In contrast, Western states emphatically rejected any possible causal relationship in this regard and resisted all attempts to remould the scope of these rights under IHRL for the sake of addressing religious sensibilities. This chapter has argued that this causal relationship is neither automatically inevitable nor absolutely impossible; rather, it should be empirically examined without predetermined assumptions. The interconnection, including possible practical overlaps and links, of the four analytic categories – defamation of religion, incitement to hatred, violation of religious freedoms, and racism against religions' adherents – should be empirically examined without predetermined or fixed assumptions, rather than conceived of in strictly normative or conceptual terms. No single determination can be made *in abstracto* on such complex matters.

The UN witnessed political power struggles to define the limits of freedom of expression in relation to religion, both through reinterpretation of the existing international norm prohibiting incitement and the introduction of new complementary standards. This chapter has analysed international normative politics associated with the recent attempts by Islamic states to influence the scope, content, and meaning of this norm. By the year 2010, standard-setting attempts had been brought to a halt, indicating that the opponents to these attempts were much more effective than their supporters in advancing their normative agendas. The United States played an important role in influencing the outcome of such attempts. It employed tools of political influence and pressure to diminish the level of support for the standard-setting initiatives and then force Islamic states to suspend these initiatives. In addition to influential states, the opponents of the proposed standards included active and dynamic international and national NGOs. The theoretical and legal underpinnings of the OIC's approach were widely rejected by experts and NGOs, which further undermined their position. Islamic states, supported by African states, were the only advocates of standard-setting efforts. They failed to acquire additional support for their normative agenda from other actors within the international law-making community. This unevenness in the capabilities and effectiveness of the advocates and counter-advocates of the standard-setting attempts ultimately contributed to the failure of these attempts.

The terminological shift in UN Resolution 16/18 on 'combating intolerance, negative stereotyping and stigmatization of, and discrimination, incitement to violence and violence against, persons based on religion or belief' does not in itself address the areas of contention between states on the regulation of hate speech. The new resolution uses the same terminology as Article 20(2). However, the debates accompanying standard-setting efforts indicate that Article 20(2) does not constitute a clear universal benchmark for assessing the content and effects of hate speech that should be prohibited. Moreover, both sides invoked other human rights norms such as freedom of religion and prohibition of discrimination to justify their polarized stances. This means that these rights also refer to different normative content, in some aspects related to the scope of limitations on freedom of expression vis-à-vis religion.[349]

The consensual adoption of Resolution 16/18 may have ended the visible diplomatic conflict between Islamic and Western states on the concept of defamation of religion, but it has by no means ended the normative struggle to define the meaning and scope of the international norm prohibiting incitement to hatred. The Resolution does not, therefore, appear to represent any substantial progress towards a new consensus on the implications of this norm.

---

[349]   Langer, *Religious Offence*, p. 259.

6

Conclusions

Reconciling protection against hate speech with the safeguarding of fundamental freedoms, particularly freedom of expression, has, historically, posed considerable regulatory challenges. Nevertheless, a number of developments have triggered a new wave of public, political, legal, and academic debates about the questions and conundrums underlying the legal regulation of hate speech. As a result of an unprecedented rise in immigration flows, most modern societies have become increasingly racially, religiously, and culturally diverse. However, in many cases this diversification has been accompanied by increased social anxieties and inter-group tensions, which provide fertile ground for hate speech and exacerbate its harms. In addition, ever-accelerating advances in information and communication technology have inadvertently provided a powerful infrastructure for the proliferation of hate speech with increasing potency, speed, and visibility. Due to the geographical dimension of globalization (rising immigration flows) and its virtual dimension (the ICT revolution), hate speech incidents now have the potential to escalate quickly from mere local controversies into global crises with wide-ranging and boundary-crossing repercussions.

Against the backdrop of these new globalized hate speech dynamics, the nature and scope of states' IHRL obligations on prohibiting incitement to hatred have taken on increased importance. As well as becoming one of the most pressing challenges confronting IHRL, incitement to hatred has also become a controversial issue within multilateral human rights diplomacy. Key questions being posed in the ongoing debates over how best to respond to the new wave of hatred include whether the international legal norm providing protection from incitement to hatred, as it currently stands, is suitable to address the contemporary manifestations and challenges of this phenomenon. Alternatively, does it need to be further developed or expanded?

These questions have drawn renewed attention to Article 20(2) of the ICCPR, which obliges states to legally prohibit advocacy of national, racial, or religious hatred that constitutes incitement to discrimination, hostility, or violence. This book has illustrated that some of the dominant approaches to Article 20(2) adopt a very narrow conception of the Article. These approaches conceive of the Article as a mere limitation clause on the exercise of freedom of expression. This book has proposed the validity of a different approach by arguing that the Article sets forth an autonomous right to protection from incitement to discrimination, hostility, or violence. It has traced the journey of the norm prohibiting incitement to hatred within IHRL in three analytical domains: its emergence, its jurisprudence as developed by supranational human rights–monitoring and adjudicatory bodies, and the recent unsuccessful attempts to create complementary international standards. It has set out a longitudinal analysis spanning multiple decades, from the late 1940s (when negotiations on the drafting of the Article started) to the first decade of the twenty-first century (when the most recent debates over the norm's meaning and the need for its development took place at the UN).

Despite the evident links, in both historical and contemporary contexts, between hate speech and gross human rights violations such as mass atrocities, the journey within IHRL of the right to protection from incitement to hatred has been problematic. The codification within IHRL of the norm prohibiting incitement to hatred has taken place without a widely shared understanding among states on how to address its definitional uncertainties and underlying tensions. The controversies that characterized the drafting history of Article 20(2) had not been reconciled by the time of the ICCPR's adoption. These old normative battles related not only to the Article's objectives and the means of achieving them, but also to its very inclusion in the Covenant. The more recent UN standard-setting efforts in the area of incitement to hatred created political tensions among states and ended in stalemate. These new normative battles indicated that states' understandings of the rationale, meaning, and scope of the norm prohibiting incitement to hatred still featured prominent gaps, which may even be widening. Moreover, the hate speech jurisprudence generated by various supranational monitoring and adjudicatory bodies is characterized by several weaknesses. This jurisprudence has not provided a systematic method of identifying incitement for the purposes of restricting the exercise of freedom of expression, nor has it developed the constitutive elements of the threshold of hatred. Clarity on the precise obligations of states pursuant to the norm prohibiting incitement to discrimination, hostility, or violence is therefore difficult to locate within existing jurisprudence.

Despite its codification in IHRL more than sixty years ago, the right's exact normative core and scope remain largely unsettled, underdeveloped, and contested. While Article 20(2) of the ICCPR established a strong international legal norm obliging, and not just authorizing, states to prohibit by law the expressive acts described therein, the norm still lacks a coherent universal meaning. It has, so far, resisted substantive evolution and appears almost frozen in a specific frame. There is a high degree of uncertainty as to the domestic legal requirements for enforcing the right, leaving a broad spectrum for states' discretionary interpretations and implementation patterns. It is often difficult to determine whether a violation has occurred in any given circumstance and, consequently, in what circumstances the right can be claimed before a court or relevant monitoring body. This has yielded a fragmented legal landscape. Thus, the translation of the claim to be – or the interest in being – protected from incitement to hatred into a specific international human right has proven fraught with difficulties. There is even a sceptical reading, deriving from strictly libertarian or individualist approaches to human rights, of the existence and validity of this right.

This book has sought not only to trace the difficult journey of the right to protection from incitement to discrimination, hostility, or violence within IHRL, but also, more importantly, to explain the core challenges which have arisen during the course of this journey. It has argued that the challenges which have faced the development and strengthening of international standards providing protection from incitement to hatred are largely attributable to five internal features of this right. These five features are the 'emotive' component, the 'incitement' component, the tensions between equality and liberty rights of speakers and members of targeted groups, the 'group identity' component, and the 'religion' component. The major areas of international contention over the meaning of the right have their basis in different national approaches to addressing the definitional uncertainties, threshold dilemmas, and tensions underlying the above-mentioned features. This five-tiered analysis of the norm exposes the skeleton around which different states' positions were constructed and shaped, both in the old and new normative battles. Moreover, these five constitutive features represent the most significant obstacles to the consolidation of supranational hate speech jurisprudence, specifically, to the articulation of strictly defined parameters or stringent tests to identify the threshold of prohibited hate speech.

The first internal feature of the right to protection from incitement to hatred – its 'emotive' component – manifests itself in the nature of expressions prohibited pursuant to the right, as well as the nature of one particular category of harms justifying such prohibition. More precisely, the right obliges states to make their national laws intolerant of an extreme emotion – *hatred* – if its advocacy incites, inter alia, the emotional harm of *hostility* towards targeted groups. In this sense, the key terms 'hatred' and 'hostility' construct the meaning of the right. However, both terms are unrelated to concrete practice, being concerned instead with intangible states of mind, attitudes, and psychological states of abhorrence, detestation, and enmity. The right's 'emotive' component represents its major definitional challenge, since it renders very difficult the clear and objective definition of the right in the context of IHRL.

The right's second feature relates to the nature of the causal or likelihood-based relationship between advocacy of hatred and its alleged harms, which is indirect, cumulative, and mentally and emotionally mediated. The complexities of proving the inciting nature of hate advocacy, given the difficulties in precisely or empirically establishing and measuring incitement, pose considerable challenges to the interpretation and enforcement of the right.

The right's implementation requires a very delicate balance to be struck between the equality and liberty rights of speakers and members of targeted groups; tensions in this regard represent the right's third internal feature. These tensions are not, as they might prima facie appear, and as the academic literature widely suggests, between the two values of liberty and equality in the abstract. Rather, they occur between the interests of members of targeted groups and speakers in enjoying both liberty and equality rights. The interaction of the two values of liberty and equality in the right is multifaceted and complex. The right takes effect by restricting speakers' freedom of expression. Yet liberty as a value is not enhanced only through the protection of a wider range of expressions; liberty can be at risk for members of targeted groups if they are not provided with protection against the harms of hate speech, as this can have a 'silencing effect' on them. Enhancing the equality of members of targeted listeners is the major underlying rationale of the right. However, equality, as a value, can also be at stake for speakers if their freedom of expression is unwarrantedly infringed upon. Thus, the interpretation and implementation of the right should not be reduced to solving perceived tensions or even conflicts between equality and liberty and then giving primacy to one value over the other.

The right's fourth internal feature is its 'group identity' aspect. It can be said of both hateful content itself and the harms of prohibited expressions that they affect specific collective identities. The right is integral to the promotion of collective goals, the prevention of communal harms, and the protection of group identities. It therefore adds another source of tension between individual and group rights. Drawing a sharp dividing line between the two categories of protection (the individualized and the collective) is inherently difficult, given that hate speech targets individuals based on their group-defining characteristics or identity. The group identity component of the right also raises the dilemma of distinguishing between the protection of groups from the collective harms of hate speech and the protection of their group-defining characteristics. The lines separating these two interlinked forms of protection are blurred ones.

The right's fifth feature relates to the prohibition of incitement to hatred on religious grounds. When it comes to the regulation of religious hate speech, a delicate, and often very difficult, balance has to be struck between freedom of religious expression, on the one hand, and protection for targeted religious adherents, on the other. This further complicates the precise determination of the threshold beyond which advocacy of religious hatred should be prohibited pursuant to the right.

Although these five internal features of the right have been presented separately, this book's analysis has highlighted the interconnections between the definitional uncertainties and tensions underlying them. These uncertainties and tensions explain the inherent interpretive and implementation problems that have arisen from the shift from moral denunciation to international legal prohibition of incitement to hatred. The interpretive conundrums are evident in a wide range of contexts, which include defining the content of prohibited speech, proving its causal relationship with proscribed harms, resolving tensions between the speakers' and listeners' rights to liberty and equality, resolving tensions between individual and group rights, and resolving tensions between the expressive and identity aspects of freedom of religion (in the context of religious-based incitement).

The regulation of hate speech involves accommodating the formal and substantive notions of equality in addition to individual and group rights. Therefore, the libertarian and egalitarian conceptions of freedom of expression and the individualist and communitarian approaches to rights greatly inform and guide the various modes of interpretation and implementation of the norm prohibiting hate speech. The libertarian-individualist approach holds that the state's prohibition of hate advocacy is generally an impermissible restriction upon the content of speech, unless such speech is directed towards an *individual* under circumstances in which an *immediate violent act* is likely to result. Contrastingly, the international norm prohibiting hate speech recognizes both the *emotional* and physical harms associated with hate speech. It limits the legitimate zone of expression available to speakers in order to protect *group* rights. The emotional and group identity aspects of the norm therefore place it in an uncomfortable position in a legal human rights edifice dominated by individual rights. The right aligns with the egalitarian notion of freedom of expression, which recognizes a wide range of harms, including non-physical harms, as justifying restrictions on hate advocacy, in order to respect the equality principle. The group identity aspect of the right aligns with the communitarian approach to rights, which seeks to protect group identities and safeguard group rights. Theories of rights which reject the notion of group rights and do not adopt an egalitarian interpretation of freedom of expression are, by definition, irreconcilable with the rationale of the right to be free from incitement to hatred as codified in IHRL.

An in-depth analysis of the structural tensions inherent in the international prohibition of hate speech, unpacking its intrinsic qualities and tracing their combined effect on its difficult journey within IHRL, is useful beyond the confines of IHRL. Indeed, any legal system that provides protection from incitement to hatred, whether at national or regional level, has to grapple with the controversies of interpretation and implementation associated with the five internal features of the norm.

Although this book has focused primarily on the impact of the internal features of the right to be protected from incitement to discrimination, hostility, or violence, it fully recognizes that the interaction of endogenous and exogenous factors shapes the evolution of international norms. It has given an account of the international normative politics that have surrounded negotiations on the norm prohibiting incitement. The historical background to the early international negotiations on the norm directly influenced its codification in the ICCPR. During the drafting phase of Article 20(2), the prevalent dynamics of the cold war, and the associated ideological and political polarization between the Eastern bloc and the West, formed an important context for the positions taken by various states. In this early phase, when the world was beginning to recover from the Second World War and establish a peaceful new world order, a clear and acute awareness developed among many states, mainly belonging to or allied with the Eastern bloc, of the link between atrocities committed against particular groups in the preceding years and hate propaganda disseminated by Nazis and fascists against those groups. The traumatic experiences of the Second World War drove those states to insist on the scope of IHRL protection being extended to hate speech prohibition in order to prevent the resurgence of similar extreme ideologies. They perceived Article 20 as an indispensable element of the new post-war world order. States that supported the inclusion of the Article believed that protection against denial or abuse of human rights should be guaranteed for every human being and should in itself constitute a principle of IHRL. States belonging to the Western bloc resisted the very inclusion of the Article in the ICCPR on the basis that it did not fall under the Covenant's substantive scope. They conceived of the ICCPR as an instrument that should set forth only individual rights of a negative nature, entailing the non-interference of states. Western states perceived Article 20 to impose unwarranted restrictions on freedom of expression, rather than setting forth a human right. Thus, they sought, during negotiations, to narrow the scope of the Article's prohibitions as much as possible.

While the Eastern bloc states were the main initiators of the codification of the norm prohibiting incitement to hatred within IHRL, Islamic states have led international advocacy efforts on the issue in recent years. The most recent phase of multilateral negotiations on the norm took place against the backdrop of a completely different international setting: the aftermath of 9/11. Islamic states reacted to the rise of hate speech targeting Muslim communities in the West during this period by promoting the development of complementary international standards on incitement to religious hatred. The standard-setting efforts led by Islamic states started with the series of UN resolutions on combating defamation of religion, adopted between 1999 and 2010. These resolutions aimed to secure recognition of defamation of religion as a human rights violation prohibited pursuant to Article 20(2) of the ICCPR. Given the non-binding nature of these resolutions, however, Islamic states regarded them as insufficient to fully address their concerns. They redoubled their efforts through the establishment, in 2006, of the UN Ad Hoc

Committee on the Elaboration of Complementary Standards, which had the explicit mandate of creating new international binding standards on incitement to racial and religious hatred. Islamic states, with the support of most African states, contended that Article 20(2) had normative gaps that necessitated the development of new complementary international legal standards. The standards proposed by Islamic states were aimed at obliging states to legally prohibit the negative stereotyping and defamation of religion, as well as the derogatory profiling and stigmatization of both individuals and groups on the basis of religion. Western states, however, strongly criticized both the general approach and conceptual framework of resolutions on defamation of religions as being incompatible with IHRL, which, in their view, should not grant protection to religions, entities, or ideologies. They did not view defamation of religion as meeting the criteria for prohibited incitement under Article 20(2) of the ICCPR. Furthermore, they resisted completely the development of new international standards providing protection from incitement to hatred.

These recent standard-setting efforts in the area of religious hate speech created tensions between Islamic states and Western states in the sphere of multilateral human rights diplomacy. Such tensions resulted largely from polarized positions on the necessity and desirability of creating new standards, exacerbated by the fact that Islamic states framed their proposals as a response to a perceived deterioration in the situation of Muslim minorities in the West. Statements made by Islamic states at the UN adopted an accusatory tone towards the West. They sought to exert political pressure on Western states to address Islamophobia and also aimed to expose what they perceived as rights deficits or protection gaps in the areas of minority rights, racism, and xenophobia in the West. They highlighted that defamation of Islam has de facto infringed upon the rights of Muslims in the West to express and practise their religion. These normative debates took place while the boundaries of freedom of expression relating to religious matters re-emerged forcefully as a contentious and sensitive issue in the West, creating friction and violence in many communities. Growing religious diversity led to demands from religious minorities, met mostly with fierce resistance, that Western democracies realign the boundaries of freedom of expression in order to advance multiculturalism. Furthermore, the Islamic states' proposals on new standards on religious hate speech occurred during a period when blasphemy offences in Western states were mostly being de jure abolished or de facto deactivated. Thus, the suggested new standards appeared oppositional to contemporaneous legal trends in the West.

While the original negotiations on the codification of the norm prohibiting incitement to hatred led, eventually, to the adoption of Article 20(2) of the ICCPR on the basis of a fragile international agreement, more recent negotiations on remodelling the norm ultimately reached an impasse. The standard-setting attempts at the UN, led by Islamic states, generated a dynamic of evolution, but this dynamic has failed to transform into actual normative evolution. A normative battle took place in the UN, mainly between Islamic and Western states, for more than a decade in an attempt to define the scope of legitimate speech vis-à-vis incitement to religious hatred. Tools of political influence were successfully employed, most notably by the United States, to pressurize the Islamic states and their allies into abandoning their standard-setting attempts. The characteristics of the advocates and counter-advocates of these efforts strongly influenced this final outcome. Despite standard-setting efforts being brought to halt, the contentious normative issues pertaining to international legal regulation of hate speech remain unresolved; they have merely been swept under the rug.

6.2 THE WAY AHEAD

Finding a universal normative framework for the right to protection from incitement to hatred is by no means straightforward. It does not appear possible to secure broad agreement on an approach that moves beyond the current level of abstraction by adding specificity to the content and effects of proscribed advocacy of hatred. Not only have the five internal features of the right significantly influenced its problematic journey within IHRL, they also appear to preclude the progressive normative development of IHRL in the area of incitement to hatred as a response to contemporary problems in hate speech regulation.

In order for the international community to overcome such paralysis, one strategy is for efforts to further develop the international norm prohibiting incitement to hatred to be directed towards approaches that place more emphasis on *procedural* development than legal or textual development. This approach would not answer the difficult question of *what* the precise legal threshold of Article 20(2) is; rather, it would address *how* to determine such threshold within different national contexts. National authorities need sufficient guidance in implementing their obligations under IHRL to prohibit incitement to hatred. Such guidance is an important factor in the avoidance of excessively prohibitive laws that suppress legitimate speech, inconsistent implementation of laws, and restrictive interpretations of laws in ways that thwart the obligation's preventive function – its central value from a policy perspective. Rather than legal or textual development, the efforts of the international community might instead be directed towards the provision of such guidance to states in the form of a *procedural manual* for enforcement of the right to protection from incitement to hatred. This would allow states to take into consideration their own national contexts when seeking to resolve the threshold dilemmas and inherent tensions underlying the five internal features of the right.

Procedural development of the norm prohibiting incitement to hatred provides a jurisdiction-specific response to that phenomenon. This can best be described as *regulatory relativism*, in which the means of achieving protection of the right is best determined in accordance with the particular context involved.

Drawing upon the analysis of the five internal features of the right to protection from incitement to hatred, it is clear that the right confronts a relativist challenge; its interpretation and implementation are highly context-dependent, undermining the possibility of reaching a universally accepted definition. The emotional aspect of the right represents a relativist challenge in light of the organic relationship between emotions and conceptions on morals. Hatred and hostility are by-products of (and triggered by) moral conceptions which, in turn, justify and rationalize them. Emotional harms are thus morality-dependent harms, as they are mediated through the moral conceptions of listeners. The right provides protection to specific sets of morals integral to national, racial, or religious identities. The emotional aspect of the right (its first internal feature) introduces an element of legal moralism into hate speech regulation. This aspect is largely responsible for the relaxed approach to scrutiny that supranational human rights–monitoring bodies have followed. Notably, these bodies have traditionally avoided giving clear directions to states regarding the protection of morals as legitimate grounds for restricting the exercise of freedoms, on the basis that morals encompass relativity and change and are shaped by cultural, historical, and societal contexts. In comparison to physical or bodily harms, international norms that provide protection from emotional harms are less likely to resonate transnationally. The incitement component (the right's second feature) represents an additional relativist challenge to the right's interpretation. The nature and strength of the causal or likelihood-based link between the content of speech and its actual or possible harms are highly contingent upon context. The wider prevailing social environment and historical context shape both the *meaning* and *impact* of speech. Notably, international norms that do not entail 'a short and clear causal chain' connecting the harms themselves with their sources are less likely to transcend cultures and acquire wide international agreement.[1] Supranational human rights–monitoring bodies have adopted, to a large extent, national author-ities' assessments of how tightly the causal relationship or likelihood-based connec-tion between advocacy of hatred and its actual or potential harms must be drawn before restricting freedom of expression. Moreover, legal traditions of different states have varying means of resolving the two sources of tension that the right embodies between speakers' and listeners' rights to equality and liberty (the right's third feature), as well as individual and group rights (the right's fourth feature). Such differences emanate from the varying levels of bias within different legal traditions towards either egalitarian or libertarian notions of freedom of expression, and their differing levels of commitment to the advancement of group rights. The religious component (the right's fifth feature) poses yet another relativist challenge to the right's interpretation and implementation. Religions' statuses within states' struc-tures vary significantly; constitutions and national legislations address the relation-ship between state and religion in a variety of ways. These variations generate different approaches to the legal regulation of incitement to religious hatred.

---

[1] Margaret E. Keck and Kathryn Sikkink, *Activists beyond Borders: Advocacy Networks in International Politics* (Cornell University Press, 1998), pp. 98–99.

Accordingly, despite the fact that hate speech is generally recognized as a universal problem, it is a problem in which particularized political, cultural, and historical national contexts play a crucial role. The hate speech phenomenon is not a static problem, but one which needs to be seen as a dynamic social process involving context. Indeed, appeals to context frequently arose during the rights' drafting history and the more recent UN debates. Supranational hate speech jurisprudence indicates that human rights–monitoring bodies have largely endorsed relativist appeals and have taken a cautious approach towards scrutiny of hate speech regulation. They have conceived of national authorities as best positioned to determine the formulation and application of hate speech laws, particularly with regard to the nature of prohibited expressions and the assessment of their likelihood to incite harms.

There are striking variations, even among liberal democracies, when it comes to the hate speech legal landscape. Different criteria are applied to define the threshold between free speech and hate speech. The legislative patterns and judicial practices related to the resolution of the hate speech problem are predicated upon different conceptions of the content of prohibited expressions, the scope of recognized harms of hate speech, the extension of protection to groups and to group-defining characteristics, the range of groups protected, and the standards of causality between advocacy of hatred and its alleged harms. The prohibition of hate advocacy that constitutes clear and unambiguous incitement to immediate violence or illegal acts is the aspect of the norm that enjoys most transnational resonance, since it easily crosses cultural and ideological boundaries. However, legal regulation of hate advocacy that falls short of incitement to violence but creates a social climate conducive to hostility and discrimination does not enjoy the same universal resonance.

After a recent comprehensive examination of the state of implementation of Article 20(2) of the ICCPR worldwide, the OHCHR characterized hate speech legislation as often 'excessively narrow or vague' and related jurisprudence as 'scarce and ad hoc'.[2] It noted the existence of a 'dichotomy' between the lack of prosecution of incitement cases and the 'persecution of minorities under the guise of domestic incitement laws'.[3]

The differing national regulatory responses to incitement to hatred are also symptomatic of the vague international normative environment surrounding the issue. Despite the fact that the international human rights paradigm is inherently aimed at establishing or influencing norms at a national level, there is a lack of clarity on precisely what Article 20(2) requires of states in practice. A procedural approach would, therefore, contribute to making Article 20(2) more practicable for states through the provision of guidance to prosecutorial and judicial authorities

---

[2] A/HRC/22/17/Add.4, paras. 11, 15.
[3] A/HRC/22/17/Add.4, para. 11.

about the sound application of national incitement legislation. The *Rabat Plan of Action on the prohibition of advocacy of national, racial or religious hatred that constitutes incitement to discrimination, hostility or violence*[4] is an important step in this procedural development path. It was the outcome of a series of regional expert workshops organized by the OHCHR during 2011 on freedom of expression and the prohibition of incitement to national, racial, or religious hatred as reflected in Articles 19 and 20 of the ICCPR. These expert workshops attracted wide participation from government representatives, civil society, academia, United Nations treaty bodies, and Special Rapporteurs of the HRC. Their objectives were threefold: firstly, 'to gain a better understanding of legislative patterns, judicial practices and policies regarding the concept of incitement to national, racial, or religious hatred, while ensuring full respect for freedom of expression as outlined in Articles 19 and 20 of the ICCPR'; secondly, 'to arrive at a comprehensive assessment of the state of implementation of the prohibition of incitement in conformity with international human rights law'; and, thirdly, 'to identify possible actions at all levels'. A 'wrap-up' expert workshop was convened in Rabat in October 2012 with the aim of bringing together the conclusions and recommendations from the previous different workshops. It led to the elaboration of the *Rabat Plan of Action*. One of the main purposes of this plan is to raise awareness and understanding of Article 20(2) and, in particular, to promote an interpretation of the Article that is consistent with other human rights; in particular Articles 18 (freedom of religion or belief) and 19 (freedom of expression) of the ICCPR. This process has brought more visibility to Article 20(2) and has sought to address some of the confusion around the Article.

The *Rabat Plan of Action* proposed a six-part threshold test as a framework for determining the threshold of 'advocacy of national, racial or religious hatred that constitute incitement to discrimination, hostility or violence' under Article 20(2) of the ICCPR. It suggested that judicial systems adopt a case-by-case analysis when applying the test to determine whether the threshold of incitement has been reached. The first of the threshold test's six elements is the social and political context prevalent at the time the expression was made and disseminated. It is interesting to note that this first element therefore refers to context. It reflects a clear recognition, after comprehensive study of relevant legislation and jurisprudence, that context is of great importance when assessing whether particular statements are likely to incite to discrimination, hostility, or violence. The *Rabat Plan of Action* recognized that context 'may have a direct bearing on both intent and/or causation'. The second element is the *speaker*, in terms of his or her position or status in society and 'standing in the context of the audience to whom the speech is directed'. The third is *intent*, in terms of the 'activation of a triangular relationship between the object and subject of the speech act as well as the audience'. The fourth is the *content and form* of expression, in terms of 'the degree to which the speech was provocative and direct, as well as the form, style, and nature of arguments deployed in the speech'. The fifth is the *extent* of speech, in terms of its reach, public nature, magnitude, size of audience, frequency, and the medium of dissemination. The sixth and final element is the *likelihood* of the occurrence of the harm, in terms of identifying 'some degree of risk of harm' and 'reasonable probability that the speech would succeed in inciting actual action against the target group, recognizing that such causation should be rather direct'.

The *Rabat Plan of Action* represents a true opportunity for systematic engagement with some of the challenging aspects of the right to protection from incitement to hatred. In contrast to the creation of substantive international standards outlining the content of expressions and harms prohibited pursuant to the right, the procedural development of the right, outlining basic guarantees for its realization, is not overloaded with navigational challenges. This procedural approach could offer a partial substitute for the development of a strong universal or consensual normative content to the right. A number of UN Special Rapporteurs, human rights experts, and NGOs have endorsed this threshold test.[5] The *Rabat Plan of Action* has also been noted in HRC resolutions on '[c]ombating intolerance, negative stereotyping and stigmatization of, and discrimination, incitement to violence, and violence around the world against persons based on religion or belief'.[6]

The greater visibility that Article 20(2) has acquired within the lexicon of IHRL during the twenty-first century has created the momentum to develop this set of principles, providing practical guidance to states on the enforcement of the right to protection from incitement to hatred. Further consolidation of this set of principles would guide national legislators when drafting relevant incitement offences in legislative form, as well as bringing much-needed discipline, consistency, and rigour to the methodologies employed by courts when reaching their verdicts on incitement to hatred cases. Greater specification of the procedural aspects of the legal interpretation of this norm helps to maintain and protect a universal normative core, instead of merely accepting its fragmentation into separate historically based, culturally defined, politically shaped, and country-specific approaches.

Understanding the considerable difficulties facing the development, strengthening, and expansion of the international norm prohibiting incitement to hatred is more pertinent now than perhaps ever before, given the hate speech challenges that proliferate throughout our globalizing world. This book has provided an explanatory framework through which to understand the origins and causes of the core challenges facing the evolution of this norm. It has illustrated the importance of examining the role that the internal features of international human rights could play in influencing their normative evolution. It provides a framework of analysis

---

[5] A/HRC/22/17/Add.4, para. 22.
[6] A/HRC/Res/37/38, para. 5.

from which further reflection and scholarship on this norm, and, by extension, the evolution of other human rights, can emerge.

Additional empirical studies on the 'push and pull' factors for normative evolution in IHRL, focusing not only on rights that witnessed successful normative evolution, but also on rights where such evolution seems to face serious obstacles or resistance, are needed to contribute to its theoretical development. As human rights challenges with global dimensions, and thus global impact, increase, questions about the normative development of the existing international human rights framework also acquire significant policy relevance. Explaining the internal and external dynamics of normative evolution in the context of IHRL is crucial to the identification of its conditions and, consequently, to the formulation, by different stakeholders, of strategies that can shape and influence such an evolution.

Bibliography

Abrams, Floyd. 'On American Hate Speech Law'. In *The Content and Context of Hate Speech: Rethinking Regulation and Responses*, edited by Michael E. Herz and Péter Molnár, 116–128. New York: Cambridge University Press, 2012.

Adhar, Rex and Ian Leigh. *Religious Freedom in the Liberal State*. 2nd ed. Oxford: Oxford University Press, 2013.

Alexander, Larry. *Is There a Right of Freedom of Expression?* Cambridge: Cambridge University Press, 2005.

Allport, Gordon W. *The Nature of Prejudice*. Cambridge, MA: Addison-Wesley Pub. Co., 1954.

Altman, Andrew. 'Freedom of Expression and Human Rights Law: The Case of Holocaust Denial'. In *Speech and Harm: Controversies over Free Speech*, edited by Ishani Maitra and Mary Kathryn McGowan, 24–49. Oxford: Oxford University Press, 2012.

Alves, Jose A. Lindgren. 'Race and Religion in the United Nations Committee on the Elimination of Racial Discrimination'. *University of San Francisco Law Review* 42 (2008): 941–982.

Appiah, Kwame Anthony. 'What's Wrong with Defamation of Religion?' In *The Content and Context of Hate Speech: Rethinking Regulation and Responses*, edited by Michael E. Herz and Péter Molnár, 164–182. Cambridge; New York: Cambridge University Press, 2012.

Baehr, P. R. *Non-Governmental Human Rights Organizations in International Relations*. New York: Palgrave Macmillan, 2009.

Bakalis, Chara. 'Regulating Hate Crime in the Digital Age'. In *Globalization of Hate: Internationalizing Hate Crime?*, edited by Jennifer Schweppe and Mark Austin Walters, 263–276. New York: Oxford University Press, 2016.

Baker, C. Edwin. 'Autonomy and Hate Speech'. In *Extreme Speech and Democracy*, edited by Ivan Hare and James Weinstein, 139–157. New York: Oxford University Press, 2009.

'Harm, Liberty, and Free Speech'. *Southern California Law Review* 70 (1997): 979–1020.

'Hate Speech'. In *The Content and Context of Hate Speech: Rethinking Regulation and Responses*, edited by Michael E. Herz and Péter Molnár, 57–80. New York: Cambridge University Press, 2012.

'Scope of the First Amendment Freedom of Speech'. *UCLA Law Review* 25 (1978): 964–1040.

Barendt, Eric. 'Religious Hatred Laws: Protecting Groups or Belief?' *Res Publica* 17, no. 1 (2011): 41–53.

Baxi, Upendra. *The Future of Human Rights*. New Delhi: Oxford University Press, 2002.

Belnap, Allison G. 'Defamation of Religions: A Vague and Overbroad Theory That Threatens Basic Human Rights'. *Brigham Young University Law Review* 2010 (2010): 635–686.

Benesch, Susan. 'Contribution to OHCHR Initiative on Incitement to National, Racial, or Religious Hatred'. Vienna, 2011. www.ohchr.org/EN/Issues/FreedomOpinion/Articles19-20/Pages/ContributionsOthers2011.aspx.

'The Ghost of Causation in International Speech Crime Cases'. In *Propaganda, War Crimes Trials and International Law: From Speakers' Corner to War Crimes*, edited by Predrag Dojcinovic, 254–268. New York: Routledge, 2012.

'Vile Crime in Inalienable Right: Defining Incitement to Genocide'. *Virginia Journal of International Law* 48 (2008): 485–528.

Benier, Kathryn. 'Global Terrorism Events and Ensuing Hate Incidents'. In *The Globalization of Hate: Internationalizing Hate Crime?*, edited by Jennifer Schweppe and Mark Austin Walters, 79–95. New York: Oxford University Press, 2016.

Berk, Richard A., Elizabeth A. Boyd, and Karl M. Hamner. 'Thinking More Clearly about Hate-Motivated Crimes'. In *Hate and Bias Crime: A Reader*, edited by Barbara Perry, 123–143. New York: Routledge, 2003.

Bertoni, Eduardo. 'Hate Speech under the American Convention on Human Rights'. *ILSA Journal of International & Comparative Law* 12 (2006): 569–574.

Besson, Samantha. 'Human Rights: Ethical, Political or Legal? First Steps in a Legal Theory of Human Rights'. In *The Role of Ethics in International Law*, edited by Donald Earl Childress, 211–245. New York: Cambridge University Press, 2012.

Beth, Loren P. 'Group Libel and Free Speech'. *Minnesota Law Review* 39 (1955): 167–184.

Beyani, Chaloka. 'Law and Judicial Practices'. Nairobi, 2011. www.ohchr.org/Documents/Issues/Expression/ICCPR/Nairobi/ChalokaBeyani.pdf.

Black, Henry Campbell. *Black's Law Dictionary: Definitions of the Terms and Phrases of American and English Jurisprudence, Ancient and Modern*. St. Paul, MN: West Pub. Co., 1990.

Blitt, Robert C. 'The Bottom Up Journey of "Defamation of Religion" from Muslim States to the United Nations: A Case Study of the Migration of Anti-Constitutional Ideas'. *Studies in Law, Politics, and Society* 56 (3 August 2011): 121–211.

Boekle, Henning. Volker Rittberger, and Wolfgang Wagner. 'Norms and Foreign Policy: Constructivist Foreign Policy Theory'. *Tubingen Working Papers* 34, no. a (1999).

Boerefijn, I. and J. Oyediran. 'Article 20 of the International Covenant on Civil and Political Rights.' In *Striking a Balance: Hate Speech, Freedom of Expression, and Non-discrimination*, edited by Sandra Coliver, 29–32. Article 19, International Centre Against Censorship, Human Rights Centre, University of Essex, 1992.

Boonin, David. *Should Race Matter? Unusual Answers to the Usual Questions*. New York: Cambridge University Press, 2011.

Bossuyt, Marc J. *Guide to the 'Travaux Préparatoires' of the International Covenant on Civil and Political Rights*. Martinus Nijhoff Publishers, 1987.

Boyle, Kevin. 'Hate Speech – The United States versus the Rest of the World'. *Maine Law Review* 53 (2001): 487.

Boyle, Kevin. 'Religious Intolerance and the Incitement of Hatred'. In *Striking a Balance: Hate Speech, Freedom of Expression and Non-discrimination*, edited by Sandra Coliver. Article 19, International Centre Against Censorship, Human Rights Centre University of Essex, 1992.

Boyle, Kevin and Anneliese Baldaccini. 'A Critical Evaluation of International Human Rights Approaches to Racism'. In *Discrimination and Human Rights: The Case of Racism*, edited by Sandra Fredman, 135–192. Oxford: Oxford University Press, 2004.

Bradney, Anthony. *Law and Faith in a Sceptical Age*. New York: Routledge-Cavendish, 2009.

Brems, Eva. 'Introduction'. In *Conflict between Fundamental Rights*, edited by Eva Brems. Intersentia, 2008.

Brennan, Fernne. 'Punishing Islamophobic Hostility: Are Any Lessons to Be Learned from Racially Hostile Crimes?' *Journal of Civil Liberties* 8 (2003): 28–50.

Brink, David O. 'Millian Principles, Freedom of Expression, and Hate Speech'. *Legal Theory* 7, no. 2 (2001): 119–157.

Brison, Susan J. 'Speech, Harm, and the Mind-Body Problem in First Amendment Jurisprudence'. *Legal Theory* 4, no. 1 (1998): 39–61.

Brown, Alex. *Hate Speech Law: A Philosophical Examination*. New York: Routledge, 2017.

Brown, Chris. 'Universal Human Rights: a Critique'. In *Human Rights in Global Politics*, edited by Timothy Dunne, 103–127. New York: Cambridge University Press, 1999.

Brudholm, Thomas. 'Conceptualizing Hatred Globally: Is Hate Crime a Human Rights Violation?'. In *The Globalization of Hate: Internationalizing Hate Crime?*, edited by Jennifer Schweppe and Mark Austin Walters, 31–48. New York: Oxford University Press, 2016.

Buchanan, Allen. 'The Egalitarianism of Human Rights'. *Ethics* 120, no. 4 (July 2010): 679–710.

Buchanan, Allen E. *Justice and Health Care Selected Essays*. New York: Oxford University Press, 2009. http://public.eblib.com/EBLPublic/PublicView.do?ptiID=472216.

Campbell, Tom. *Rights: A Critical Introduction*. New York: Routledge, 2006.

Cannie, Hannes and Dirk Voorhoof. 'The Abuse Clause and Freedom of Expression in the European Human Rights Convention: An Added Value for Democracy and Human Rights Protection?' *Netherlands Quarterly of Human Rights* 29, no. 1 (2011): 54–83.

Catlin, Scott J. 'Proposal for Regulating Hate Speech in the United States: Balancing Rights under the International Covenant on Civil and Political Rights'. *Notre Dame Law Review* 69 (1994): 771–816.

Cerone, John. 'Inappropriate Renderings: The Danger of Reductionist Resolutions'. *Brooklyn Journal of International Law* 33 (2008): 357–378.

Chayes, Abram and Antonia Handler Chayes. *The New Sovereignty: Compliance with International Regulatory Agreements*. Cambridge, MA: Harvard University Press, 1995.

Checkel, Jeffrey. 'Norms, Institutions, and National Identity in Contemporary Europe'. *International Studies Quarterly* 43, no. 1 (March 1999): 84–114.

Clapham, Andrew. *Human Rights: A Very Short Introduction*. Oxford: Oxford University Press, 2007.

Clarke, B. 'Freedom of Speech and Criticism of Religion: What Are the Limits?' *Murdoch University Law Journal* 14, no. 2 (2007): 94–121.

Conte, Alex. 'Democratic and Civil Rights'. In *Defining Civil and Political Rights; The Jurisprudence of the United Nations Human Rights Committee*, edited by Alex Conte and Richard Burchill, 65–110. Aldershot: Ashgate, 2009.

Conte, Alex. 'Limitations to and Derogations from Covenant Rights'. In *Defining Civil and Political Rights: The Jurisprudence of the United Nations Human Rights Committee*, edited by Alex Conte and Richard Burchill, 39–64. 2nd ed. Aldershot: Ashgate Publishing Limited, 2009.

Conte, Alex and Richard Burchill. 'Introduction'. In *Defining Civil and Political Rights; The Jurisprudence of the United Nations Human Rights Committee*, edited by Alex Conte and Richard Burchill, 1–18. Aldershot: Ashgate, 2009.

Cotler, Irwin. 'State-Sanctioned Incitement to Genocide: The Responsibility to Protect'. In *The Content and Context of Hate Speech: Rethinking Regulation and Responses*, edited by Michael E. Herz and Péter Molnár, 430–455. New York: Cambridge University Press, 2012.

Cox, Neville. 'Blasphemy, Holocaust Denial, and the Control of Profoundly Unacceptable Speech'. *American Journal of Comparative Law* 62 (2014): 739–734.

Cram, Ian. 'The Danish Cartoons, Offensive Expressions, and Democratic Legitimacy'. In *Extreme Speech and Democracy*, edited by Ivan Hare and James Weinstein, 311–330. New York: Oxford University Press, 2009.

Crawford, Neta. *Argument and Change in World Politics Ethics, Decolonization, and Humanitarian Intervention*. Cambridge: Cambridge University Press, 2002.

Cumper, Peter. 'Inciting Religious Hatred: Balancing Free Speech and Religious Sensibilities in a Multi-Faith Society'. In *Does God Believe in Human Rights? Essays on Religion and Human Rights*, edited by Nazila Ghanea-Hercock, Alan Stephens, and Raphael Walden, 233–258. Leiden: Martinus Nijhoff Publishers, 2007.

'Outlawing Incitement to Religious Hatred — a British Perspective'. *Religion and Human Rights* 1, no. 3 (2006): 249–268.

Danchin, Peter. 'Defaming Muhammad: Dignity, Harm, and Incitement to Religious Hatred'. *Duke Forum for Law & Social Change* 2 (2010): 5–38.

De Jong, Dennis. 'Freedom of Religion and Belief in the Light of Recent Challenges: Needs, Clashes and Solutions'. In *Does God Believe in Human Rights? Essays on Religion and Human Rights*, edited by Nazila Ghanea-Hercock, Alan Stephens, and Raphael Walden, 181–206. Leiden: Martinus Nijhoff Publishers, 2007.

Defeis, Elizabeth F. 'Freedom of Speech and International Norms: A Response to Hate Speech'. *Stanford Journal of International Law* 29 (1992): 57–130.

Deflem, Mathieu. *Sociology of Law: Visions of a Scholarly Tradition*. New York: Cambridge University Press, 2008.

Delgado, Richard. 'Words That Wound: A Tort Action for Racial Insults, Epithets, and Name-Calling'. *Harvard Civil Rights – Civil Liberties Law Review* 17 (1982): 133–182.

Delgado, Richard and Jean Stefancic. 'Four Observations about Hate Speech'. *Wake Forest Law Review* 44 (2009): 353–370.

Understanding Words That Wound. Boulder, CO: Westview Press, 2004.

Diehl, Paul F. and Charlotte Ku. *The Dynamics of International Law*. Cambridge: Cambridge University Press, 2010.

Dobras, Rebecca J. 'Is the United Nations Endorsing Human Rights Violations?: An Analysis of the United Nations' Combating Defamation of Religions Resolutions and Pakistan's Blasphemy Laws'. *Georgia Journal of International and Comparative Law* 37 (2008): 339–380.

Donders, Yvonne. *Towards a Right to Cultural Identity?* New York: Intersentia, 2002.

Donnelly, Jack. *Universal Human Rights in Theory and Practice*. Ithaca: Cornell University Press, 2002.

Dorsen, Norman. 'Is There a Right to Stop Offensive Speech? The Case of the Nazis at Skokie'. In *Civil Liberties in Conflict*, edited by Lawrence O. Gostin, 122–135. New York: Routledge, 1988.

Douglas-Scott, Sionaidh. 'Hatefulness of Protected Speech: A Comparison of the American and European Approaches'. *William & Mary Bill of Rights Journal* 7 (1999): 305–346.

Drinan, Robert F. *Can God & Caesar Coexist?: Balancing Religious Freedom and International Law*. New Haven: Yale University Press, 2004.

Dworkin, Ronald. *A Matter of Principle*. Cambridge, MA: Harvard University Press, 1985.

Dworkin Robert. 'Forward.' In *Extreme Speech and Democracy*, edited by Ivan Hare and James Weinstein, 1–10. Oxford University Press, 2009.

Taking Rights Seriously. London: Duckworth, 1977.

Eltayeb, Mohamed Saeed M. 'The Limitations on Critical Thinking on Religious Issues Under Article 20 of ICCPR and Its Relation to Freedom of Expression'. *Religion and Human Rights* 5, no. 2–3 (2010): 119–135.

Emerson, Thomas I. *The System of Freedom of Expression*. Random House, 1970.

Farrior, Stephanie. 'Molding the Matrix: The Historical and Theoretical Foundations of International Law Concerning Hate Speech'. *Berkeley Journal of International Law* 14 (1996): 1–98.

Feinberg, Joel. *Harm to Others*. New York: Oxford University Press, 1984.

Harmless Wrongdoing. New York: Oxford University Press, 1988.

Offense to Others. New York: Oxford University Press, 1985.

Feldman, David. *Civil Liberties and Human Rights in England and Wales*. 2nd ed. Oxford: Oxford University Press, 2002.

'Freedom of Expression'. In *The International Covenant on Civil and Political Rights and United Kingdom Law*, edited by D. J. Harris and Sarah Joseph, 391–437. Oxford: Clarendon Press; Oxford University Press, 1995.

Fergenson, Laraine R. 'Group Defamation: From Language to Thought to Action'. In *Group Defamation and Freedom of Speech: The Relationship Between Language and Violence*, edited by Monroe H. Freedman and Eric M. Freedman, 71–86. Westport: Greenwood Press, 1995.

Feyter, Koen De. 'In Defence of a Multidisciplinary Approach to Human Rights'. In *The Tension Between Group Rights and Human Rights: a Multidisciplinary Approach*, edited by K. de Feyter and George Pavlakos, 11–38. Portland: Hart Publishing, 2008.

Finnemore, Martha and Kathryn Sikkink. 'International Norm Dynamics and Political Change'. *International Organization* 52, no. 04 (1998): 887–917.

Fiss, Owen M. *The Irony of Free Speech*. Cambridge, MA: Harvard University Press, 1996.

Foster, Joshua. 'Prophets, Cartoons, and Legal Norms: Rethinking the United Nations Defamation of Religion Provisions'. *Journal of Catholic Legal Studies* 48 (2009): 19.

Foxman, Abraham H. and Christopher Wolf. *Viral Hate: Containing Its Spread on the Internet*. New York: Palgrave Macmillan, 2013.

Freeman, Mark and Gibran van Ert. *International Human Rights Law*. Toronto, ON: Irwin Law, 2004.

Freeman, Michael. 'Are There Collective Human Rights?' In *Politics and Human Rights*, edited by David Beetham, 25–40. Wiley-Blackwell, 1995.

Garland, Jon and Corinne Funnell, 'Defining Hate Crime Internationally: Issues and Conundrums'. In *The Globalization of Hate: Internationalizing Hate Crime?* edited by Jennifer Schweppe and Mark Austin Walters, 15–30. New York: Oxford University Press, 2016.

Gaudreault-DesBiens, Jean-Francois. 'From Sisyphus's Dilemma to Sisyphus's Duty – A Meditation on the Regulation of Hate Propaganda in Relation to Hate Crimes and Genocide'. *McGill Law Journal* 46 (2001): 121–140.

Gearty, Conor A. 'The Internal and External "Other" in the Union Legal Order: Racism, Religious Intolerance and Xenophobia in Europe'. In *The EU and Human Rights*, edited by Philip Alston, Mara R. Bustelo, and James Heenan, 327–358. Oxford; New York: Oxford University Press, 1999.

Gelber, Katharine. 'Reconceptualizing Counterspeech in Hate Speech Policy (with a Focus on Australia)'. In *The Content and Context of Hate Speech: Rethinking Regulation and Responses*, edited by Michael E. Herz and Péter Molnár, 198–216. Cambridge; New York: Cambridge University Press, 2012.

Gerards, Janneke H. 'Fundamental Rights and Other Interests: Should It Really Make a Difference?' In *Conflict Between Fundamental Rights*, edited by Eva Brems, 655–689. Intersentia, 2008.

Ghanea, Nazila. 'Expression and Hate Speech in the ICCPR: Compatible or Clashing?' *Religion and Human Rights* 5, no. 2–3 (2010): 171–190.

'"Phobias" and "Isms": Recognition of Difference or the Slippery Slope of Particularisms?' In *Does God Believe in Human Rights? Essays on Religion and Human Rights*, edited by Nazila Ghanea-Hercock, Alan Stephens, and Raphael Walden, 211–232. Leiden; Boston: Martinus Nijhoff Publishers, 2007.

Goldberger, David. 'Sources of Judicial Reluctance to Use Psychic Harm as a Basis for Suppressing Racist, Sexist and Ethnically Offensive Speech'. *Brooklyn Law Review* 56 (1990–1991): 1165–1212.

Goodall, Kay. 'Incitement to Religious Hatred: All Talk and No Substance?' *The Modern Law Review* 70, no. 1 (2007): 89–113.

Gordon, Gregory S. *Atrocity Speech Law: Foundation, Fragmentation, Fruition*. Oxford University Press, 2017.

Gostin, Larry. 'Collective and Individual Rights: Toward Resolving the Conflict'. In *Civil Liberties in Conflict*, edited by Lawrence O. Gostin. New York: Routledge, 1988.

Graham, L. Bennett. 'Defamation of Religions: The End of Pluralism'. *Emory International Law Review* 23 (2009): 69–84.

Graumann, Carl F. 'Verbal Discrimination: A Neglected Chapter in the Social Psychology of Aggression'. *Journal for the Theory of Social Behaviour* 28, no. 1 (1998): 41–61.

Gray, John. *Liberalism*. Buckingham: Open University Press, 1995.

Green, James Frederick. 'Changing Approaches to Human Rights: The United Nations, 1954 and 1974'. *Texas International Law Journal* 12 (1977): 223–238.

Greenawalt, Kent. *Fighting Words: Individuals, Communities, and Liberties of Speech*. Princeton, NJ: Princeton University Press, 1995.

'Speech and Crime'. *Law & Social Inquiry* 5, no. 4 (1980): 645–685.

Grey, Thomas C. 'Civil Rights vs. Civil Liberties: The Case of Discriminatory Verbal Harassment'. *Social Philosophy and Policy* 8, no. 02 (1991): 81–107.

Griffin, James. *On Human Rights*. Oxford; New York: Oxford University Press, 2008.

Grimm, Dieter. 'Freedom of Speech in a Globalized World'. In *Extreme Speech and Democracy*, edited by Ivan Hare and James Weinstein, 11–22. New York: Oxford University Press, 2009.

Grinberg, Maxim. 'Defamation of Religions v. Freedom of Expression: Finding the Balance in a Democratic Society'. *Sri Lanka Journal of International Law* 18 (2006): 197–222.

Guerra, Luis Lopez. 'Blasphemy and Religious Insult: Offenses to Religious Feelings or Attacks on Freedom?' In *Freedom of Expression: Essays in Honour of Nicolas Bratza President of the European Court of Human Rights*, 307–320. Wolf Legal Publishers, 2012.

Gunn, T. Jeremy. 'The Complexity of Religion and the Definition of Religion in International Law'. *Harvard Human Rights Journal* 16 (2003): 189–215.

Hall, Nathan. *Hate Crime*. New York: Routledge, 2013.

Haraszti, Miklos. 'Forward: Hate Speech and the Coming Death of the International Standard before It Was Born (Complaints of a Watchdog).' In *The Content and Context of Hate Speech: Rethinking Regulation and Responses*, edited by Michael Herz and Peter Molnar. Cambridge University Press, 2012.

Hare, Ivan. 'Blasphemy and Incitement to Religious Hatred: Free Speech Dogma and Doctrine'. In *Extreme Speech and Democracy*, edited by Ivan Hare and James Weinstein, 289–310. New York: Oxford University Press, 2009.

Hare, Ivan and James Weinstein, eds. *Extreme Speech and Democracy*. New York: Oxford University Press, 2009.

Harel, Alon. 'What Demands Are Rights? An Investigation into the Relation between Rights and Reasons'. *Oxford Journal of Legal Studies* 17, no. 1 (1997): 101–114.

Hassan, Parvez. 'International Covenants on Human Rights: An Approach to Interpretation'. *Buffalo Law Review* 19 (1969): 35–50.

Hawkins, Darren. 'Explaining Costly International Institutions: Persuasion and Enforceable Human Rights Norms'. *International Studies Quarterly* 48, no. 4 (2004): 779–804.

Heinze, Eric. 'Toward a Legal Concept of Hatred: Democracy, Ontology, and the Limits of Deconstruction'. In *Hate, Politics, Law: Critical Perspectives on Combatting Hate*, edited by Thomas Brudholm and Birgitte Schepelern Johansen, 94–112. Oxford University Press, 2018.

'Viewpoint Absolutism and Hate Speech'. *The Modern Law Review* 69, no. 4 (2006): 543–582.

Henkin, Louis. 'Group Defamation and International Law'. In *Group Defamation and Freedom of Speech: The Relationship between Language and Violence*, edited by Monroe H. Freedman and Eric M. Freedman, 123–134. Greenwood Press, 1995.

'International Human Rights and Rights in the United States'. In *Human Rights in International Law*, edited by Theodor Meron, 25–67. Oxford: Clarendon Press, 1992.

'Introduction'. In *The International Bill of Rights: The Covenant on Civil and Political Rights*, edited by Louis Henkin, 1–31. Columbia University Press, 1981.

Herz, Michael E. and Péter Molnár, eds. 'Interview with Kenan Malik'. In *The Content and Context of Hate Speech: Rethinking Regulation and Responses*, 81–91. Cambridge; New York: Cambridge University Press, 2012.

eds. 'Interview with Robert Post'. In *The Content and Context of Hate Speech: Rethinking Regulation and Responses*, 11–36. Cambridge; New York: Cambridge University Press, 2012.

'Introduction'. In *The Content and Context of Hate Speech: Rethinking Regulation and Responses*, edited by Michael Herz and Peter Molnar, 1–7. Cambridge University Press, 2012.

eds. *The Content and Context of Hate Speech: Rethinking Regulation and Responses*. Cambridge; New York: Cambridge University Press, 2012.

Higgins, Rosalyn. 'The United Nations: Still a Force for Peace'. *The Modern Law Review* 52, no. 1 (1989): 1–21.

Howard, Erica. *Freedom of Expression and Religious Hate Speech in Europe*. New York: Routledge, 2018.

Howard-Hassmann, Rhoda E. 'Canadians Discuss Freedom of Speech: Individual Rights Versus Group Protection'. *International Journal on Minority and Group Right* 7, no. 2 (2000): 35–64.

Ingram, Attracta. *A Political Theory of Rights*. Oxford; New York: Clarendon Press; Oxford University Press, 1994.

Jeremy, Anthony W. 'Religious Offences'. *Ecclesiastical Law Journal* 7, no. 33 (2003): 127–142.

Joseph, Sarah. 'A Rights Analysis of the Covenant on Civil and Political Rights'. *International Legal Studies* 5 (1999).

Judson, Janis L. and Bertazzoni, Donna M. *Law, Media and Culture, the Landscape of Hate*. Peter Lang, 2002.

Kalin, Walter. 'Examination of State Reports'. In *UN Human Rights Treaty Bodies: Law and Legitimacy*, edited by Helen Keller and Geir Ulfstein, 16–72. Cambridge; New York: Cambridge University Press, 2012.

Kapai, Puja and Anne SY Cheung. 'Hanging in a Balance: Freedom of Expression and Religion' *Buffalo Human Rights Law Review* 15 (2009): 41–79.

Keane, David. 'Cartoon Violence and Freedom of Expression'. *Human Rights Quarterly* 30, no. 4 (2008): 845–875.

Keck, E. Margaret and Kathryn Sikkink. *Activists beyond Borders: Advocacy Networks in International Politics*. London: Cornell University Press, 1998.

Keller, Helen and Leena Grover. 'General Comments of the Human Rights Committee and Their Legitimacy.' In *UN Human Rights Treaty Bodies: Law and Legitimacy*, edited by Helen Keller and Geir Ulfstein, 116–198. Cambridge: Cambridge University Press, 2012.

Keller, Helen and Geir Ulfstein. 'Conclusions'. In *UN Human Rights Treaty Bodies: Law and Legitimacy*, edited by Helen Keller and Geir Ulfstein, 414–425. Cambridge: Cambridge University Press, 2012.

Keipi, Teo, Matti Näsi, Atte Oksanen, and Pekka Räsänen. *Online Hate and Harmful Content: Cross-national Perspectives*. New York: Routledge, 2017.

Kennedy, Randall. *Nigger: The Strange Career of a Troublesome Word*. New York: Pantheon Books, 2002.

Kiss, A. C. 'Permissible Limitations on Rights'. In *The International Bill of Rights: The Covenant on Civil and Political Rights*, edited by Louis Henkin. New York: Columbia University Press, 1981.

Klabbers, Jan. 'International Legal Histories: The Declining Importance of Travaux Préparatoires in Treaty Interpretation?' *Netherlands International Law Review* 50, no. 03 (2003): 267–288.

Klausen, Jytte. *The Cartoons That Shook the World*. New Haven, CT: Yale University Press, 2009.

Klotz, Audie. *Norms in International Relations: The Struggle against Apartheid*. Cornell University Press, 1999.

Kratochwil, Friedrich V. *Rules, Norms, and Decisions: On the Conditions of Practical and Legal Reasoning in International Relations and Domestic Affairs*. Cambridge; New York: Cambridge University Press, 1989.

Kretzmer, David. 'Freedom of Speech and Racism'. *Cardozo Law Review* 8 (1986–1987): 445–514.

Kretzmer, David and Frederick Schauer, eds. 'Speech, Behaviour and the Interdependence of Fact and Value.' In *Freedom of Speech and Incitement Against Democracy*, 43–62. Kluwer Law International, 2000.

Kubler, Friedrich. 'How Much Freedom for Racist Speech?: Transnational Aspects of a Conflict of Human Rights'. *Hofstra Law Review* 27 (1998): 335–376.

Laborde, Cecile. 'The Danish Cartoon Controversy and the Challenges of Multicultural Politics: A Discussion of the Cartoons That Shook the World'. *Perspectives on Politics* 9, no. 3 (2011): 603–605.

Langer, Lorenz. 'Recent Development: The Rise (and Fall?) of Defamation of Religions'. *Yale Journal of International Law* 35 (2010): 257–263.

Religious Offence and Human Rights: The Implications of Defamation of Religions. Cambridge University Press, 2014.

Lasson, Kenneth. 'Group Libel Versus Free Speech: When Big Brother Should Butt In'. *Duquesne University Law Review* 23, no. 1 (1984): 70–130.

Lawrence, Charles R. III. 'If He Hollers Let Him Go: Regulating Racist Speech on Campus'. *Duke Law Journal* 1990 (1990): 431–483.

Lawrence, Frederick M. 'Violence-Conducive Speech: Punishable Verbal Assault or Protected Political Speech'. In *Freedom of Speech and Incitement against Democracy*, edited by David Kretzmer and Francine Kershman Hazan, 11–32. Kluwer Law International, 2000.

Legro, Jeffrey W. 'Which Norms Matter? Revisiting the "failure" of Internationalism'. *International Organization* 51, no. 01 (1997): 31–63.

Leigh, I. Damned if they do, Damned if they don't: the European Court of Human Rights and the Protection of Religion from Attack. *Res Publica* 17, 55–73 (2011).

Lerner, Natan. *The UN Convention on the Elimination of All Forms of Racial Discrimination.* 2nd ed. Alphen aan den Rijn [u.a.]: Sijthoff & Noordhoff, 1980.

Lester, Anthony. 'The Right to Offend'. In *Freedom of Expression: Essays in Honour of Nicolas Bratza President of the European Court of Human Rights*, 297–306. Wolf Legal Publishers, 2012.

Levey, Geoffrey Brahm and Tariq Modood. 'The Muhammad Cartoons and Multicultural Democracies.' *Ethnicities* 9, no. 3 (1 September 2009): 427–447.

Levin, Abigail. *The Cost of Free Speech: Pornography, Hate Speech and Their Challenge to Liberalism.* New York: Palgrave Macmillan, 2010.

Limon, Marc, Nazila Ghanea, and Hilary Power, 'Freedom of Expression and Religions, the United Nations and the 16/18 Process.' In *Blasphemy and Freedom of Expression Comparative, Theoretical and Historical Reflections after the Charlie Hebdo Massacre*, edited by Jeroen Temperman and András Koltay. 645–680. Cambridge University Press, 2018.

MacCormick, Neil. *Legal Right and Social Democracy: Essays in Legal and Political Philosophy.* Oxford; New York: Clarendon Press; Oxford University Press, 1982.

Machan, Tibor R. 'Considerations of the Libertarian Alternative'. *Harvard Journal of Law and Public Policy* 2 (1979): 103–124.

MacKinnon, Catharine A. *Only Words.* Cambridge, MA: Harvard University Press, 1993.

MacKinnon, Catharine A. 'Pornography as Defamation and Discrimination'. In *Group Defamation and Freedom of Speech: The Relationship between Language and Violence*, edited by Monroe H. Freedman and Eric M. Freedman, 253–265. Greenwood Press, 1995.

Mahoney, Kathleen E. 'Speech, Equality, and Citizenship in Canada'. *Common Law World Review* 39, no. 1 (March 2010): 69–99.

Mahoney, Paul. 'Universality versus Subsidiarity in the Strasbourg Case Law on Free Speech'. *European Human Rights Law Review* 4 (1997): 364–379.

Maitra, Ishani and Mary Kathryn McGowan, eds. *Speech and Harm: Controversies over Free Speech.* Oxford: Oxford University Press, 2012.

Malik, Maleiha. 'Extreme Speech and Liberalism.' In *Extreme Speech and Democracy*, edited by Ivan Hare and James Weinstein, 96–121. New York: Oxford University Press, 2009.

Marsh, Elizabeth. 'Working Paper No. 3: "General Comments"'. *International Council of Voluntary Agencies*, December 2001. https://icvanetwork.org/doc00000486.html.

Massaro, Toni M. 'Equality and Freedom of Expression: The Hate Speech Dilemma'. *William and Mary Law Review* 32 (1991): 211–266.

Massey, Calvin R. 'Hate Speech, Cultural Diversity, and the Foundational Paradigms of Free Expression'. *UCLA Law Review* 40 (1992): 103–198.

Matsuda, Mari J. 'Outsider Jurisprudence: Toward a Victim's Analysis of Racial Hate Messages'. In *Group Defamation and Freedom of Speech: The Relationship Between Language and Violence*, edited by Monroe H. Freedman and Eric M. Freedman, 87–121. Greenwood Press, 1995.

Matsuda, Mari J. 'Public Response to Racist Speech: Considering the Victim's Story'. *Michigan Law Review* 87, no. 8 (August 1989): 2320–2381.

McDougal, Myres S., Harold D. Lasswell, and Lung-chu Chen. 'Human Rights and World Public Order: A Framework for Policy-Oriented Inquiry'. *The American Journal of International Law* 63, no. 2 (April 1969): 237–269.

McGoldrick, Dominic and Thérèse O'Donnell. 'Hate-speech Laws: Consistency with National and International Human Rights Law'. *Legal Studies* 18, no. 4 (1998): 453–485.

McGonagle, Tarlach. 'A Survey and Critical Analysis of Council of Europe Strategies for Countering "Hate Speech"'. In *The Content and Context of Hate Speech: Rethinking Regulation and Responses*, edited by Michael E. Herz and Péter Molnár, 456–498. Cambridge; New York: Cambridge University Press, 2012.

Minority Rights, Freedom of Expression and of the Media: Dynamics and Dilemmas. Cambridge; Portland: Intersentia, 2011.

Meer, Nasar and Tariq Modood. 'Refutations of Racism in the "Muslim Question"'. *Patterns of Prejudice* 43, no. 3–4 (2009): 335–354.

Mendel, Toby. 'Does International Law Provide for Consistent Rules on Hate Speech?' In *The Content and Context of Hate Speech: Rethinking Regulation and Responses*, edited by Michael E. Herz and Péter Molnár, pp. 417–429. Cambridge; New York: Cambridge University Press, 2012.

Mengistu, Yared Legesse. 'Shielding Marginalized Groups from Verbal Assaults without Abusing Hate Speech Laws'. In *The Content and Context of Hate Speech: Rethinking Regulation and Responses*, edited by Michael E. Herz and Péter Molnár, 352–377. Cambridge; New York: Cambridge University Press, 2012.

Meron, Theodor. *Human Rights in International Law*. Oxford: Clarendon Press, 1992.

Human Rights Law-Making in the United Nations: A Critique of Instruments and Process. Oxford; New York: Clarendon Press; Oxford University Press, 1986.

Mill, John Stuart. 'On Liberty.' In *J. S. Mill, On Liberty in Focus*, edited by John Gray and G. W. Smith, 23–130. New York: Routledge, 1991.

Modood, Tariq. 'The Place of Muslims in British Secular Multiculturalism'. In *The Challenge of Religious Discrimination at the Dawn of the New Millennium*, edited by Nazila Ghanea-Hercock, 223–244. Leiden; Boston: Martinus Nijhoff Publishers, 2003.

Modood, Tariq, Randall Hansen, Erik Bleich, Brendan O'Leary, and Joseph H. Carens. 'The Danish Cartoon Affair: Free Speech, Racism, Islamism, and Integration'. *International Migration* 44, no. 5 (2006): 3–62.

Molnar, Peter. 'Responding to "Hate Speech" with Art, Education, and the Imminent Danger Test'. In *The Content and Context of Hate Speech: Rethinking Regulation and Responses*, edited by Michael Herz and Peter Molnar, 183–197. Cambridge University Press, 2012.

Molnar, Peter. 'Towards Improved Law and Policy on "Hate Speech": The "Clear and Present Danger" Test in Hungary.' In *Extreme Speech and Democracy*, edited by

Ivan Hare and James Weinstein, 237–264. Oxford; New York: Oxford University Press, 2009.

Moon, Richard. *Putting Faith in Hate: When Religion Is the Source or Target of Hate Speech*. Cambridge University Press, 2018.

Mutua, Makau. 'Standard Setting in Human Rights: Critique and Prognosis'. *Human Rights Quarterly* 29, no. 3 (2007): 547–630.

Nagtzaam, Gerry. *The Making of International Environmental Treaties: Neoliberal and Constructivist Analyses of Normative Evolution*. Edward Elgar Publishing, 2009.

Nash, David and Chara Bakalis. 'Incitement to Religious Hatred and the "Symbolic": How Will the Racial and Religious Hatred Act 2006 Work?'. *Liverpool Law Review* 28, no. 3 (1 November 2007): 349–375.

Nathwani, Niraj. 'Religious Cartoons and Human Rights – A Critical Legal Analysis of the Case Law of the European Court of Human Rights on the Protection of Religious Feeling and Its Implications in the Danish Affair Concerning Cartoons of the Prophet Muhammed.' *European Human Rights Law Review* 4 (2008): 488.

Nettheim, G. '"Peoples" and "Populations": Indigenous Peoples and the Rights of Peoples'. In *The Rights of Peoples*, edited by James Crawford, 107–126. Oxford; New York: Clarendon Press; Oxford University Press, 1988.

Nifosi-Sutton, Ingrid. *The Protection of Vulnerable Groups under International Human Rights Law*. New York: Routledge, 2017.

Noorloos, Marloes van. *Hate Speech Revisited: A Comparative and Historical Perspective on Hate Speech Law in the Netherlands and England & Wales*. Cambridge; Portland: Intersentia, 2011.

Norris, David. 'Are Laws Proscribing Incitement to Religious Hatred Compatible with Freedom of Speech?' *UCL Human Rights Review* 1, no. 1 (2008): 102–117.

'Note: A Communitarian Defense of Group Libel Laws'. *Harvard Law Review* 101 (1988): 682–701.

Nowak, Manfred. *U.N. Covenant on Civil and Political Rights: CCPR Commentary*. 2nd ed. Kehl, Germany; Arlington, VA: N.P. Engel, 2005.

Nowlin, Christopher J. 'The Protection of Morals under the European Convention for the Protection of Human Rights and Fundamental Freedoms'. *Human Rights Quarterly* 24, no. 1 (2002): 264–286.

Oetheimer, Mario. 'Protecting Freedom of Expression: The Challenge of Hate Speech in the European Court of Human Rights Case Law'. *Cardozo Journal of International and Comparative Law* 17 (2009): 427–444.

Oliva, Javier García. 'The Legal Protection of Believers and Beliefs in the United Kingdom'. *Ecclesiastical Law Journal* 9, no. 01 (2007): 66–86.

Osiatynski, Wiktor. *Human Rights and Their Limits*. Cambridge; New York: Cambridge University Press, 2009.

'Outcome Document of the Durban Review Conference'. April 2009. www.un.org/en/durbanreview2009/pdf/Durban_Review_outcome_document_En.pdf.

Oyediran, J. 'Article 13 (5)of the American Convention on Human Rights'. In *Striking a Balance: Hate Speech, Freedom of Expression, and Non-discrimination*, edited by Sandra Coliver. Article 19, International Centre Against Censorship, Human Rights Centre, University of Essex, 1992.

Parekh, Bhikhu. 'Group Libel and Freedom of Expression: Thoughts on the Rushdie Affair'. In *Striking a Balance: Hate Speech, Freedom of Expression and Non-discrimination*, edited by Sandra Coliver, 358–362. Article 19, International Centre Against Censorship, Human Rights Centre University of Essex, 1992.

'Is There a Case for Banning Hate Speech?' In *The Content and Context of Hate Speech: Rethinking Regulation and Responses*, edited by Michael E. Herz and Péter Molnár, 37–56. Cambridge; New York: Cambridge University Press, 2012.

Parekh, Bhikhu C. *Rethinking Multiculturalism: Cultural Diversity and Political Theory.* Cambridge, MA: Harvard University Press, 2000.

Parmar, Sejal. 'The Challenge of "Defamation of Religion" to Freedom of Expression and the International Human Rights'. *European Human Rights Law Review* 3 (2009): 353–375.

Partsch, K. J. 'Racial Speech and Human Rights: Article 4 of the Convention on the Elimination of All Forms of Racial Discrimination'. In *Striking a Balance: Hate Speech, Freedom of Expression, and Non-discrimination*, edited by Sandra Coliver, 21–28. Article 19, International Centre Against Censorship, Human Rights Centre, University of Essex, 1992.

Partsch, Karl Josef. 'Freedom of Conscience and Expression, and Political Freedoms'. In *The International Bill of Rights: The Covenant on Civil and Political Rights*, edited by Louis Henkin, 209–245. New York: Columbia University Press, 1981.

Petrova, Dimitrina. '"Smoke and Mirrors": The Durban Review Conference and Human Rights Politics at the United Nations'. *Human Rights Law Review* 10, no. 1 (1 March 2010): 129–150.

Pinto, Meital. 'What Are Offences to Feelings Really About? A New Regulative Principle for the Multicultural Era'. *Oxford Journal of Legal Studies* 30, no. 4 (21 December 2010): 695–723.

Post, Robert 'Cultural Heterogeneity and Law: Pornography, Blasphemy, and the First Amendment'. *California Law Review* 76, no. 2 (March 1988): 297–335.

'Hate Speech'. In *Extreme Speech and Democracy*, edited by Ivan Hare and James Weinstein, 123–138. Oxford University Press, 2009.

'Racist Speech, Democracy, and the First Amendment'. *William and Mary Law Review* 32 (1991): 267–328.

'Religion and Freedom of Speech: Portraits of Muhammad'. *Constellations* 14, no. 1 (2007): 72–90.

'The Constitutional Concept of Public Discourse: Outrageous Opinion, Democratic Deliberation, and Hustler Magazine v. Falwell'. *Harvard Law Review* 103, no. 3 (January 1990): 601–686.

Price, Richard. 'Moral Limit and Possibility in World Politics'. *International Organization* 62, no. 02 (2008): 191–220.

Redish, Martin H. *Freedom of Expression: A Critical Analysis.* Charlottesville, VA: Michie Co., 1984.

Rehman, Javaid. *International Human Rights Law.* Harlow; New York: Longman/Pearson, 2010.

Reichman, Amnon. 'Criminalizing Religiously Offensive Satire: Free Speech, Human Dignity, and Comparative Law'. In *Extreme Speech and Democracy*, edited by Ivan Hare and James Weinstein, 331–356. Oxford; New York: Oxford University Press, 2009.

Richards, David A. J. *Free Speech and the Politics of Identity.* Oxford; New York: Oxford University Press, 1999.

Riesman, David. 'Democracy and Defamation: Control of Group Libel'. *Columbia Law Review* 42, no. 5 (May 1942): 727–780.

Risse-Kappen, Thomas, Stephen C. Ropp, and Kathryn Sikkink. *The Power of Human Rights: International Norms and Domestic Change.* Cambridge University Press, 1999.

Rosenfeld, Michel. 'Hate Speech in Constitutional Jurisprudence: A Comparative Analysis'. *Cardozo Law Review* 24 (2002): 1523–1568.

'Hate Speech in Constitutional Jurisprudence: A Comparative Analysis'. In *The Content and Context of Hate Speech: Rethinking Regulation and Responses*, edited by Michael E. Herz and Péter Molnár, 242–289. Cambridge; New York: Cambridge University Press, 2012.

Roth, S. J. 'CSCE Standards on Incitement to Hatred and Discrimination on National, Racial or Religious Grounds'. In *Striking a Balance: Hate Speech, Freedom of Expression, and Non-discrimination*, edited by Sandra Coliver, 55–60. Article 19, International Centre Against Censorship, Human Rights Centre, University of Essex, 1992.

Rowbottom, Jacob. 'Media Freedom and Political Debate in the Digital Era'. *The Modern Law Review* 69, no. 4 (2006): 489–513.

Rytina, Nancy. *Estimates of the Legal Permanent Resident Population in 2012*, July 2013. www.dhs.gov/sites/default/files/publications/ois_lpr_pe_2012.pdf.

Sadurski, Wojciech. *Freedom of Speech and Its Limits*. Springer, 1999.

Moral Pluralism and Legal Neutrality. Dordrecht; Boston: Kluwer Academic Publishers, 1990.

'On Seeing Speech through an Equality Lens: A Critique of Egalitarian Arguments for Suppression of Hate Speech and Pornography'. *Oxford Journal of Legal Studies* 16 (1996): 713–724.

Sandel, Michael J. *Liberalism and the Limits of Justice*. Cambridge; New York: Cambridge University Press, 1982.

Sandholtz, Wayne. 'Dynamics of International Norm Change: Rules against Wartime Plunder'. *European Journal of International Relations* 14, no. 1 (1 March 2008): 101–131.

'Globalization and the Evolution of Rules'. In *Globalization and Governance*, edited by Aseem Prakash and Jeffrey A. Hart, 77–102. New York: Routledge, 1999.

Sandholtz, Wayne and Kendall W. Stiles. *International Norms and Cycles of Change*. Oxford; New York: Oxford University Press, 2009.

Schabas, William. *Genocide in International Law: The Crimes of Crimes*. Cambridge; New York: Cambridge University Press, 2000.

Schabas, William A. *Genocide in International Law: The Crime of Crimes*. 2nd ed. Cambridge: Cambridge University Press, 2009.

Schauer, Frederick. 'The Phenomenology of Speech and Harm'. *Ethics* 103, no. 4 (1993): 635–653.

Schauer, Frederick. 'Slippery Slopes'. *Harvard Law Review* 99 (1985): 361–383.

Schlutter, Birgit. 'Aspects of Human Rights Interpretation by the UN Treaty Bodies'. In *UN Human Rights Treaty Bodies: Law and Legitimacy*, edited by Helen Keller and Geir Ulfstein. Cambridge: Cambridge University Press, 2012.

Schweppe, Jennifer and Mark Austin Walters, 'Introduction: The Globalization of Hate'. In *The Globalization of Hate: Internationalizing Hate Crime?*, edited by Jennifer Schweppe and Mark Austin Walters, 1–12. New York: Oxford University Press, 2016.

Scolnicov, Anat. *The Right to Religious Freedom in International Law: Between Group Rights and Individual Rights*. New York: Routledge, 2011.

Scordato, Marin and Paula A. Monopoli. 'Free Speech Rationales after September 11th: The First Amendment in Post-World Trade Center America'. *Stanford Law & Policy Review* 13 (2002): 185–206.

Seeley, James J. 'Article Twenty of the International Covenant on Civil and Political Rights: First Amendment Comments and Questions'. *Virginia Journal of International Law* 10 (1970): 328–347.

Segerlund, Lisbeth. *Making Corporate Social Responsibility a Global Concern: Norm Construction in a Globalizing World.* Farnham; Burlington: Ashgate, 2010.

Sen, Amartya. 'Elements of a Theory of Human Rights'. *Philosophy & Public Affairs* 32, no. 4 (2004): 315–356.

Shany, Yuval. 'Toward a General Margin of Appreciation Doctrine in International Law?' *European Journal of International Law* 16, no. 5 (1 November 2005): 907–940.

Sieghart, Paul. *The International Law of Human Rights.* Oxford: Oxford University Press, 1983.

Sim Kok Eng, Amy. 'Preventing Hatred or Silencing Voices: Making the Case for a Rigorous Threshold for the Incitement to National, Racial or Religious Hatred'. Bangkok, 2011. www.ohchr.org/Documents/Issues/Expression/ICCPR/Bangkok/AmySim.pdf.

Simpson, Evan. 'Responsibilities for Hateful Speech'. *Legal Theory* 12, no. 02 (2006): 157–177.

Skorini, Heini í, 'The OIC and Freedom of Expression: Justifying Religious Censorship Norms with Human Rights Language'. In *The Organization of Islamic Cooperation and Human Rights*, edited by Marie Juul Petersen and Turan Kayaoglu, 114–141. Pennsylvania: University of Pennsylvania Press, 2019.

Smelser, Neil J. *Theory of Collective Behavior.* New York: Free Press; Collier-Macmillan, 1962.

Smith, Karen E. 'The European Union at the Human Rights Council: Speaking with One Voice but Having Little Influence'. *Journal of European Public Policy* 17, no. 2 (2010): 224–241.

Smith, Rhona K. M. *Textbook on International Human Rights.* 4th ed. Oxford: Oxford University Press, 2009.

Sohn, Louis B. 'New International Law: Protection of the Rights of Individuals Rather than States'. *American University Law Review* 32 (1982): 1–64.

Sottiaux, Stefan. '"Bad Tendencies" in the ECtHR's "Hate Speech" Jurisprudence'. *European Constitutional Law Review* 7, no. 01 (2011): 40–63.

Steiner, Henry J., Philip Alston, and Ryan Goodman. *International Human Rights in Context: Law, Politics, Morals: Text and Materials.* Oxford; New York: Oxford University Press, 2008.

Sternberg, Robert J. and Karin Sternberg. *The Nature of Hate.* New York: Cambridge University Press, 2008.

Stone, Geoffrey R. 'Content Regulation and the First Amendment'. *William and Mary Law Review* 25 (1983): 189.

'Content-Neutral Restrictions'. *The University of Chicago Law Review* 54, no. 1 (1987): 46–118.

Sumner, L. W. 'Incitement and the Regulation of Hate Speech in Canada: A Philosophical Analysis'. In *Extreme Speech and Democracy*, edited by Ivan Hare and James Weinstein, 204–220. New York: Oxford University Press, 2009.

Sumner, Wayne. 'Hate Speech and the Law: A Canadian Perspective'. In *Pluralism and Law*, edited by Arend Soeteman, 37–54. Sits-Stuttgart: Springer, 2011.

Taylor, Paul M. *Freedom of Religion: UN and European Human Rights Law and Practice.* New York: Cambridge University Press, 2005.

Teff, Harvey. *Causing Psychiatric and Emotional Harm: Reshaping the Boundaries of Legal Liability.* Portland: Hart Publishing, 2009.

Temperman, Jeroen. 'Blasphemy, Defamation of Religions & Human Rights Law'. *Netherlands Quarterly of Human Rights* 26, no. 4 (2008): 517–545.

Religious Hatred and International Law: The Prohibition of Incitement to Violence or Discrimination. Cambridge: Cambridge University Press, 2015.

Thomson, Judith Jarvis. *The Realm of Rights*. Cambridge, MA: Harvard University Press, 1990.

Thornberry, Patrick. 'Forms of Hate Speech and the Convention on the Elimination of All Forms of Racial Discrimination (ICERD)'. *Religion & Human Rights* 5, no. 2 (1 January 2010): 97–117.

Timmermann, Wibke Kristin. 'Incitement in International Criminal Law'. *International Review of the Red Cross* 88, no. 864 (2006): 823–852.

Incitement in International Law. New York: Routledge, 2015.

'Incitement, Instigation, Hate Speech and War Propaganda in International Law'. LL.M. Thesis, Centre Universitaire de Droit International Humanitaire. Accessed 12 July 2013. www.geneva-academy.ch/docs/memoires/memoire_timmermann.pdf.

'The Relationship between Hate Propaganda and Incitement to Genocide: A New Trend in International Law towards Criminalization of Hate Propaganda?' *Leiden Journal of International Law* 18, no. 02 (2005): 257–282.

Tobin, John. *The Right to Health in International Law*. New York: Oxford University Press, 2012.

Tsesis, Alexander. 'Dignity and Speech: The Regulation of Hate Speech in a Democracy'. *Wake Forest Law Review* 44 (2009): 497–532.

'Hate in Cyberspace: Regulating Hate Speech on the Internet'. *San Diego Law Review* 38 (2001): 817.

Tuck, Richard. *Natural Rights Theories: Their Origin and Development*. Cambridge: Cambridge University Press, 1979.

Tulkens, Francoise. 'When to Say Is to Do Freedom of Expression and Hate Speech in the Case-Law of the European Court of Human Rights'. Strasbourg, 2012. www.ejtn.net/Documents/About%20EJTN/Independent%20Seminars/TULKENS_Francoise_Presentation_When_to_Say_is_To_Do_Freedom_of_Expression_and_Hate_Speech_in_the_Case_Law_of_the_ECtHR_October_2012.pdf.

Türk, Danilo. 'Introduction: Group Rights and Human Rights'. In *The Tension between Group Rights and Human Rights: A Multidisciplinary Approach*, edited by K. de Feyter and George Pavlakos, 1–8. Portland: Hart Publishing, 2008.

Tyagi, Yogesh. *The UN Human Rights Committee: Practice and Procedure*. New York: Cambridge University Press, 2011.

Vance, Susannah C. 'Permissibility of Incitement to Religious Hatred Offenses under European Convention Principles'. *Transnational Law & Contemporary Problems* 14 (2004): 201.

Verkhovsky, Alexander. 'Data-Collection and Fact-Finding'. Vienna, 2011. www.ohchr.org/Documents/Issues/Expression/ICCPR/Vienna/CRP2Verkhovsky.pdf.

Vrielink, Jogchum. 'Islamophobia and the Law: Belgian Hate Speech Legislation and the Wilful Destruction of the Koran'. *International Journal of Discrimination and the Law* 14, no.1 (2014): 54–65

Waldron, Jeremy. *Liberal Rights: Collected Papers 1981–1991*. Cambridge: Cambridge University Press, 1993.

'Mill and the Value of Moral Distress'. *Political Studies* 35, no. 3 (1987): 410–423.

The Harm in Hate Speech. Cambridge, MA: Harvard University Press, 2012.

Walker, Samuel. *Hate Speech: The History of an American Controversy*. Lincoln: University of Nebraska Press, 1994.

Walzer, Michael. *Spheres of Justice: A Defense of Pluralism and Equality*. New York: Basic Books, 1983.

Weber, Cynthia. *International Relations Theory: A Critical Introduction*. New York: Routledge, 2009.

Weinstein, James. *Hate Speech, Pornography, and the Radical Attack on Free Speech Doctrine*. Boulder, CO: Westview Press, 1999.

Wendel, W. Bradley. '"Certain Fundamental Truths": A Dialectic on Negative and Positive Liberty in Hate-Speech Cases'. *Law and Contemporary Problems* 65, no. 2 (2002): 33–85.

Werbner, Pnina. 'Islamophobia: Incitement to Religious Hatred – Legislating for a New Fear?' *Anthropology Today* 21, no. 1 (2005): 5–9.

West, Caroline. 'Words That Silence? Freedom of Expression and Racist Hate Speech'. In *Speech and Harm: Controversies over Free Speech*, edited by Ishani Maitra and Mary Kathryn McGowan, 222–248. Oxford: Oxford University Press, 2012.

Yang, Tseming. 'Race, Religion, and Cultural Identity: Reconciling the Jurisprudence of Race and Religion'. *Indiana Law Journal* 73 (1997): 119.

Zeno-Zencovich, Vincenzo. *Freedom of Expression: A Critical and Comparative Analysis*. 1st ed. Oxon: Routledge-Cavendish, 2008.

Index

Lightning Source UK Ltd.
Milton Keynes UK
UKHW020659160522
403054UK00004B/79